TECHNOLOGY PLACE & ARCHITECTURE
The Jerusalem Seminar in Architecture

1996

TECHNOLOGY, PLACE & ARCHITECTURE

1994

ARCHITECTURE, HISTORY & MEMORY

1992

THE PUBLIC BUILDING: FORM & INFLUENCE

TECHNOLOGY PLACE & ARCHITECTURE

The Jerusalem Seminar in Architecture

Edited by Kenneth Frampton
with Arthur Spector
and Lynne Reed Rosman

First published in the United States of America in 1998 by
Rizzoli International Publications, Inc.
300 Park Avenue South, New York NY 10010

Copyright © 1998 by Rizzoli International Publications, Inc.

All rights reserved.
No part of this publication may be reproduced in any manner whatsoever
without permission in writing from Rizzoli International Publications, Inc.

Library of Congress Cataloging-in-Publication Data

Jerusalem Seminar in Architecture
    Technology, place & architecture : the Jerusalem Seminar in Architecture : 1996, Technology, place & architecture, June 9–11 : 1994, Architecture, history, and memory, November 7–10 : 1992, The public building, form and influence, November 8–11, Jerusalem, Israel / edited by Kenneth Frampton, with Arthur Spector and Lynne Reed Rosman.
       p.   cm.
    ISBN 0-8478-2085-8 (pbk)
    1. Architecture and technology—Congresses. 2. Regionalism in architecture—Congresses. 3. Space (Architecture)—Congresses. 4. Architecture, Modern—20th Century—Congresses. I. Frampton, Kenneth. II. Spector, Arthur. III Rosman, Lynne Reed. IV. Title.
NA2543.T43J47 1998   97-48254
720' .1'05—dc21   CIP

Designed by Abigail Sturges Design

Printed and bound in Singapore

Page 11 illustration: Details of transept roof, Crystal Palace, Great Exhibition of the Works of Industry of All Nations, London, 1851. From a drawing by Charles Downes, reprinted from *The Building erected in Hyde Park for the Great Exhibition 1851* [sic] (London: John Weale, 1852; reprinted by the Victoria & Albert Museum, London, 1971), plate 18.

Page 201 illustration: Ruins of Bethshemesh (Ain Shems), Middle-Late Bronze-Age city, Caanan (now Palestine). Drawing from the Haverford expedition, 1928-30, reprinted from *Cities and Planning in the Ancient Near East* (New York: George Braziller, 1968), fig. 109.

Page 235 illustration: Le Corbusier, travel sketch from 1910-1918, reprinted from *Creation is a Patient Search* (New York: Frederick A. Praeger, 1960), p. 39.

CONTENTS

6 *Foreword*
Lord Rothschild

7 *Preface*
Arthur Spector

10 **1996**
TECHNOLOGY, PLACE & ARCHITECTURE

12 *Introduction*
Kenneth Frampton

16 Raimund Abraham
34 Enric Miralles
56 Glenn Murcutt
76 Jean Nouvel
94 Patricia Patkau
118 Renzo Piano
138 Álvaro Siza
160 Peter Walker

182 *Technological Euphoria vs. Critical Practice*
Stanford Anderson

190 *The Daemons of Place*
Robert Oxman

194 *Technological Change and the Fate of the Public Realm*
Kaarin Taipale

200 **1994**
ARCHITECTURE, HISTORY, & MEMORY

202 *Introduction*
Julian Beinart

204 Dimitris Antonakakis
208 A.J. Diamond
212 Balkrishna V. Doshi
216 James Ingo Freed
220 Arata Isozaki
224 Antoine Predock

228 *Memory in Architecture*
Stanford Anderson

230 *The Atrium as Surrogate Public Form*
Kenneth Frampton

232 *History and Memory*
Joseph Rykwert

234 **1992**
THE PUBLIC BUILDING:
FORM & INFLUENCE

236 *Introduction:*
Julian Beinart

238 Henry N. Cobb
242 Charles Correa
246 Romaldo Giurgola
250 Herman Hertzberger
254 Ram Karmi and Ada Karmi-Melamede
258 José Rafael Moneo
262 Richard Rogers
266 Moshe Safdie

270 *Louis Kahn and English History*
Stanford Anderson

272 *The Case for the Tectonic as Commemorative Form*
Kenneth Frampton

274 *The Contemporary Civic Building and the Public Work of Art*
Joseph Rykwert

276 *Biographies*
286 *Project Credits*
288 *Illustration Credits*

FOREWORD
Lord Rothschild

For more than a century, my family and Yad Hanadiv, our family foundation, have initiated public projects throughout Israel. The most significant, architecturally, are the Supreme Court, the Knesset, and Hemda, the Tel Aviv Center for Science Education. For the past thirty years, education has been Yad Hanadiv's principal focus. The Jerusalem Seminar in Architecture, established in 1992 at the time of the dedication of the Supreme Court building, joins our interests in architecture and education. The Seminar offers the architectural community edification and inspiration through an interaction with the world's finest practitioners of architectural theory and design. At its biennial conferences distinguished architects and theorists discuss their ideas and projects with thousands of colleagues. The Seminar creates a unique forum in Israel which enables architects and students to reflect on fundamental issues of their profession and to be confronted with the best work in the field of architecture.

Jerusalem, an ancient and modern city, is a particularly appropriate venue for the Seminar. Central to the three monotheistic religions, it is endowed with a mystique and spirit which have long served as a catalyst for new ideas. Its rich three-thousand-year architectural history combined with new architectural challenges make it both an architectural museum and a laboratory.

The Seminars have produced an impressive body of written and visual material. With the fourth conference scheduled for June 1998, during the celebration of Israel's Fiftieth Anniversary, it is appropriate to take stock and record in permanent form what the Seminars have achieved. This book, intended as an educational tool, will bring the deliberations of the Jerusalem Seminar in Architecture to a wide audience. Ideally, its contents will stimulate discussion, criticism, and the generation of new approaches.

It is my pleasure to thank my cousin Béatrice de Rothschild Rosenberg, a Yad Hanadiv Trustee, for taking a special interest in the Jerusalem Seminar in Architecture and, by doing so, ensuring its success.

PREFACE

Arthur Spector

The Jerusalem Seminar
1992–1996

The Rothschild family has been involved in the life of Israel since 1882, making seminal contributions in the fields of education, science, technology, culture, and welfare. Yad Hanadiv, their family foundation, has implemented the construction of two of the most significant public buildings in Israel, the Knesset (Parliament) and the Supreme Court.

In 1992, to celebrate the inauguration of the Supreme Court building, the Foundation sponsored a symposium on the architecture of the public building. The intent was to create an ongoing international forum for important topics in architecture and urbanism. Prominent architects, historians, and theorists from around the globe came to Jerusalem that year, and for subsequent biennial meetings, to discuss key topics through case studies of their own work.

This book, which documents these discussions, is being published during the fiftieth year of the State of Israel. At the turn of the century, Israel began to establish its social and political foundations. When the State was formed in 1948, it was hardly a cultural *tabula rasa*. Many Central European and Eastern Jews brought with them to Palestine skills, cultural traditions, and a burning desire to build a new and better society. This was particularly relevant in the case of architecture. The early migrant architects, such as Richard Kaufmann, Erich Mendelsohn, Leopold Krakauer, and Austen Harrison, were trained in Germany and England and brought to Palestine the emerging principles of modern architecture. Today, the International Style continues to be abundantly represented in Israel, much of it in its original form and clarity. These early pioneers transformed the architecture of the Mandate period and established a sound foundation of modern, white, cubic, flat-roofed architecture that was technically and climatically appropriate and suited to the idealism of the emerging state.

In the years following the establishment of the State, a successive generation of architects born and educated in Europe, such as Ze'ev Rechter, Dov Karmi, and Arieh Sharon, built on this tradition and produced much of the finest early architecture in Israel. While there were a number of very successful buildings in the early years of the State, the main concern was putting a roof over the heads of the streams of new immigrants arriving too fast to allow measured settlement or careful absorption. The new State was burdened with crippling security costs, allocating over sixty percent of its annual budget for defense. Architecture was not a priority, and there was neither the time nor the money to invest in implementing an architecture of quality or place.

Since the Six-Day War in 1967, Israel has suffered continuous debilitating terrorism. In response, most public architecture was, and still is, influenced by the need to build safe and protective buildings. Our public work has layers of barriers, giving a defensive character to most contemporary public buildings. This is hardly conducive to producing a welcoming or friendly built environment. It has inhibited the emergence of the public's identification with its civil architecture.

Given these contexts, it has been increasingly difficult to nurture and sustain a subtle discourse on Israel's architecture. This was the reason for Yad Hanadiv to sponsor a biennial seminar in architecture and urbanism. At the same time, Israel's emergence as a high-tech society with a strong economy and hopes for peace in the region has created an appetite for an architecture of quality and invention. It became essential to expose Israeli architects as directly as possible to the work and thinking of some of the most prominent architects in the world.

Jerusalem is a natural venue for such an exchange of ideas. As one of the world's eminent cities, its history and traditions have influenced the human spirit for over three thousand years. Its physical beauty and magnetism have the capacity to uplift and energize visitors.

The first two seminars, in 1992 and 1994, were chaired by Julian Beinart and myself. We strongly felt that the focus should be on built architecture. This allowed us to examine realized projects and gauge their impact on the communities they were intended to serve. We tried to ensure that the presentations would be as concise and as coherent as possible. We aimed for interaction among the lecturers and their formal respondents, and between the architects and the audience (largely comprised of Israeli architects), in smaller discussion sessions. As a complement to the main presentations, we invited a number of architectural historians and theorists to respond to the lectures and to present their own contributions on the topics.

The success of the first three seminars was unexpected. Close to one thousand architects participated in each of the first two seminars and an equal number had to be turned away for lack of space. For our third seminar, we moved the venue to a larger facility to accommodate the more than two thousand architects who eventually attended from many different countries.

Each seminar was audio- and videotaped; these largely unedited recordings were sent to universities and libraries around the world. Originally, we thought that this would be sufficient documentation. By 1996, we realized that the significance of the seminar proceedings merited more systematic and effective dissemination. We therefore decided to publish full-length, edited versions of the 1996 lectures and discussion sessions in this book. Lacking sufficiently edited documentation for the 1992 and 1994 proceedings, we present them here in an excerpted form which we believe indicates their essential content and conveys something of their impact.

This biennial seminar, consisting of three intensive days of highly stimulating and exhausting discussion of current issues vital to the practice of the profession, has demonstrated its capacity for enlivening architectural culture within Israel and beyond. In focusing on built work, frequently against the background of the larger urban or regional fabric, we have had the opportunity to cover a wide range of architectural topics with concise and articulate presentations. Seminar participants have been treated to intense and direct examination of many innovative architectural ideas.

Listening to the measured and precise observations of Harry Cobb, to Arata Isozaki's revelatory account of his early career, or to the culturally specific observations of Herman Hertzberger, Charles Correa, and Antoine Predock were for me moments of revelation. James Ingo Freed's emotionally charged description of his design for the United States Holocaust Memorial Museum was both deeply moving and of a special relevance to us. Later, I felt a special affinity for Renzo Piano when he convincingly implored the audience to avoid a linear process in design, much as Louis Kahn had done some forty years earlier. I cannot forget the refreshing modesty and understatement that characterized Álvaro Siza's presentation, or the way in which Stanford Anderson's scholarly contributions added an academic dimension to each seminar.

I want to thank Lord Rothschild and Yad Hanadiv for their vision and continuing support of the seminar series. Representing the Yad Hanadiv Board of Trustees, Béatrice de Rothschild Rosenberg has assumed particular responsibility for this project. Her intensive personal involvement has conferred an élan on the entire event. Arthur Fried, of Yad Hanadiv, has lent his invaluable advocacy and assistance throughout the six years of our tenure. My personal gratitude also goes to my colleague and conference co-chairman for the years 1992 and 1994, Julian Beinart, whose participation was, and is, very much part of the spirit of this symposium. An inestimable debt is also due to Lynne Rosman, our seminar coordinator and co-editor of this book; her boundless energy and organizing ability have assured the precision and quality of the proceedings. Lastly, I have to thank the twenty-seven distinguished practitioners who have participated in this seminar series to date. They have all taken time out from busy and intense schedules to be with us and give freely of themselves.

Kenneth Frampton, who was the chairman for the 1996 seminar, has edited this book so as to provide a clear sense of the interrelatedness of the presentations and the exchange among discussants which are characteristic features of the seminar. We are grateful to him for his involvement in the conference series since its inception. He has given generously of his professional knowledge, intellectual acumen, and ability to mediate in delicate situations.

1996

TECHNOLOGY, PLACE & ARCHITECTURE

June 9–11
International Convention Center Jerusalem

Seminar Chairman
Kenneth Frampton

Session Chairs
Shlomo Aronson
Julian Beinart
Pe'era Goldman
Arthur Goldreich
David Reznik
Moshe Safdie
Arthur Spector
Avraham Yaski

Discussion Moderators
Shlomo Aronson
Zvi Efrat
Omri Eytan
Pe'era Goldman
Andres Mariasch
Robert Oxman
Arie Rahamimoff
Tony Rigg

Presenters
Raimund Abraham
Enric Miralles
Glenn Murcutt
Jean Nouvel
Patricia Patkau
Renzo Piano
Álvaro Siza
Peter Walker

Commentary
Stanford Anderson
Robert Oxman
Kaarin Taipale

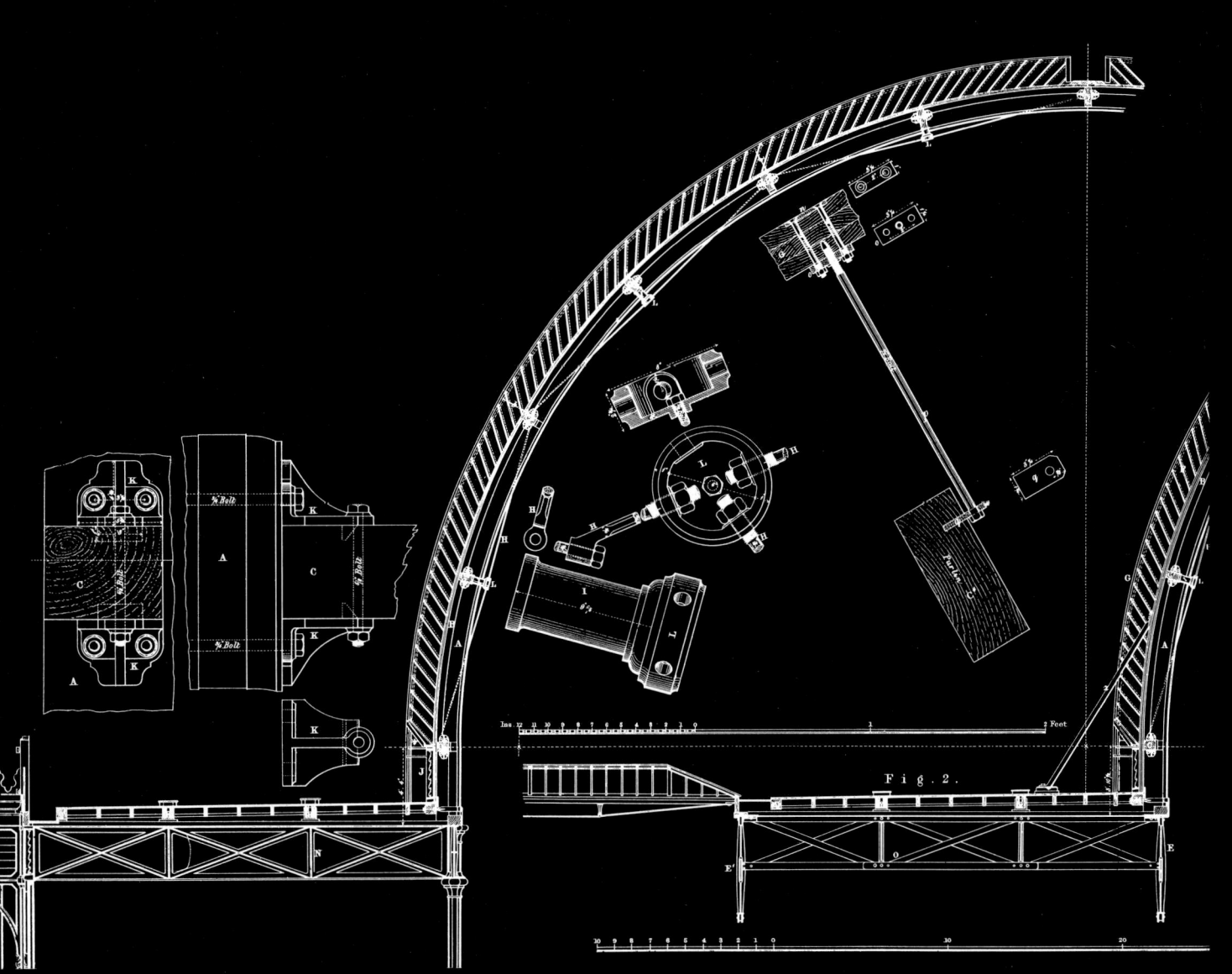

Fig. 2.

INTRODUCTION
Kenneth Frampton

Since the emergence of the profession, a salient, often undeclared aspect of architectural practice has been the reconciliation of conflicting values through the creation of inflected form, irrespective of whether the work be a private dwelling, a public institution, or a piece of urban development. This critical dimension has become more difficult to sustain due to the constantly escalating rate of technological change and the greatly increased scale of urbanization. The deleterious environments of the nineteenth-century industrial city notwithstanding, architecture and planning in the first half of this century still aspired to achieve a balance between industrialization and more traditional forms of agrarian land settlement and use. The turn of the century was attended by a proliferation of attempts to mediate between the two economies, largely through the creation of satellite communities designed by such garden city pioneers as Ebenezer Howard and Georges Benôit Lévy, or through the semi-spontaneous emergence of the dormitory suburb that followed in the wake of extending rail transit out into the countryside.

With the advent of universal car ownership after 1945, accompanied by the exponential expansion of tertiary industry and the maximization of agricultural production, this promise of achieving a new environmental equilibrium was constantly frustrated. Over the last fifty years, large areas of the so-called developed world have become placeless domains where each shopping mall looks like the next and a disjointed conglomeration of exurban fragments spreads across the landscape. This has been accompanied by intense but random levels of commercial high-rise speculation in one downtown after another.

One needs to set these transformations within a wider context, one which, while recognizing the broader consequences of regional urbanization, also acknowledges the way in which building technology has radically changed over the last half century. These innovations have brought about a dematerialization of building together with a literal mechanization/electrification of its fabric. The development of tungsten lighting, electrical elevators, two-pipe plumbing, central heating, and air-conditioning between 1880 and 1904 coincided with the simultaneous perfection of steel-frame and reinforced concrete construction. These innovations had the effect of separating the non-load-bearing skin from the structural frame of the building. As R. Gregory Turner has shown in his 1986 study, *Construction Economics and Building Design*, these changes shifted the focus away from undifferential masonry mass toward the articulation of built form into *podium, services, framework,* and *envelope.* Turner shows that, during the past thirty-five years, these sectors have grown increasingly independent, each with its own criteria and consultants. He also demonstrates that while the cost of the podium has remained relatively stable at twelve and one-half percent of the budget, the cost of electro-mechanical services has risen since the turn of the century to some thirty-five percent of the total. The chances are that this figure will only increase with the emergence of telematic communication. Conversely, the amount devoted to the basic structure has dropped from approximately eighty percent in the previous century to some twenty percent today. That we tend to spend more today on electro-mechanical equipment than on any other single item is surely indicative of the importance we now attach to comfort and communicative efficiency rather than to durability and the representational value of built form.

Despite the undeniable progress of techno-science and the beneficial effect it has had on the quality of human life, one has sufficient reason to be apprehensive about the tendency of technology to become a new nature covering the surface of the earth while simultaneously destabilizing both the natural and the man-made worlds.

Admittedly we have an overall tendency rather than an absolute condition applying to all building everywhere at any given historical moment. Moreover, as Cecil D. Elliot has written in his book, *Technics and Architecture* (1992):

> It would be convenient, but only somewhat accurate, to attribute twentieth-century changes in architecture to the influence of technology as it was applied to building. Architecture is a complex art having many a master. A building is at the same time an object, an investment and a cultural and personal expression of beliefs. Any change in the way buildings are built or the way they look must be tested by a variety of standards, their relative importance being somewhat different for every project. This truism explains why certain technological aspects of architecture have been readily adopted and others have been long delayed. . . .

What Elliot does not say is that building, like agriculture, tends to be a somewhat anachronistic procedure, one that by standards of techno-science cannot be truly regarded as being "high-tech." We need look no further than to the typical foundation in order to have proof of this. I am alluding to the tangled mass of mud, rock, and preexisting pipes, etc., that even today is still the prelude to almost every building operation. It is precisely this schism between wet and dry construction, together with the split between craft-practice and industrial technique, that compels one to acknowledge the hybrid character of building. Within this mixed activity, it is possible to apply various levels of production to different parts of a given work, not only for reasons of economy and efficiency but also for the realization of certain expressive values. Technological maximization as an end in itself is categorically opposed to the expressive potential of the consciously hybrid approach, since this last yields a range of forms that are more open to inflection. The very opposite of this mediatory attitude is made evident by the maximization of technique. I am thinking, say, of the optimization of air-conditioning in hot-dry climates where protection from the sun has been traditionally provided by thick walls, overhangs, and cross-ventilation, or in this century by the provision of *brise soleil* and by the possibility of opening and closing windows and shutters at will. The capacity to open a structure to natural ventilation is equally crucial in temperate climates. Who has not experienced the situation where in fine weather it is impossible to open a window because the fenestration has been fixed in order to maximize the efficiency of the air-conditioning system? Similar observations may be applied to the traditional roof and its capacity to shield a building from inclement weather. Moreover, all such responsive elements can be said to be automatically expressive of the climate and hence of the place in which the structure happens to be situated.

From this it follows that technological maximization as such is often antithetical to the creation and maintenance of the place-form. We may note how the maximization of one technique will sometimes necessitate the equally excessive use of another. Thus, the prevalence of air-conditioning is in part a compensatory response to automotive noise and petro-chemical pollution. This double bind of using one technique to correct a dysfunction caused by another may be compared to similar syndromes in other fields. I have in mind the overprescription of antibiotics together with the optimized use of invasive high-tech surgical methods in the practice of allopathic medicine, or, let us say, the excessive use of artificial fertilizers in agriculture with the corresponding undermining of the immune system and equally deleterious effects on the water table and long-term fertility of the land. As against such maximizing techniques, often applied for economic or ideological reasons, we may posit the judicious application of technology to the real issues confronting society. The challenge is to maintain cultural *quality* in an epoch largely devoted to the instrumentalization of *quantity*.

Thus, one is brought to recognize the perennial demand for rationalized production and constructional innovation, including such recent developments as the use of structural glass over wide spans or the employment of high-strength glues and sealants in almost every aspect of building construction. Such new materials and jointing methods have shifted the focus away from load-bearing masonry towards "dematerialized" modes of assembly. This transformation has been accompanied by the proliferation of other "dry" techniques from gypsum plasterboard to glass-reinforced fiber, from heat-resistant glass to thin, machine-cut stone capable of simulating heavy-weight masonry. Whether or not one elects to exploit such applications to unsatisfactory ends is one of the ethical and cultural dilemmas confronting architectural design today. The ubiquitous curtain wall is a case in point, for it has often been applied in unsuitable cultural and climatic situations—ostensibly for economic expediency. In India, for example, the intense radiant heat gain and the accompanying glare make it a questionable technique.

Technological maximization, irrespective of whether it is bureaucratically enforced or ideologically adopted, also has the tendency to reduce the creation of built-form to the production of freestanding objects, whether the object in question is merely a technological instrument or the occasion for a spectacular aesthetic display. Against this, we may posit the critical strategy of the place-form, the ecological obligation that each new structure be inscribed into its site in such a way as to permit the creation of an articulated earthwork. Thus Mario Botta's slogan "building the site" means to engender a condition in which it is all but impossible to discern where the ground ends and the building begins. Hence the critical import of the *tectonic* and the *topographical* values in the development of built form, or, to put it more directly, the protective value of the *roofwork* and sustaining value of the *earthwork*.

This evocation of the earthwork returns us to the issue of global urbanization and to the fact that the reintegration of land-form into built-fabric is crucial today if we are to be able to mediate in any way the consequences of megalopolitan development. Aside from the application of minimum standards, as these are essential to the regulation of highway construction and suburban zoning, regional urbanization over the past fifty years has shown little regard for the cultural and ecological impact that scattered suburban settlement has had on the overall character of the landscape. This impact has been felt on land that, within living memory, was almost exclusively devoted to agriculture or forestry, and on areas previously classified as desert, which have been transformed into verdant automotive suburbs largely through the profligate use of irrigation. While much of this rapacious development will be difficult to reintegrate in cultural and ecological terms (one thinks of the infinitely extended American strip, most of which will become ruined long before it is either demolished or rebuilt), it is nonetheless desirable that every architectural commission be conceived as a potential place-form, or that, where necessary, the work should create its own micro-environmental context. In this sense, the art of landscape is absolutely critical. At the same time one must remain open to the use of advanced techniques, particularly where judiciously applied and inflected so as to create a culturally significant work.

All of the above accounts for the range, type, and caliber of the architects and critics who have been invited to participate in this seminar. In one way or another, they have all been involved in the conscious creation of critical work. Moreover, they have each displayed their own specific capacity for balancing the use of modern technology with a particular sensitivity towards the value of topographical form. Thus, all of them point in their respective ways to a future in which technique, in all its aspects, will come to be mediated by architecture for the purposes of sustaining the identity of a place.

LECTURE
Raimund Abraham

I would like to express my gratitude for the privilege of having participated in this conference and for the special hospitality I have been shown. I think all of us who participated here have lectured and participated in seminars in many cities all over the world. But this is not any city: this is Jerusalem. For me, this is so overwhelming that it makes it almost impossible to casually return to the conventional engagement in an academic discourse on architecture. Jerusalem is a city unlike any other, a city which has been violated radically and repeatedly over millennia, its edifices erased, rebuilt, or inscribed into the imaginary world of memory, while all European capitals have either succumbed to preservation or become showcases of architectural design, giving birth at a breathtaking pace to the newest trends and their stars.

This morning I happened to read that Frank Gehry has been selected as one of the twenty-five most influential people in America. Imagine: it was not Madonna, or Michael Jackson, or Mick Jagger; it was Frank Gehry. While this event may be celebrated by professionals as a public triumph of their profession, it may be that architecture will be more and more removed from the humility of its task as it is projected into the limelight of show business—seemingly elevated, but actually absorbed by the world of commodities. This is a betrayal of the realm of ideas rooted in the inevitable challenge of authenticity, ideas which have always been and always will be born in the desperate loneliness and within the hermetic world of the singular artist.

I shall present today, through texts and images of my work, a singular position in architecture which does not claim to impose a collective ideology. I do not claim to present answers, but rather questions, in a continuous search for the truth, my truth, in architecture.

When everything has become possible through technology, it might be that nothing is possible anymore. The methodology of sequential thought will encounter the resistance of thought itself. Development exhausts itself in the impossible. But hope, hidden in the impossible, may provide a new vision: to embark on unpredictable journeys, to generate impulses of resistance, to create images, which, by going beyond the signification of resistance, become resistance. Images, by denying obedience to the boundaries of historic memory, become memory, not to remember, but to be remembered.

Borders are essential to pass judgment, borders are metaphors to be dissolved when judgment has been passed: moments of critical positions. Borders: to probe, to surmise, yet indecipherable; to embody borders by their absence. Borders: conceived as passages, compressed, shattered within their own density, to become fragments of new borders. Object and image appear inseparably interlocked by invisible and inseparable borders. Yet the awareness of the separability, incapable of liberating their own density, becomes the essential impulse toward reality, a continuously changing reality, in which space and time are inseparable yet exchangeable.

Transplantion II
Project, 1967

In what direction is architecture going? Architecture moves toward itself to dissolve in itself, to become speechless for the sake of silence, yet filled with the desire to signify its solitude: silent, unknown, sign. In the written image: immutable. In the drawn image: unspeakable. In the built image: uninhabitable. The mystery of these images becomes the myth of the journey of architecture, and the odyssey of the imaginary inhabitants who attempt to decipher them. The Sirens were conquered by Ulysses, by his obstinacy and by his deception, by the harmless power of technology. Yet the power of their songs made them imperishable.

One ought to try to reduce everything to dot zero. The search for dot-zero is the surveyor's odyssey. All spatial properties lie hidden in this point. Yet it is this point—inaccessible, defiant of any methodology—that would make it worthwhile to search for and cherish its revelations. The spaces of the imaginary have no dimensions. In the solitude of silence, whisper screams.

The temple had to yield first to destruction before one could contemplate its palingenesis. Architecture must remind itself how vulnerable the surface of the earth has become: the horizon; magic site of all beginnings.

The theorems of geometry are text. Its translatability into physiological signs and images constitutes the ontological task of architecture. Writing music: vision of sounds. Drawing architecture: sounds of vision.

Wittgenstein's proposition that architecture perpetuates and glorifies (yet if there is nothing that deserves glorification, there is no need for architecture), can be refuted by the fact that architecture has already crossed the threshold of glorification by its own negation. Architecture takes care of itself. In the depth of speechlessness: the manifestation of silence.

Technology meets tradition:
Led by its master, this camel carries solar panels on its back which power a compact refrigerator underneath.

Before I break this silence with my own work, I would like to project an image that encompasses my thoughts, or rather clarifies my position toward technology. And it might help, by its poetic irony, to dispel the anxiety of those who fear the diabolic consequences of technology, and to discourage those who are willing to embrace technology as the savior of our future existence. This image, as you see, is of a camel and its master; the camel carries a solar panel to power a refrigerator, which is carried underneath. I believe that, unless we retain this irony in the face of the almost apocalyptic development of technology, we are going to lose our hope.

In my search for architecture, I try to cut through that which we call the History of Architecture, namely, an accumulation of edifices, their dates, and the names of their inventors. I rather want to cut back to the beginning of time and space, exactly that ontological site which provides us with the possibility of regaining our sensibility toward the interventions caused by architecture. Whether you like it or not, whatever we do—in thought, in drawing, in writing, or in the actual implementation of buildings—we are going to violate that horizon, we are going to violate the equilibrium between the sky and the earth.

The site is the generating force that produces or should produce architecture. I cannot conceive of any formal manifestation that is not rooted in the site. The site is a manifold phenomenon. It is first a place of immediacy, a place of confrontation of our most basic sensibilities, our most basic needs, the most basic need for shelter, while the power of ideal language empowers us to transmute, to transform that immediate physiological space defined by our senses and our most basic desires into places where the rituals of life can be celebrated.

In that search, I discovered that architecture, which has been associated with the other visual arts (with painting and sculpture, and particularly the erroneous assumption that when architecture reaches the complexity of sculpture it becomes art), is a language that has more essential affinities to other structural languages, such as literature, cinema, and music. In that context, I would like to read a text that I translated from *Die Schrift* by Vilém Flusser, one of the most important thinkers of our time, a Jewish philosopher who fled Prague in the 1930s and lived most of his life in Brazil. I believe that thus far, none of his texts has been translated from the German.

> One of the fundamental mythologies of the Western world confirms the etymological precedence of excavating, cutting, carving, or painting. According to this myth, god formed his own image out of clay (in Hebrew, *adamah*) to create man (in Hebrew, *adam*) by imprinting his spirit into matter. God took matter (clay) in his hand, touched it, transformed it and finally carved forms into it—he in-formed it.
>
> To inform becomes as such an active gesture directed against matter and object.
> To write is to in-form by excavating, carving furrows of the spirit into objects of matter.
> To write is the gesture of carving information with the intent and desire to excavate shafts into the prison walls in order to escape the imprisonment of the objective world.

Born into the landscape.

To touch it, to smell it, to let the eyes graze over it, to let the eyes dig into it, to scratch signs into the earth, to excavate cavities, to pile up mounds, to bury the entire body in the earth, to measure with groping steps, to feel space, to draw scales and to engrave them eternally into Stone.

To sharpen the eyes like a sword, not only to caress the landscape, but to dissect it, to measure between the heavens and earth, to create horizons.

To let lines vanish into points, immaterial, but with greater precision than any known tactile or visual reality before.

Torn from the power of gravity. Torn from the terror of the endless landscape. Memory and desire: that is Architecture, Built or Unbuilt. A collision of irreconcilable thoughts and interventions.

In entering the images of my work, I would like to reflect upon the very important beginning in my work. These were the heroic times of the

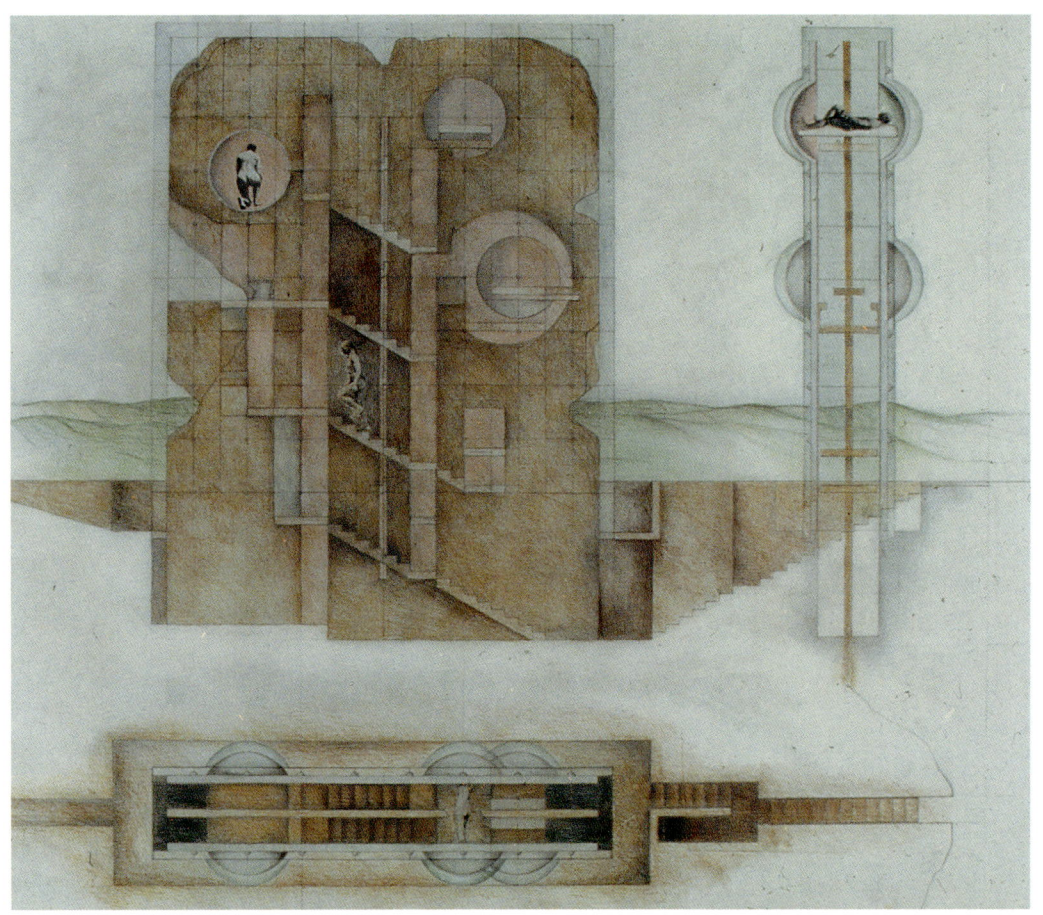

House Without Rooms
Project, 1974
Sections (above)
and skeleton model (right)

House for Euclid
Project, 1983
Fragment (left)
and rendering of transformation (below)

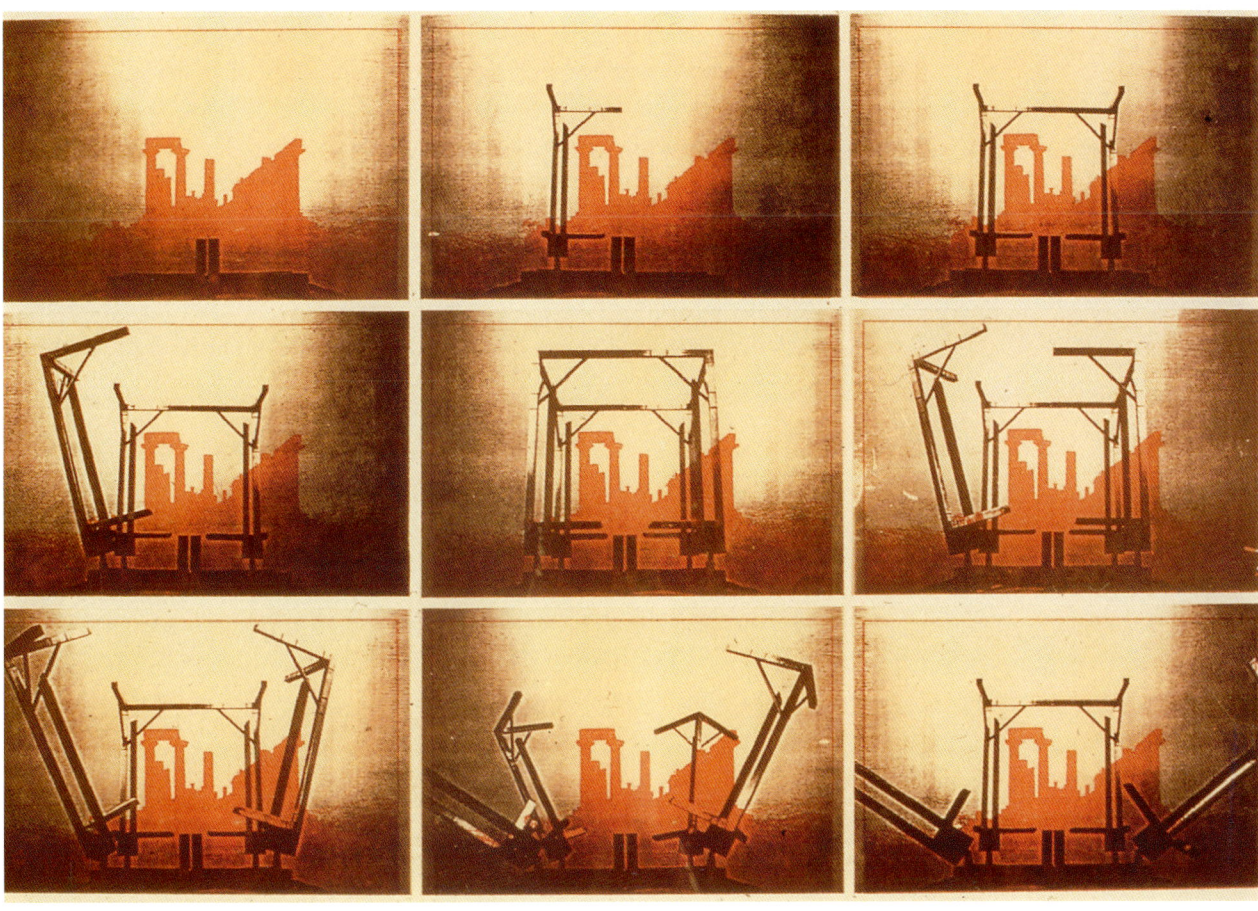

1960s. The projects have been falsely interpreted as utopias, as fantasies. For me, they are simply visual poems, poems that were carried by the impulses of a fascination with technology—not as a savior, not as a tool for progress, but as an enigmatic phenomenon of magnificent structures. These images were created by my romantic notion of and attachment to the technology of that time.

The first project is a Crater City. The second, a tower hanging into the water from the surface of the earth. Each work implied a different intent, but both ultimately embodied exactly that spirit which allowed me to depart from the conventional task of becoming a practicing architect. For while I am not a practitioner, I practice the discipline of architecture.

From this series of imaginary projects, which were highly influenced by the fascination with technology, in the 1970s I returned to the problem of the house. The house is one of the ever-haunting origins of architecture. The primal necessity to dwell becomes the need to transcend the notion of dwelling with the poetic desire to conquer and inhabit unknown abodes, to recall an architecture that is rooted in the metaphoric notion of elemental tectonic interventions in imaginary or memorized landscapes. While my early projects testify to my determination to search for an architecture that has its origins in the collision of fundamentally abstract forms with the topography of landscape, my later series, *Houses,* manifests my obsession to encompass and project the archetypal ritual of dwelling.

The first of these dwellings is the House without Rooms, in which the fragmented elements of the house—archaic by their own nature—become inseparably compressed within a fragile cosmology that denies the conquest of habitation. Space is stripped of its Euclidean dimension. Then the house is virtually born: submerged and erect, receiving and rejecting, fertile sediments of an unknown intimacy. Eyes barter vision for touch, perpetuating memories for the future embedded in layers of the past. Walls are transformed into sensory constructs, defining movement through tactile sensations.

Horizons appear tilted, verticalized. Strips of sky are buried in shadows of the earth's crust. Gravity loses its eternal dominance. Light is filtered through stairs toward the inner parts of the house, barely illuminating motionless landscapes of flesh and stone: fossils of an unchallenged presence. The inner silence remains protected by the armor of the outer walls, metallic reminiscence of ancient shelters.

The second House is the House for Euclid. It is based upon a dream. My recollection of dreams has usually been vague, fragmentary, and distorted, but this particular dream left a precise and lasting imprint on my memory. A man who strongly resembled Jim Stirling guided me toward, as he described it, a mysterious construction site. A soft and barren hill, detached from any recognizable geographic identity, revealed on its flattened top a square concrete slab with sides approximately twelve feet long raised one foot above the soil. Its surface was marked by an orthogonal grid parallel with the sides of the square plane. Four cubes, approximately eighteen by eighteen inches, were placed one on each corner of the slab. They seemingly floated above the surface of the square. Each steel cube was supported and connected by a steel joint that functioned as a pin hinge, turning 180 degrees within a vertical plane, and as a vertical axle, turning 360 degrees within the horizontal plane with independent sockets in the cube as well as the slab. Each of the cubes was turned against the orthogonal sides of the slab and appeared slightly tilted along the vertical axis, as if to defy the accepted rules of gravity. The number of possible juxtapositions seemed infinite. It was the precision of my memory that enabled me to demystify the imaginary quality of the dream: surreal and real became interchangeable metaphors.

Next, I have chosen to present a series of towers, some built and some in the process of being built. These are towers that are defined not by the possibilities of technology, of meaning, of reaching the limits of the sky, but rather partially by their materiality, by a new definition of a vertical shaft. They are actually all very small.

The first tower is a simple stair tower attached to an old house belonging to friends of mine who wanted independent access to each floor. For me, despite its rather simplistic function, the tower became a guardian of the house, a witness, hermetically enclosed as any guardian has to be, only accessible to light, but offering the softness of a space that is inhabitable by the moving body of the occupant, defining the movement from the darkness to the light.

The second is an unbuilt tower, the Times Square Tower. This was an entry to an ideas competition to find a replacement for the old Times Square Tower in New York City. There was a time in New York when one never had to look in the newspaper for the movies. All the movies were shown in Times Square shortly after they were released and you could see them cheaper there than anywhere else in town. So I proposed a tower consisting of seven cinemas stacked on top of each other. This project is particularly important for me since it demonstrates, first of all, that I never arrive at a formal manifestation without confronting it with the program. For me this is a confrontational process, not "form follows function" or vice versa. I believe architecture has the power to deny habitation, to deny illumination, to deny all known properties that would conventionally qualify it as habitational, but it nonetheless has to be confronted with that as a program.

In the process of stacking the cinemas, there were affinities I had not anticipated, affinities to the "Endless Tower" of Brancusi as a tower of rhythmically changeable or interchangeable elements reaching to infinity, yet crowned by another object.

This is the stair tower of a building that is located at the end of the city of Graz in southern Austria, adjacent to a park. I wanted to create a building that almost directly responds to the forces of the site, a rather noisy street; this results in that very protective windowless shield with the terraces oriented toward the park. In this deconstruction of a building into its basic tectonic elements, the tower itself became the crucial pivot

Above and right
Stair Tower
Lanz, Austria, 1985

Facing page
Times Square Tower
Site montage, 1984

around which all other elements moved. In this case, the tower is not like the first stair tower, the guardian. It is a sign that defines the vertical movement within the structure of the building.

The next tower occurs as a repetitive element in a row housing project in Vienna, where I tried to expand on the idea of the tower as a guardian, as a sign for vertical access, and also as a repetitive form that demonstrates the almost fatalistic aspect of living next to one another.

The next tower is perhaps the tower of my destiny. It is the tower for the Austrian Cultural Institute on 52nd Street in New York. The classical building protruding out of the building line is the site, which may be one of the most unique sites for a tower in the city. It is seven meters sixty wide and the tower is going to be about eighty meters tall. It was the result of a competition.

As this tower is a rather small object within the vertical topography of the city of New York, I tried to develop a tectonic vocabulary that would not make the tower rise, but rather the opposite; the point was to make it fall—that falling notion projecting the sense of suspension. The origin of the scheme has been inspired by the most trivial circumstances of the so-called zoning envelope that defines the limits of any vertical building in New York. I simply took the exact angle of the sloping zoning envelope, decomposed it, and structured it in autonomous planes, which, by their layering, created that sense of suspension and not of ascension.

By the nature of the site, the smallness and proximity of the adjacent building, the tower can be decomposed into three basic elements: to the rear, the staircase, which I have called the vertebrae; the supporting tower; and the transparent mask. All the light in the interior spaces of the tower is projected through the outer skin. The lateral compression of the site, I wrote, defines the latency of its vertical thrust.

Three elementary towers:

> The Vertebra / Stair Tower
> The Core / Structural Tower
> The Mask / Glass Tower

Signifying three counterforces of gravity:

> The Vertebra—Ascension
> The Core—Support
> The Mask—Suspension

The entire Tower rests on the cavity of its public spaces.

So it is not like the conventional segmentation of a column into base, shaft, and capital; rather it is a lateral definition. This means there are actually three towers contained in one. This drawing demonstrates the statement about the whole tower resting on the cavity of its public space. There are two kinds of public spaces: inter-flowing spaces of galleries leading up to a small theater and library, and repetitive loft spaces for offices and apartments.

This drawing shows the rather complex solution to the required means of egress from the tower out to the street inside the seven-meter-sixty frontage. It was a struggle working within the severe limitations of the New York City building code, and the tectonic gesture of the tower to provide spaces that would justify its construction, would justify its use. So for me, from the very beginning of this project with the competition, finding the most efficient and economical solution was inseparable from my architectural vision.

This is a tower that was never intended to be built, the tower of my imagination, the *Tower of Wisdom*. This realm of drawing and imagination is the world that keeps me sane when I despair in the trivial world of professionalism.

A drawing for me is a model that oscillates between the idea and the physical or built reality of architecture. It is not a step toward this reality, but an autonomous act to anticipate the concreteness of the ideal. An architectural drawing can never be rendered, but has to submit to the laws of construction, revealing the idea of the inherent syntactic form through the grammar of lines. The line demands the precision of geometry, while the layering of pigments expresses the inner and outer qualities of materiality through texture. The first markings on a white sheet of paper, the first carvings in stone, the first engravings in metallic plates represent the beginnings of architecture, the primal act of construction moves toward the realization of an idea.

> To draw is to cut an idea into a body, violating its silence.
> To draw is to map the world through signs, locating the absence of the eyes.

When you build you have to submit to the fate of architecture. Idea and matter are the poles of architecture. Their futures differ. For thought, the idea prevails. For matter, it turns to waste. The idea is the manifestation of thought totally encased and protected by the individual power of its inventor, but violated by the intention of implementation, and consequently, its realization. The utterance of thought is silenced as soon as it is pronounced, while the silence of matter is violated by its own fate of decay. Knowing that only what appears evident can be translated, the enigma of unknown fragments remains. Matter will only survive its own fate through the memory of desire: an adventure across the real and the imaginary, an adventure of work in pursuit of itself.

> While you build the wall you shall destroy the stones
> while your eyes long for the window you shall destroy the wall
> while you form sheets of glass you shall destroy the crystals
> while you extrude the iron bar you shall destroy mountains of ore
> while you reach for the sky you shall destroy the earth.

Stair Tower
Residential building, Graz, Austria, 1990–1993

Austrian Cultural Institute
New York, 1992–
Site montage (facing page)
and model (right)

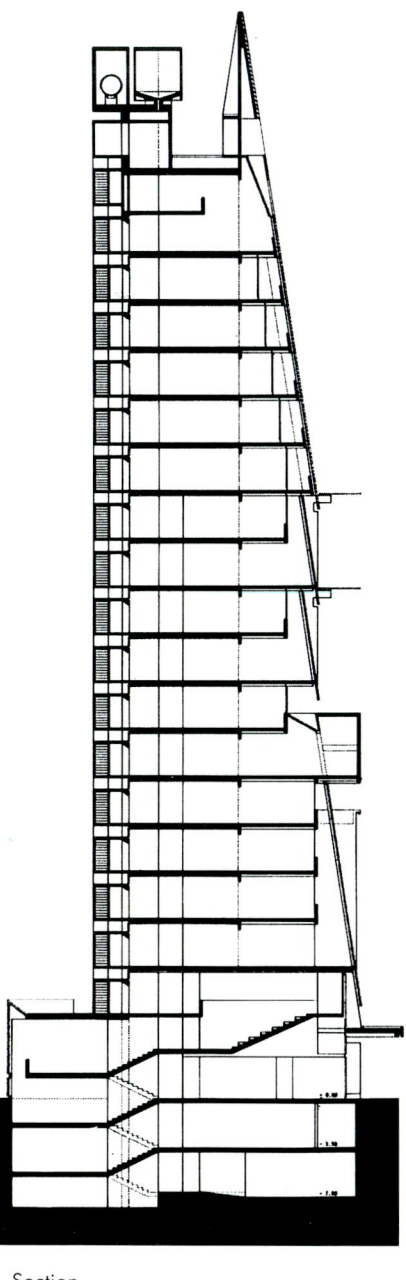

Section

29

DISCUSSION
Raimund Abraham
Omri Eytan

Omri Eytan: *Could you begin by saying something about* Technology, Place & Architecture?

Raimund Abraham: I am suspicious of the triadic title because in a trilogy, one of the three terms can always be negotiated with the other two. Thus we may say that on the one hand technology threatens the identity of place and that without place, there's no architecture. Alternatively, we may say that technology itself is our salvation and that we no longer have any need for place. The fact is that none of us has any possibility of influencing the apocalyptic development of technology. This is simply a consequence of the human condition. Man is a thinking animal, and thought, while dangerous, cannot be limited or censored. In science there is a predictable evolution of thought, which is entirely different from architecture—which I consider an art without possibility for evolution. I am totally bemused by Jean Nouvel's question, namely, how does one go beyond Mies van der Rohe, because Mies reached his own limits. Moreover, Mies's work had nothing to do with transparency, because he treated glass as a crystalline material in order to reduce architecture to an utmost clarity. Hence Philip Johnson's total misreading of Mies in his own Glass House—he thought that Mies was after transparency.

When I was a student we had clearly defined adversaries. Our professors were conservatives. They believed in a certain kind of building typology derived from historical precedent, so it was an easy position to revolt against. But now we have teachers like myself who encourage the students to imagine their own limits and to experiment continually. They are urged to be completely free, except that I insist on clarity and craft discipline. So today it is difficult to revolt.

I practice the discipline of architecture, but I'm not a practitioner. I teach architecture, but I'm not a teacher. I engage in theory, but I'm not a theoretician. I have refused to become absorbed by any kind of movement, by any kind of collective enterprise. My work comes into being under rather hermetic conditions. I try to isolate myself, and I think this is possible for every student or architect, because it doesn't take much to make architecture. All you need, ultimately, is a piece of paper, a pen, and a room where you can lock your door. I think that if everyone took that seriously, there would be resistance against the public relations professions of our time; against a world dominated by star architects who have become their own promoters. As far as technology in architecture is concerned, we are still referring to a very primitive technology. Comparatively speaking, architecture is still based on principles that are thousands of years old. The cutting edge of technology today is the invisible technology of genetic engineering, of microchips. This technology has one real danger: with its seductive power, it can undermine authenticity. Recently, in a discussion with a friend, I said, "I don't worry about virtual reality. I worry about virtual authenticity." We may say that virtual reality is simply a consequence of more complex machines. The issue is that advanced technology can help us produce very seductive images, images of buildings that appear to be floating, transparent. Jean Nouvel remarked yesterday evening that he is striving for an architecture that is magic. I'm also striving for an architecture that is magic; but my magic lies in the mystery, whereas his magic derives from magicians. As long as you don't know the tricks of a magician, it's all very fascinating. The moment we find out how it works—when the rabbit comes out of the hat—it's all over.

With his invention of illusion in film, another Frenchman, Georges Méliès, became the greatest living magician at the beginning of the century. While films tried to simulate movement, Méliès was the first filmmaker to realize that film's potential was in something different; namely, the possibility to let singular frames, as images, collide in time. In this way Méliès as magician could have been the greatest producer of virtual reality in his day. Instead, he decided to go for the truth: to not exploit the technology of cinema to simulate movement but rather to discover the truth of the medium. That has always been a great inspiration for me. I had many friends who were independent filmmakers, and they infused me with the idea that one may become a practicing architect without waiting for commissions. You can make architecture simply by drawing your ideas on a pad or building a model. I still don't believe that architecture necessarily has to be built; it can also be quite literally written.

Habitation is a ritual that is thousands, maybe millions of years old, and we simply have to reinterpret it: there has to be a difference in meaning between the term "house" as used today versus a thousand years ago. There is a different program for which one has to invent a new tectonic language. The technology of our time is leading us toward architecture composed totally of images, while I believe that the truth of architecture lies in the invisible part of the building, how it has been constructed, how the material meets other material. Only the one who makes something ultimately knows its essence, and this is true of any other discipline.

On the other hand, architecture has the advantage of embodying abstraction in its own syntax. This means that when you find a ruin of a temple somewhere in the fields, you are able to reconstruct the whole because the logic of the whole was already embedded in the fragments. It's impossible to do that with a painting or sculpture.

A month ago I made a presentation of a book on my work in my home town, Bolzano, in the mountainous region of Austria. I was talking to people whom I had known since my childhood, and it was a very strange feeling because I had left this place long ago. I realized that in retaining my memory of the mountains I had climbed, the people I had known, I had in fact left nothing behind. It is this memory that reappears in your work. At the same time, I am not a sentimental person. Sentimentality comes when you don't succeed in creating your memory. There is a poem which says that the only memory that counts is the memory that remembers you.

Growing up in a world like the one in which I grew up, where you had to climb mountains in order to get beyond the treeline to be free; where your life depended on the cracks in the rock, I found that what I learned in school is incomparably less important than what I learned through experience with the soil I grew up on. Many of my relatives were wine growers, and I grew up with the experience of watching the earth being cut and tilled. I smelled the earth, the cow shit, the animals; and I touched the rocks. This is the kind of memory that re-emerges in one's work.

Eytan: *Your works tend not to be ephemeral in nature, as opposed to the projects by Jean Nouvel. You deal with a place, and you want to define your relationship with this place. You build as part of an overall context, which is also social; that is, it is built for people. So you must have some notion of the nature of your social intervention as an architect.*

Abraham: First we should talk about gravity, and then about the social component. When I build I draw very little, because I never considered drawing as a means to determine reality but rather as an autonomous reality. Thus, when I build, I draw a little and I build models. I build large-scale models because I want to sense the weight of the elements I am going to use in the construction. So even if technology provides us today with means by which weight seemingly can be overcome, where gravity is not an issue anymore, I instinctively go against such a trend. I believe that one of the challenges of our time is to build differently with archaic materials, while being affected by the modern sense of transparency and lightness. We should strive for reinterpretation in which we recognize what is archaic in our nature and what is archaic in the nature of architecture. I don't doubt that we will enter a time when architecture is no longer necessary. It may be that we are not necessary anymore, and this is the ultimate confrontation between entropy and immortality. Science puts its faith in immortality, while architecture has to reflect entropy; it has to concern itself with the fragility of our lives, of our survival. Technology aims to give us the hope that we may overcome death, that we may live forever. Those who fear death embrace technology; those who celebrate death in a hopeful way are surely architects. I believe that if as an architect you try to convey and transform your own humanity, you don't have to worry about not transferring your social conscience into your architecture.

In the last analysis, perhaps housing is not a suitable subject for architecture. I felt that way when I entered Jerusalem and saw all those instant housing projects without any infrastructure, without any feeling for the subtleties of the place. They are, for whatever reason, simply imposed on the landscape. Maybe we can call most of them ugly; maybe they're not architecture. Alternatively, they are architecture in a different way. I've never experienced anything like that.

Eytan: *Would you intervene in a living, historical city that is trying to be modern by using high-tech architecture? How do you see the work of Jean Nouvel and others like him with regard to maintaining indifference toward the specific character of a place?*

Abraham: I'm afraid that I cannot talk about Jerusalem and Jean Nouvel in the same context, but what I experienced yesterday, looking from the Mount of Olives, is that there is such a powerful presence of violation in this city, historically speaking, and with any violation there is always some truth. Today when you go to any one of the capitals of Europe, particularly Vienna— which I know better than the others—you walk through an alien city, because it has been renovated; it has been preserved. Any violation has been camouflaged. The old buildings have new skins, but the skins are all wrong, because the wrong stucco, the wrong paint, and the wrong color have been used. So they *look* like the buildings I remember, but they are not the buildings I remember. I am drawn to look at all the ugly highrises even if doing so violates my aesthetic sensibilities.

We live at a time when we have perhaps never been closer to actually experiencing the apocalypse. The apocalypse is not this wonderful event where the heavens come down and the earth is swallowed up. Instead, the apocalypse is a very slow process, much like cancer, and it is happening every day. The only way each of us can function is if we recognize its presence and still succeed in making beautiful things. There have always been times when wars were raging over the land yet somewhere in a monastery a monk was making a book or somebody else, a painting. And what is left from those wars? Not the heroes; they are all gone. What is left is the book, the painting, and the sculpture that were made. Nothing has really changed, except we become more and more aware of the consequences of thought, the consequences of inventions, the consequences of technology. I think that if we have the courage to recognize it, this is a wonderful time.

Without any question, Jean Nouvel is a very good architect. I don't believe that his architecture doesn't make places; they are just different kinds of places. Jean Nouvel attempts to use his own designs, his own vision and invention, as a new ideology for making architecture. I don't want to be part of that. I don't believe in magicians' architecture. He does. There is a difference between those who embrace technology and those who simply use it. I am not convinced by an ideology that hopes for a future of light, dematerialized architecture. It is a rather naive hope, because with the exception of Albert Speer, architects never had any power. As to an architecture capable of influencing the spiritual life of any culture, there were only a few architects who had the courage, the endurance, and the vision to make such an architecture. There were times—short periods of time—when some architects in different parts of the world shared collective support for those visions. For example, take the historical context of the birth of modern architecture and modern art: it was characterized by a collective breakdown of all known social systems and the beginnings of an experiment in democracy. This monumental change led to collective support for a new revolution in the disciplines of the arts. Unfortunately, we are not in a time like that. There is no collective support, and we should not be so unrealistic as to look for it. The only chance we have is to be as radical, as individuals, as we can.

I was shocked when the Soviet Union collapsed. In the period of oppression, Soviet artists had the chance to make an art that was as powerful as the revolution itself, but what they had produced was imitation Andy Warhol. Just as you can never blame your parents for your failures, so you cannot blame the circumstances in which you are asked to make your architecture. You must have the courage to do your own thing. Thinking is dangerous, and imagining is even more dangerous. Opportunism starts already in kindergarten. When you go to kindergarten you realize that at a certain moment all kids are equally imaginative; they all make wonderful paintings and drawings. Then along comes the teacher and says: "The tree is not blue, it's green. The sky is blue, not red." And so out of twenty kids, maybe three will say, "No! My tree remains blue." Can you imagine the ratio of kids who succumb to the pressure of authority when it comes to elementary school and then to high school and university? Needless to say, very few of them survive; not because they don't have the same possibility for imagination but because they have abandoned it.

Eytan: *In what way can we be radical as architects at this moment in history?*

Abraham: I think we have to define "we." I think you have to have the courage to say "I," because the "we" is ultimately undefinable. You refer to "they," which are always the others, while "we" are the ones in the know. What I understand by the term radical is striving to achieve utmost clarity in one's work. Radical, in my opinion, means is that you honestly pursue your own limits and the limits of the discipline in which you try to express yourself. That, I think, is what each of us has to do in his own way. What is not radical is to go with the fashions and the trends and lament about the lack of support you get, collectively or otherwise.

Eytan: *Which leads us back into the ground and to the idea of being rooted.*

Abraham: Yes. You can uproot a plant, pull the roots out. Each plant has a completely different root, each root a different resistance. I am alluding to the root of a tree—that's what the word radical originally reffered to. When I talk about history, what I have in mind is not the history in books, because that is too comforting. Books give you the illusion that the events of the past are logically related to one another and that you can measure the present by means of the past. When I talk about the origins of architecture, I have in mind a horizon. A horizon is a phenomenon that is not physical. It doesn't belong either to the heavens or to the earth. Whatever you do in the slightest produces a change in that horizon, a violation of the site. When we become aware of that exactly, we become susceptible to what it means to make a hole in the ground and put a building on top of it. I believe that if architects became conscious of this violation, maybe they would think twice, and we would have fewer buildings and more architecture.

LECTURE
Enric Miralles

At the outset I would like to say that I do not take style to be the systematic repetition of formal gestures. It is something that derives from a particular way of operating. The gestures that determine my work come from a set of specific interests, irrespective of the spatial results that ensue. I believe that systematic repetition and variation can provide things with a certain coherence, and in this regard, a great deal of my work depends upon accumulation and repetition. Every sketch of mine is worked over at least thirty times, and my colleagues do the same. My repetitive method is aimed at revealing the underlying structure of the site, its scale, and its basic coordinates. In my view, repetition is essential to the embodiment of an architectural idea. I work with constructive rather than visual criteria, and in this respect, repetition assumes a statical importance. We may say each new sketch is an act of forgetting, while geometry is important as a basic tool, affording a means to articulate specific situations. It enables me to come up with forms that could not have been anticipated.

I believe that one of the most characteristic things about my work is that I never have an a priori idea of the space I am trying to create; I always posit some kind of ground plan as a point of departure, rather than working from elevations or three-dimensional configurations. Multi-level plans afford the coordinates from which the sections are automatically derived. The three-dimensional form only arises at the end of the process, never prior to the generation of these plans and sections. This method of designing is more abstract and conceptual than working directly from sectional profiles. Sectional thinking has an archaic character, as if we were still working with the classical orders. I am much more attuned to the idea of a productive accumulation in plan rather than to working in section.

Place may be seen as one of those moments when thought becomes integrated into reality. In this sense, a drawing, even a sheet of paper, becomes a kind of place. And yet one only accepts the confines of a piece of paper in order to forget it, to treat it as a kind of invisible backing. In the process of designing, one shifts, and then construction returns us to this origin. As it comes to be enclosed, empty space expresses the absence of what once existed there. Simultaneously, that which we would have thought to be impossible comes into existence.

The experience of walking may be seen as a kind of writing on the surface of the ground. It is a trace of the movement which we seem to discover in a particular place. Fragments of various hypothetical movement patterns generate a geometry that becomes woven into reality in such a way that it is capable of engendering new shapes. These traces occupy the entire space. They have nothing to do, however, with the boundary markers with which one establishes a piece of property.

Our 1985 project for the Igualada Cemetery Park near Barcelona was a concept that assumed the form of a path. It was structured by a dualistic there-and-back movement that covered the entire terrain, leaving it essentially untouched. In developing this trajectory, we had to forego any kind of narrative dimension, since such narration would be unbearable in a cemetery. It meant working with hypothetical movement across the site in

Igualada Cemetery-Park
Barcelona, Spain, 1985–1997

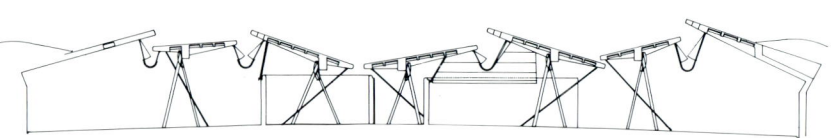

Olympic Archery Range
Competition and Training Building,
Barcelona, Spain, 1989–1992

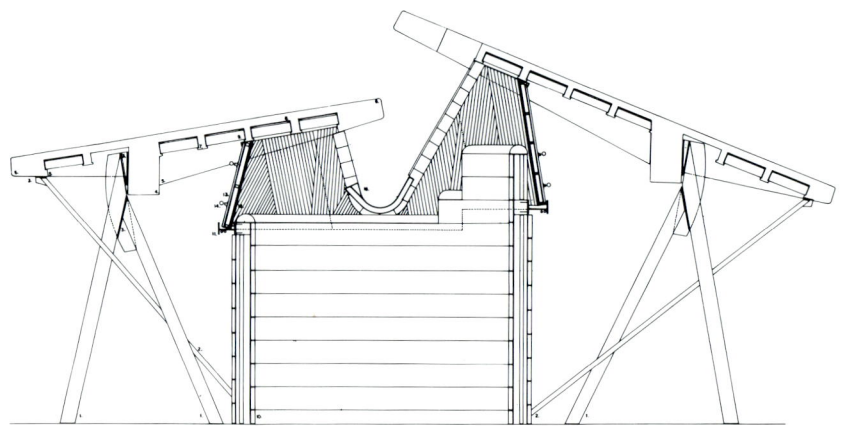

Cross sections

36 ENRIC MIRALLES 1996

Site plan

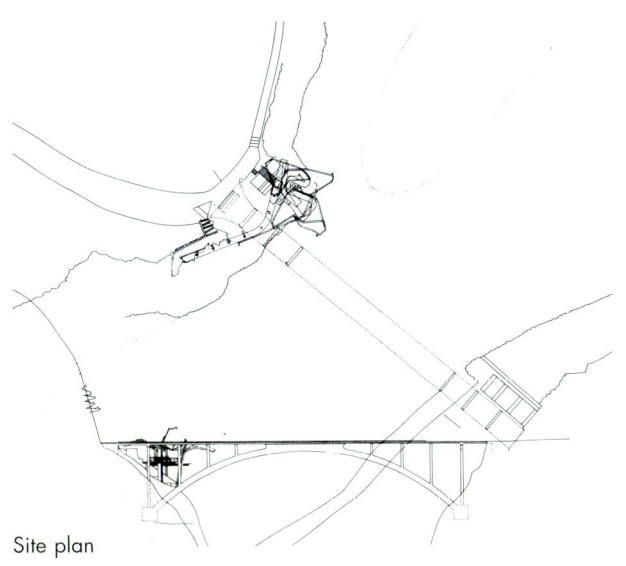

Unazuki Meditation Pavilion
Unazuki, Japan, 1991–1993

Copenhagen Auditorium
Project, 1993

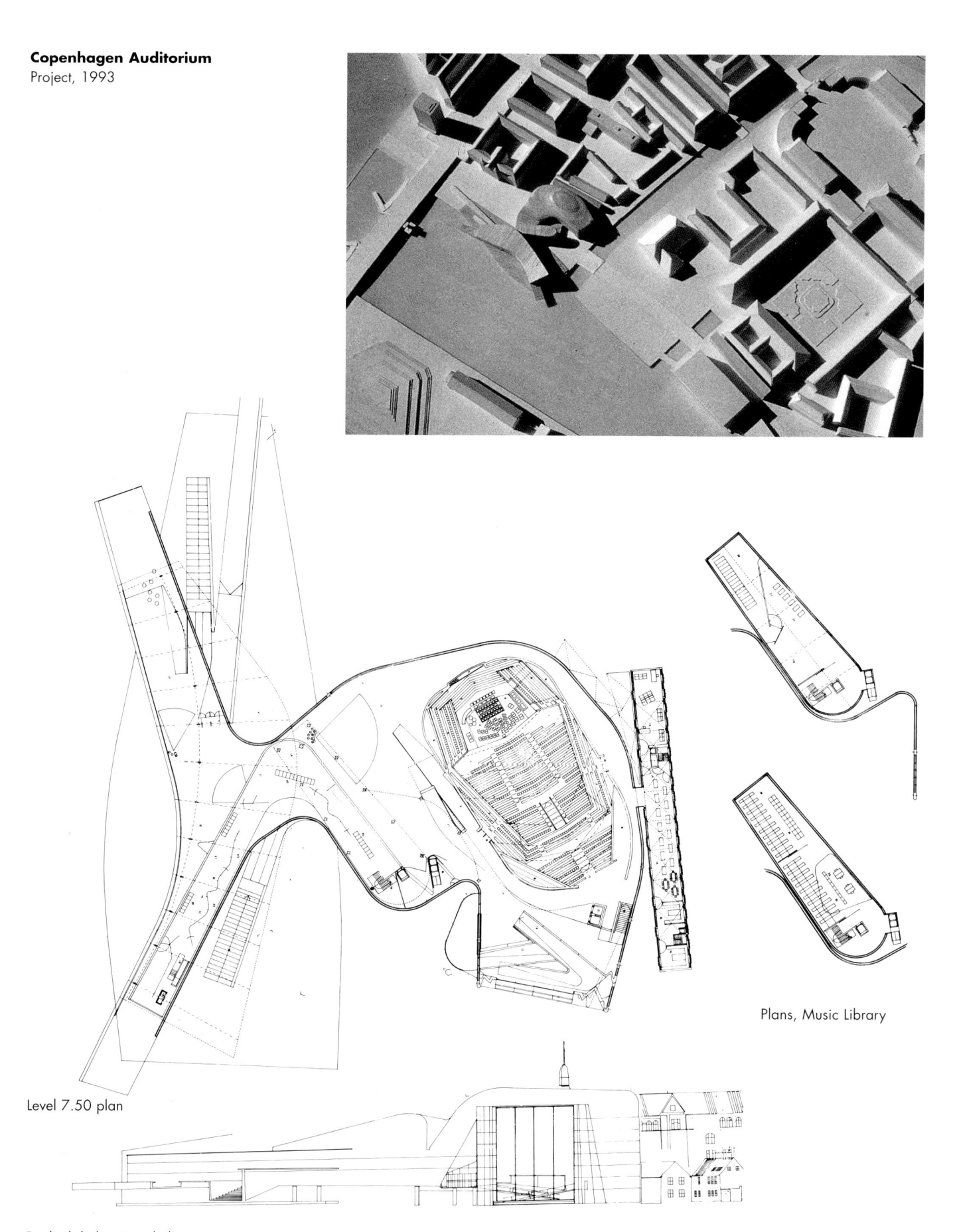

Level 7.50 plan

Plans, Music Library

Frederiksholms Kanal elevation

38 ENRIC MIRALLES 1996

such a way as to multiply the number of dividing paths. We had to insert intermediate spaces and various kinds of escape routes.

In our 1993 proposal for Bremerhaven, as in our other urban work, the specific form of the proposal derived in large part from the brief. However, in formal terms, the design initially derived from a series of gestural figures, from intuitive hieroglyphics that I have on occasion called "blots." These helped us to uncover and/or represent the labyrinthine order of the old port. The project was broken down into a series of thematic zones that were given evocative names, such as "labyrinth," "promenade," and "crystal palace." Among other things, the labyrinth served to accommodate a small zoo at the northern end of the old port. The promenade was conceived as a series of terraces overlooking the harbor. The crystal palace was designed as an activity center capable of receiving the energy coming from the surrounding urban fabric. Each of these elements created a new topography, of which the earth mounds that formed part of the labyrinth were the most dramatic.

Our 1993 proposal for twin concert halls in Copenhagen also arose from the suggestion of a "blot." This gestural form evoked the way people spontaneously gather in order to listen to music. The concert halls were situated in the most sheltered part of the site. They were stacked on top of one another to form a dense assembly, a kind of microcosmic urban form. The surface was treated as a mnemonic device with the large window and the ramps recalling the ancient surroundings of the city.

Like the undulating metal entrance that we designed for the Takaoka Railway Station in Japan (1993), the meditation pavilion at Unazuki, near Toyama (1991–1993), was conceived as redefining the topography of the site. The tubular metal structure echoed in its arabesque form the complex structure of the original pilgrimage routes leading to the site. A bridge, a small path, and an old pilgrim route are brought together in this sculptural space-form conceived as a complement to the rugged beauty of the site. By attaching this tubular construction to the abutment of an existing bridge, the bridge becomes spatially linked to the landscape.

The Igualada Cemetery is a necropolis built in an unused quarry on the outskirts of a rather nondescript industrial estate not far from Barcelona. It is largely made up of different types of retaining walls, ranging from in-situ reinforced concrete construction to the so-called *gablon* technique, in which wire mesh sustained by steel rods is back-filled with mortarless rubble. This method is only used for low rise at the end of the cemetery, whereas the deeper excavations are close to the point of entry and held in place by a mixture of in-situ and pre-cast concrete construction. These retaining walls, which incline both inward and outward, provide the necessary depth for a columbarium. Pre-cast niches set into the in-situ framework accommodate the coffins. Large family mausoleums are set into the gablon walls on two separate levels.

The lower floor of the cemetery, paved in unused railway sleepers set in weak cement, also has a number of spots reserved for individual burial. Near the main entrance there is a charnel pit, a morgue, a sacristy, and

**National Training Center
for Rhythmic Gymnastics**
Alicante, Spain, 1989–1993

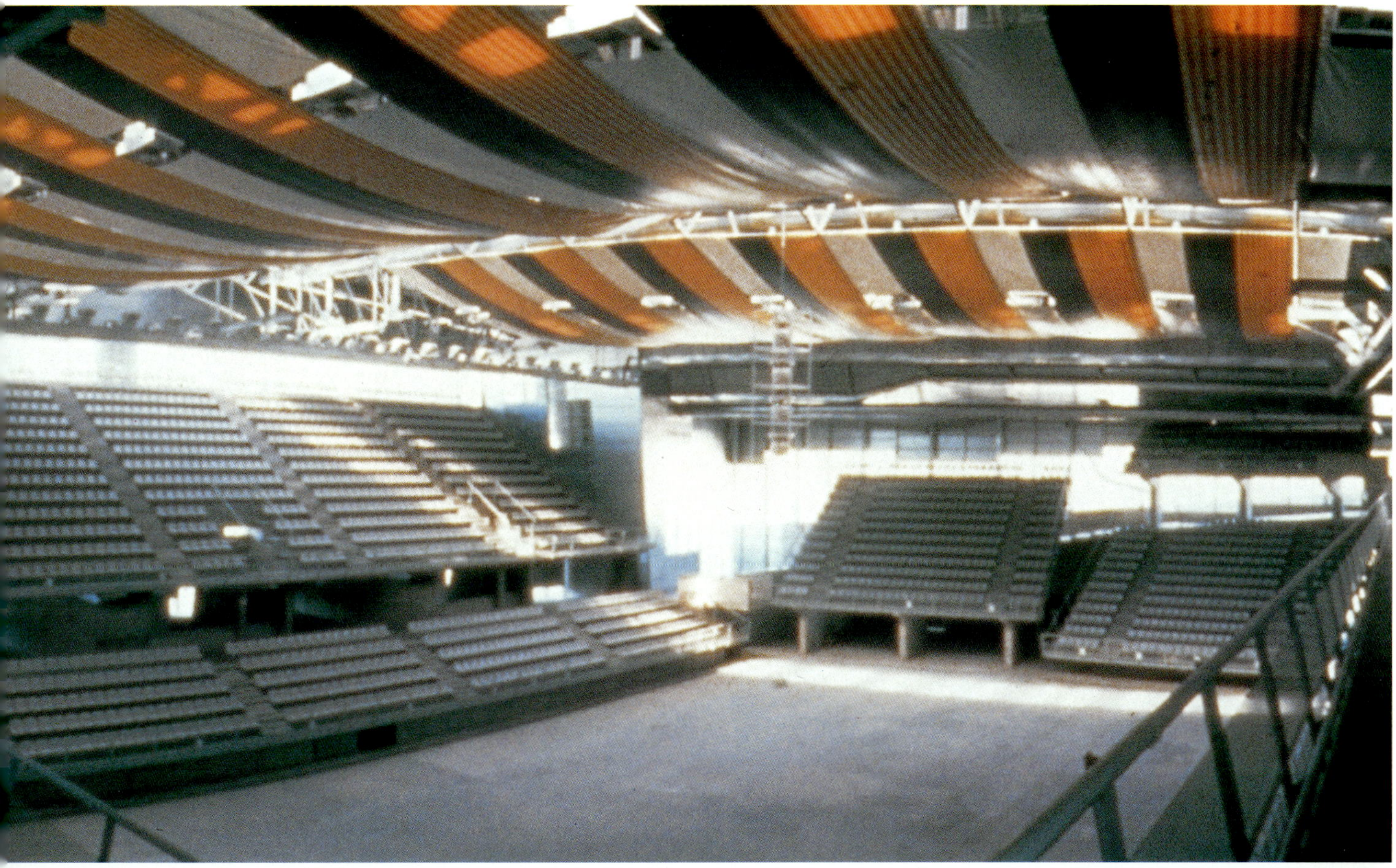

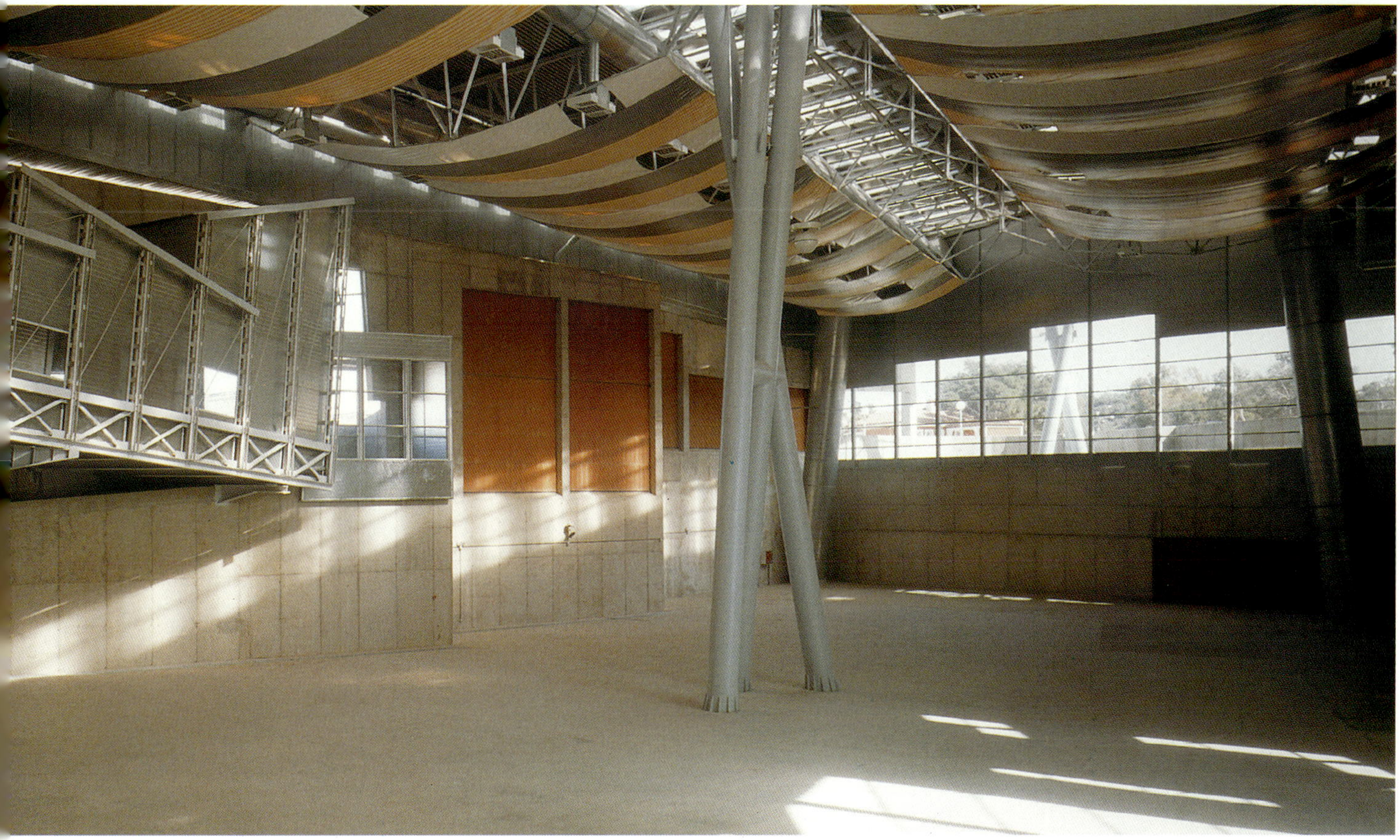

Floor plan

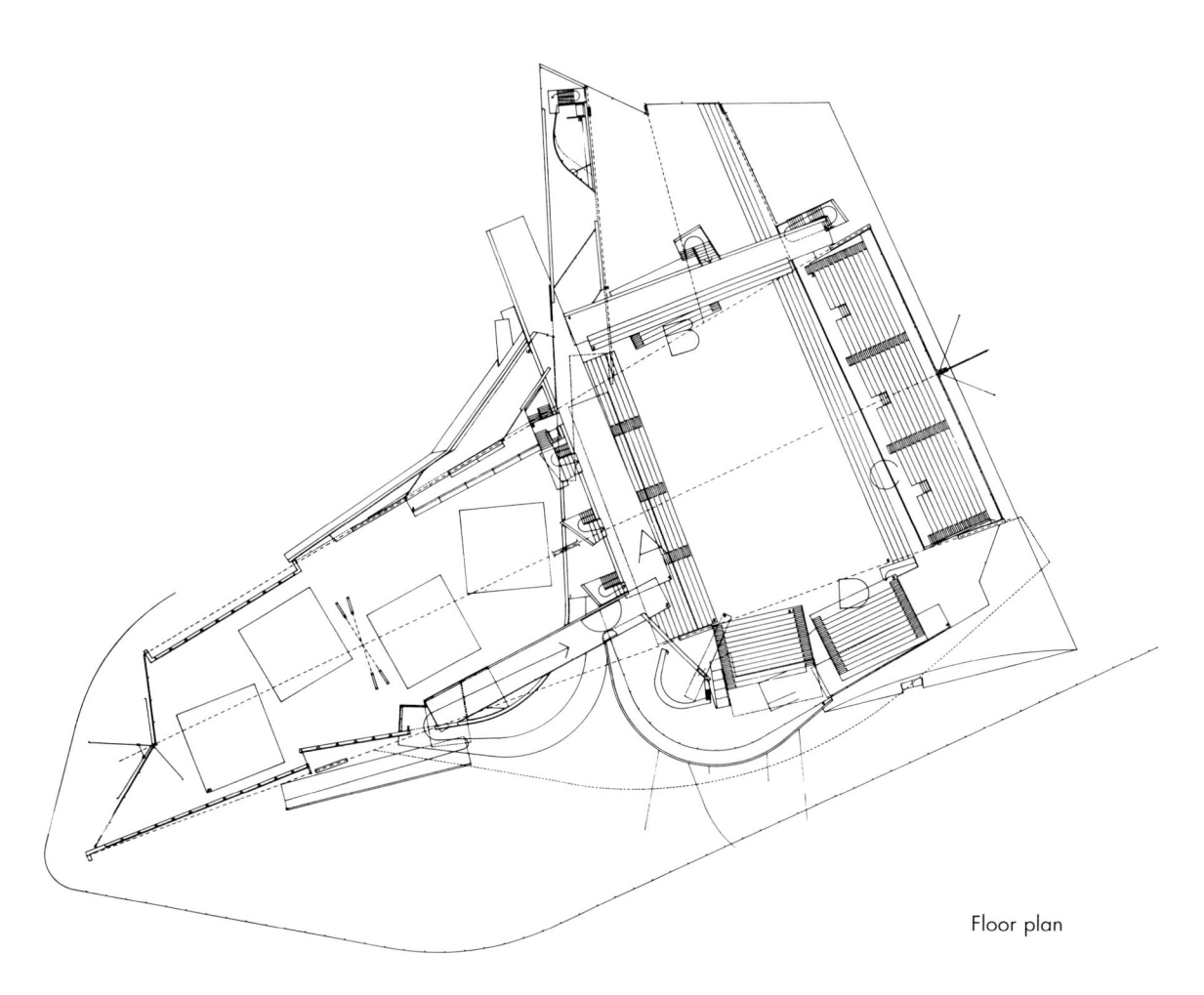

a chapel. The lowest level of the site has a melancholic mood which is transcended as one rises up out of the cutting on leaving the site.

The Archery Range realized for the Barcelona Olympics of 1992 was our first attempt at an earthwork. Both the competition and the training buildings serve the open target range immediately in front of them. In each instance, a sectional profile is integrated with an earthen embankment. The form of both structures arises in part out of a need to contain the earth. They are in fact bunker buildings. Where the training building mimics the flight of arrows across the site, with its concatenation of spread-eagle concrete roofs covered in tiles, the competition building assumes a more undulating and articulate form. Both buildings are conceived as land-forms that extend the formations of the topography. Indeed, the design emerged out of a conscious interplay between the building and the site, through a kind of automatic writing in which various calligraphic propositions appear to interact with the contours of the ground. This is evident in the competition building, where supported concrete shells loosely combine with a metal pergola. In the training building, tubular metal pylons and cylindrical concrete columns support tile-faced roof slabs. The columns, bounded by screen walls in terra-cotta blocks, weave in and out under the warped roof to generate a series of dressing rooms for the competitors.

The Morella boarding school was built outside the medieval hill town of Castellon between 1986, the date of the competition, and 1994, the date of completion. The school, which faces out over spectacular unspoiled countryside, was conceived so that its triangular cellular form echoes the spiraling structure of the town. This rotational movement of the plan facilitated the staggered arrangement of the classrooms and dormitory spaces. The larger common space establishes the boundary of the building on one side. As in the archery complex, when the building is seen from above the roof becomes the fourth facade. From this vantage point, one becomes aware of the building's labyrinthine configuration, the dormitories being accessed by a serpentine corridor as they descend the hill. Different levels are linked by ramps, terraces, and courts as they cascade down the slope.

Between 1990 and 1994, we built two sports facilities in Huesca and Alicante. Developed in succession, these two stadiums were closely interrelated. In Huesca, the arena is formed out of the ground, while expressive steel trusswork spans the stadium in section. In Alicante, the stadium is raised off the ground. Whereas Huesca functions like an open-air amphitheater, Alicante is an introverted structure centered around an athletic activity. The main arena in Alicante is roofed over by three long-span trusses. These trusses, built up from laminated steel angles and tubes, are resolved according to different statical models: those that are subject to simple bending have a variable profile in section, while others subject to torsion have an asymmetrical cross section designed to accommodate the twisting action. An undulating roof form is suspended between these lines of support. An existing football stadium constitutes one end

Above and overleaf
National Training Center for Rhythmic Gymnastics
Alicante, Spain, 1989–1993

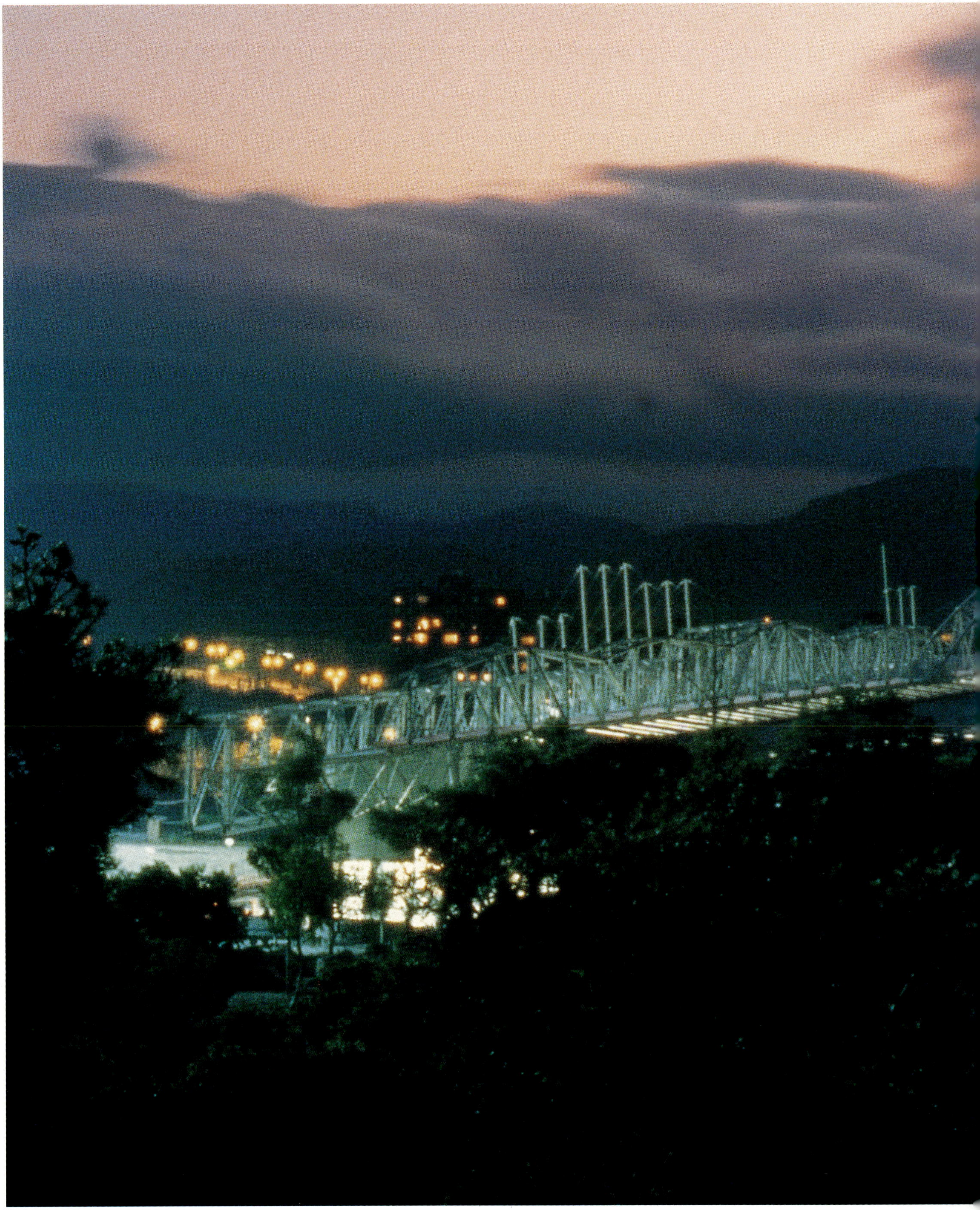

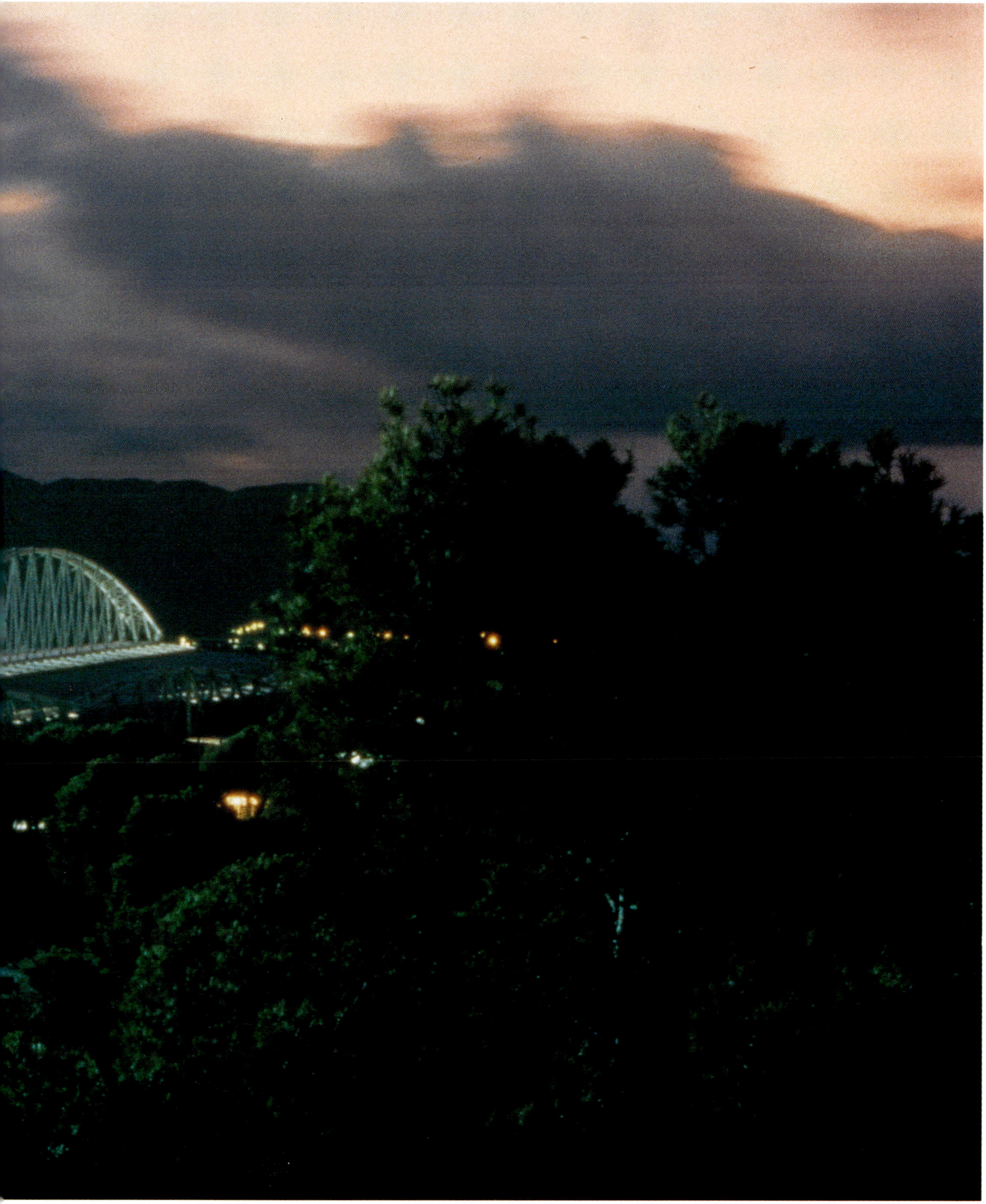

46 ENRIC MIRALLES 1996

of the complex while the other is established by the classrooms, dining rooms, and dressing room facilities. The elevated amphitheater is executed in reinforced concrete, while the tribune itself is supported on cylindrical supports.

I feel I am part of a tradition that values the process of manufacturing as the origin of creative thought. For example, one rotates a sheet of drawing paper in such a way as to make it lose its sheet-like nature. In part, it is a question of capitalizing on a single intuition: of seeing it appear in all its possible forms, of aligning different elements acrobatically, as in a game. One tries to represent all the aspects of one's project within the confines of a single page. It is not a question of accumulating data in the most efficient way, but rather of multiplying forms, thereby enabling the generation of forms which you had not thought of at the beginning. Thus one advances the project through a series of successive beginnings, as if each one were definitive, all the while constantly dismantling the assembly and modifying the scale. The best aspects of a sketch are its intermediate states, where the kaleidoscopic potential emerges in all its aspects, where one discerns what might be left over from the project for use on another job. The new situations that arise almost spontaneously are what distances a work from its point of departure. It is a heuristic method that pursues an abstract idea as a way of arriving at the form of a building.

I have recently been looking at Bruno Taut's own house, built in Berlin-Dahlewitz in 1927. Because of the peculiar radial plan of the house, each room is virtually pentagonal in shape. This means it would be difficult to reconstitute the form of the house from its independent elements. Given the isolated pieces, you would hardly know how to set one room beside another. Each room thus has its own independent logic irrespective of the quasi-symmetrical form of the house as a whole. I think that Taut is part of a tradition in which one is more interested in surprise and variation than in the overall concept of the project. In this instance, the house has a particularly sharp character due to its skillful detailing, the location of the rooms, the furnishing of the space, the relationships between door, table, window, radiator, etc. It is a tradition which, instead of making you heir to a set of forms and ideas, teaches you to observe in a certain way and to discover things. At the same time, it is important to note that this commitment to variation and surprise does not necessarily imply geometric or material complexity.

Facing page
National Training Center for Rhythmic Gymnastics
Alicante, Spain, 1989–1993

Morella Boarding School
Castellon, Spain, 1986–1994

National Training Center for Rhythmic Gymnastics
Alicante, Spain, 1989–1993

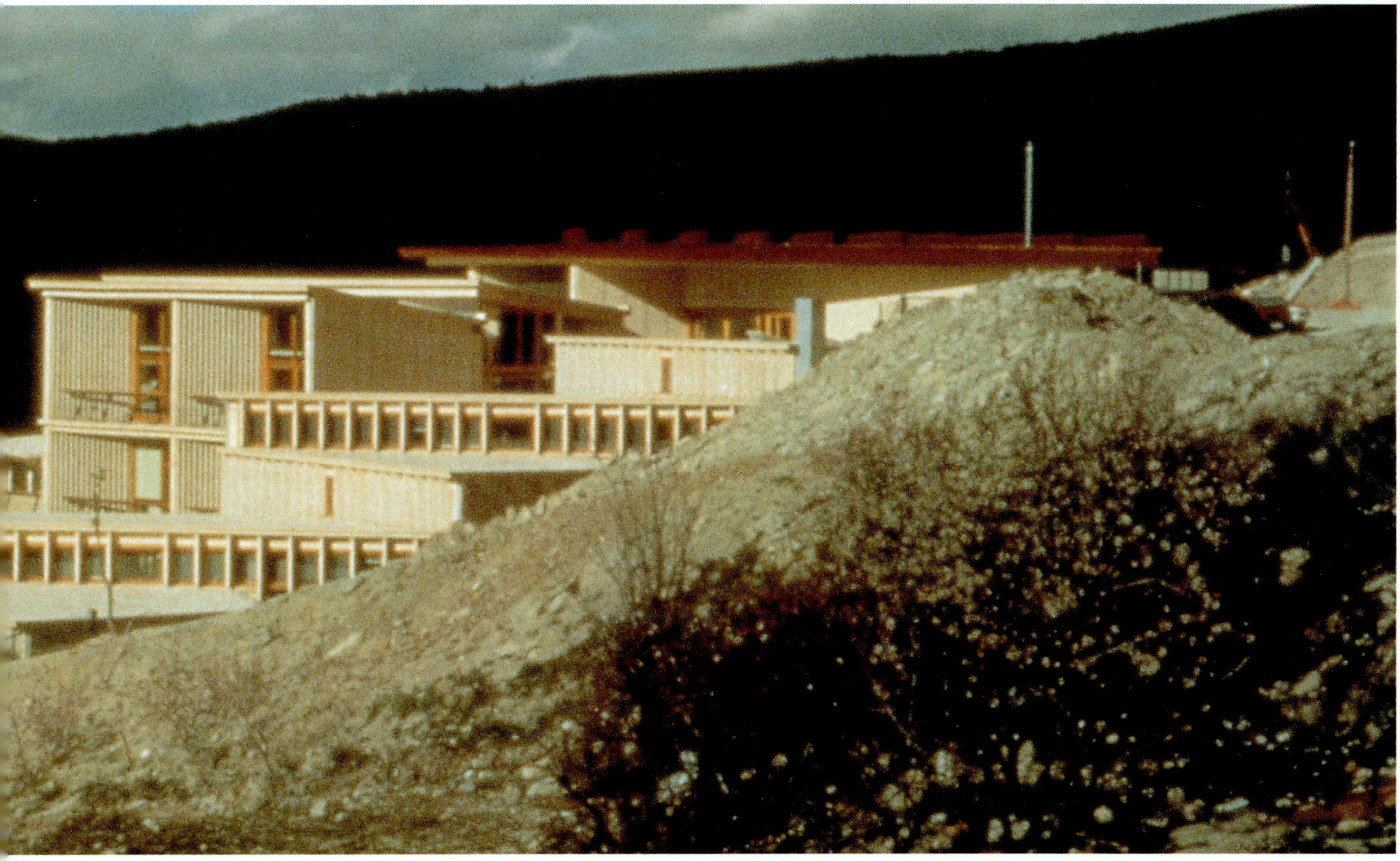

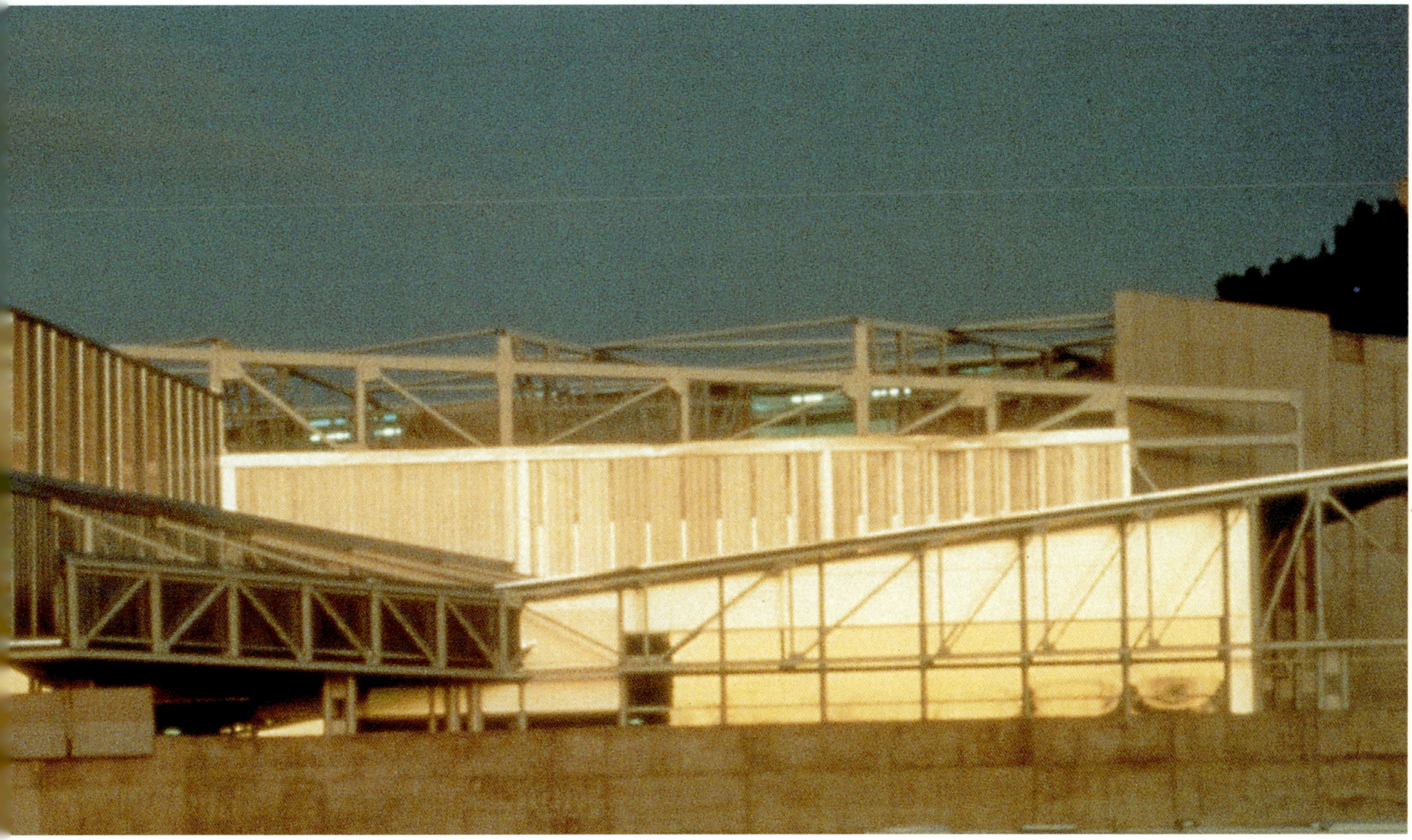

DISCUSSION
Enric Miralles
Andres Mariasch

Andres Mariasch: *The first time I saw a work of Enric Miralles I didn't know anything about him. I was surprised by the Igualada Cemetery, recognizing that its concrete retaining walls were the profiles of a master architect. Although the forms were free, they were not at all casual. The entire structure was a kind of non-building that was combined with the topography in an impressive way. Later, I was astonished to learn that Miralles doesn't work with a preconceived idea. Instead he works pragmatically, trying to rationalize the procedure in post facto terms. This is an architect who cares about technology and about the spatial-tectonic expressivity of his work. My primary question is, how can one design without a concept? Does the main impetus come from the site? Does it depend upon the function of the building? Or, does technology provide the point of departure?*

Enric Miralles: My practice derives from the new situation that arose in Spain after the demise of Franco. It was one of those rare moments when, for political reasons, people from different generations came together and shared in the work that had to be done. Our ideas and impulses were largely collective. My goal at that portentous time was to learn. Learning meant jumping from one idea to the next, from one discovery to the next, and even from one project to another. I was lucky enough to have the common sense not to allow this restlessness to destroy my work. When you are a student, you have to maintain a difficult balance between what you need to know and what you want to do. For this reason I have always tried to leave my projects somewhat open, to resist the tendency to structure them around one particular closed idea. What I like about Jean Nouvel is that he is so good at characterizing the kind of project he wants to realize. He establishes a set of priorities rather than depending upon causal reasoning. He is able to demonstrate how light is a kind of miraculous aesthetic. I agree with such a conceptual approach.

Mariasch: *But in the case of Nouvel, aren't we dealing with a somewhat authoritarian approach to architecture? Isn't the open-ended way you practice architecture a more effective way of establishing a dialogue between place and technology?*

Miralles: I once asked students to design a table as a project, but soon realized that this problem was too difficult and sophisticated even for myself, particularly from the point of view of understanding the importance of all the details. After that, we looked into all the different kinds of cutlery produced by designers through the century. I particularly like the idea of achieving new form through the process of a *répétition differente*, of realizing a new work through a small variation. My point is that you don't always have to start by thinking about the complete form of a building. There is a lot of strategic work to accomplish before completing a project. In that sense, I am not so preoccupied with the point of departure. I am concerned much more with what I would like to call "the center of the continuity." I feel that we should not underestimate the importance of time in architecture, that is, the time it takes to initiate the work.

Mariasch: *Can you explain a little bit more clearly what you mean by "time." Do you mean the moment when you really understand the nature of the problem?*

Miralles: No, I mean the physical time that obtains in a particular place. What is the time of Jerusalem for instance? Who knows the answer to this, despite the fact that everything is built in stone? When you start working, the first question to be asked is what is the nature of the moment in which you begin. This doesn't mean seeking continuity with the past. If you think of the past as an aspect of the future, then you may be surprised about what you can do.

Mariasch: *Don't you think that in this post-modern age we are in danger of falling into such extreme individualism that it will no longer be possible to find a common language with which to confront such issues as ecology, place, tradition?*

Miralles: Well, this is a matter of individual responsibility. I think that many of us try to respond to the complexities of reality and not just to ecological considerations. If you understand reality in all its complexity, then you are compelled to respond to a wide range of issues. The activity of projecting is a fantastic means for understanding reality. To enter fully into problems you have to have absolute connections with the real world. This doesn't mean that we should all agree about programmatic issues. It is demagogic, for example, to justify mediocre architectural work in the name of ecology. Once you stress a single factor in this way, it always leads to disastrous results. All these questions are very subtle. For instance, we encounter a serious problem in Germany with the extensive recuperation of the poisoned land, land polluted as a result of mining, mostly in East Germany, around Leipzig and Dresden. These problems are so complicated that it is essential to enter into their full complexity and not to settle for a solution that is only successful from a particular point of view.

Mariasch: *I really like your meditation place in Japan, and I think that there you play with materials in a unique way. For example, it seems to be plastic, but in fact it is iron. It is situated on a site suspended between the forested mountains and the sky, a conjunction that invites meditation. This pavilion establishes a path for pilgrims who camp at the end of a deck or overlook the landscape. It is both interesting and bucolic. But at the same time, I feel it would be more comfortable to have a place for meditation in the mountain itself or in a more enclosed site without the presence of stimulating objects.*

Miralles: The first thing we thought of with this work was the Japanese tradition of pilgrimage routes, which we interpreted as a form of haiku where every step of the way is indicative of something to be borne in mind. In a way, the entire landscape is permeated by thought. The client proposed that we build a meditation pavilion on a mountain path. Instead of merely accepting this, I proposed that we shift the site to a place that is completely overwhelming because of its proximity to the gorge. This site was so strong that I could start by responding to the context alone and thereby avoid the difficulty of trying to interpret the unknowable secret sentiments of my client. In fact, one might say that this entire work was based on physical gesture. Most of my work is grounded in physical actions. The Igualada Cemetery is nothing but a deep cut into the earth, just as this pavilion is simply a platform for metaphorically jumping into the void. I think that all such actions amount to a dialogue between the architect, the people, and the particular place. In this project, it is a matter of moving from a concealed silence by way of a movement to one side of it. I usually attempt to construct some kind of hidden equilibrium. This conditions my basic working method at the parti stage, a kind of dialogue with the topos through an initial gesture or action. If you look carefully at my work, you can perhaps see those places to which I was more spontaneously sympathetic than others. This evocative empathy finds a direct reflection or expression in the tectonic elements employed in the work. I am particularly susceptible to doors and windows, with which I always try to unify the character of the project. In this regard, I always try to avoid orthogonal rooms, because such volumes entail difficult corner conditions. When one starts thinking in terms of cubic form, this entails past precedent and one runs the risk of losing the spirit of the work. My aim is to weave all the components into a whole like the woof and warp of a carpet. For this reason I resort to different forms of repetition. In a way, I always follow the initial action or gesture and then try to reveal its full dimensions by uncovering and developing it in all its aspects. There are always certain doubts, as in the National Training Center for Rhythmic Gymnastics in Alicante.

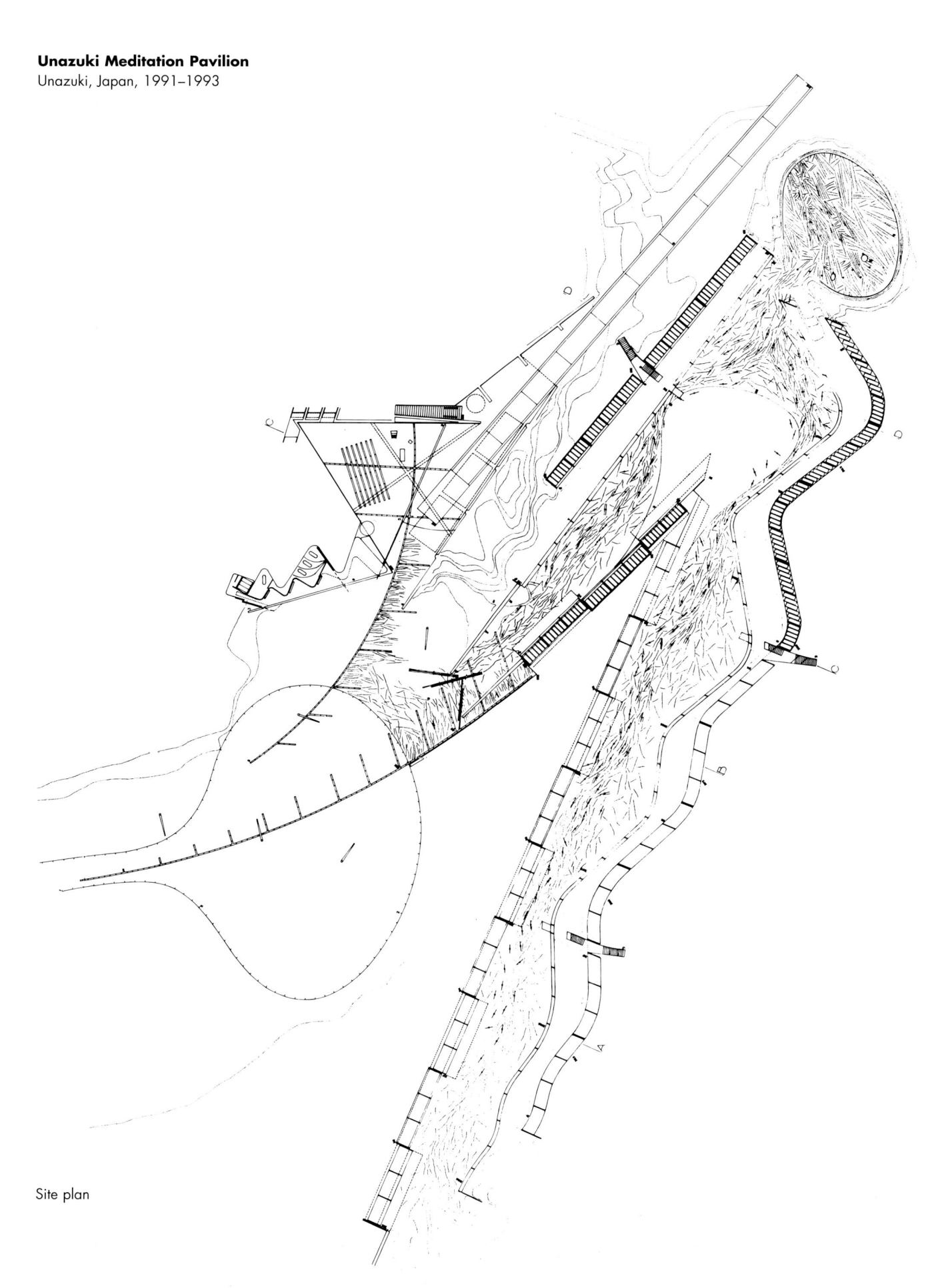

Unazuki Meditation Pavilion
Unazuki, Japan, 1991–1993

Site plan

Audience: *Looking back on the past eighteen years of your production, can you identify a principle that comes through all of your work at the conceptual level? For example, when you start a project conceptually, is it the geometry, the space, or the light that comes to the fore, and what exactly is the role of place in your work?*

Miralles: My approach in general is very pragmatic. For me, place creation entails a relatively simple process. Even before drawing a line, I try to establish a kind of ideal quality. Take the Igualada Cemetery. It looks fantastic, but in fact it is only a cul-de-sac at the end of a narrow, somewhat polluted industrial parcel. It is a piece of marginal land on the edge of the city which the municipality bought very cheaply. I realized that it could be transformed into a kind of ideal valley. The geometry involved in this concept established an interrelationship between specific dimensions, but this is quite different from cubist geometry. In spanning a space I always think in terms of spanning more than this particular space. I think in terms of bearing points, rather than discrete rooms. It then becomes a matter of choosing which points to connect and how to effect these connections structurally. A twenty-meter span is rather difficult to achieve in reinforced concrete, and with forty meters, it is imperative to use steel. At the same time, the geometry is constantly transformed through the length of the project in terms of its transverse sections. In the cemetery, the angle of the retaining walls is initially rather steep, but as the depth of the cut diminishes, it becomes almost perpendicular. To some extent, the transformation of the geometry derives from accepting random conditions. This acceptance is crucial, for through it, it is possible to define and express the boundaries of a project in topographical terms, calibrating the dimensions in terms of the contours from the very beginning. I feel out the potential profile of a given topography almost as though I were blind. In this sense, my approach is extremely tactile. A given topos or body of material invariably suggests a kind of continuity. Concrete is an important material from this point of view, particularly since it always constitutes the foundations. The creation of the basic earthwork is absolutely fundamental in this regard; for this is the point at which the initial geometrical potentialities are established. Everything tends to grow logically out of this initial gesture. Rising up from the base, the design continues in concrete or changes over to some other structural material depending on the circumstances. In the last analysis, everything stems from the initial shaping of the ground.

Most of my work today happens to be outside Spain. I'm working in places as different from each other as Salonika and Copenhagen. In such different places, you carry your own modus operandi with you and then develop the continuity from a core centroid that you discover within the site. In some respects this is a reciprocal process, since after working in Japan, for example, I will bring back to Spain something from the particular experience I had in Asia. I feel that, when Japanese clients give commissions to foreign architects, it is reminiscent of the medieval period when traveling troupes of players went from city to city and village to village, representing via the theater narrative histories drawn from the outside world. I believe that this is just the kind of exchange we need: cross fertilization rather than a therapeutic response based upon simply fulfilling the relatively low levels of local expectancy. Of course we have to be sensitive and responsible and discover what is appropriate to the specific situation. We also have to respond to the realities of the budget and to other indispensable objective factors. In Salonika, we are trying to build a ferry terminal out of pre-cast concrete units, a technique I would not envisage using in Spain, where pre-cast concrete is rather expensive.

The aim of this seminar is certainly not to arrive at specific answers to questions concerning the interrelationship of technology, place, and architecture. For me, technology has much more to do with conceptual processes than with technique in the literal sense. This surely is one of the main themes of this seminar. Technology cannot be conceived of solely in terms of lasers or other forms of high-speed communication, above all because the time of each place is somewhat different. In Salonika someone suggested installing an enormous television screen with which to announce the arrival and departure of the boats. Then the client said to me, "If you want to build this ferry terminal out of marble, that is fine, but please don't introduce large TV screens." Here we can surely sense the difference between an abstract image of technology in general and the culture of a particular place and clientele. On the other hand, when we look at the communications tower in Barcelona, we realize that Norman Foster handled it in a very intelligent way. He made an appropriate sketch design and then a very good Spanish engineering firm took over and completed the work. In both instances we may speak of a technology that was appropriate to the subject.

Audience: *I would like to hear something of your impressions of Jerusalem and especially about the policy of building here in one unique material, namely stone.*

Miralles: I suppose that this is one of those constraints which are so absolute and decisive that paradoxically it assures a great deal of freedom once the principle is fully accepted. Today we saw Mendelsohn's Bank Leumi on Jaffa Road, which is a remarkable achievement in stone. However, it is somewhat painful to see a reinforced concrete building faced in stone which is not operative tectonic material. Personally I hate stone details, and to tell the truth, I cannot imagine putting stone on top of a window. But in Spain there are many architects who are obsessed with making things out of stone, so perhaps you should ask them to come here.

Audience: *It seems that you and other Spanish architects whom I admire very much were never influenced by post-modern ideas, whether they be architectural or philosophical. If that's so, what would you say kept you uninterested in that phenomenon?*

Miralles: The post-modern approach was seen as irrelevant in Spain. This was perhaps due to the fact that, in Spain, architecture was a living tradition that people carried with them into the 1980s. Aside from this, Spain has not yet experienced the kind of economic boom that would have attracted big speculators into the region. Another factor is that, in Spain, architectural design is very influenced by technology.

Audience: *You referred previously to the poor technology in Spain. Is your architecture really affected by this? I come from a country where the level of building technology is even worse.*

Miralles: Spain had excellent civil engineers up to the 1950s and 1960s. Eduardo Torroja was one of the world's leaders in the field of concrete shell structures. We also had some very good bridge engineers who did consistent work. However, it was not structural engineering in the architectural sense, nor did we have the kind of combined firms of architects and engineers that emerged first in London in the 1950s and then later in France. While so-called high-technology depends on a close collaboration between architects and engineers, I prefer to keep using a practical if rather primitive technology. The fact that the Igualada Cemetery was built slowly and that there were usually no more than three workers on the site at any one time is perhaps a reflection of this.

Audience: *Could it be that one of the reasons why your projects are perpetually somewhat unfinished is that they are built over a long period of time?*

Miralles: Sometimes this occurs for practical reasons, but I have to confess that I have elected to work in a way that enables the project to continue, as it were, of its own accord. This continuation is both literal and figurative. Since any particular project may be on the boards in our office for as long as eight years, there is inevitably a lot of overlap among the different projects that come into the office. In any case, I try not to work on any project in isolation from the next, even if a particular room in the office may be given over to a single project. I prefer to think that all the projects are interrelated as part of a common research endeavor that is pursued without any rupture across time, irrespective of the technology employed or the peculiarities of the site.

Audience: *Are you influenced by any living architect?*

Miralles: The problem with living architects is that you are too close to them, you share too many things in common. I was always attracted to those who are more remote, where you have to make an effort at interpretation. In general I am more susceptible to being influenced by a group of architects, or by places in which people work together, where there is a lot of interaction and an intense exchange of ideas.

Audience: *Is there some concept in your work that you would like us to pay particular attention to?*

Miralles: Like Jean Nouvel, I am interested in dematerialization, however I am equally interested in a tactile reading of my work, that is to say in terms of the body moving over the ground. I would like you to pay particular attention to that and to the abstract aspect of my surfaces.

Audience: *Mr. Miralles, it strikes me that when you talk about your work you frequently utilize metaphors that belong to tailoring, you have a tendency to use such words as thread, cloth, and textile.*

Miralles: Well, yes, in a certain sense I am like a tailor. I like a tailored jacket when it is half done. I like the cutting tables on which tailors work. I also like the way in which they attain precision, from the marking of the material with chalk, to the cutting of the cloth, to the assembly of the piece.

LECTURE
Glenn Murcutt

Facing page
Magney Country House
Moruya, New South Wales, Australia,
1982–1984

In Australia we still enjoy a largely egalitarian society. The land is vast and powerful, and even with its current population of eighteen million people concentrated in the principal cities on the coast, you don't have to go too far into the outback to realize that the human being is an ant in the landscape and a giant in the built environment. As the Australian painter Lloyd Rees put it: "The land made the aboriginal people, and the land is now making European Australians."

On the one hand we have the land, while on the other we have the impact of vernacular modes of building, be they aboriginal or European. Of this last, as the great Egyptian architect Hassan Fathy wrote in his book *Natural Energy and Vernacular Architecture*:

> Fortunately, recent "discoveries" of the value of traditional forms of medicine, technology and agriculture have led to a revived interest in pre-industrial knowledge. The field of vernacular architecture offers an abundance of concepts that can be used today.

In Australia we are acutely conscious of the changing patterns of the earth's climate. We are painfully aware that we are poised beneath a large hole in the ozone layer and that we have the highest incidence of skin cancer in the world. This alarming reality makes us particularly sensitive to health problems that arise from our rapacious consumption of resources. For every line we draw there is a true cost and this cost has not yet been measured properly. We are aware that it takes one megajule to process one kilogram of rough-sawn timber and five megajules to process a kilogram of dressed timber from rough-sawn material. It takes about thirty-five megajules for a kilogram of steel and 145 for a kilogram of aluminum. We know the price of electricity, but we do not realize the cost of things for which we do not receive a discrete bill. Take commercial transport. The maintenance costs on the road systems per annum for a twenty-two-wheel vehicle in Australia vary between eighteen thousand and sixty thousand Australian dollars, and are carried by the Australian taxpayer. But this accounting does not take into consideration health costs or the costs associated with the heavy vehicle accident rate. These are costs that should be measured, and only when we finally do understand the real costs to the planet will we alter our entire way of thinking about the built environment.

Sustainable architecture is virtually impossible, with the possible exception of architecture based on renewable resources such as timber, or on the expenditure of human effort. You may use wool for insulation and think of it as environmentally responsible, but we in Australia know that, with the exception of human occupation, there is no greater damage done to our landscape than that inflicted by sheep. They compact the ground, they discharge toxins that are sprayed on the wool—not to mention the scouring process which leaches additional toxins into our water systems.

Australia is an enormous continent. Comparatively speaking, it extends north-south from Scandinavia to North Africa and east-west from Spain almost to Israel. It is approximately four thousand kilometers north-south and four thousand kilometers east-west. The climate therefore varies enormously, from the monsoonal tropics, wet tropics, subtropics, warm

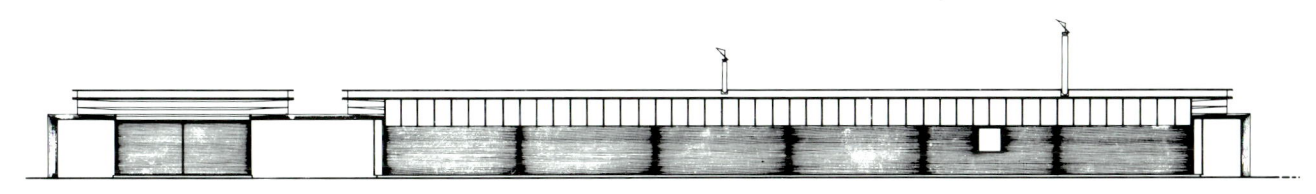

South elevation

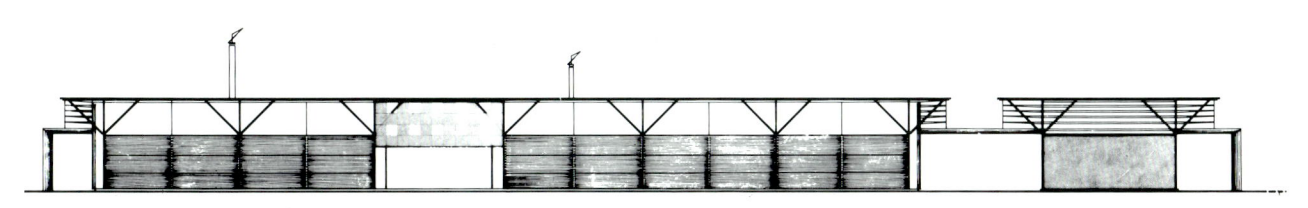

North elevation

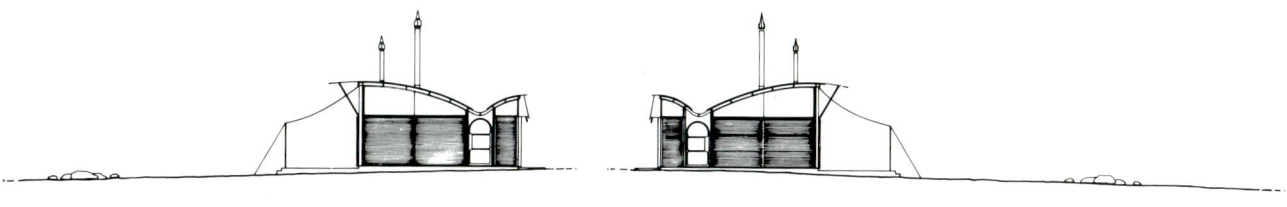

West elevation

East elevation

57

temperate, temperate, hot arid, and cool temperate, and combinations of several climes at the interface of systems. The sun, throughout seasons, is in the northern sky for all parts of Australia except for the tropics, where in mid-summer the sun's position is in the southern sky. The rainfall varies from less than six hundred millimeters to above two thousand five hundred millimeters per annum and the landform from sea level to Mt. Kosciusko at 2,228 meters. In wintertime, there is a cooling in the center of the land mass. This draws warm air inland with corresponding wind patterns. In summer, the center, which is constantly exposed to the sun, heats up, bringing in the cool air from the coast. In wintertime, cold air comes in from the South Pole and moves across the country to the north-west, providing the prevailing wind of the Australian tropics. The center is an arid region with minimal rainfall, dry climate, and temperatures reaching forty to forty-five degrees Celsius. Winds vary from calm to the cyclonic conditions in northern Australia, where velocities reach sixty-three meters per second accompanied by tidal surges in excess of two thousand millimeters. Most Australians live in the urban centers, while about ten percent live in townships and the country regions.

My works are sited in all regions and climatic conditions throughout Australia (except for the cool temperate), and range from the coastal urban and rural to the inland urban and rural. Culturally, I have designed for Aboriginal, Asian, and European Australians. I have built at latitudes between eleven and a half and thirty-eight degrees south of the equator. In 1987, after twenty-seven years of developing climatically responsive buildings, it came as an extraordinary shock to me to discover the structures of the aboriginal people which respond to the climatic conditions and bear some clear similarities to the work I had pursued. The principles embodied in the shelters of the aboriginal peoples are timeless and relevant.

The landscape of Australia, like the climate, varies greatly as one moves through the land. During the monsoon season in the escarpment country in northern Australia, the impervious rock transfers fresh water to the lowlands, then on to the mud flats and estuaries, and finally into the ocean. In the hot, arid region, the landscape is tough and it can be harsh. In the moister coastal regions, the Eucalypt are large and often lush, tall, and straight. The form and height of the Eucalypt and other flora informs us about the wind, the water table, leaching, and general soil depths and conditions. Melaleucas indicate a high level of moisture. In the hot, arid regions, the leaves of many trees turn their edges to the sun, which reduces transpiration and thus ensures survival, whereas trees in the cooler climes present the face of their leaves to the sun for survival. A consequence of leaves turning their edges to the sun is that a greater level of light penetrates the structure of the flora, providing at once a legibility and transparency in the landscape. The clarity of the light in Australia serves to separate the elements in the landscape. In my architecture, I aspire to a similar legibility and transparency.

We have to exercise extreme care when siting buildings. To excavate too deeply can interrupt water patterns. Disturbing the site unduly changes water distribution and augments soil erosion. Varying the water patterns can kill many of the established, more sensitive Australian native plants.

The architecture that the British brought with them forms part of the Australian tradition, particularly as this architecture came to be modified in response to the climate. Even the most primitive, utilitarian, early industrial buildings in Australia were responsive to place and climate. Some early vernacular structures in the hot, arid regions, for example, respond marvelously to the environment, exploiting such devices as running water over timber screens combined with air movement to cool the environment. Nothing could be further from such principles than the appalling suburban prototypes now built throughout the country irrespective of differences in climate and landscape.

I completed the Magney House at Moruya, New South Wales, in 1984. The site, some 350 kilometers from Sydney, is at about latitude thirty-eight degrees south; the site is coastal with the altitude at sea level. The clients, who had been coming to camp on the site for twenty-five years, commissioned me to design a beach house which maintained a certain tent-like quality. During the winter, cold winds often come off Mt. Kosciusko. In summer, the site enjoys the southeastern and the northeastern cooling sea breezes. With temperatures during the summer months varying from twenty to twenty-eight degrees Celsius, the cooling breezes are used to advantage. In winter, cold winds are from the southwest and the temperatures can drop from twelve to five degrees. The insulated, mass thermal wall is placed to the south, providing protection from the winter cold as well as picking up the deeply penetrating winter sun. Since there is no water on the site, the rain water is collected in tanks. The inner walls throughout the house are brick; outside, they are insulated and metal clad. The fenestration to the north lets in the winter sun, provides ventilation, and affords views of the coastline and lake to the north. Glass walls open the house to the landscape through a series of layers including insect screens and external mobile venetian blinds. The house is zoned to provide two independent areas: one for the parents and the other for children, family, and friends. The house is set directly on the ground to benefit from the thermal mass of the earth. The concrete slab is faced in dark gray tile, which absorbs warmth from the sun during the winter daytime and releases it during the night.

The Murcutt House in Belrose, Sydney, dating from 1972, was designed for my brother and his wife. Situated in the suburbs of Sydney, the house is rotated sideways, orienting the living spaces away from the street and to the north. My brother and his wife are musicians and they needed a public entry so they could receive their pupils at the front of the house where they teach, and retreat to the sitting area where they enjoy the privacy of the courtyard garden. The garden captures the sunlight and the cooling northeast sea breezes in summer and provides protection from the cold southwesterly winds in winter.

The Simpson-Lee House in Mount Wilson, New South Wales, completed in 1994, is located in the Blue Mountains, two hundred kilometers west-southwest of Sydney at an altitude of one thousand meters. The plan is based on the idea of a path. For aboriginal people the path was of the utmost importance. In far north Australia the aboriginal people lived in caves during the wet season. These cave spaces were never entered

Magney Country House
Moruya, New South Wales, Australia,
1982–1984

Simpson-Lee House
Mount Wilson, New South Wales, Australia,
1989–1994

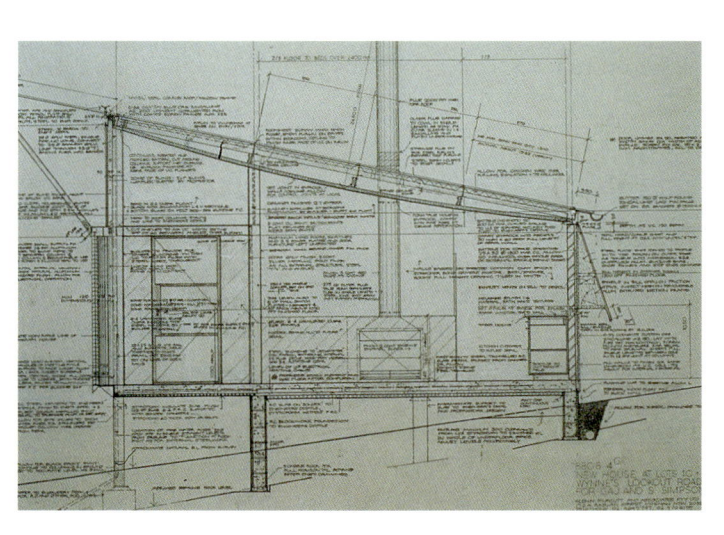

Marie Short House
Kempsey, New South Wales, Australia,
1974–1975 and 1980 (extension)
Extension (above) and cross section (left)

frontally but rather from behind or from the sides, after the guardian spirits were asked for permission. From within the cave both prospect and refuge are experienced. Unlike occidental civilization concepts of beginning, middle, and end, the aboriginal people responded to time, dimension, and path as a continuum. Like that of the traditional northern Australian aboriginal notion of entry, the entry of this building has been planned to the side of the main space and to the edge junction with the landscape.

The house was designed for clients in their seventies: he, a retired head of school and professor of economics; and she, a horticulturist and potter. The brief outlined a modern house. The climate in winter can be cold, temperatures falling to one degree Celsius at night, but in the daytime it rises from twelve to twenty degrees. During the change of seasons, there is good rainfall accompanied by moderate nighttime temperatures and wonderfully comfortable daytime temperatures. During summer, the nights vary from twelve to eighteen degrees and days eighteen to thirty degrees, occasionally reaching thirty-eight degrees. The humidity is low throughout the year. This house has insulated, reversed-brick-veneer external walls and brick internal walls which mediate between climatic extremes. This section of the house has its roof reaching for the light in the same way as do the mountain Eucalypt. The section determines spaces of refuge and prospect; the fenestration provides for ventilation, light, outlook, and inclusion of the large weathered rock and the forest and valleys beyond into the main living spaces. With the external venetian blinds fully raised and the doors and insect screens opened back to the air-lock zones, the main living, dining, and kitchen space becomes an open veranda platform and space.

From the simple mono-pitched roof, the rainwater is collected and stored in water tanks and a reflecting pool with a combined capacity in excess of one hundred thousand liters. The pottery studio doubles as a garage and overflow space for accommodations. The rainwater is stored not only to provide domestic water but also to serve as an emergency reservoir in case of a bush fire. The house and studio/garage were supplied with sprinklers, which not only keep the house wet on the outside but also soak the flora. They protect the house during a bush fire and provide water for firefighting for the houses adjacent to it as well.

Built in 1975 and extended for myself in 1980, the Marie Short House, 450 kilometers north of Sydney, sits lightly on a New South Wales coastal landscape that is subject to high rainfall, and, during the floods, is prone to invasion by snakes, lizards, frogs, and insects, each one preying on the other. To provide a dry and safe platform, the house is raised above the ground. The curvature of the roof is directly responsive to wind flow and wind pattern, providing positive pressure on the windward side of the roof and negative pressure on the leeward side of the building, and thereby generating air movement within the roof leaves to the prevailing cooling, northeastern coastal winds. The roof is opened to the north for the entry of light into the very core of the house. During the summer months, the roof glazing is protected by the external louver screens, which block out the sun, while in winter these static louvers deliver light directly through the glazing into the belly of the house. The northern facades of the house are layered with external blinds, then insect screens, and finally adjustable louvers on the inside. This early house, designed in 1974, was constructed to allow for alteration, and in 1980 it was extended without wasting a stick of timber or a single louver. No element was lost, and only some new and recycled timber—as well as human effort—was required for the additions. The gable end, veranda, deck, stairs, doors, louvers, and blinds were all reused in the building extension.

I'm very interested in buildings that adapt to changes in climatic conditions according to the seasons, buildings capable of responding to our physical and psychological needs in the way that clothing does. We don't turn on the air-conditioning as we walk through the streets in high summer. Instead, we change the character of the clothing by which we are protected. Layering and changeability: this is the key, the combination that is worked into most of my buildings. Occupying one of these buildings is like sailing a yacht: you modify and manipulate its form and skin according to seasonal conditions and natural elements, and work with these to maximize the performance of the building. This involvement with the building also assists in the care for it. I am concerned about the exploitation of the natural environment in order to modify the internal climate of buildings. Architects must confront the perennial issues of light, heat, and humidity control yet take responsibility for the method and the materials by which, and out of which, a building is made. These considerations, context, and the landscape are some of the factors that are constantly at work in my architecture.

Two projects designed for northern Australia are located in the monsoonal tropics twelve and a half degrees south of the equator, where the seasons are well defined. Although the seasons are divided into four in European terms, they are not so classified in aboriginal terms. For the aboriginal peoples, there are six seasons: the pre-wet season, the season of the heavy rain and growth, the flowering season, the fruiting season, the early dry season, and the main dry season. This region is a landscape of escarpments, caves, creeks, waterfalls, rivers, billabongs, lagoons, estuaries, coastlines, and extraordinary flora and animals. The caves are invariably painted, depicting legends involving all sorts of mythology and dream images as well as the availability of traditional foods.

One project is the Kakadu Visitors' Information Centre and Park Headquarters, a center for the interpretation of the landscape in the Kakadu National Park in the Northern Territory (1992–1994). I worked on this building with a group of young architects from northern Australia known as Tropo-Architects. The site is east of Darwin. Winter to summer, temperatures vary from twenty-eight to thirty-three degrees Celsius with high humidity during summer and low in winter. With the build-up of heat from November to March, there is the threat of cyclones with a wind velocity that can reach forty meters per second, accompanied by thunderstorms and torrential rain with constantly shifting winds. The first sketches began with ideas about airflow moving through the building. Air passages were introduced into the buildings, providing for airflow and cooling with both the summer northwest and the winter southeast prevailing winds. The sketches related to the pressurization of air, creating a venturi effect, speeding up the

Overleaf
Visitors' Information Center and Park Headquarters
Kakadu National Park, Northern Territory, Australia, 1992–1994

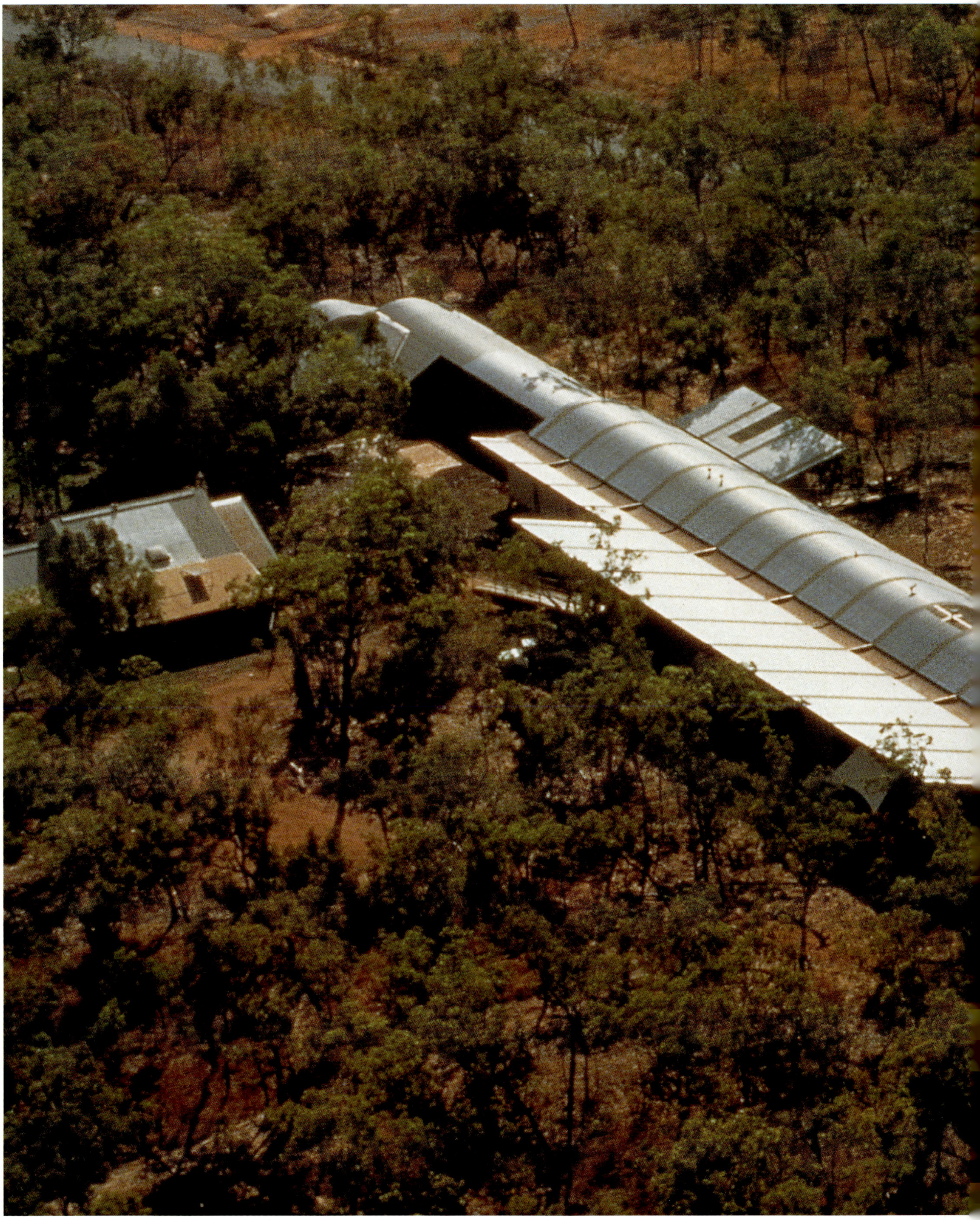

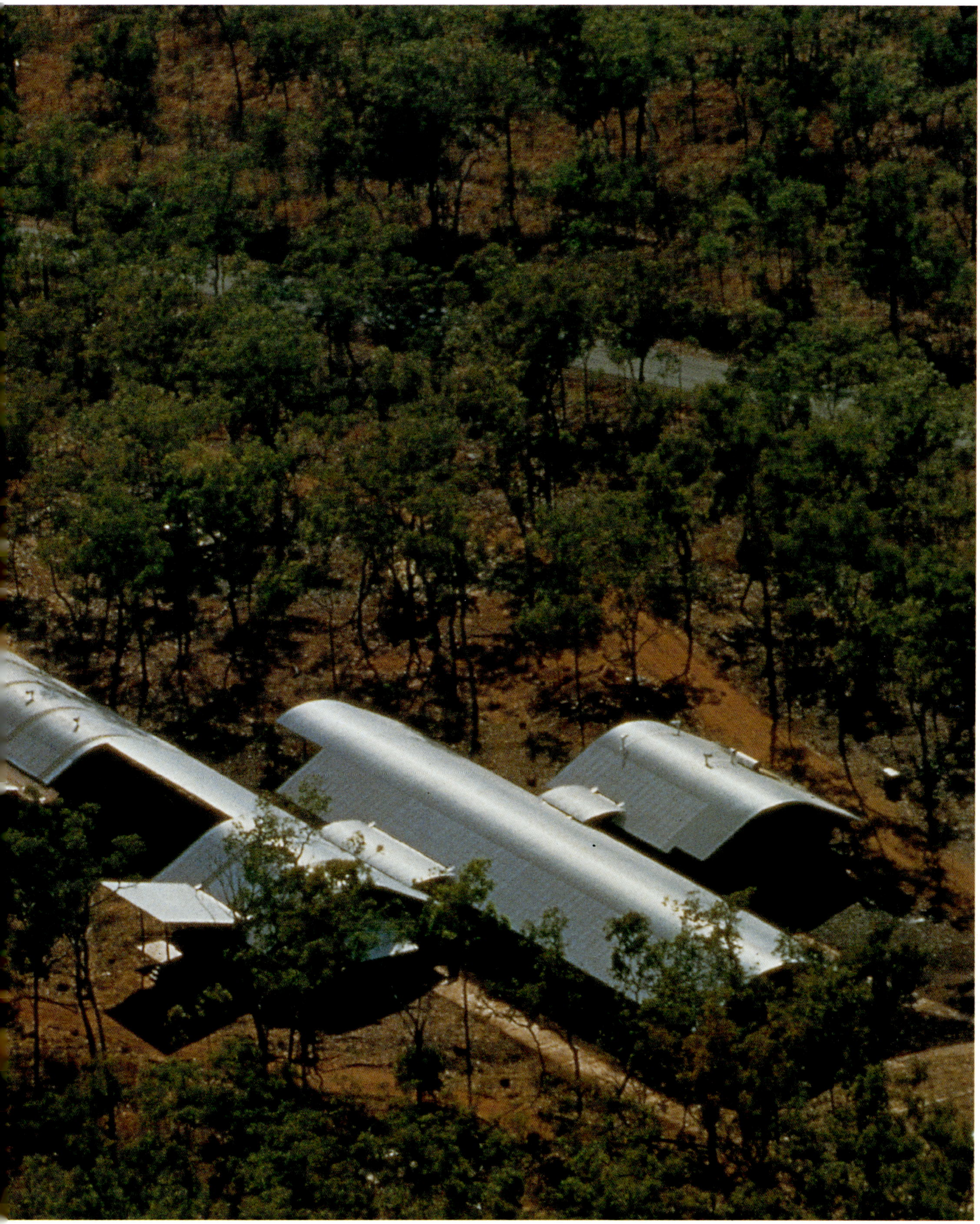

Above
Arnhem Land, Northern Territory, Australia
Bark painting by Australian aboriginal artist

Facing page
Visitors' Information Center and Park Headquarters
Kakadu National Park, Northern Territory, Australia, 1992–1994

passage of the air by compressing it at the level of human occupation. The increased air velocity combined with the evaporation of perspiration from the skin provides for a perceived cooling effect. The section relates closely to many of the natural cave profiles in the region. Rammed earth was used in the floors and walls to provide mass, thereby achieving thermal lag keeping these unventilated areas of the building cool.

The other building, to the east of the interpretive center, is for the Marika-Alderton family in the Yirrkala Community in Eastern Arnhem Land in the Northern Territory (1991–1994). This was built for an aboriginal client, Marmburra Banduk Marika and her husband Mark Alderton. In this part of Australia, temperatures vary from twenty-two degrees Celsius in winter to thirty degrees in summer; there is low humidity in winter and ninety-five percent in summer, and cyclonic wind velocities can reach sixty-three meters per second. The aboriginal people in this community still spear fish and gather food in the traditional way. Yet they are very much part of the twentieth century. An aboriginal leader, representing the indigenous people of Australia both nationally and internationally, this is Marika's country. She is affiliated with a university, is a member of the Australia Council, and has served on the board of the National Gallery of Australia. She travels widely while remaining part of the culture which she is intent on preserving.

The houses that aboriginal people have traditionally built for themselves are very different in form and placement from the disgraceful bunkerlike

Marika-Alderton House
Yirrkala Community, Eastern Arnhem Land,
Northern Territory, Australia, 1991–1994

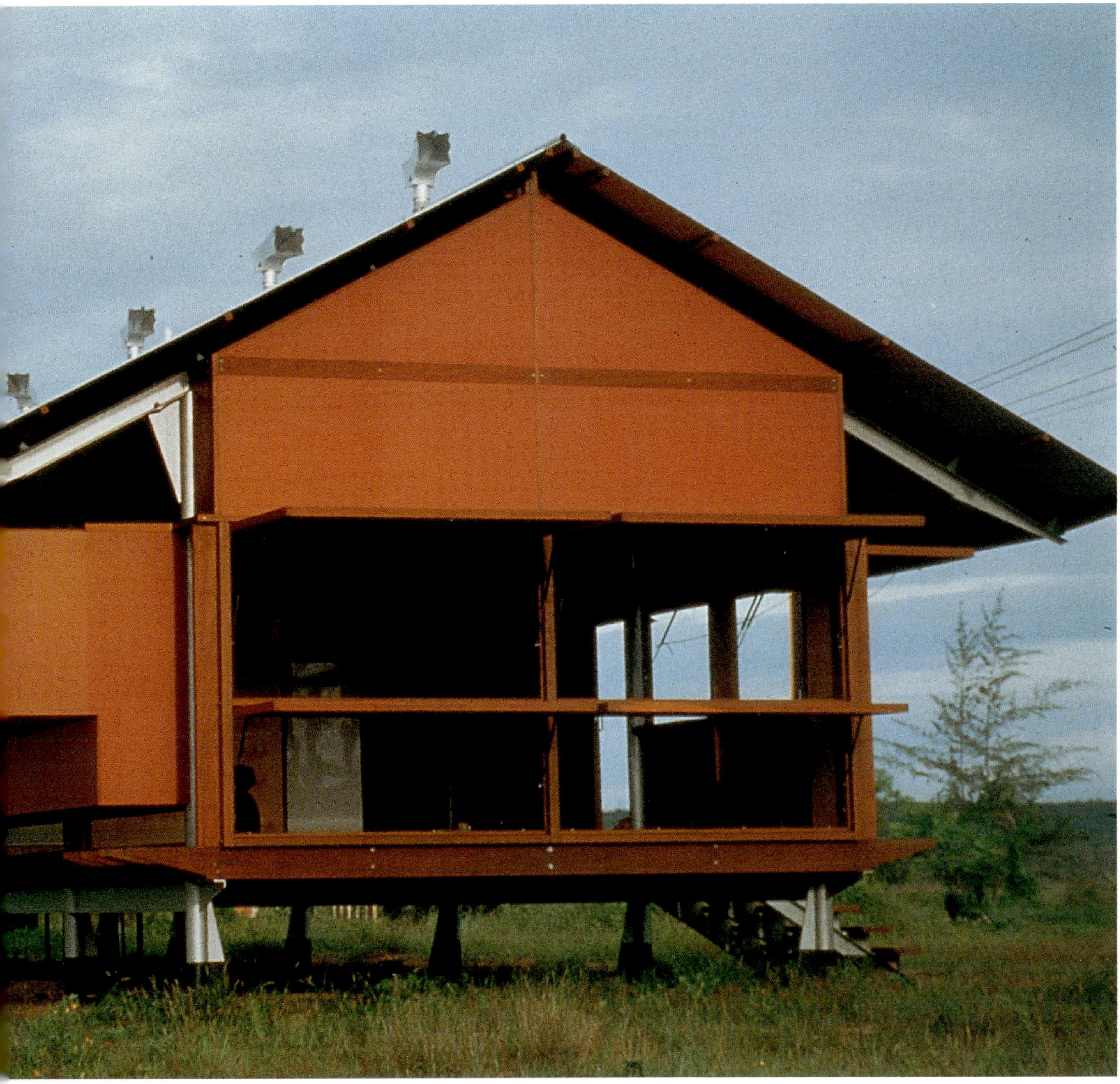

buildings provided in the last half century by the state. Many cultural issues are involved in the design of aboriginal housing. Aboriginal people find our cellular planning unhealthy, yet they do not want an architecture so different from that provided for European Australians. The aboriginal people like to observe the horizon and the patterns of the weather and to watch the outside without being seen.

Culturally, parents occupy the west end of the building, as they correspond to the time of the setting sun, to the age when life is at an end. Children live to the east of the parents, where one sees the birth of the day, since they correspond to the beginning of life. Traditionally, sons and daughters avoid eye contact and communication with each other. Bathing spaces are placed deep inside the house, providing isolation from the sitting area, food preparation, television, and video.

During the daylight hours, it is hard to see into this house through the ventilating slatted doors and shutters if they are closed, but it is very easy for the occupant to see what is happening outside from inside. After dark, the reverse is true; however, the daytime level of privacy is not required at night since the inhabitants spend most of the evening around a campfire on the beach with family, relatives, and friends.

For the cyclonic periods, the Marika-Alterton house is braced and held down against the tremendous wind pressures. The southern fins break the wind velocities and provide privacy from bedroom to bedroom as well as shade over the house for the first few hours after the summer sunrise and sunset. They frame views and direct ventilation through the house. The site is close to a bauxite mine, so it was important to find an ultraviolet stabilized color to match the earth red of bauxite. The venturi roof ventilators equalize the pressure between the inside and the outside, so the positive-negative pressure differential is minimized. The house is raised ten meters off the ground to protect it from tidal surges during the conjunction of a cyclone and high tide, when half a meter of water can flood the area of the site. Hence the necessity of the dry platform and the open slatted floor, where sand that is tracked and blown into the house can easily fall through.

As a child, I was raised on the principle that, since most of us spend our lives doing ordinary tasks, the most important thing is to carry them out extraordinarily well. Sometimes extraordinary means different. I was initially prevented from building the Marika-Alderton House by government housing advisers. They disapproved of my design, which opposed the European concrete bunker mentality. They also objected to the timber used in prefabrication. The building was constructed in Sydney and transported across Australia on barges and trucks; this clearly challenged local government thinking. With my clients' initiative, together we have won a battle, and having erected the first such house, it has become a building which defines some principles for lightweight and economical dwellings. With another similar house under construction and others commissioned, we have established a new type of building for the Northern Territory.

Marika-Alderton House
Yirrkala Community, Eastern Arnhem Land,
Northern Territory, Australia, 1991–1994,
Childrens' wing

DISCUSSION

Glenn Murcutt
Robert Oxman

Robert Oxman: *Could you address the practical aspects of being a sole practitioner?*

Glenn Murcutt: I work very closely with my engineer, James Taylor, and the reassuring thing is that his father was also my engineer in an earlier period. It is of primary importance for an architect to have a fine engineer who can respond to his creative demands. The next most important thing, of course, is to have a wonderful client.

The salient feature of a one-person practice is that one is solely responsible for the design and for the building at every stage of the process. One has to answer to everyone involved: the builder, the client, and above all oneself. It is extraordinarily demanding, and if one is planning some ten to fourteen buildings a year by oneself, it is really a difficult task. On top of this, I can have twenty to thirty inquiries a week from students, architects, universities—all wanting something.

In twenty-six years of private practice, one gets to know a lot of contractors. All told, I have probably worked with some forty builders, ten to fifteen of whom I would trust with everything. We are always told: "Never get close to the builder; never strike up a friendship—they'll take advantage of you." I can honestly say that this has never happened to me. I have worked with Finns, Dutch, English, Serbs, and New Zealanders. I even have worked with the odd Australian builder. I have been with my Finnish builder in the sauna on a Friday night, and after hours of drinking and talking, I am not able to drive myself home. However, there is no conflict of interest whereby the friendship is allowed to affect the quality of the work or vice versa.

Audience: *What influence has Mies van der Rohe's tectonic world-view and quest for ideal form had on your work?*

Murcutt: At the age of sixteen I was introduced to the work of Mies van der Rohe by my father, and in particular the Farnsworth House. Early in my career I reacted very positively to this work. I loved it because of its simplicity. However, one has to be careful with simplicity: it must contain the essence of everything it has initially set out to do and simultaneously represent its latent complexity. This complexity has to be distilled in such a way that the essence retains all the elements of the original paradigm. When any of these elements are left out, the simplicity becomes merely simplistic.

There is no doubt that Mies has been very important to me, and I have spent some forty years trying to exorcise him from my psyche. By now, I realize that this is not going to happen entirely; the principles of his work are too deeply embodied within me. However, other factors of equal importance have redirected the Miesian influence, and I believe that I am no longer designing Miesian buildings. Modern architecture is wonderful, as long as you don't make it into dogma. I first went to Europe in 1962, and I saw a house in Paris which possessed some Miesian qualities. A decade later I received a scholarship and finally got inside the building, which happened to be Pierre Chareau's Maison de Verre. I realized that modern architecture didn't have to be a rigid dogma, but on the contrary could be open-ended.

There are principles, however, which lie beyond the influence of Mies or his American follower Craig Elwood, fundamental issues that turn on such questions as: Why air conditioning? Where does the wind come from? What is the temperature range? What is the condition of the land? What is the water-table level and the geological structure? What is the history of the indigenous people's occupation of the site? What is the reason for the form of the indigenous architecture?

What did the early European and present-day farmers do? What are the patterns of movement of animals that have lived here over time? What are the fire regimes in this place? What does the landscape require for propagation? These are questions that one can ask in the name of any society, for any piece of land. There are answers to every one of these questions, and within these answers lie principles that must be addressed. One needs to assume responsibility for what is embedded in the site and its environs if for no other reason than that it has been there since time immemorial.

I find great satisfaction in the elegance of a solution when it embodies all the things that are required of the brief and also all the multitude of things that are not in the brief, but are inscribed in the land. Very few clients are going to tell you anything about the land and their responsibility for it. I have said to clients who bought land adjacent to a national park: "Look, the government has a policy whereby they are prepared to purchase these sites at the true market value. My recommendation is that you offer it to the government, because I'm not prepared to design a house on it; to me the land comes first." After some hesitation these clients eventually sold the land. They followed my recommendation and bought another beautiful site, and on it I built a house for them.

Oxman: *How do you work? What for you is the meaning of the famous phrase "creation is a patient search"?*

Murcutt: I was very gratified to learn that Álvaro Siza thinks that architects don't invent anything, that they transform reality. I have often gotten into trouble for saying much the same thing, as once when I spoke in the presence of the head of a school of architecture in Canberra, who wrote me a most terrible letter about this issue. My point is that every work that doesn't already exist comes into being out of the potential for its existence; so we don't actually create architecture. Our role is one of discovery, just as a scientist discovers. The important issue about discovery is that it is non-elitist; we all have the potential to discover. The core of the creative process is how we go about the act of discovery. From this point of view I can claim that I have happened upon a sun-shading device which sits outside a glass roof and resolves the sun for summer-winter geometry in different parts of Australia to a north-facing roof—the sun is in the northern sky in the southern hemisphere—one installs the slats at an angle to the horizontal of thirty-one degrees, thirty-three minutes in the Sydney area with a fifty-five degree cut-out overlap. It works perfectly for winter and perfectly for summer. With this kind of sunscreening, throughout the summer the sunlight is reflected and bounced into the interior of a building; during the rest of the year the sun enters the building directly. The principles behind the relationship of the sun's position to any point on earth were found long before me; I have simply found a way of harnessing them.

Intuition is an important factor in all this. When there are many known factors, one can have a hunch about a solution and then make a leap beyond the known in order to find a "solution" and test it. The empirical method in science works much the same way. In my childhood, I worked with wind patterns in the designing of model boats and aircraft, and later I sailed racing skiffs and did some flying. In the design of boats and aircraft, there is little room for error. Architecture is more forgiving; nonetheless I do have some of my buildings wind-tunnel tested.

Australia is an isolated land. As a result, Australian architects tend to be thirsty for knowledge, their offices having some of the best libraries of international journals in the world. When I worked in large offices, I saw how the magazines would come into the office, how the ideas would be absorbed, and then in a matter of two weeks the influence manifested itself in all the new designs. I used to say to myself, "God, I don't know how they can have the nerve to do this. It is so obvious and so awful, and it's mostly not about where we are in Australia." I decided that when I went into practice I would not subscribe to a single architectural journal from anywhere in the world. For twenty-six years I maintained this abstention, which puts me at a disadvantage when I come to conferences such as this one, because people talk about architects who are doing this and that and I'm unfamiliar with their work. The important thing about my withdrawal from the latest fashions exhibited in journals is the fact that, unless one is skilled at seeing through these images to the underlying principles (or the absence thereof), they are not going to be understood. Most photographs that you see in journals greatly exaggerate the quality of the building. For a start, the spaces are totally misrepresented through the use of the wide-angle lens.

Observation is as important as intuition and discovery. Above all, know yourself, observe what you do, the things you enjoy, even write it down, and then ask yourself: Why do I do this? Go to a restaurant and be there early. Go to a table, sit down, and then ask yourself: Why did I go to this table? What can I observe of the quality of life here? Where is the service coming from? What sort of privacy can I enjoy in this setting? The important thing to observe is how each of us reacts to space, the quality of light, the inevitability of movement, the flow patterns, the dimensions, the color, and so on. Ventilation is a key issue, but not air-conditioning, since this usually flattens an environment. I don't talk about space that much, but space is, of course, critical. It must, however, be the result of all the other factors working in unison, no factor being of greater import than the others. For example, the fins shielding the face of the house designed for the aboriginal people in eastern Arnhem Land not only block the entry of the early morning and late afternoon summer sun, but also serve to break down the force of the high-velocity winds. They provide privacy to the sleeping spaces, define the structural order, frame the views, and direct ventilation patterns.

When I returned from visiting Europe in 1964, there was something of a renaissance in Sydney with Ross Thorne, Ken Wooley, Bruce Ricard, Bill Lucas, Neville Gruznan, Ian McKay, and Harry Howard, among many other fine Australian architects at that time. Some came out of the tradition of the Case Study houses in the United States or evoked Frank Lloyd Wright, Charles Eames, or Craig Ellwood. Some were also influenced by Japanese culture and architecture. Some had studied landscape architecture in the United States, principally at the University of Pennsylvania. In contrast to the work of the 1960s, many of the more recent "isms" seem to me to be detached from reality. Their adherents don't seem to have an understanding of people, of modern technology, or of modern spatial relationships.

The so-called Sydney School of architects, on the other hand, favored materials that harmonized with the colors of the weathered Sydney sandstone and the olive-purples of the landscape. However, when the design of a building in the Australian landscape was refused by a town council because the work supposedly didn't blend with the natural environment, I got myself into an interesting legal argument based on English semantics. Blending is what can be done to an egg or to a cake, but how can architecture and the landscape be blended? How do the two mix? One certainly can harmonize with the landscape. But what is harmony? Disparate sounds which when put together, create a pleasing whole. Repeating the same sound or same element is monotonous. My question was: are you asking me to produce monotony or are you asking me to produce harmony? Fortunately, I have won ten out of the eleven cases that arose from local authorities refusing my applications for a building permit, each more or less on the same grounds.

Technology is an important aspect of building, but is clearly problematic when it becomes an event, an end in itself. In general terms, I don't like an architecture of events because it means that the architecture becomes extraordinarily self-referential, and it is tiresome to be in a place where one has to look at the work all the time. When a building becomes desperately interesting I find it enervating. I like an architecture where the technology is incidental or, alternatively, is integrated in such a way as to be mute.

Audience: *How do you approach a context that is more complex than those of most of your work? What if, in addition to space and climate, you must contend with factors of urban setting, roads, history, etc.?*

Murcutt: The complexity of any program is dependent upon one's ability to perceive complexity. As I have indicated, the true resolution of complexity is simplicity. What might look simple is often highly complex. My works cover a great range of sites in urban, suburban, and rural areas, at different latitudes and altitudes; some works are at a great distance from the cities, others occur on the immense Australian coastline; there are great variations in the cultural contexts as well. It is an extremely complex and difficult thing to design for the scale of the Australian landscape; you're like an ant in this environment, and comparatively, a giant in the built environment. One needs to respond to the zonal and scalar changes, to fundamental changes in light levels, etc. What I am suggesting is that there is a great complexity within my own country in designing with the land, because in each region, one has to respond to totally different conditions and contexts.

Urban and rural contexts present equal but different complexities that have to be addressed. In every context, one needs to address scale, typology, morphology, materiality, wind, light, and the surrounding built environment. The real constants in Australia are the climate and the land. I imagine it must be much the same here. A solution for Tel Aviv is not a solution for Jerusalem and vice versa. At this very moment, Tel Aviv has a temperature of, say, thirty degrees Celsius and a humidity of eighty percent, and that's different from the conditions here in Jerusalem, where it is cooler with lower humidity. Different conditions demand different responses.

National cultural differentiation is a mysterious thing. Can you imagine the French ever designing a Mercedes-Benz? Can you imagine the Germans designing a Citroen? It must be something in the psyche and the language that brings about a different way of dealing with these mechanisms, a different way of doing things. It is important to remember this when dealing with people from different cultures, even if the nation is supposed to be homogenous, as in the case of Australia or Israel.

I detect that many people here are close to the spirit of this land; I sense that very clearly. It is similar to what I have felt with Finns in Finland, who also enjoy a very close relationship with their land. You can't talk to a Finnish architect for more than three minutes without discussing nature. For me the universal continuity of the natural environment is the great bond that we all share. I think you have great potential with the natural energy systems and raw materials here. I know there is a lot of discussion at the moment about the imposition of having to use stone. But you know, stone is versatile; it can be used either for cladding or for a load-bearing component, or for a unit in a modular form. When put into compression, stone can span dimensions which make for wonderful spaces. When combined with other materials, its potential is enormous. Understanding the nature of stone may allow us to deal poetically not only with the material, but also with the place, be it urban, suburban, or rural. The questions I ask are questions about principles, and those questions are as appropriate to the urban as they are to the rural context.

PRESENTATION BY
Jean Nouvel

Facing page
Institut du Monde Arabe
Paris, 1981–1987

The question of technology is hardly new. As long as humanity has existed on this earth, people have tried to dominate matter and materials; to overcome gravity, weather, and fate; to increase their control over the physical environment. Man started by putting one enormous stone on top of another. At the time, this was a technological achievement. Then, two more were placed on top of these stones, then three, four, and so on, until the vault came into being. In much the same way, fenestration progressed from greased animal skins to oiled paper to glass, which was first produced in small, not very translucent pieces. Glass eventually became clearer and people were able to join the pieces together with lead beading. Finally, it became transparent and much larger in size. Today we can produce a single sheet of glass which is ten meters long and three meters wide. We enter into a kind of architectural Darwinism in which our knowledge is used to eliminate useless matter and to increase performance in the areas of loading, lightness, and insulation. As a result of a series of amazing inventions in the twentieth century, people have come to realize that almost anything is possible. In all domains, this century has been one of technological and formal exploration. With the technological creation of new forms of images, such exploration is reaching new heights.

Like the plastic arts, which have tested every conceivable medium, architecture, once content to copy classical models, has changed direction completely and experimented with practically all possible built forms. There was once a well-established academic system involving the slow improvement of cultural paradigms. Then, suddenly, these forms were no longer applicable. A new system had to be adduced, a system of diagnoses in which architecture had to relinquish a number of its ambitions.

It can be said that the ambition of architecture at the turn of the twentieth century was to construct a totally new, artificial world in which people could live. However, architects soon discovered the impossibility of designing an entire city and were compelled to reassess the range of technologies that could be applied readily to building. Architecture found that it could do no more than alter the world piecemeal, rather than transform it as a totality. Confronted with chaos, architecture—like contemporary science or philosophy—had to contend with something which could not be dominated, and thus it took refuge in a metaphysical dimension.

Throughout this technological century we have been understandably fascinated by machines: by high-speed aircraft, by telephones which enable people to talk to one another across the globe, by dynamos of enormous power. Among the first to be struck by this was Le Corbusier, whose *Vers une architecture* takes us back seventy years. Much of modern expressionism stemmed from this fascination and a philosophy arose based on the expression of technology and structure. Since that time, modern architecture has constantly oscillated between austere abstraction, which typified expression at its simplest, and a dynamic expression of fluid movement and structural form. The fascination with machines came to a head with the work of Archigram in the late 1950s, with the ideological apotheosis of the city as a machine. And in many respects, we can say that the Centre Pompidou in Paris, dating from 1972, was the most

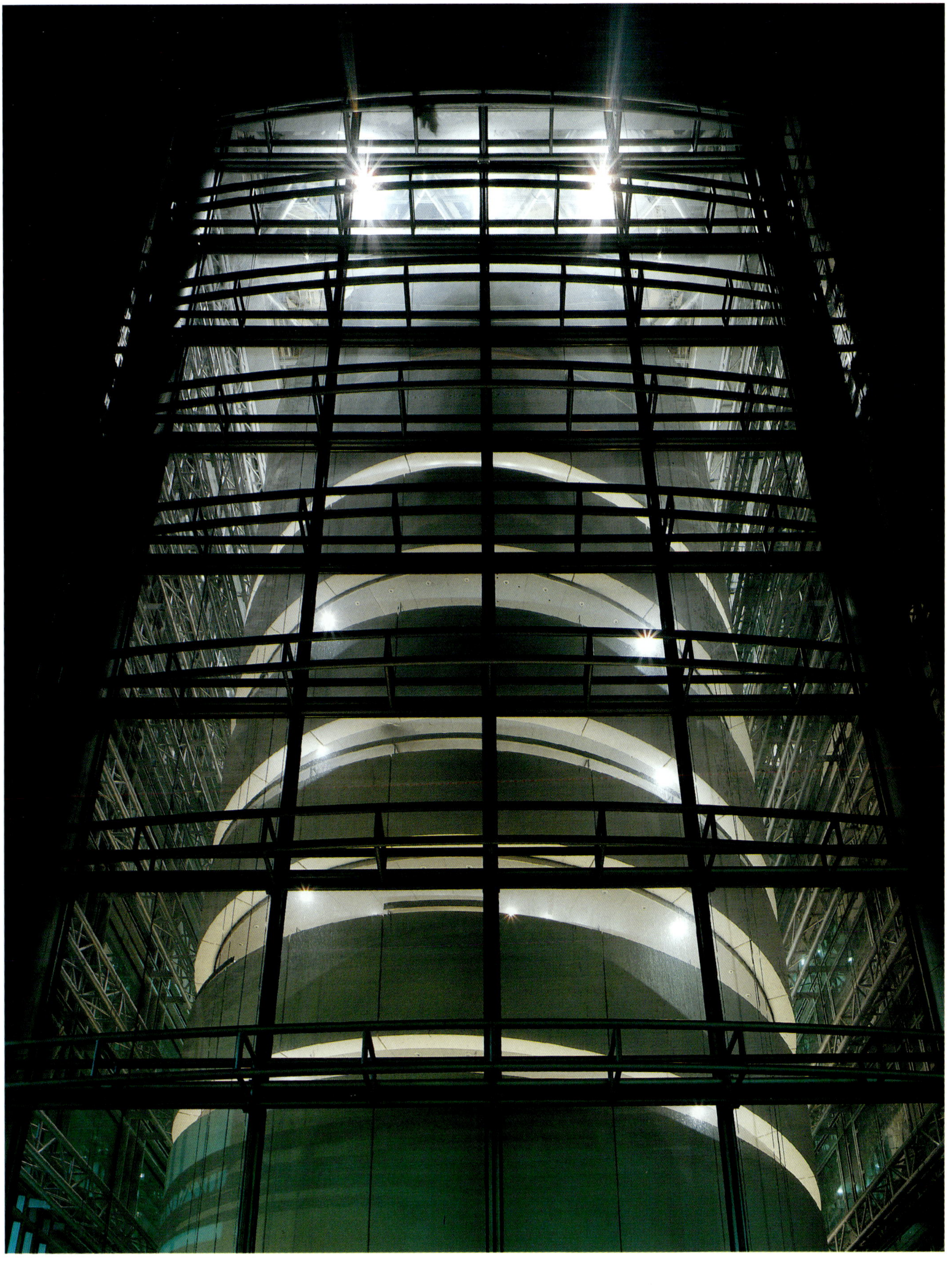

accomplished example of the technological expressionism derived from Archigram. However, at the time, architects still subscribed to a theory of functionalism. Today we are entering a period in which form gains its independence from function. Increasingly, function has come to be technologically satisfied without making any reference to form.

Today, the simpler things appear in formal terms, the more complex they often are in design and manufacture. This holds true for cars, computers, sound systems, and television sets. There is a growing tendency toward mechanization, electronization, miniaturization. Everything is becoming increasingly compact, light, and small. Ultimately, the only thing left will be the result. In architecture—a field traditionally based on craft, where monumental scale is often regarded as a virtue—there is a great deal of resistance to this new trend.

It is always difficult to integrate fundamental changes. Even in automobiles, it took a long time to get rid of the concept of the coach. For thirty or forty years we seemed to be unsure whether our cars were being pulled by steam horses or by real horses. There were still spoked wheels—people balked at eliminating them. In architecture, it is more or less the same: for as long as possible it patently resists the integration of the new. New techniques must prove themselves and become better understood psychologically in order to be accepted. Architectural forms that integrate these aspects today are all linked to electronics and to images. There is more and more talk of automation, and this is slowly but inexorably asserting its presence. There has been talk of "smart buildings," about offices that can manage their energy autonomously. In my estimation this kind of "smartness" isn't very sophisticated. It is possible to go much further. If, however, we look toward the integration of systems, in particular the significatory systems such as photography, then it would appear to be difficult to integrate the most advanced technological systems into architecture.

Probably the greatest technological revolution in architecture involves the fundamental changes that have taken place in the nature of building materials. This is the area where we can identify the buildings of the next generation. Today, when we discuss steel, it is usually high-performance steel, not nineteenth-century steel. When we talk about glass, we no longer refer to simple transparent sheets. Glass now possesses ever-more sophisticated characteristics. Soon there will be ultra-sophisticated glass, which, as a result of built-in micro-bubbles of air, will provide more thermal insulation in a few centimeters than is currently available in dozens of centimeters of glass wall—let alone the stone wall of earlier times. There is wood that can be molded and reconstituted, optical fiber, plastics, carbon fiber, etc. So the main change in technology involves change in material itself rather than in application or in our philosophy of material. Material is now subject to new issues: for example, people are increasingly preoccupied with recycling. They are loathe to use materials that will not decompose. Indestructible materials are the root cause of urban pollution, which prevents and obstructs change in the built environment. Thus, material recyclability is rapidly becoming a moral question.

Facing page and overleaf
Institut du Monde Arabe
Paris, 1981–1987

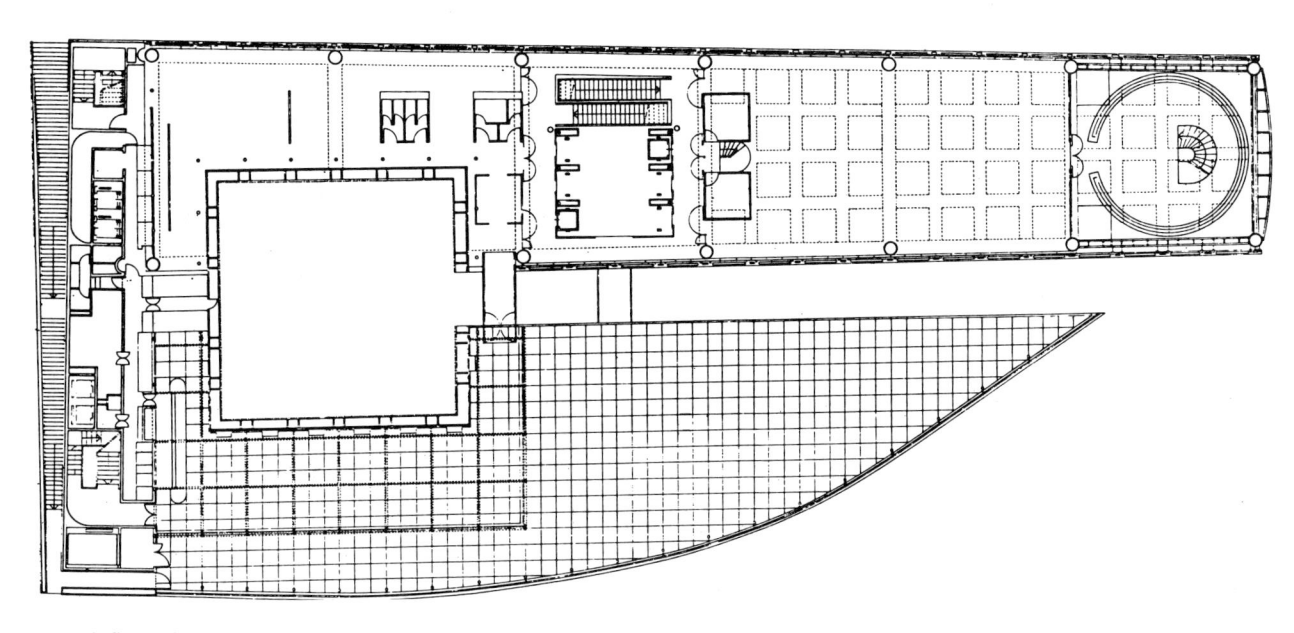

Ninth floor plan

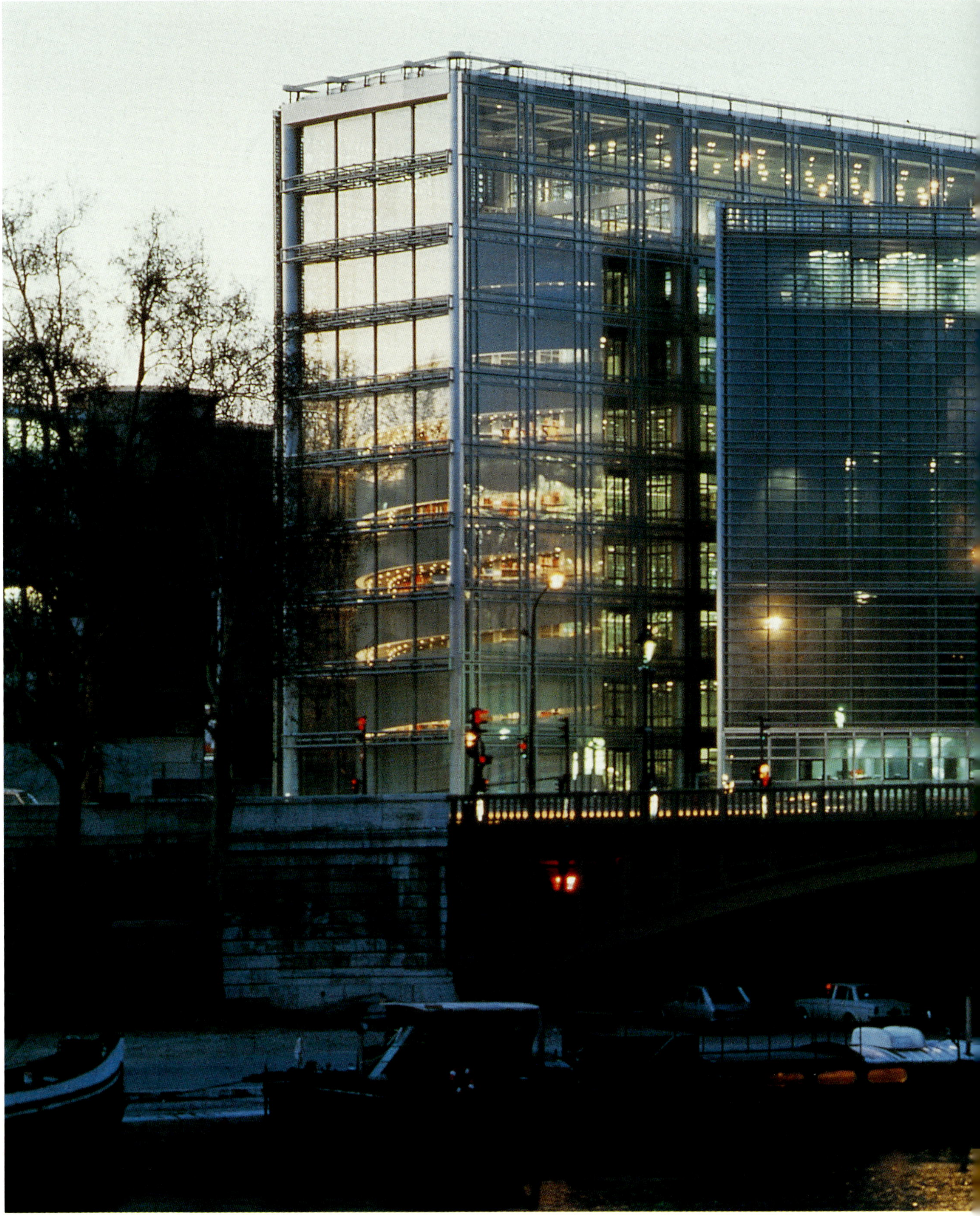

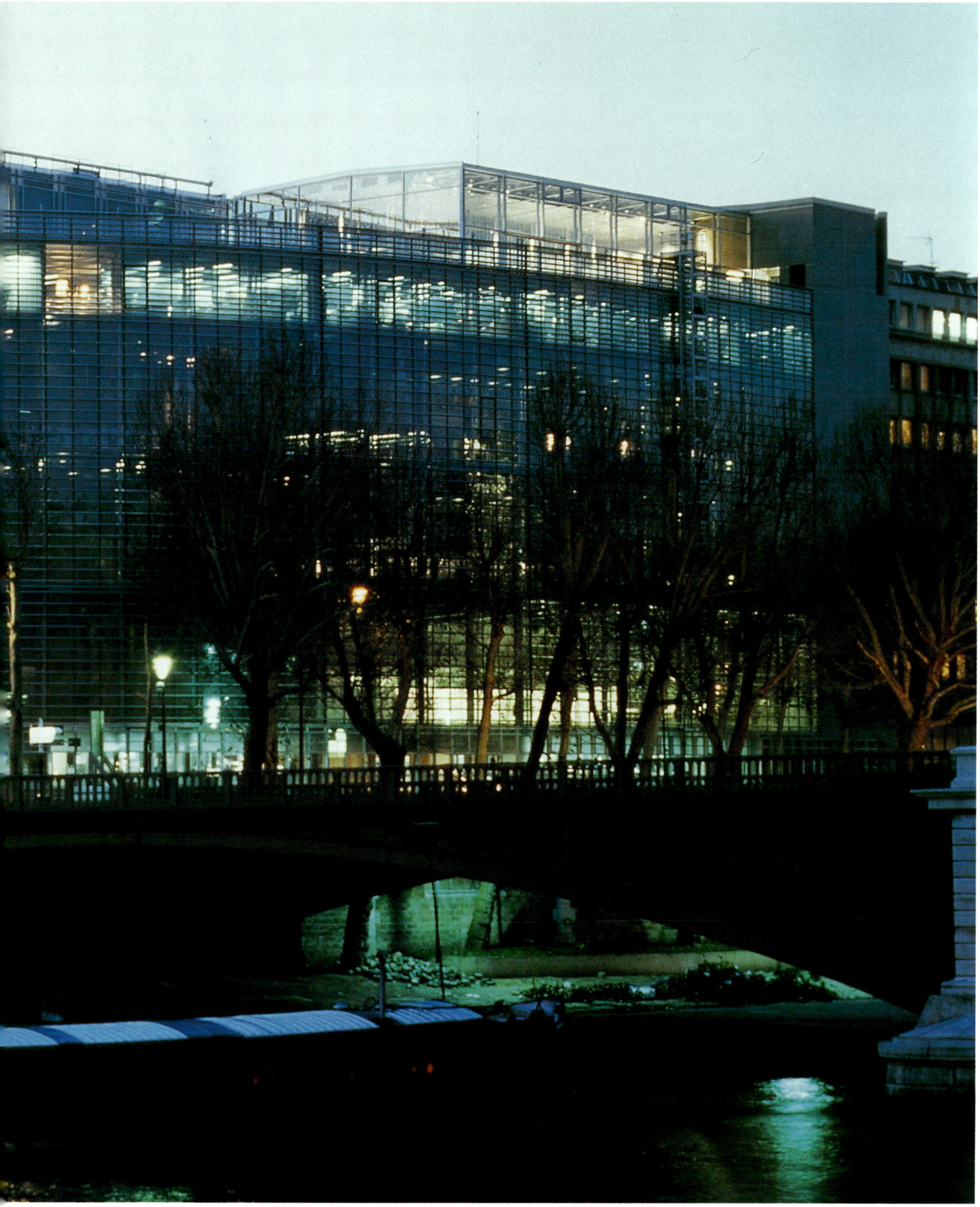

Materials can also be used to change perception and create a fleeting impression. A material may take on different aspects under varying conditions according to whether it is raining, foggy, or sunny. There is contemporary interest in light, darkness, wind, and plant life. The latter is now becoming an architectural material in the full sense of the word. The trend towards immateriality originates with a technology-based architecture that tends to favor virtual effects. A symbiotic opposition arises between the visible and invisible; between that which can be perceived and that which is imperceptible; between the clear-cut and the blurred.

The shape-scale-material relationship is becoming increasingly strong because this is what most forcefully announces the presence of new materials. You know, for instance, that a particular quality can only be achieved with carbon fiber. Hence, an entirely new architecture emerges out of new material qualities.

The question of technology, then, is not simply one of form—it is a question of the limits of a particular material characteristic. The treatment of light as a material is also an issue. Today this involves pixels, digital images, aligned images, light screens, the solar spectrum, light refraction, the use of colors present in light, the utilization of cold light with optical fibers, etc. Light is increasingly involved as an element that destroys materiality. A city can now be translated into a cosmic pointillism. It is obvious that night—darkness—destroys materiality; but at night everything depends on what is shown and what is concealed. There are images that come into their own only at night—the light images which are increasingly present, either as luminous lettering or as projections.

We have begun a race to eliminate form. For a number of years now architects wondered how they could go beyond Mies van der Rohe. Mies was clearly on the same wavelength as the artists of his epoch—perhaps ahead of many of them—in developing minimalism, working toward an absolutely reduced formal vocabulary. Can we achieve a similarly rigorous reduction of form without the structural frame as the main means of expression? An important element in all this is the size of the components. As soon as one aims at immateriality, there is a tendency to make the various components, particularly glass, inordinately large to eliminate the transition between outside and inside. By using large-scale walls and strong colors, Lluis Barragan attained a level of abstraction that caused one to question the reality of his material; you want to touch the wall to know whether it is thick or not, if it's truly "there" in a material sense.

We are confronted by an order that restructures elements through the scale and hierarchy of signs, whether these are images, advertisements, or a series of constructional elements that could be used equally as signs or constructional components. What enters at this point are questions concerning our traditional notion of space. We may say that space is no longer solely constructed. It is becoming dematerialized and global, and in this global space there floats an increasing number of signs and images that give rise to a new poetics.

In general we may claim that certain building techniques are archaic because they express the tactility of the particular material. This is as true of stone and brickwork as it is of prefabricated concrete. Such structural expression is in the process of vanishing. What appear instead are microsystems, textures, monochrome tones, images, kinetic graphic forms; in short, interfaces hide the underlying structure. The objective is to blur, erase, and even eliminate the constraint of material.

We approach a modernity that might be defined by an aesthetics of the miraculous. This is evident in the computer industry with the miniaturization of computers. The application of liquid crystals enables one to pass, at the push of a button, from a glass surface that is opaque to one that is colored or translucent. In addition, images may be projected onto partitions which penetrate our walls to the depth of a couple of millimeters. Increasingly, room is being made for a poetics and metaphysics of space in the constant drive toward immateriality. Here, too, we need to look in the direction of the plastic arts. Take an artist like James Turrell, who creates a sense of immensity using very little, actually, a mere framework. Behind the framework, you are no longer certain what there is. One tries to get there, to touch the material, but it's not there. His work has major architectural consequences because it deals with that which is both perceivable and automatically related to a new body of a physical and metaphysical knowledge.

The absolute image of technology today is the non-image: an absence, the invisibility of all technical solutions. The extreme aspiration is that of human as conjurer, who can make anything appear or disappear at will according to need or desire; who can travel instantly to any location by lighting up windows on the world, or by ever-faster self-propulsion. As analyzed by Paul Virilio, speed and technology eliminate barriers between people and nature, between the world and the universe. People want there to be nothing—nothing at all—between the heavens and us, between the countryside and us, and all of this is going in a direction that entails a reorganization of our relationship to nature. We want the absence of materiality to put us in touch again with the non-synthetic world. This necessarily leads to the rejection of certain materials or substances that I would call negative.

In contrast, we see the development of what to me are positive materials: both natural and artificial elements which are liberating in that they offer sustainable ways to control the world through either solar energy or photosynthesis. There are miniaturized materials which are closer to the body and will soon be incorporated into the body. This too takes us back to Virilio's argument that, ultimately, the people with the most complex physical challenges—say a fighter pilot or a disabled person—
will perform every function by just moving a finger.

It is through technology and modernity that it will be possible to solve the ecological crisis and the problems of cities. Pollution will only be overcome by means of electric or hybrid forms of automotive movement. Third World housing problems can only be tackled if technical development takes the form of a number of ready-made solutions that can be dispatched for manufacturing in already inhabited localities to replace or to change the

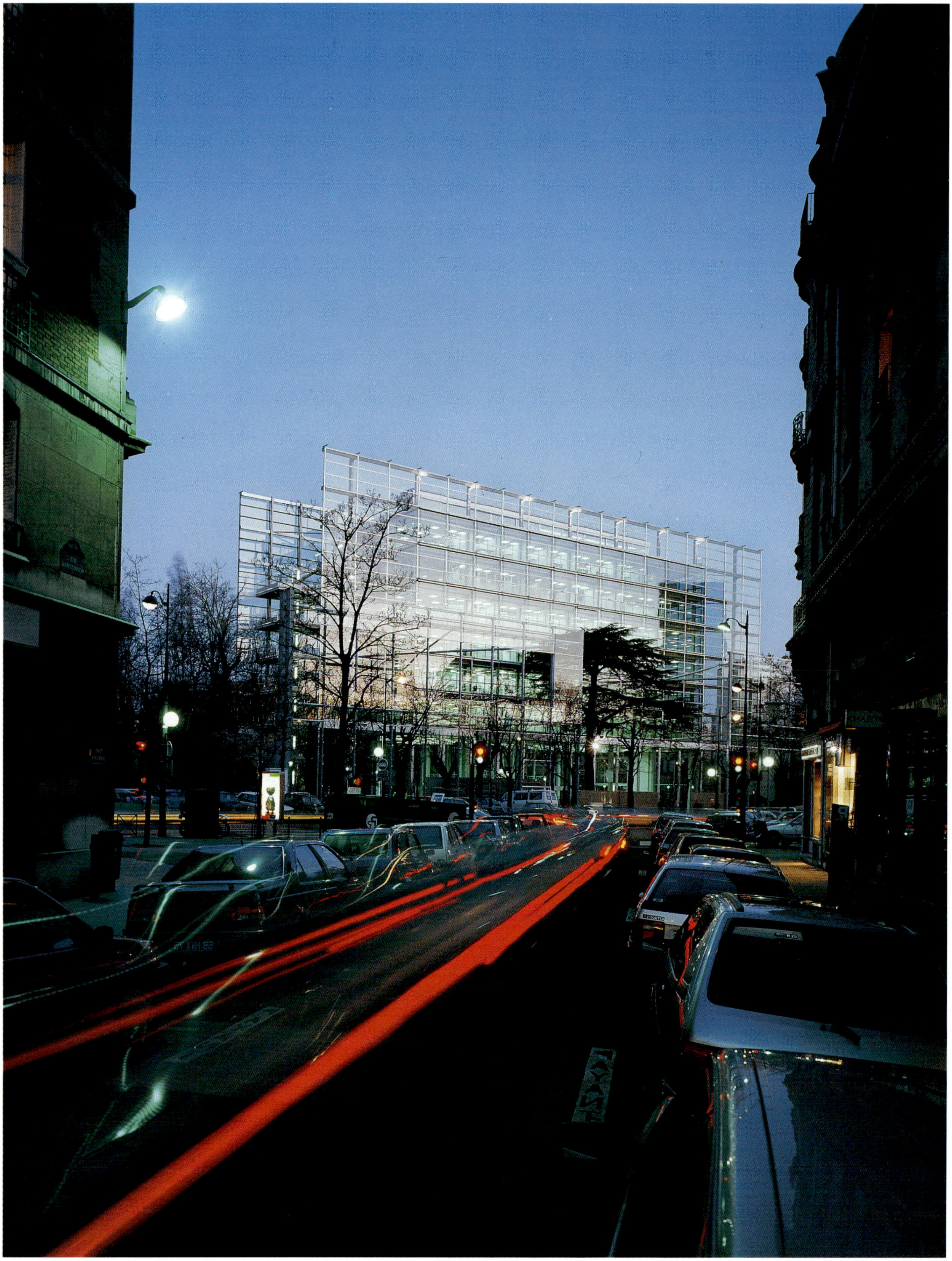

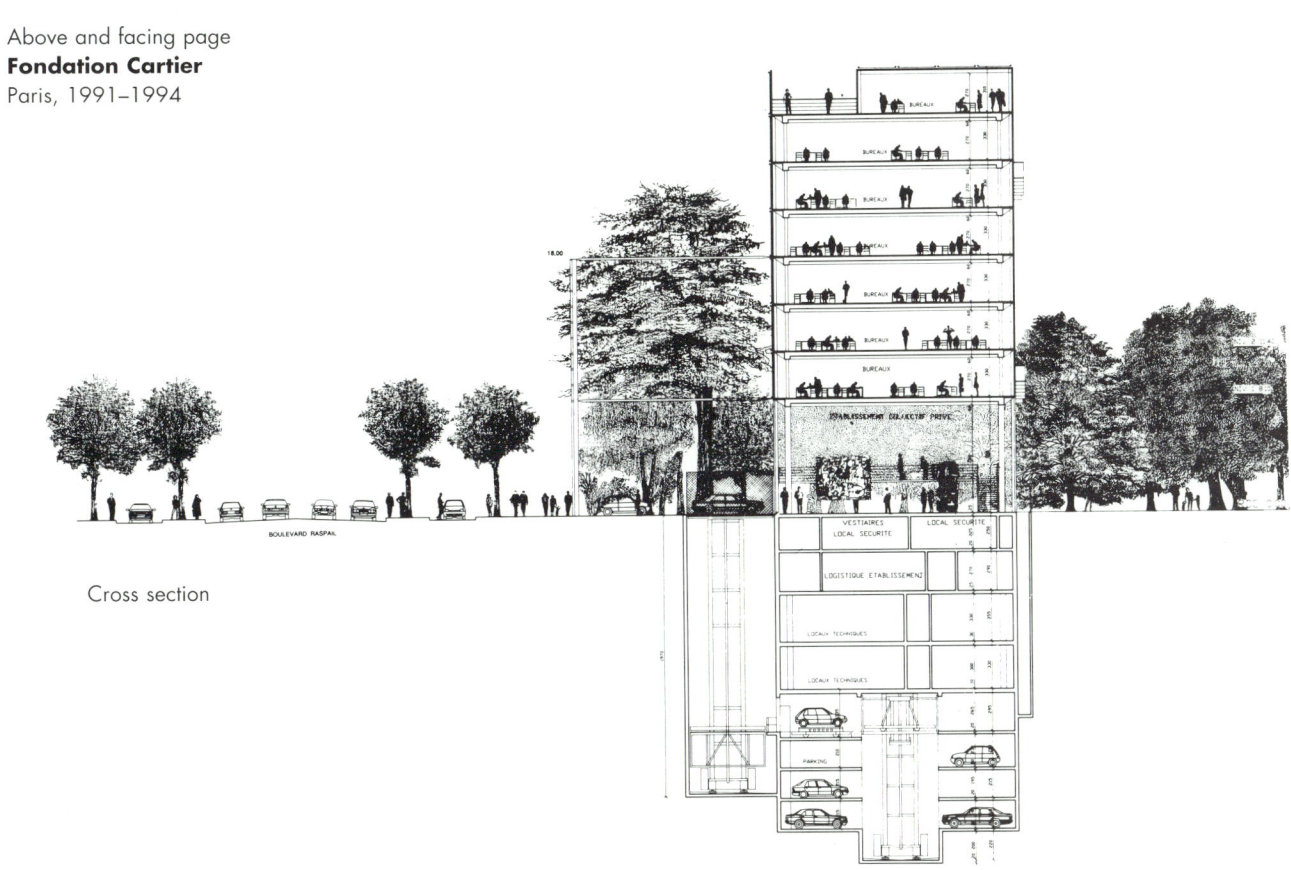

Above and facing page
Fondation Cartier
Paris, 1991–1994

Cross section

current deployment of material. This will be accomplished if these elements are utterly flexible and light, if they can be cut and shaped. One realizes that today in the Third World, it is already much easier to possess a television set or a transistor radio than a kitchen sink. The conclusion is that immaterial networks and sources of energy must be cultivated. This will be best accomplished by architects who have already been moving in this direction. Glenn Murcutt, for example, explores the versatility of corrugated iron to solve problems of cost, climate, energy, transport, design, and construction.

Between overarching theoretical discourses and the cold light of reality, a gap remains, and, despite our daily attempts to bridge it, this gap continues to widen. An architect is continually faced with small questions, progressively and selectively localized. Some of these issues can be illustrated by projects I have designed.

In the Institut du Monde Arabe, completed in Paris in 1987, I resorted to the use of mechanical jalousies reminiscent of Islamic decoration. These screens were composed of a series of rotating metal apertures that could be opened or closed down by electro-mechanical means. In fact, the entire building, when viewed from the Right Bank of the Seine, seems under certain conditions to be a gigantic, translucent sunscreen. Inside, one encounters a similar dissolution of space and matter achieved in part through transparency and in part through bright surfaces and reflections. The selection of aluminum as the main material was largely based on the fact that it responds to every changing nuance of ambient light.

Von Sprekkelsen, the architect of La Grande Arche in Paris, wanted a minaret for his arch. I projected a minaret that was perhaps somewhat higher than he had been anticipating. It was a 425-meter-high cylinder of curved glass, forty-three meters in diameter, with a width to height ratio of one to ten. Here, once again, one encounters a dematerialization through material, beginning with the black marble that, turning into black granite and gradually becoming polished, progresses from dark gray to light gray and eventually to glass. The glass, in its turn, is gradually overprinted with a silk screen so as to become a virtual mirror. You don't quite know where this cylinder begins and ends because it rises from an excavation and dissipates into the sky. It is a metaphorical link between the center of the earth and the cosmos.

In 1990 I designed a headquarters building for the German publisher Dumont Schauberg, owner of several newspapers and publishing houses. I proposed erecting the building beside a lake so one could clearly see the reflection of the building in the water. The transparent facade of the building would have been silk-screened with important slogans referring to the cultural, political, and scientific events of the epoch. This typographic screen would also have helped to protect the interior from the sun. A wall of water descending from the top of the building was to have been installed as a means of screening the noise from the nearby highway.

In 1993, I was commissioned to expand and refurbish the Opera House in Lyons. I proposed building on top of the classical structure, covering the volume with a glazed volume to be used largely as a rehearsal space. The double-glass roof is composed of a layer of green glass with silk-screen overprinting to provide protection from the sun. From a distance this roof appears to be faced in copper. Inside the existing shell I suspended a volume that was lacquered black throughout. Every seat within the forty-meter-high auditorium volume is provided with an optic fiber light. The space is thus illuminated at certain moments by "candles," which recalls the Lyons festival celebrating the Virgin Mary who saved Lyons from a plague some centuries ago. Since that time, the inhabitants of Lyons annually commemorate their salvation by putting candles in their windows. Each member of the audience is provided with an optic fiber candle so that when these lights are randomly illuminated the auditorium is transformed and the architecture is then made up of the people themselves.

The Fondation Cartier, completed in 1994, is built within the street frontage of a Hausmannian boulevard. A large cedar tree on the site, planted in 1823 by the French poet Chateaubriand, had to be preserved along with most of the trees on the site. This, and a requirement to build on the exact footprint of the previous building, largely determined the design. I didn't want to build high, out of proportion with the street, so I created an eighteen-meter-high glass screen, aligned with the frontage of the boulevard. This screen is higher than the glass prism of the building. There are in fact three layers of glass through which one can see simultaneously both the sky and the sky in reflection. Similarly, it is hard to tell if one sees a tree or the reflection of a tree. The crystalline structure of the glass also responds to the ambient color of the day. Here forty-five-centimeter-deep beams spanning sixteen meters entailed using special prestressed steel to gain a high performance with less material. The size of the glass panels was also stretched to the limit. Here we have eight-by three-meter glass walls that may be slid open or completely removed easily. It is a building that repudiates the idea of being "designed in detail." Inside, the glass is irregularly sanded so the interior seems somewhat ghostly when seen through the glass.

Through works such as these, I believe we can see the emerging "ethos of modernity." To me being modern means making the best possible use of our memory. It means connecting the most ancient facts with the most recent. It means moving at the quickest pace set by our new knowledge. It means paying attention to the evolution of what already exists and not

Institut du Monde Arabe
Paris, 1981–1987

Below and facing page
Lyon Opera House
Lyon, France, 1986–1993

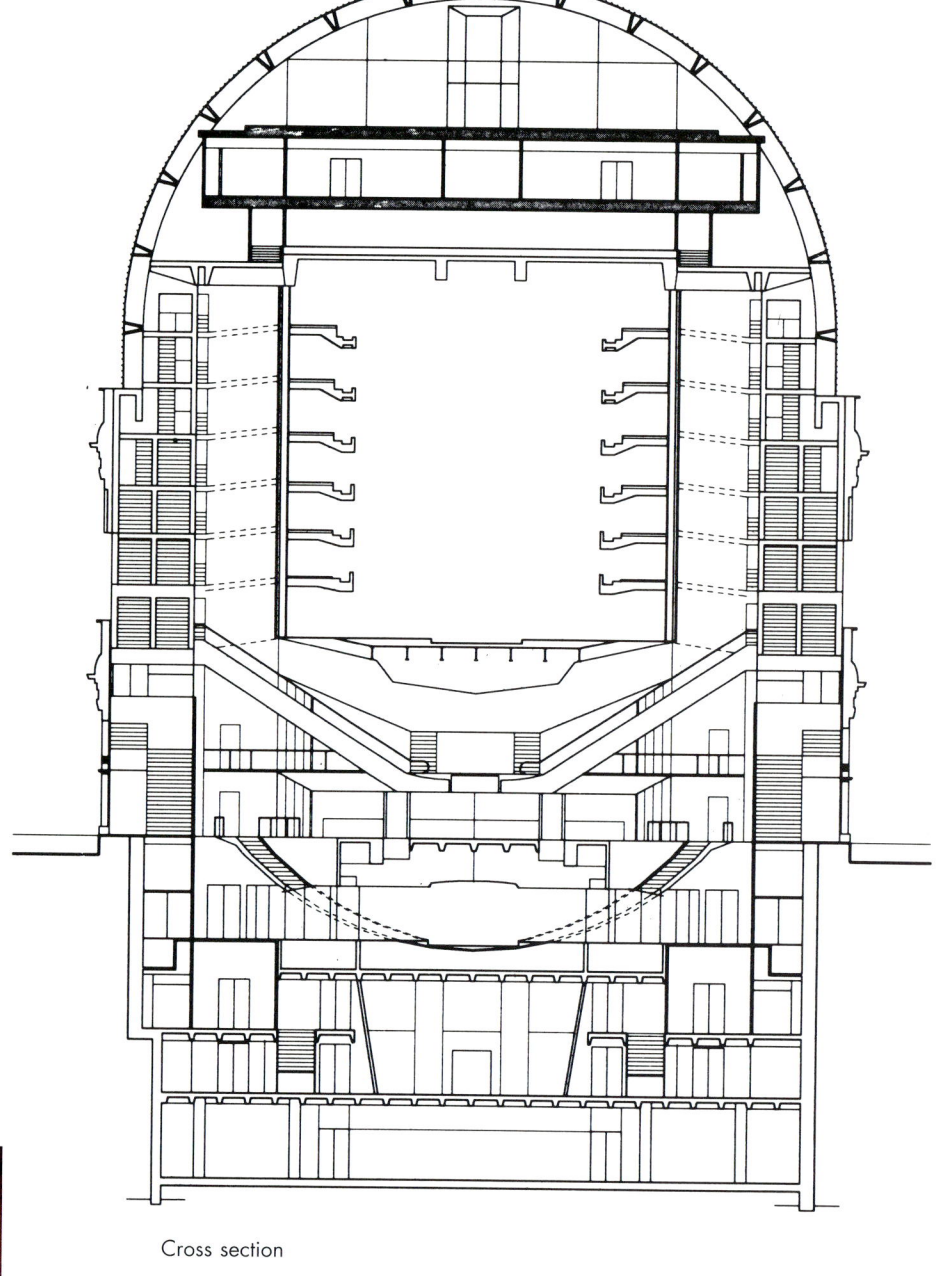

Cross section

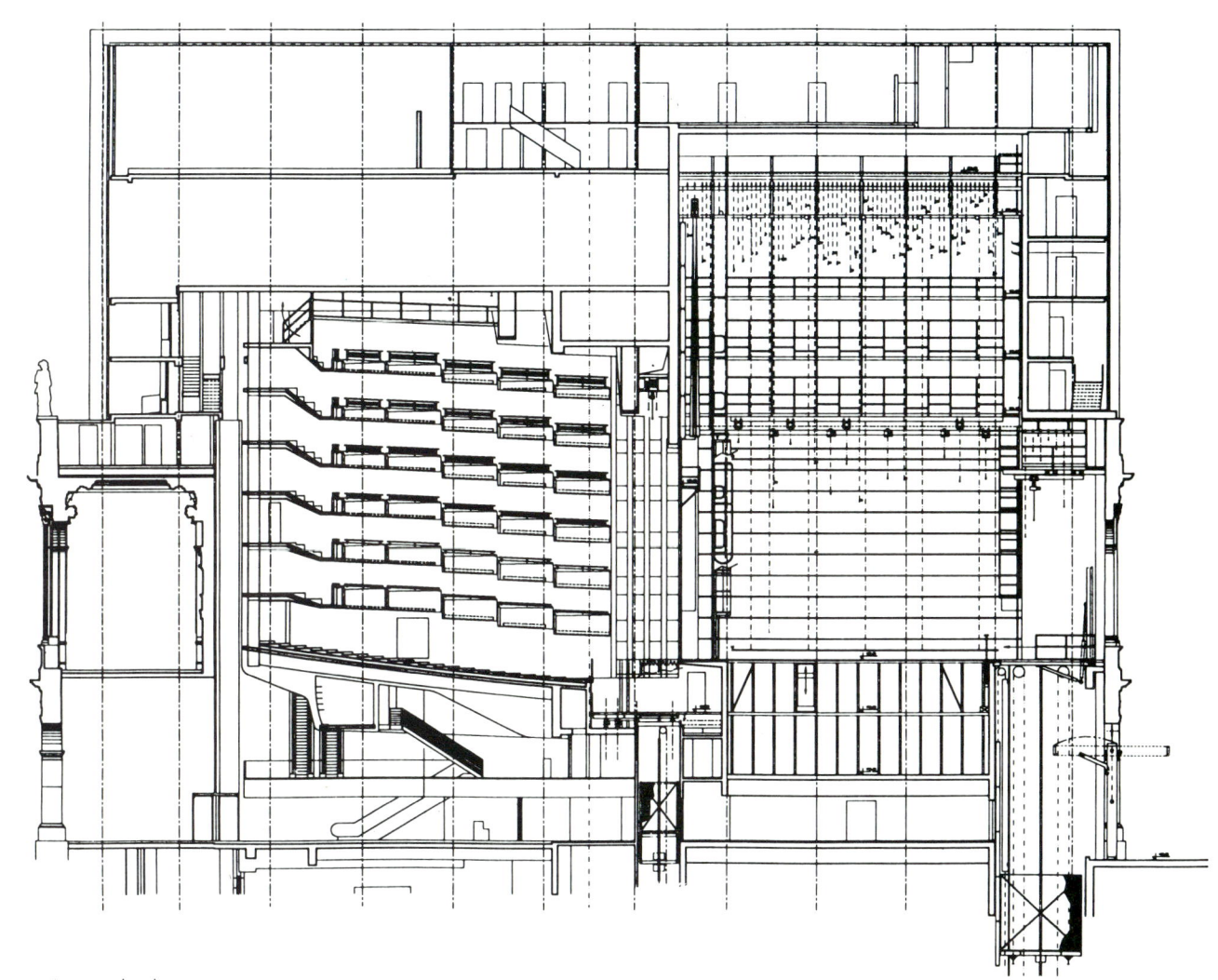

Longitudinal section

DISCUSSION
Jean Nouvel
Zvi Efrat

Zvi Efrat: *I would like to begin the discussion by asking you to what extent do you think of architecture as an autonomous discipline?*

Jean Nouvel: Architecture was an autonomous discipline a century ago, or even seventy or eighty years ago, but not today. Previously, architecture had its own manifest rules. It could always build with the same techniques and systems, generally in stone and wood. All the theories were very clear and the educational curriculum for the architect was self-evident. It was easy to build a building because there were accepted recipes. There was also a distinct urban typology. Today, however, after the hyper-development of all the cities around the world, there is a new system which we may call chaos. There are no simple rules and no simple typologies. Every case requires a specific diagnosis of the situation in relation to its parameters. Now architecture must be practical in relationship with other cultural disciplines. This century is notable for all of the images it has created, and architecture is one way of collecting and arranging some of these images. In the past, we thought of architecture as the art of organizing space. Today, we know it is a means by which we record and represent living culture. For contemporary architects history and the mastery of technology are not enough. An architect must understand the living culture. An architect must live a full life and see a lot of things. It is impossible to practice architecture if you don't understand the world, if you have never seen the most important cities in the world under different human conditions: the cities of the Third World, the industrial cities of America and Japan, and so on. To ignite your imagination when you are building in an urban situation you need an understanding of urbanization in general. For all these reasons, I think that the autonomy of architecture is untenable.

Efrat: *Several months ago, Peter Eisenman was in Jerusalem at a different conference. In one of his asides, he remarked that you and he represented the two leading opposed or divergent positions in architecture today. He asserted that he treats the issue of space and form, while you deal with surface, with the envelope, what he called the architecture of spectacle and information. Would you comment with that?*

Nouvel: For me, the main question about the work of Peter Eisenman turns on his involvement with deconstruction and postmodern philosophy. I don't think philosophy has helped us understand what may be possible architecturally after the demise of modernity. I fail to understand the relationship between postmodern philosophy and postmodern architecture. For me, Peter Eisenman behaves like a painter. He's a good artist. However, should an architect behave like an artist? An artist always displays the same personal vocabulary. An architect cannot build every building with the same vocabulary. Perhaps such a painterly approach was valid during the first fifty years of this century. But today, if you decide that all your buildings are white or are composed of circles or triangles, or that all your buildings are fractured, I can only respond with the greatest skepticism. I want to know why the building form is subsumed to a seemingly arbitrary artistic or philosophic conception. With the Peter Eisenman building in Berlin, my first question is, why is the building like this?

There is no doubt that some architects have involved and subtle systems for the generating plastic form. For me, the main issue is the specificity of each particular set of circumstances. We must rigorously analyze every situation and every building program. We have to think and talk endlessly with the client and with everyone else affected by the project. We need to articulate sound reasons for building in a particular way and not in another. Strictly formal questions should be left for later. We can't say that because my style is like this, the building has to assume this form. We often talk about the resemblance between the task of the filmmaker and that of an architect because they have to tackle similar questions.

Stanley Kubrick made films about a variety of subjects: war in *The Paths of Glory*, delinquency and terror in *A Clockwork Orange*. The subjects were quite different, as were the formal and structural character of the respective films. All the same, I can identify a movie by Kubrick because there is a common style irrespective of the diverse themes and techniques. This surely is how it should be with architects. Currently, architects are very insecure about the question of style. They want to achieve a clear a priori style. However, architects should be more like doctors, for whom the diagnosis is the most critical moment of their practice. We cannot base our work on a premature answer to a given question, and Peter Eisenman is much too involved with such preliminaries.

Efrat: *I suspect that your notion of a place or a context is very different from my idea of innate architectural or geographical character. It seems your concept has to do more with broader cultural questions.*

Nouvel: I think that today, cities can only develop through small modifications. I think that most of the buildings of the last fifty years are like geographic falsifications of the city. For my part I try to discern the poetic character of the situation in which I have to build. It is not simply a question of integrating the building into the existing context. I find that a literal, imitative contextual approach is usually disastrous, since it is very important for a new building to impart its own intrinsic quality to the other buildings around it. This is the real issue that confronts us when we talk about integration. It is not simply a question of similarity; it is a question of responding intelligently to the situation. With this approach you have to understand clearly the precise character of the context. You have to know what is possible in relation to your client, what is allowed by the authorities, etc. In this way you can perhaps adopt a positive attitude towards the construction of a city step by step.

Efrat: *You mentioned your skepticism vis-à-vis the discipline of urbanism. However, in your actual practice your conclusions seem to be quite different. In a developing country like Israel, your skepticism with regard to urbanism and the modern project is relevant because here we still design new towns. Modern urbanism is still part of our culture. We believe in the possibility of building cities.*

Nouvel: Yes. I have often thought about architects who say they want to design new cities. I think it's like a writer saying I want to write a library. It's an ambitious project. If we build entire neighborhoods, as architects in this century have often tried to do, the results are generally quite awful. As far as I am concerned, urban design is dead today. It is not possible, for example, to go on creating streets and squares or to reconstruct the European city. Attempts to do so end up as surrealist nostalgia. Both the utopian modern city of the thirties and the post-modern nostalgic city are equally impossible today.

I believe a third way is possible: one should try to discover the essential poetry of the new city form. I think that contemporary filmmakers are very important influences in this regard, like for example Wim Wenders, who makes you understand the poetic dimension of electrical wires, of the macadam road, of the desolate suburbs that are not so automatically bad. We have to find ways of giving quality to the existing urban reality.

Efrat: *I would like to come back to the issue of technology, or perhaps in your case we should say microtechnology or nanotechnology or even alchemy. For your exploitation of notions like flatness, lightness, transparency, translucency, disappearance, evaporation, liquidation, unstable materiality, mutation, deformation, velocity, fragility, illusion, vertigo, and so on, we could employ the one*

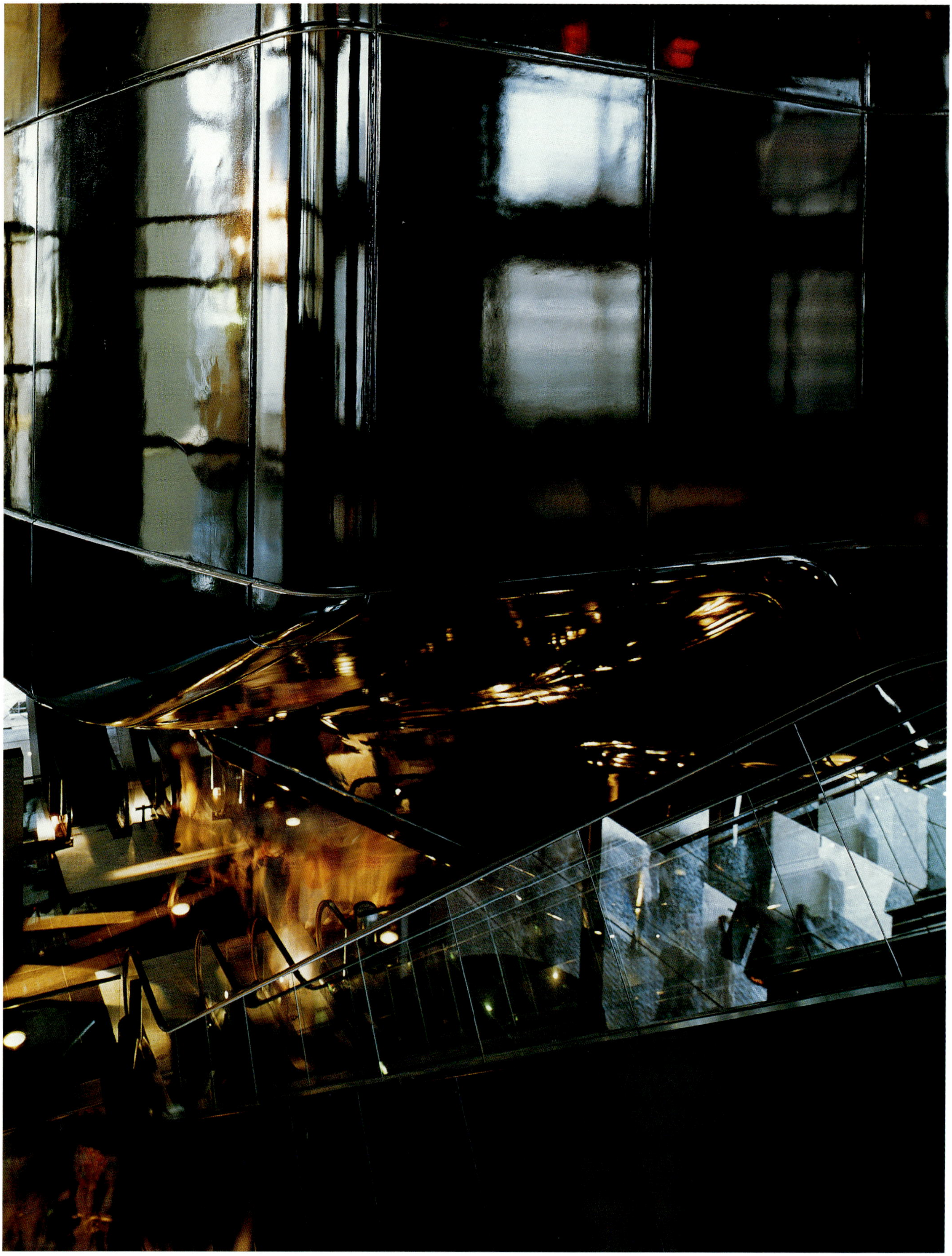

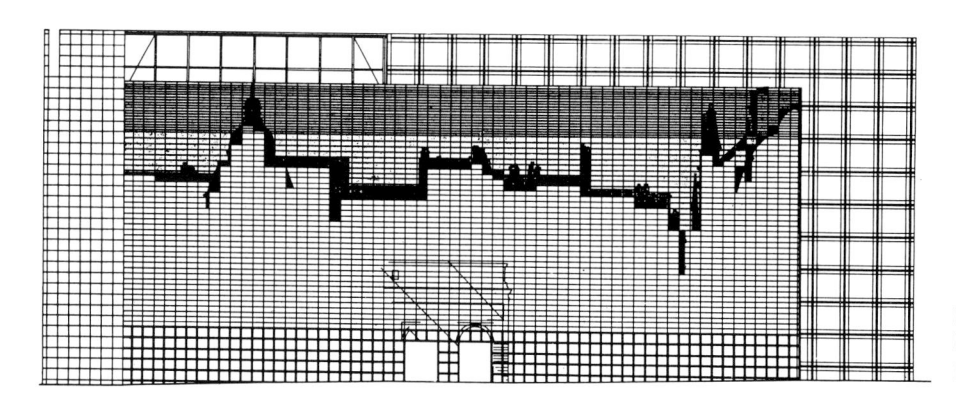

Institut du Monde Arabe
Paris, 1981–1987,
North elevation

word "metaphysical." Would you please comment further on the way you tinker with our contemporary perception.

Nouvel: I am convinced that we now have to create architecture in relation to the actual context in which we live. This is not as simple as it was a century or two centuries ago. We are part of a very volatile and dynamic system, and the dynamic culture of the cinema is a strong influence on our mode of being. We cannot approach architecture in the same static way as we did before. There is the overwhelming experience of velocity, of the relationship between space and speed, between time and space. This affects our perception of everything. Our memory of a person in space is like recalling an image in a movie. You cannot appreciate a film if you see only one image just as you cannot have an appreciation of architecture if you see only one facet, one detail. What counts today is the dynamic continuity of space, and architects and urbanists have to take our new sense of perception into account. This change must be the foundation for the new city and the new neighborhood and a new public architecture.

Facing page
Lyon Opera House
Lyon, France, 1986–1993

Efrat: You talk about a technology, about a technoculture or tectonic culture that is so refined, so sophisticated and committed to high-performance that sometimes it's almost invisible. There is only an image left, or, perhaps more precisely, an after-image, a virtual image of the technology. I would like to ask how you can protect your buildings from a rapid amortization. Some people would say that your sense of architectural technology is totally ephemeral. Traditionally, architecture has been concerned with precisely the opposite, with being durable. What do you have to say about the apparent fragility of your work?

Nouvel: Do you think we have to build a building in concrete or stone, with very thick walls, for it to withstand the passage of time? I don't think so. I think that if an architect wants to create buildings with durability, the main objective must be to design a structure which has a strong symbolic character. When people love a building, they keep it alive for a long time. Look at the Eiffel Tower. If it were not constantly painted it would have disintegrated long ago. It's the same thing for all architecture. The most difficult time for a building is the first thirty years of its life, because during that period you don't know if the building will acquire cultural importance or not. It is difficult of course to maintain a building with an external structure, but even with a fluctuating budget, the Institut du Monde Arabe has proved easy to maintain. Its glazed surface is completely smooth. As long as the surface is not damaged, glass resists the passage of time extremely well. For this very reason it is bound to be one of the primary materials of the future. But I think its ephemerality is also important, because the image of the building changes under different conditions, in rain or in fog, or under a gray or sunny sky, etc. I think that qualities of ephemerality have a direct effect upon our desire to maintain a building over a long period of time.

LECTURE
Patricia Patkau

One of the domains where a culture defines itself is the sphere of interaction between the general and the particular, an interaction which establishes associations that allow us to make sense of both. The two extremes to which any culture tends may be defined as follows: a condition of extreme particularity, where everything is different, and a condition of extreme generality, where everything is the same. Where the first may be recognized for its predisposition to chaos, the second may veer toward a trivial or meaningless order. In the context of chaos or extreme particularity, meaning is created by association, by organizing things in such a way that patterns arise which make it possible to understand the relationships between entities. In this way, similarities are the key to understanding. In the context of extreme generality, meaning is created by differentiation, by introducing vital nuances within the patterns defining relationships between things. Because all cultures exist in a dynamic state, meaning must constantly be created to avoid degeneration toward either chaos or triviality. This involves a complex balancing act in which both similarities and differences must be maintained and developed simultaneously. In his book *The Philosophy of Symbolic Form*, Ernst Cassirer wrote: "It is the fundamental principle of cognition that the universal can be perceived only in the particular, while the particular can be thought of only in reference to the universal."

The particular grounds us in the local; the general engages us in associations beyond our immediate situation. The interaction between them within a specific cultural context yields understanding. Far from being an anachronism, such a balance is essential to maintaining structures of cognition and meaning. However, as Western society is increasingly dominated by the homogenizing effects of mass production and mass media, as a result of global capitalism, the balance between the general and the particular is jeopardized. As technological change tends toward a self-hybridization that denies our ability to control its course, much less to assimilate its potential, increasingly we face a world that is self-fulfilling, out of place, and generalized. In this context, an emphasis on meaningful differentiation and the creation of the particular becomes more critical.

Our firm's work over the past ten years has been consciously conditioned by a confrontation with this predicament. We begin each project with a search for localized particular characteristics within the basic data of the project. This "found potential" may include such aspects as site, climate, building context, program, local culture, or anything that will facilitate the development of an architectural order that is evocative of the particular circumstance. The mechanism through which this is achieved is differentiation. This approach can be illustrated by five projects that have helped us explore this evocation of circumstance. The projects to be discussed are taken from the last decade of our practice, designed with my partner John Patkau, and more recently, with a third partner, Michael Cunningham.

In 1991, we realized the school for a Coastal Salish Indian band on delta land in the Fraser River, a few hours' drive from Vancouver, at the point where the valley disappears into the coastal mountain range. The aboriginals of western Canada have suffered tremendously from the forced superimposition of European culture. Our client, the Seabird Island band, represents a struggling culture. It is a community in some disarray with many social problems. Yet in light of Canada's new policy providing indigenous peoples with a degree of self-governance, the band is looking to the future with some degree of hope.

The new school presented a major opportunity for them. It was to be their most significant resource and their largest community building. As such, the school program described a hybrid, communal-cum-educational space. The construction process was to be organized by the band manager. The school itself was to be built by band members and used as a training program in construction. Finally, the faculty of the school was to be staffed largely by a diverse group of indigenous teachers.

The school is situated at a point in the Fraser Valley where the mountain range closes in on the agricultural plain, forming a huge room with a flat floor. To situate the building in this immense landscape, we provided it with an internal scale, the scale of a body with its own references independent of the landscape. While the mass of the building assumed a zoomorphic form, it was not meant to be representative of any actual animal. Its external shape simply supplied the internal scale.

The local climate is severe, with winds coming down from the mountains and driving across the plain. We placed the school across the path of the prevailing wind to shelter an existing cluster of band buildings on the leeward side. Our purpose was to stabilize this core, no matter what its intrinsic quality, so the space created could become a focal point for community events.

The other point of departure was the mixed nature of the program. The plan permits several ways of managing space. The school operates at the scale of the whole while a sequence of spaces (the gym, reception area, service areas, and home economics room) can be partitioned off for community use. The kitchens of the home economics room also serve large events catered by the community that take place in the assembly room/gym.

In addition to an academic curriculum, the school provides training in traditional indigenous skills. Teaching gardens and salmon-drying racks are located near the front porch of the building. As such, the building acts as a framework for outdoor instruction. All the classrooms face south and open to the porch, enabling the band elders to enter directly into the classrooms and participate in the teaching.

This project was also quite clearly meant to be a cultural site. When the band first approached us, they expressed an antipathy toward orthogonal architecture, which they took as a symbol of the repression their people had suffered. So there was a certain difficulty in bringing our modernist background to the project. We had to find some common ground whereby actions in one culture could be seen positively in the other. We were able to establish this shared frame of reference by encouraging an awareness of the sculptural traditions of both cultures and an appreciation for the tradition of large, wooden structures that are part of indigenous culture

96 PATRICIA PATKAU 1996

along the coast. (Coastal Salish artifacts are characterized by abstract representations of zoomorphic forms, almost unrecognizable as the animals or birds they represent, more essences than depictions of reality.)

The porch on the south side of the school was meant to recall the urbanity of certain coastal villages with their boardwalks, elaborated building fronts, and rows of welcoming totemic figures fronting the water's edge. We built a series of sculptural armatures that would support garden vines and salmon-drying racks as a kind of echo of that urbanity.

Due to the limitations of unskilled labor, the design was conceived without significant detail, its power residing in the basic framing and form. Yet the form was quite complex, and in a sense, this school could not have been built with the normal means of production. The average contractor would undoubtedly have found the complexities of its form intimidating, and would have set his or her price accordingly. Band members didn't have any construction experience, so they simply asked for instructions and got started. The building had to serve as a training program for unskilled labor, and since band members could not readily read the construction documents, we built a model of the school indicating all the framing systems. Technologies were of the kind that could be achieved on site with a chain saw.

Facing page
Seabird Island School
Agassiz, British Columbia, Canada, 1988–1991

The means of construction here were in the service of a community's future, and their purpose was to facilitate this overarching goal. The process reminded us of traditional barn raisings, where the relationship between a community and its technology resides in the hands and bodies of each of its members. This directness lent an enabling capacity that is remarkable in an age where the sophistication of our tools tends to distance, and even disenfranchise, the greater public from the act of building.

Our next project was the Canadian Clay and Glass Gallery, won in competition in 1986. The Seabird Island School and the Clay and Glass Gallery, located in two radically different places in Canada, were worked on simultaneously in the office. These two projects reflect a contrast of construction technologies and material use due to their different contexts. The site for the gallery was in Waterloo, Ontario, beside Barton Myer's Seagram's Museum, the world headquarters of Seagram's whiskey. Our site was located at the entrance to a recreational lake and park system, linked to the university beyond and bordered by the linear structure of the old town center.

When we entered the competition, we were interested in encouraging a more critical approach to institutionalized culture by revealing the complete process involved in the production of an artwork, from creation to collection to validation to exhibition. Inspired by reading Brian O'Dougherty's *Inside the White Cube, The Ideology of Gallery Space*, we attempted to remove the authoritarian character of the white cube and return artwork to the context of everyday life. We began to look for ways to make the value judgments implicit in curatorial work explicit and to connect the viewers in the gallery to the work so they might feel like active participants in the cultural judgments being made. To do this, we developed certain spatial

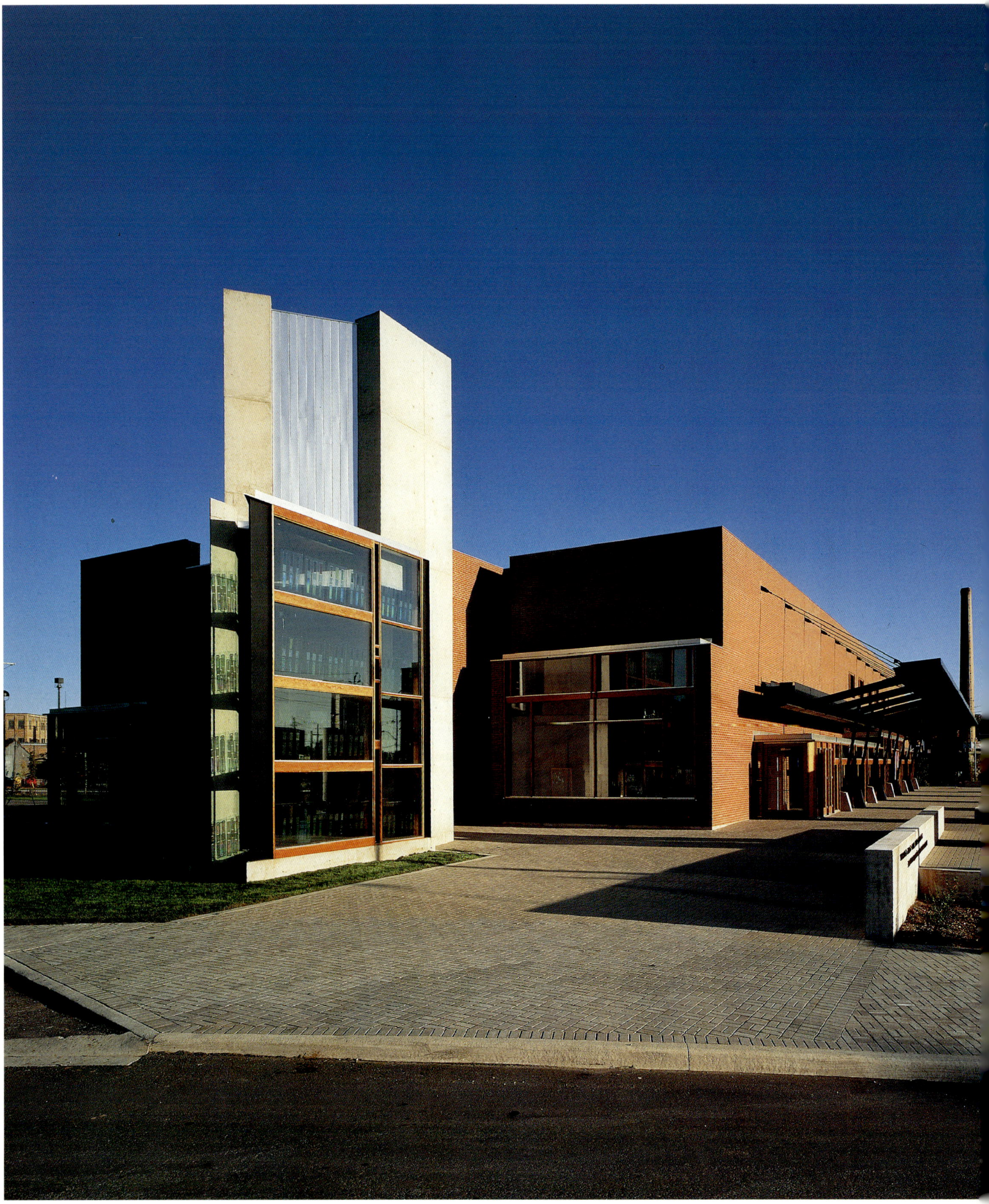

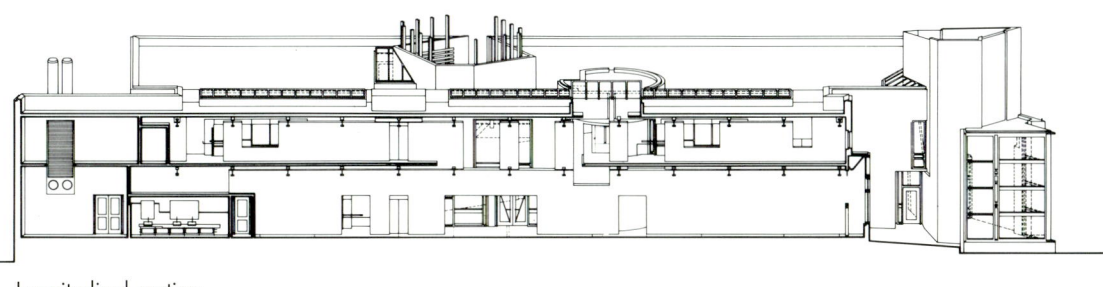

Canadian Clay and Glass Gallery
Waterloo, Ontario, Canada, 1988–1992

Longitudinal section

and constructional strategies: natural light, views, and a courtyard brought the changing seasons and the time of day into the heart of the gallery; staff areas were configured to maximize their accessibility; the building was detailed to reveal the laminations of its own making; and building construction was intended to demonstrate the craft-making that characterizes objects in the gallery.

This museum was the first of our projects that attempted to demystify the process of construction while simultaneously enriching the experienced vocabulary of parts. Tectonically, the building was understood as an anatomical procedure that didactically singles out parts of construction. A process of de-lamination reveals and explains each layer of construction. The brick layer abuts an aluminum reveal that explains the space of the insulation and separates brick cladding from block back-up. Structure is evident, its layers expressed. In the courtyard gallery, a layer of climbing vines on a trellis was added to recall the formwork of construction. This process of revealing through de-lamination goes against the common Canadian practice of concealing bad workmanship through cladding. It takes less effort to add a "surface" than to take care in the initial phases of construction.

Our experience in the Clay and Glass Gallery led us to reflect on the possible role for tectonic expression within the conventional construction process. We privileged certain areas for expression, while accepting the potential of skins in others. We began questioning the degree to which a building should be about its own construction, and where construction might come to be "about" something else by muting its own fabric. This issue was taken up in a small branch library in Newton, a suburb of Vancouver.

The Newton librarians were adamant that the library be open and accessible to the diverse ethnic groups of their community. An exposed structure sliding through from interior to exterior suggested ways of being in the field of influence of a building before even entering. The overall layered tectonic was dialogical with both cladding and exposed construction. Wherever the building went outside it became a simple skeleton. Inside, where it was needed, we added a layer of drywall "skin." The cross-sectional voids created by these skins accommodate mechanical services or serve as light reflectors.

The Barnes House was built on Vancouver Island in 1993 for a psychiatrist and a landscape architect. The program essentially called for a small, one-room house with a lower-level studio and guest area, and an upper-level living area and master bedroom. The upper floor is a simple, large volume with areas separated by low screens. The site is located on the edge of an open rocky outcrop overlooking the Strait of Georgia, a body of water separating the island from the mainland. We read the site not only as the outcrop upon which the house is situated, but also as the platform for a regional panorama. The site is complex, with moss and fern micro-landscapes constituting miniature tapestries that cover the surface of the rock, and there is a swale running through it filled with remarkable red-barked arbutus trees. This gave onto a panorama of the Strait.

Barnes House
Nanaimo, British Columbia,
Canada, 1991–1993

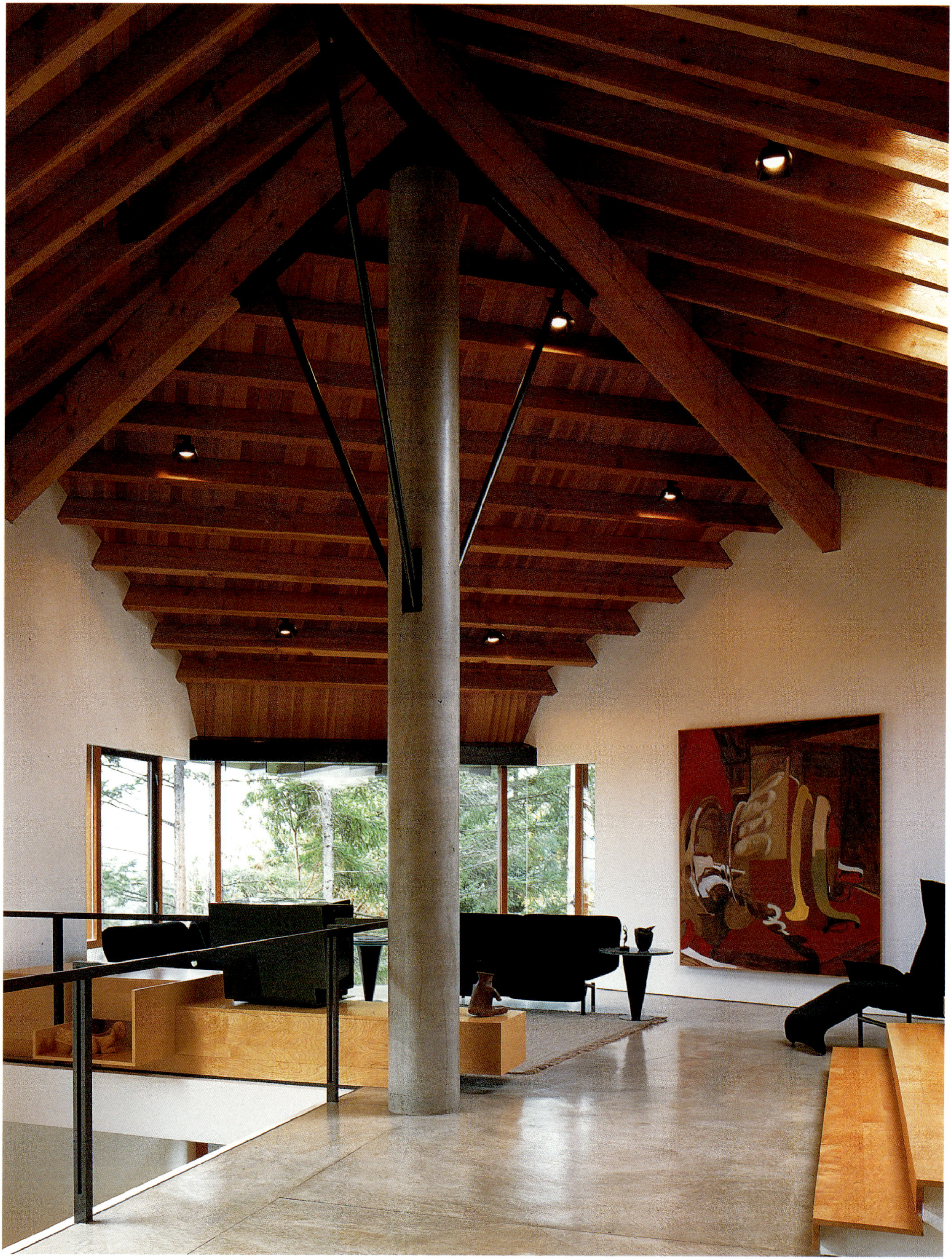

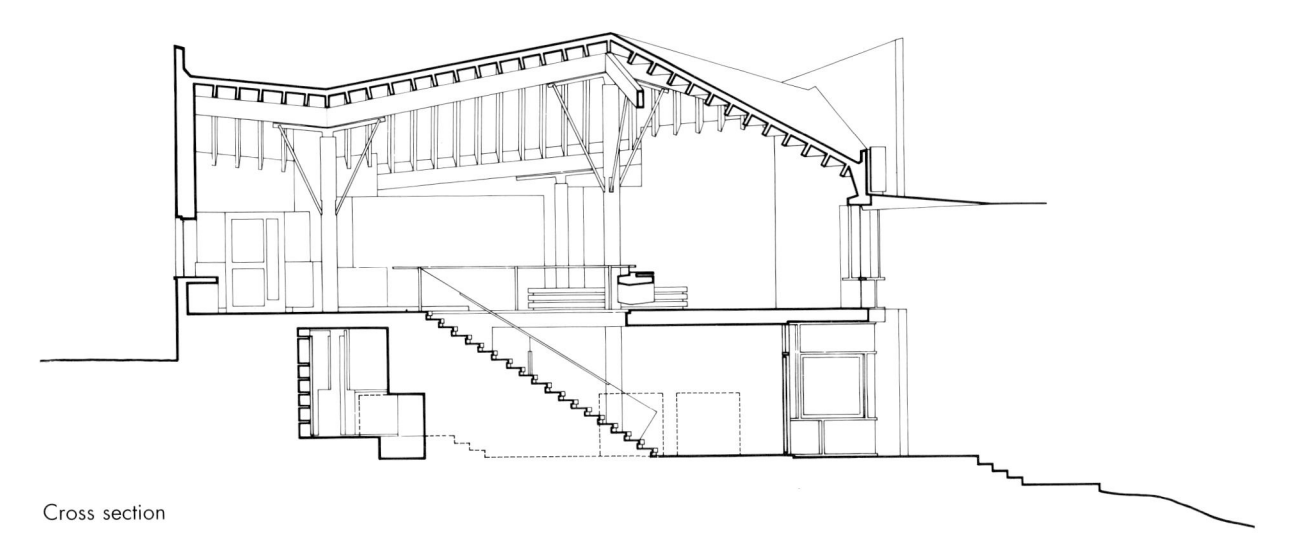

Cross section

In siting the house, we attempted to form a binding condition between the structure and its multiple landscapes. We wanted an active reading that would allow the site to be perceived in a new way. We wanted to bring its particular qualities to the fore, from the small-scale textural character of the rock to the large-scale expanse of the sea. We conceived of the building as a focusing device for establishing an awareness of ourselves in place. We sited the house in the swale itself, with the entrance at a low level between two masses of rock with their surfaces hard up against the house as a material presence. Two views, one higher and one lower, bisect the grove of arbutus trees from their roots to the canopy. Finally, when you turn at the top of the stairs on the upper floor, an expansive view of the Strait is revealed.

The project attempts a non-didactic use of material, one that could be said to be relational. Like most of our work, this house is of wood-frame construction. The stud walls are covered by sheets of drywall, suggesting a kind of immateriality distinguishing the framing of the roof from the earthwork below. The house uses systems of construction that are simultaneously "real" and abstract. On the upper levels, the walls lose their materiality to emphasize the presence of shelter. At the point of spatial release under the steel canopy, you feel the force of the projection at the scale of your body as the roof descends to compress the space of release. The details are most elaborate where the body operates parts of the building: its doors and windows. This is clearly a change from earlier uses of material which were more didactic, systematic, and self-reflexive.

The Strawberry Vale Elementary School is a public school, approximately 3,300 square meters in size, containing sixteen classrooms and support areas for students from kindergarten through seventh grade. It serves a neighborhood of single-family homes in an "edge" suburb that is closely connected to its rural past. In addition to addressing the conventional programmatic requirements typical of all schools, the design of the site attempted to address two further issues: the history of the site and the impact of building on the environment.

Above and facing page
Barnes House
Nanaimo, British Columbia, Canada, 1991–1993

Facing page and overleaf
Strawberry Vale Elementary School
Victoria, British Columbia, Canada,
1992–1995

The existing site contained two earlier school buildings, one of which was in very bad shape and needed to be torn down, the other being a one-room schoolhouse. We moved the small building, the first school built in this location, to the front of the site to mark the entrance. It has been restored and serves as a preschool building. The foundation of the second building was kept as a memory of the past and as a teaching and play area. With the completion of the new building, a child walking to school can experience a three-school historical sequence.

The new school is situated to the south of a large neighborhood park which has a very beautiful grove of indigenous Gary Oaks. A slope along a rock rift runs through the park draining down toward the school. We exploited this watershed as a means of teaching children about hydrology and biodiversity. The water is collected along a series of concrete transfers situated to the south side of the school. Water from the roof also drains into this system, and then all of the water is carried under the school to reappear in ditches that are planted to filter it as it flows into a retention pond. Along the water route, birds provide fertilizer and seeds and a local landscape is reinstating itself. As you approach the building through the park, you are struck by a wild meadow with its stand of Gary Oaks—an enduring sign of the fragility of the site. The school maintains a low profile against the monumental rock rifts that are extensions of the courtyards. A large rock face fills the view through a glass wall and is the first surface you see upon entering the school.

As in our first school, the classrooms are arranged facing south, grouped into pods of four and separated by the rock rifts that penetrate the site. All classrooms have doorways opening directly onto the site, providing access to the outside teaching areas. Views are aligned in multiple directions according to diagonals passing through the school and into the peripheral landscape. Each single classroom is associated with the three adjoining classrooms through a communal interior space and with three other classrooms through an exterior space. In this way, each classroom belongs both to its pod and to a larger community, relating in some way to almost half the classrooms in the school via these in-between spaces. The classrooms and communal spaces are organized along a linear spine that provides circulation below and servicing above. The plan shifts at the rock rifts, encouraging an intimacy of social space. The services above are both accessible and visible, revealing the workings of the building to both children and adults. This servicing void also provides for extra space wherein future technological changes may be easily accommodated.

The tectonics of this school are very much derived from previous experience. Here the concrete earthwork as abstract topography flows easily from exterior to interior. The site slopes in two directions, from the gym across to the park and along the spine of the building. The concrete earthwork takes up these sectional changes. Steel is used for large spans, with wood framing elsewhere. Material layers are added or deleted according to need. The roof profile steps down as a layer of insulation is deleted over exterior spaces. Drywall is added to drive daylight into the building. A layer of boarding holds acoustic material where needed. A millwork layer lines the building at the level of touch. The selection of

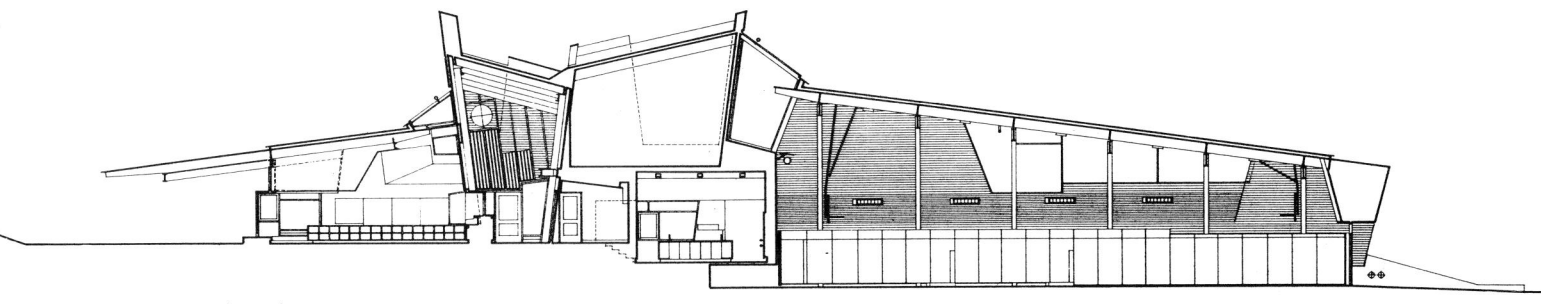

Cross section through gym

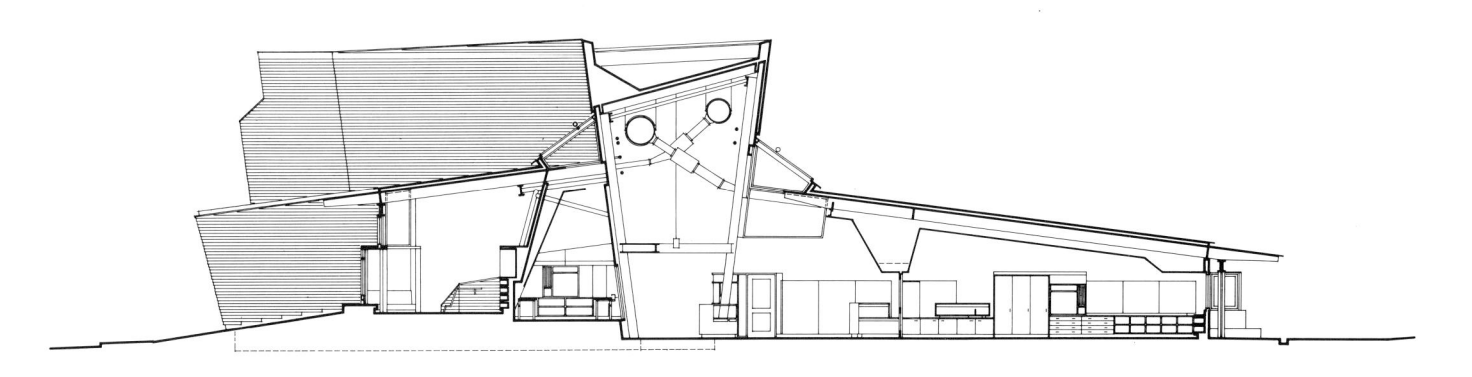

Cross section through library, corridor, and classroom

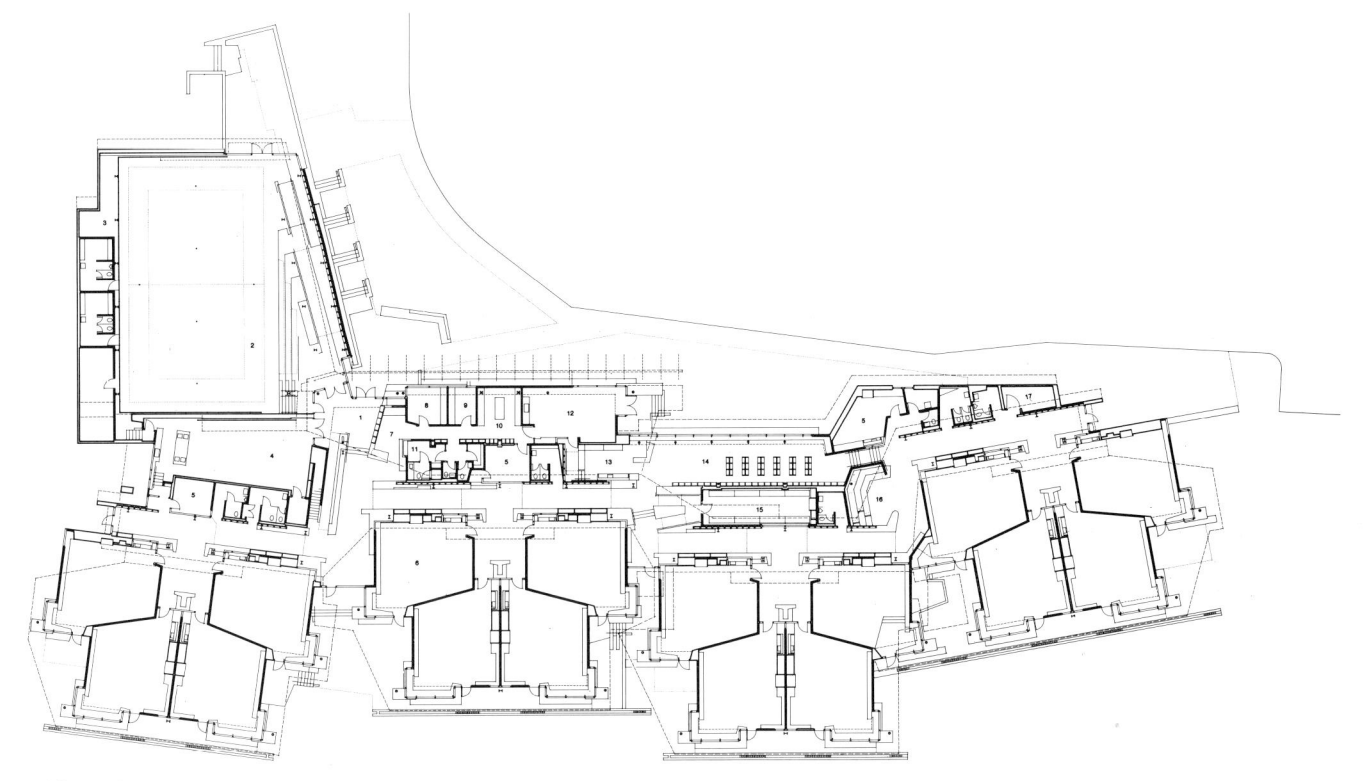

Ground floor plan

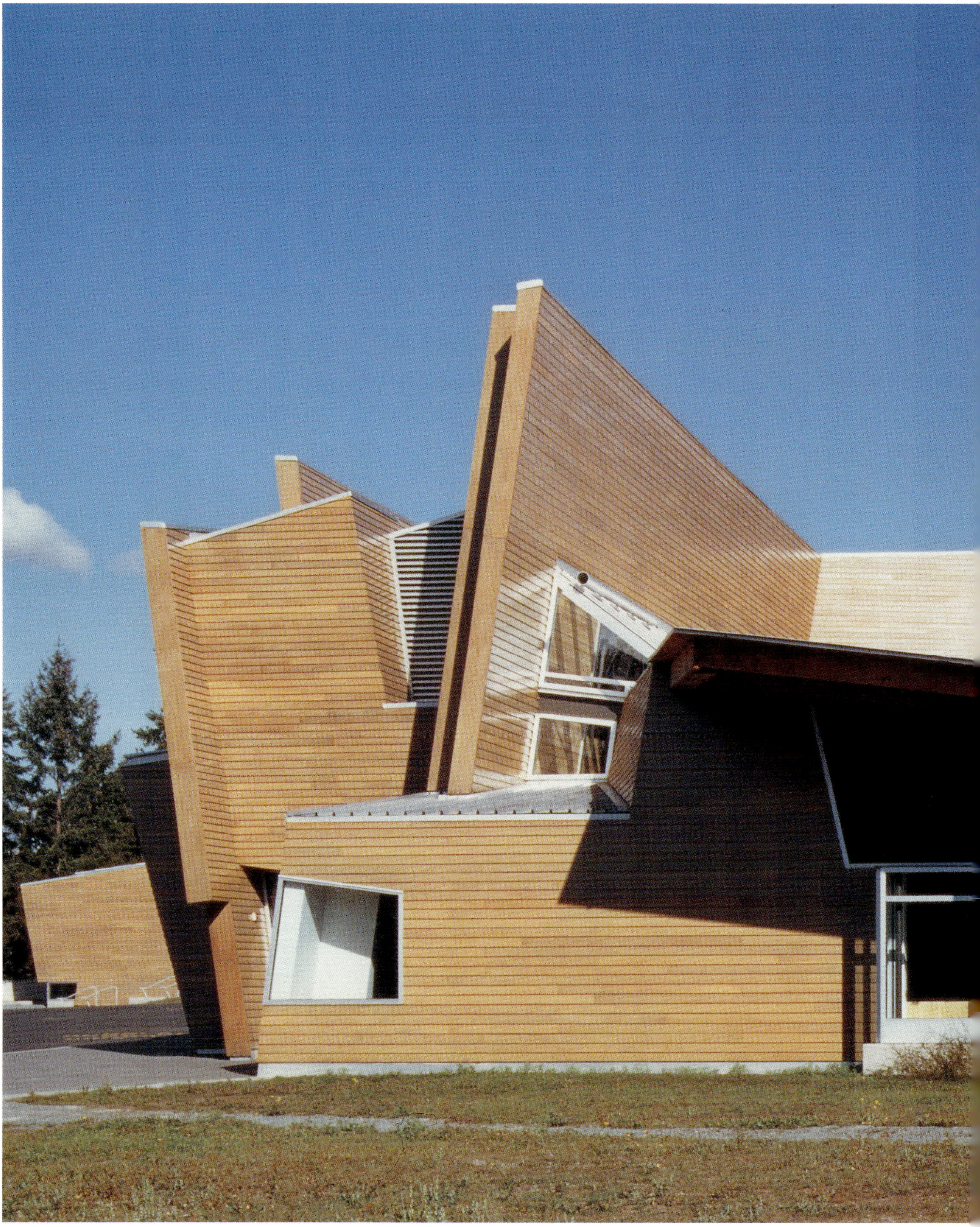

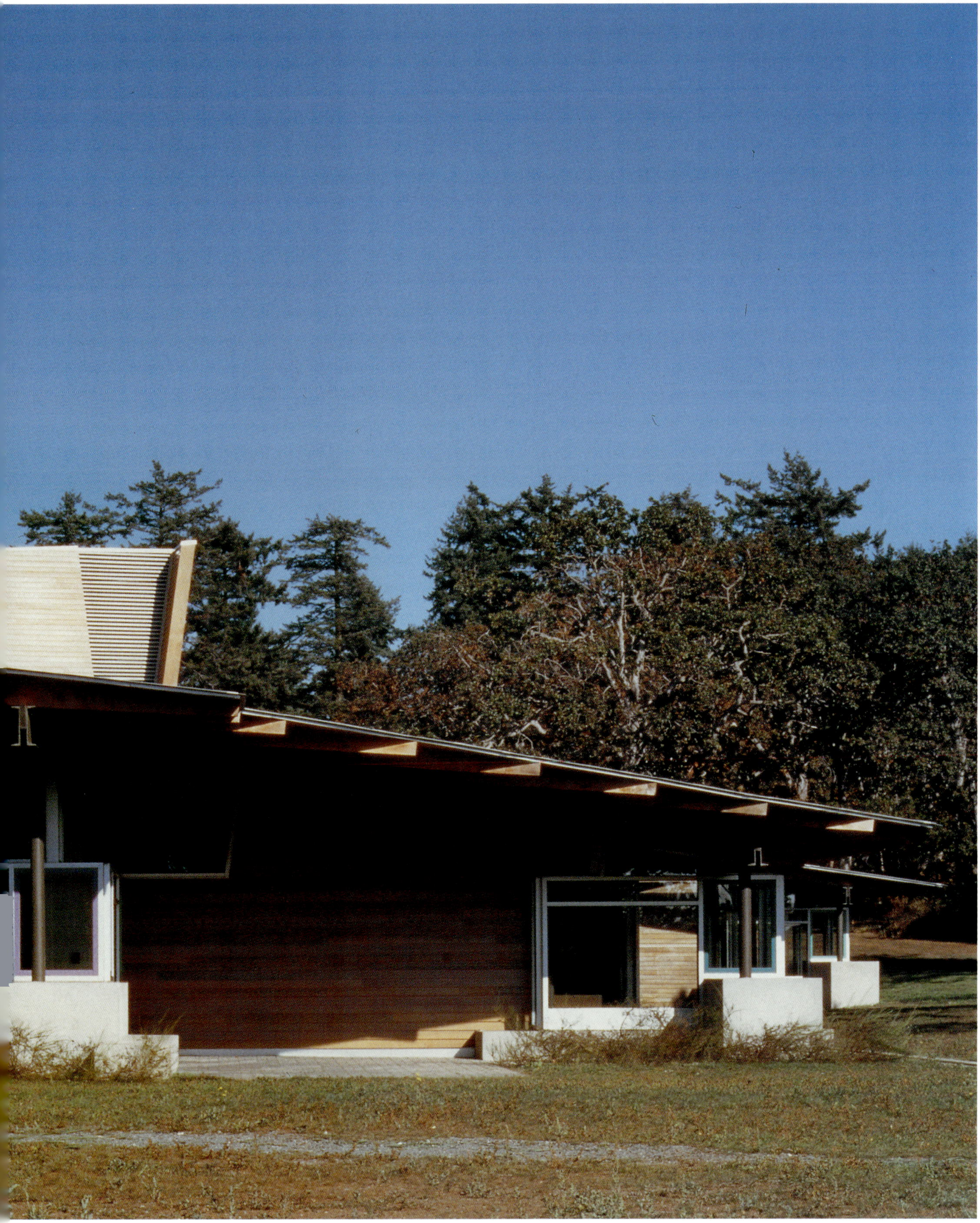

Facing page
Strawberry Vale Elementary School
Victoria, British Columbia, Canada,
1992–1995

material, from the concrete foundations to the laminated timber roofwork, responds to multiple and complex factors (the environment, economics, pragmatic considerations) while simultaneously attempting to focus the direct experience of place.

Our practice acknowledges that architecture is part of a complex at once affecting and affected by the world, that it is part of a dynamic changing condition, and that its measure lies in that relationship. An important consequence of this attitude is that architecture is not viewed as something distinct from the natural world. Just as the forces of nature act upon building, we, through building amplified by technology, work upon nature. While architecture is the product of human thought and work, it must also be understood as part of a greater whole, responding through its relational character to varying contexts. Another consequence of this attitude is that architecture is viewed as heterogeneous. The differentiation implicit in a search for the particular leads to an acceptance of simultaneous presences; the regular with the irregular, the weak with the strong, the dynamic with the static.

Our experience suggests that buildings can add up to much more than themselves. Construction can convey salient intuition that renders the world comprehensible. Acts of construction can help a community gain a sense of pride in its accomplishments. A site and a building can be bound to a situation both physically and culturally. Architecture can begin to inscribe a relationship between our bodies and what we construct—a tracing of ourselves in our world that is specific and non-instrumental. In this sense, technology can be said to produce only the moment. Its commodifying drive is thwarted by architecture that intervenes to convert aspects of the immediacy which are neither transferable nor commodifiable into the powerful direct experience of a place. It is possible to begin imagining a technology imbued with architectural intent. It remains the architect's role to discover alternate ways of "thinking" construction, establishing relational conditions, tracing an empathetic response to the things we build, rendering architecture a necessary act, one that is essential to the maintenance of cognition and meaning.

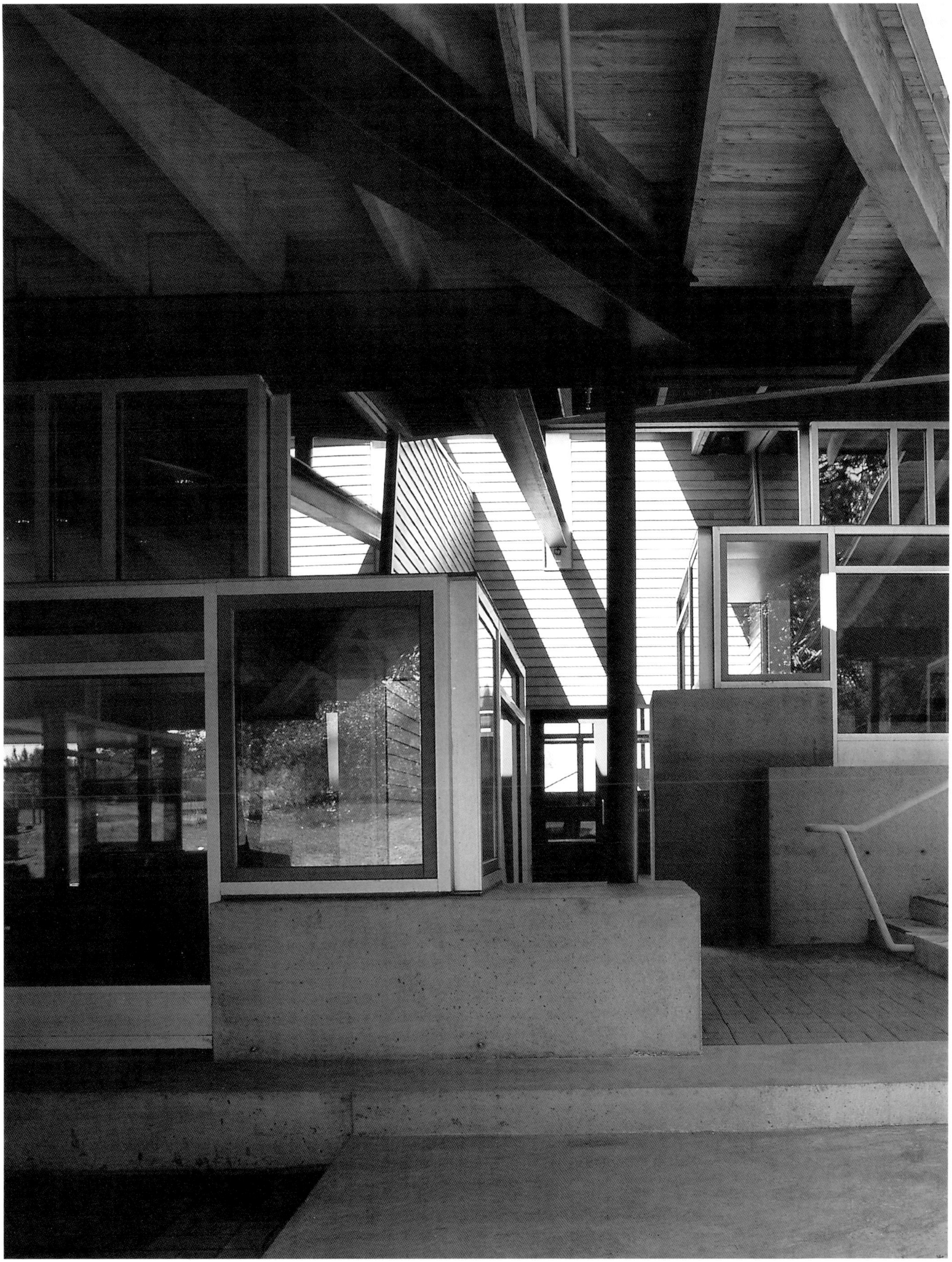

**Strawberry Vale
Elementary School**
Victoria, British Columbia, Canada,
1992–1995

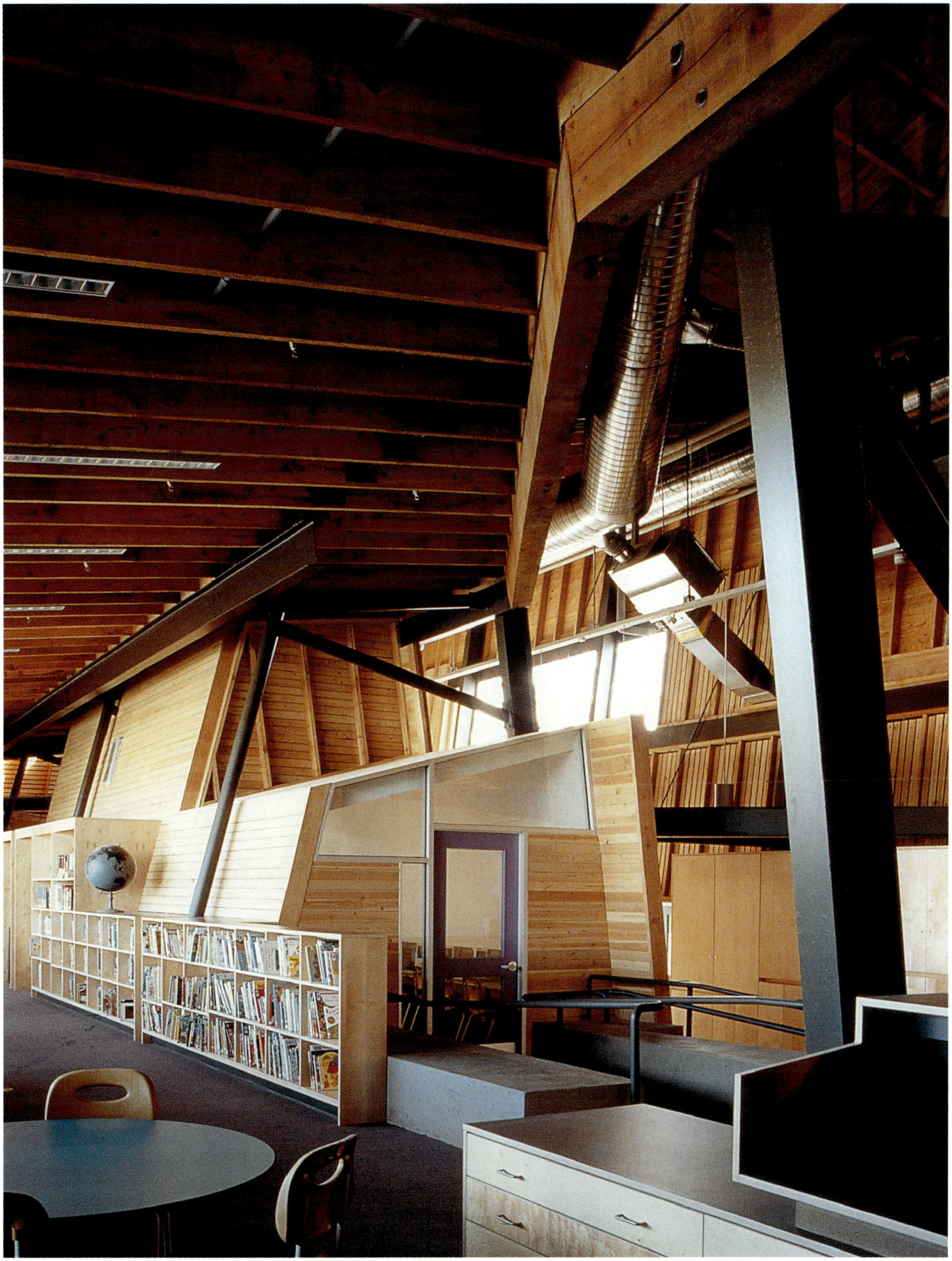

DISCUSSION
Patricia Patkau
Tony Rigg

Tony Rigg: *We have much to learn from the way in which Patkau Architects have achieved works of cultural sensitivity responding simultaneously to context, climate, and micro-climate. They have succeeded in synthesizing these layers in an architecture that is at once complex and integrated, somewhat akin to a living organism. I would like to ask Patricia Patkau to explain the process by which this layering is achieved.*

Patkau: Together with my partner, John Patkau, who is also my husband, I started to practice about fifteen years ago. Due to our limited experience we had to learn everything the hard way. We began by discovering how two boards fit together, investigating traditional systems of detailing for their logic rather than for their stylistic characteristics. Fortunately, we knew one or two older people in the profession whom we consulted in moments of stress or anxiety. The history of our practice has been one of slow, incremental learning. I wish it were faster. However, there is satisfaction in reviewing our last decade of practice and seeing that virtually every year has brought growth in our work. One of the things we do at the beginning of any project is to reflect on our past work and ask what it is we haven't included in our architecture to date. Continual reassessment of past architecture pushes us to get beneath surface considerations.

In our early experience, working on the Canadian prairie, we were compelled to respond critically to climatic extremes. We had to learn to mediate between the intentions of the project and the nature of the elements. Today, we practice on the Canadian West Coast, which has the mildest climate in the country but also the wettest. The annual rainfall is sufficient to designate parts of the coast as rain forest. This is nothing like the prairie where we both grew up, a Siberia-like climate where it is forty below for six months, with summer lasting only two months before the return of the harsh weather. So from the beginning, we have had a great respect for the conditions of the place in which we are building.

In school, one learns that the real richness of architecture is its wide diversity. In school, one talks about philosophy, technology, sociology, and environmental issues, and the amazing thing is that the discipline itself eventually confronts you with all of them. Since every project takes a number of years, the learning process is slow, but with each one knowledge advances. Then you start to wonder how many working years remain to address the full diversity of which the discipline is capable.

Audience: *Do you find that teaching and working influence each other?*

Patkau: At the moment I'm the only one in the firm teaching full-time, at the University of British Columbia. For me this is compelling. First, the students are quite remarkable. They haven't yet faced the realities of the profession and all kinds of idealism are possible. With students, I can discuss the best set of possibilities, and such discussions balance the daily routine of practice. Teaching is also my way of staying in touch with the younger generation. I never think about myself as old, simply because I am immersed in a culture that is constantly changing. I don't have children, so for me it's important to have this connection to the future.

Audience: *A certain amount of design flexibility during the construction process represents a significant difference between practice in England and practice in Israel.*

Patkau: To me it's a critical difference. You can only anticipate so much prior to construction, and so the possibility of allowing time to inform the process of realization necessarily produces a better building. There are always things that happen during construction which can't be foreseen. The potential to respond to such factors is a privilege generally unavailable to North American practitioners.

Practice in Canada, like practice in the United States, is constantly inhibited by the threat of litigation. For all our projects, we have had to produce a set of working documents describing the building precisely and absolutely before construction begins. If during construction a problem arises and you want to change things, it immediately becomes contentious. The various parties have very different interests and each tries to exploit the new situation to their advantage. So it's not a cultural situation in which you are able to develop the project in depth during the process of realization.

As far as the restriction regarding the use of stone in Jerusalem, I feel there is a dimension to construction here which is not fully utilized by architects. As I understand the process, there is a layer of stone, and then a space, and then a layer of concrete, with the final layer often being a block that serves as a kind of interior finish. It seems that either the block or the concrete layer could be considered redundant; however, this is surely a system that proffers a certain wall depth with tremendous potential that I don't feel is sufficiently acknowledged.

Audience: *The concrete layer is the load-bearing element of the building. Traditionally, in Jerusalem, the mode of construction is not a column-beam system, but mass concrete load-bearing walls.*

Patkau: The very fact that the layering exists holds potential for architecture. In our work, for example, we take the stud-frame construction and peel away the layers by which it is concealed, so that at times you see the skin and bones and at other times the building is fully covered and becomes volumetric. This expression in depth can give a kind of edge condition through which it is possible to explore how things are built. The building is thus no longer reduced to mass and void. It becomes a series of layers impregnated with constructional meaning in a didactic way.

Most of the projects we have built are on the coast of the Pacific Northwest, close to where we live in Vancouver. When we moved from the Canadian prairies with their cold air, blue sky, and bright sunlight to the very moist climate, actually almost a rain forest, of Vancouver, we tended to overreact to the grayness of the light and the amount of rainfall. I think a lot of our early forms came from that concern. We started to look to the roof as the prerogative form, one that could deflect wind, shed rain, and provide overhung spaces with windows that can be opened, because when it rains there is also a very soft, beautiful, cedar-scented air. It is important to be able to open windows without letting in the rain; to have an intermediate threshold between the exterior and the interior.

Many of our buildings have covered porches for various purposes: to modify the sun, to shed rain, or to provide a sense of shelter. Most of our roofs come down low at their edges; some, however, go up to capture light at the top. Most cover an interior volume that is in shadow and lightens toward the edges as an intermediary zone. Our first school was quite cognizant of indigenous culture in this regard, with an interior that has very subdued light. Traditional structures have densely-centered spaces with minimal openings and often amazing entryways. One type of ceremonial entrance took the form of the beak of a giant bird. Closed during daily use, the beak would be open only on ceremonial occasions when participants entered through the mouth. I always imagined the inside would feel like animal innards because it had rib-like exposed construction and there was little light. When we first saw the historic photographs of these buildings we were profoundly affected, and I suspect that this was a subliminal influence on our first school.

Many of the same issues also arise in our most recent school, but the form is somewhat different. It's in a semi-rural area surrounded by farms even though the area has been overtaken by suburban development. A feeling for local history remains in the very simple shed roofs, a tradition reflected in our school. The central spine space, however, has more to do with the idea of hollowing out a building to provide shadow. The sides of the spine have shafts of light coming through to pull your eye into the depth of the building and to confront it with a layered and shadowed space. That kind of depth of light in relation to shadow has been virtually erased from our received way of building today. You can find it in Alvar Aalto's cultural center for Wolfsburg, Germany, and in Herman Hertzberger's buildings, particularly in his Centraal Beheer office building in Apeldoorn. There, shadow is used in the public walkways that do not require much light. In our case, it is not bright light that you are moving into from the darkness; rather you're moving toward the normally gray light of the West Coast. I am reminded in this connection of Le Corbusier's monastery of La Tourette near Lyons, with its three side chapels illuminated by light cones successively painted black, red, and white. Entering the chapels through a dark tunnel, initially you can't see anything. The first cone of light to appear is painted black yielding a level of light the eye can just barely perceive. Moving through these dimly-lit chapels, the light gradation changes from black to red to white. There are very few instances in contemporary architecture where darkness is used in such a powerful manner.

Audience: *You spent two years in Los Angeles where light conditions are very different from the Northwest. In the Kustin house design I detect a completely different approach to the use of light, not only in sophistication, but also in technique.*

Patkau: It took us a long time to realize that in Los Angeles you ought not to seek the sun, but rather to protect yourself from it. However, in some ways, this condition was conducive to some of our intuitive attitudes toward light, because the small openings enabled us to develop a rather mute solid wrapped around an interior that receded from the light. The only area accorded more light was the rift that cut diagonally through the middle of the house, which was meant to reveal the section of the site and to allude to rifts in the landscape. The major west-facing window openings were shaded by huge, sail-like net constructions suspended from rods reminiscent of the fishing tackle that Mr. Kustin designs.

Audience: *In your private houses, particularly, you seem to insert the building into the natural landscape without touching it. Nothing could be in greater contrast to what happens in Israel, where the first thing a contractor does upon arriving on site is to bulldoze it flat. Later it is necessary to reconstruct the landscape and integrate it with the building. I look at what you have achieved with a certain amount of amazement. Is it that your contractors work in a more*

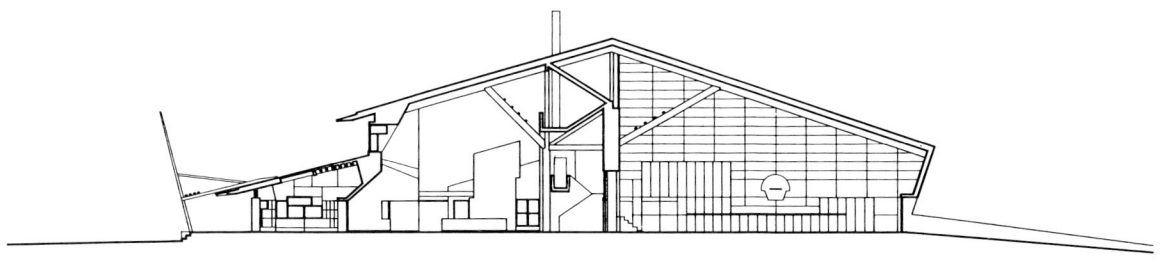

Cross section

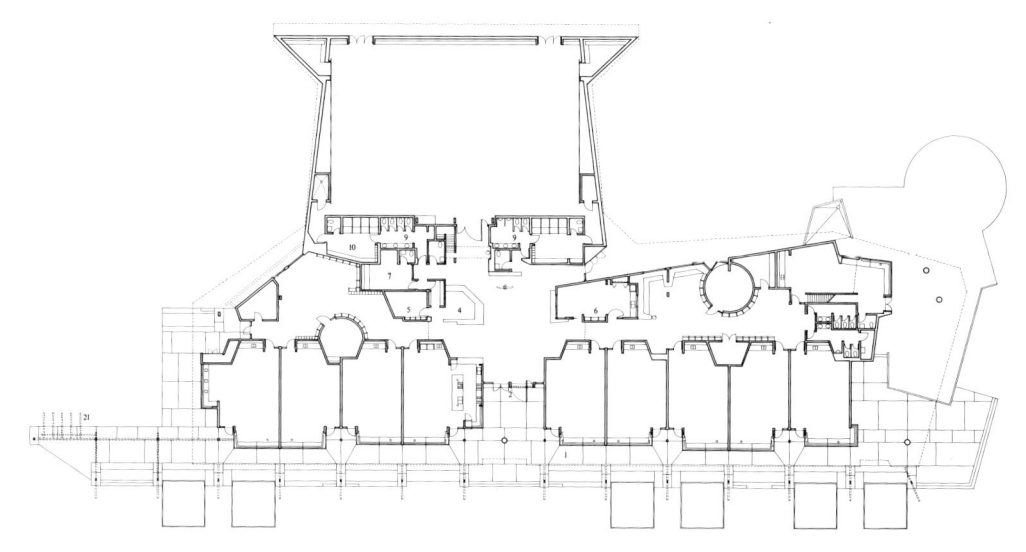

Ground floor plan

delicate way, or is it also a major challenge for you to leave the natural landscape more or less undisturbed?

Patkau: There is an optical illusion here. The first thing we do is blast the site. We affect the site more than most residential designers would. There was a tradition of early modernist houses in Vancouver which had quite a beautiful siting strategy. The houses barely touched the site. They were often set up as platforms on posts. Our houses are very distant from that tradition. We try to remake the site, to allow it to be seen in a more powerful way and not simply as it was before building began. All our houses meet the ground more or less solidly, as in wall architecture. Some of them are even cut into the rock. We've had to do a significant amount of blasting for most of them. After the fact, you don't notice that it's been blasted. But the site is severely affected and the house reflects this modification.

Audience: *How much influence do your clients have over design and choice of materials?*

Patkau: This varies from client to client. For private houses, we have long and intimate discussions with the clients in an effort to understand them as much as possible. We are very careful about whom we take as house clients. Our contract stipulates that we will do the preliminary design and at that point assess whether we are the right architects for the project. Houses take an incredible amount of time and energy, so that the compensation is not commensurate with the effort. You have to come out of it with something that matters to you more than money: the

Seabird Island School
Agassiz, British Columbia,
Canada, 1988–1991

quality of the project. We also recognize that the house will be there long after the clients have gone, and we also have obligations to neighbors and to the principles we believe in. Most of our houses have been in wooded landscapes, an environment that imposes responsibilities quite different from those of an urban setting.

Institutional clients are different. With the Seabird Island band, we had to have many meetings; but these weren't really discussions, because the native community doesn't respond very much verbally. We would explain; they would listen and nod. Then, they would go away and discuss the situation among themselves and return with a few comments. There were a few aspects of the program that they articulated, such as the need for a dual-purpose community building/school. In general, I think institutional clients are difficult and complex bodies, often changing key personnel during the process of construction. Occasionally, the person in charge (as with the Seabird Island School building program) has a commitment to the project and is willing to take personal responsibility; but for many institutional clients, at least in Canada, the main concern is that the process proceed smoothly. This places the responsibility for determining the nature of the building squarely and inappropriately on the architect. The task then is to attempt to respond to the historical and local context, and to understand how a given institution has evolved over time. In designing the Clay and Glass Gallery in Waterloo, we were much influenced by Brian O'Dougherty's book, *Inside the White Cube*, which criticizes the institutional white gallery (which, of course, also refers to a material presence). We tried to present the O'Dougherty thesis to the museum board, which precipitated an intense and difficult discussion but clarified deeply held attitudes toward institutionalized culture.

Audience: *I love your detail work. Could you tell us more about your working method and when you begin to work on details?*

Patkau: Our process used to be rather linear. We went from the concept to the plans and sections, and then materials entered the discussion. Now everything happens simultaneously. While producing conceptual sketches, we consider materials; while drawing a section, we also anticipate details. We try to use all our tools at once. At any given moment, on our boards there are plans, sections, elevations, and detailed sketches, while elsewhere we are building experimental models. We work in three as well as two dimensions and at multiple scales. In the case of Seabird Island School, we began with the program because of the particular client. Even then, we tried to make the discussion three-dimensional, and went through many models before we arrived at the final version. Quite early on, we did some fairly large-scale detailed framing pieces to resolve our approach to the construction. The final model was about eight feet long, revealed all components of the structure, and was used on-site as a reference model.

Audience: *As opposed to Israel where there is little building tradition, Canada seems to possess time-honored practices. Can you say something about that?*

Patkau: It is amazing to come here and be asked that question. I always think of the North American tradition as being so young. In Canada, there are very few traces of aboriginal culture because it was both fragile and nomadic. There are very few sites where you get a sense of inhabitation for hundreds of years. In most instances, our construction is the first "permanent" construction on that land. It's hard to define Canadian architecture, a Canadian tradition. I usually fall back on cultural explanations, the way people interact. There are differences concerning the way people act toward each other which you only understand over time.

Audience: *I wonder if you could explain how you acquire your commissions. Do they have public competitions in Canada? What are your hopes as far as your future practice is concerned?*

Patkau: We have never known how to get work. It's been very difficult for us. We are not well-connected in any way. Our first commissions were private homes. That is the way many young architects begin. We moved to Alberta during the oil boom for the opportunities that such a local economy might offer. When we first started practicing, there was so much building going on in Alberta that we thought we could get a few crumbs. We eventually managed to win a school commission, but it was never built. Most firms were building entire cities, so they didn't care if we got a tiny school. We only stayed in Alberta during the oil boom. Once oil prices dropped and provincial spending was reduced, we moved to Vancouver, British Columbia. A client who was building a house for his retirement on Vancouver Island happened to be active in the arts. This led incidentally to our next commission, which was won through competition. Canada has very few competitions except in the province of Quebec, which is interested in promoting its own culture. Young architects in Quebec have received many commissions, and I envy them. In Canada, in general, most of the competitions are invited and go to established firms, such as Moshe Safdie and Arthur Erickson. There's little chance for any young firm to gain access to this work. There was, however, a design competition for the Canadian Clay and Glass Gallery, and we managed to get on the list thanks to a referral from our client. We won the competition and built a building in central Canada, the national power base, so everybody saw it. Our career has been shaped by circumstance and a great deal of luck. Most of life is just serendipity. Our other small public commissions have not come through competition, but because of a particular individual, someone like Marie Odile-Marceau, for example, who was in charge of Indian and Northern Affairs for about six years when she created the indigenous communities program. She wanted the best architecture she could find locally to help the indigenous peoples produce the first school buildings on their reserves.

Audience: *Your approach includes a response to climate, which you take for granted as being an inherent and essential part of the design process. Do your colleagues in Canada share this view?*

Patkau: It is certainly not universal in Canada, although I think there is a growing awareness due to the environmental crisis. With such consciousness, however, architecture has the possibility of becoming issue-based and committed ideologically, and this is no less problematic than the tendency to ignore climate and the environment. A dichotomy has arisen, with some architects promoting themselves as environmentally responsible, and others thinking of themselves as designers. I think that questions of sustainability and design are critical for everyone; but sustainability is only one of the issues that has to be taken seriously. Environmental issues must be confronted in conjunction with, and balanced against, all the other cultural responsibilities to the client and the community.

LECTURE

Renzo Piano

About thirty years ago, fresh from my studies, I began experimenting with lightweight structures. At the time I didn't understand that lightness is something more than just physics, so these experiments were carried out in the spirit of trial and error. Some of these works had a truly innovative character, such as the shell structures that I made in 1967 for the Fourteenth Triennale of Milan. These were important lessons for me in the art of *technē* (technique), as they say in Greek. I began to understand the way in which image, expression, and construction could be integrated.

In 1978, in cooperation with UNESCO, we established a local field workshop for the rehabilitation of the historical core of Otranto, a beautiful small town in Southern Italy. It was a small, dismountable workshop structure within which people could meet and work together in a participatory process. This was a second important experience for me: the art of listening to and understanding people. I have worked in a collaborative way ever since, above all in my present building workshop in Genoa, which is the counterpart of a similar atelier we have in Paris. We engage in a considerable amount of craft work at both workshops, in the course of which we make models and full-scale prototypes for various buildings and building components. Thus, for me, architecture is a profession based on craft.

Our workshop is actually something between a workshop, an office, and a seminar space; we work together with architects and engineers from our Paris and Berlin offices and collaborate with outside specialists. People come, stay for a few days or a week, and we hold seminars that are referential to the work at hand. Situated on a steep hill sloping down to the sea, our workshop is a place of calm and meditation. While it is a totally transparent building, the fact that there is no direct access from the street assures a level of almost monastic seclusion. We are connected to the lower coastal access road by a small glazed cable car. Lightness and immateriality are the overriding themes of the entire building, so much so that it is difficult to discern where the building stops and nature begins.

We terraced the slope on which this building stands, and at the top of the contoured slope, we erected a simple shed of wood and glass. This building is an indispensable retreat from a world in which we are exposed to too much information, and as a result have less and less time in which

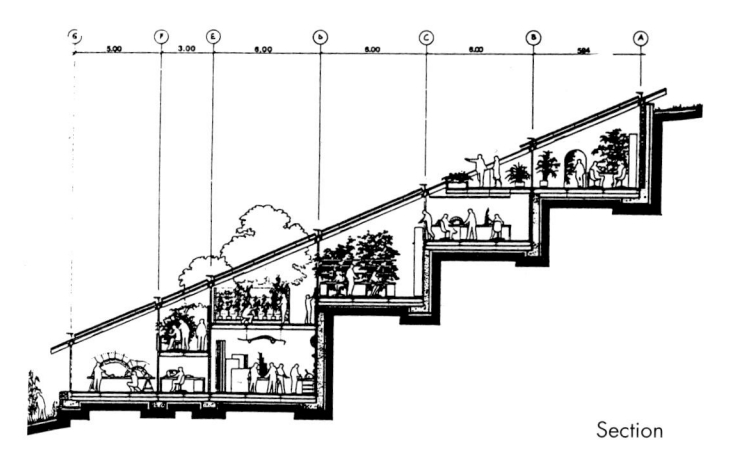

Section

Renzo Piano Building Workshop
Genoa, Italy, 1989–1991

Above and facing page
The Menil Collection Museum
Houston, Texas, 1982–1986

to think. I feel that it is absolutely essential to maintain a balance between information and meditation.

A few years after the completion of the Centre Pompidou, I began work on a much different kind of museum commissioned by Dominique DeMenil to house her remarkable art collection in Houston, Texas. The situation in Houston is the antithesis of that in Paris: Paris is too full of history and Houston is devoid of memory. Both Mrs. DeMenil and I wanted to build a museum as a place of contemplation, which is completely contrary to what I had attempted in the Centre Pompidou, where we took a stand against the traditional institution. In Houston, we wanted to create a sort of sacred place for art. It is a village museum, situated in a small-scale residential area. Our building was merely the largest structure set amid a series of two-story houses that also belong to the museum.

Following a system we developed with the late Peter Rice, the light-filtering elements on top of this structure were made of ferro-cement. The rationale for using such elements is that, while they are very thin, they are nonetheless capable of spanning a full twelve meters. Each blade is only twenty-five millimeters thick, and the resultant light inside is exceptionally good and helps to dematerialize the museum space. Since the galleries are top-lit throughout, the visitor constantly senses the time of day and the changing seasons of the year. The secret to this is that the works of art are kept in a storeroom on the roof of the museum. They are brought down and exhibited in groups of two or three hundred for a few months

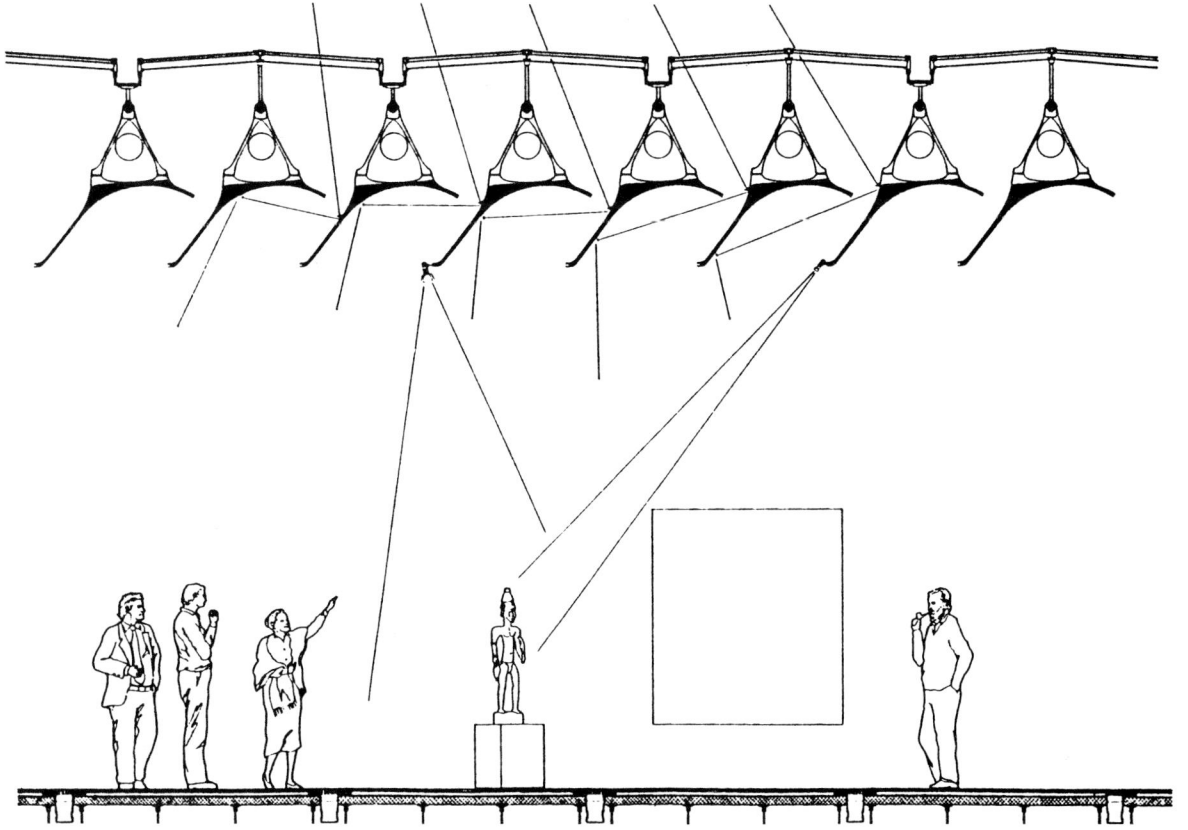

Partial section through gallery

Rue de Meaux Housing
Paris, 1987–1991

at a time. By adopting this rotational strategy we were able to admit natural light up to seven thousand lux: too much for a permanent exhibition of works of art, but acceptable with this rotational approach.

In 1991, we realized a housing project in the rue de Meaux in Paris. It consisted of 250 dwellings clustered around a central courtyard. In this complex we invented a new way of employing terra cotta, in which large tiles are hung on specially molded GRC (glass-reinforced cement) panels. By mixing two traditional materials, concrete and terra cotta, by adding fiberglass reinforcement, instead of steel, to the concrete, and by using a special technique for molding the terra cotta, we were able to develop the "grain" of the building in terms of both its complexity and its color. The warm, light color that results from this surface treatment is modulated by the light-filtering qualities of the birch trees planted within the court.

Nothing could be a greater contrast to this than the sixty-five-thousand-seat soccer stadium we built in Bari, Italy. This was a landscape operation, since we made a hill first and then placed the stadium on top. The structure is indirectly related to the nearby Castel del Monte, a strange, one might say secret, castle built by Federico di Svevia in the thirteenth century. On its hill it appears as a spaceship, like something between a fortress and a symbolic building. This became an important reference for us when we were asked to build the stadium in like fashion, similarly raised up on an earthwork.

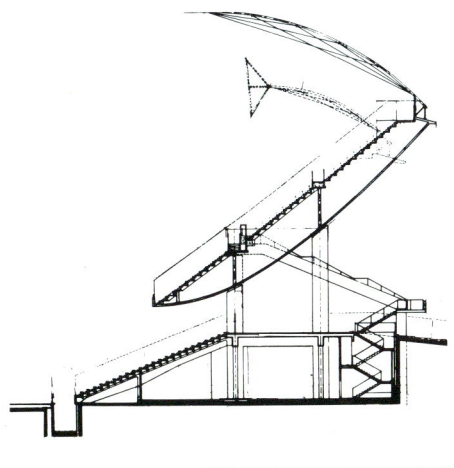

The structure itself, designed, once again, in collaboration with Peter Rice, consists of twenty-six "petals." Each petal seats two thousand people, and together with the provision for spectators in the amphitheater around the playing field, comprises the total capacity of sixty-five thousand. It's an immense building, designed in this particular way for two main reasons. The first objective was to induce natural ventilation—and for this we conducted numerous wind-tunnel tests. This makes it a rather Mediterranean building, meant to interact with the sun and the wind. The second consideration was security, based on the assumption that groups of up to two

San Nicola Football Stadium
Bari, Italy, 1987–1990

thousand people can be fairly readily controlled. It's a mono-material building built almost entirely of concrete. As you might imagine, supporting the weight of fifty thousand people on a cantilevered concrete superstructure was quite a feat from an engineering standpoint. However, despite its enormous size, the stadium was largely constructed out of prefabricated components. The overall shell structure is composed of a series of complex elements capped by a Teflon sunshade and supported on a light steel frame.

In 1988, our workshop won the competition for the new airport at Kansai, Japan, situated in the Bay of Kansai, close to Osaka, Kobe, and Kyoto. This is a huge region with a population of some twenty million people. The airport had to be built offshore, because Japanese environmental legislation restricts flight over land between 11 P.M. and 6 A.M. Therefore the airport had to be built in the sea, five kilometers from the nearest coastline, on an artificial island 4,370 meters long by 1,250 meters wide. It was an immense job. The ocean at this point is twenty meters deep and the island is sustained by some one million piles. The ground itself was largely compacted by transporting rocks on barges from neighboring islands. The building is raised on jacks, which must be adjusted to compensate for the rate of differential settlement. For the first ten years, these adjustments are being made constantly in order to keep the foundation level. To facilitate this process, the variable statical loading of the structure became extremely complex. Some idea of the scale of this undertaking may be gleaned from the fact that, for most of the construction period, we employed approximately ten thousand workers on the site. They met in the morning, exercised, changed, listened to the brief, and then went to work.

The airport terminal is a vast building designed to receive around one hundred thousand passengers a day. There are currently about fifty thousand, in addition to more than ten thousand daily visitors who travel out just to admire the airport terminal facility. At any given time, you will find thousands of children visiting the building, something which adds a dimension of vitality. We gave the terminal shed the form of a giant glider some 1.7 kilometers in length. The curvature of this structure is actually part of a toroid 16.5 kilometers in diameter; that is to say, it's a portion of a shell structure. This shape arose from a mixture of formal and technological considerations. First, there was the need for lightness, both as a technical necessity and as an aesthetic reference. Then, there were the earthquake regulations and the fact that we were building on a freshly constructed island. There were also compositional considerations, for when you create a colossal structure like this in the middle of the sea, surrounded at any one time by forty-five jumbo jets, you have to maintain the perceivable unity of the work as a whole. The building was sectioned throughout its length every 13.6 meters, to control the progressive modification of its shape during the design process. A good measure of the integrity of the structure is that the building did not suffer any damage in the 1995 Kobe earthquake, despite the fact that it moved close to fifty centimeters during the tremor. This explains why one must have structural flexibility and light construction in earthquake regions, especially when facing the risk of large horizontal forces.

Facing page and overleaf
Kansai International Airport
Osaka, Japan, 1990–1994

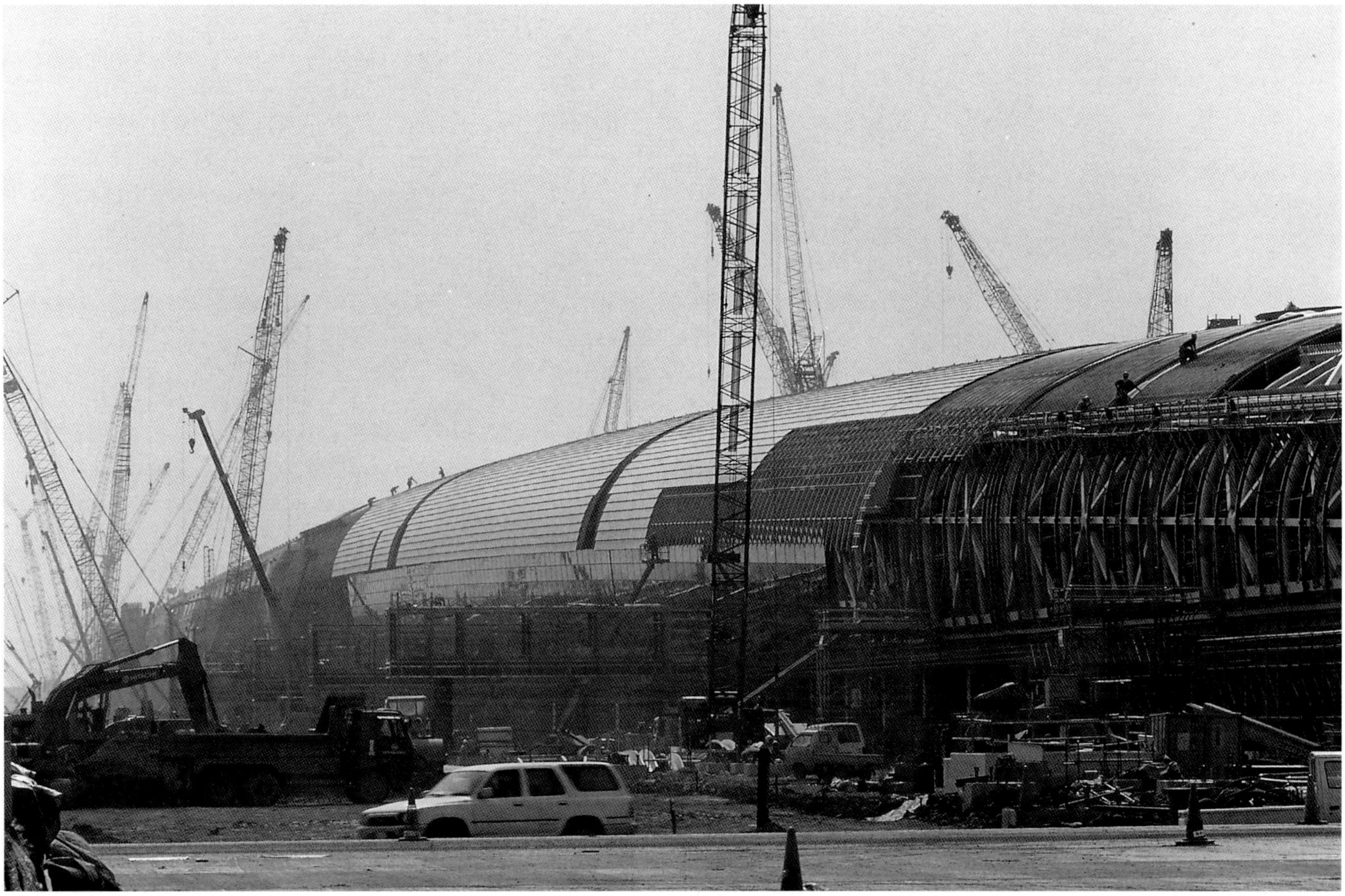

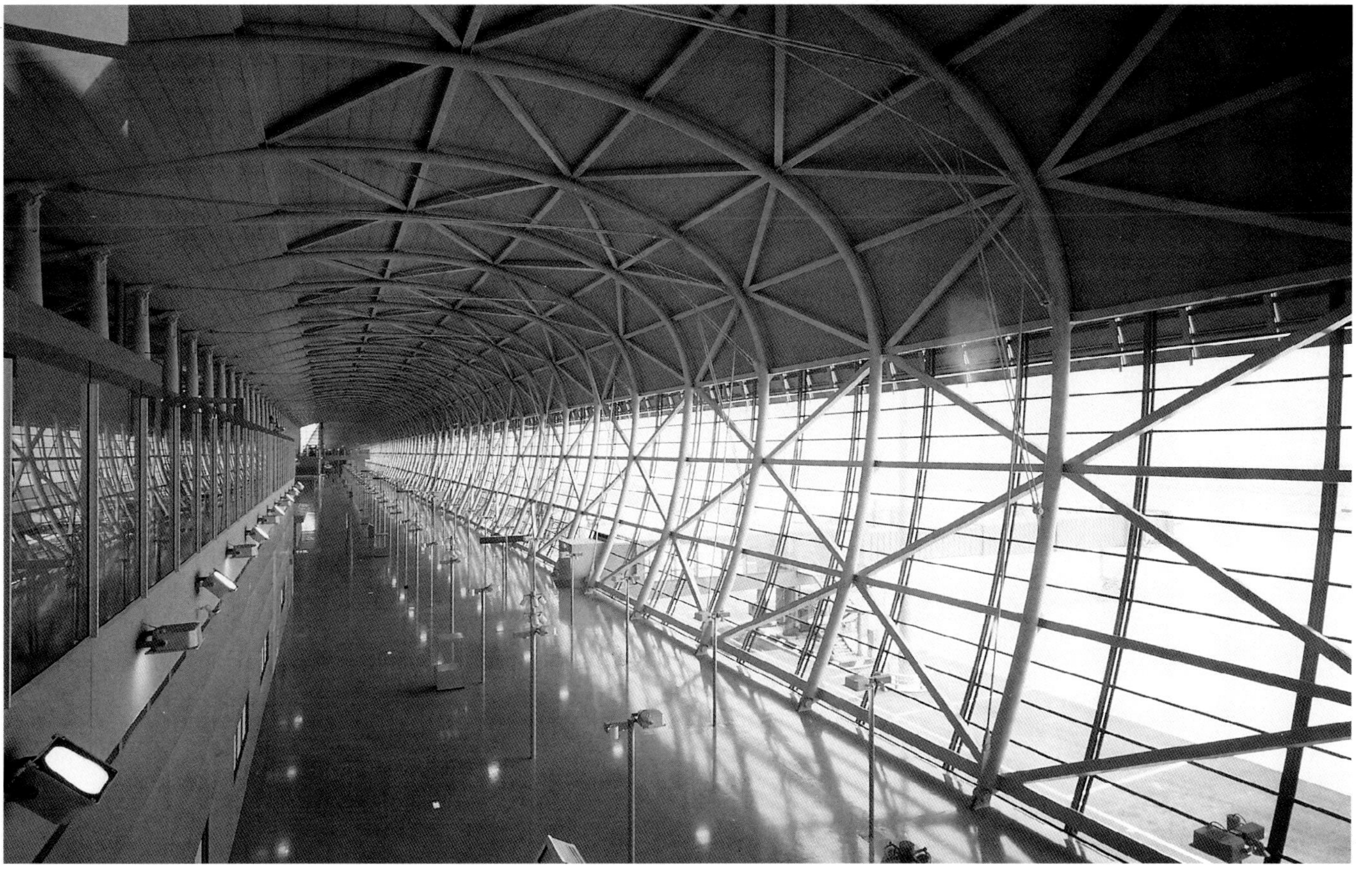

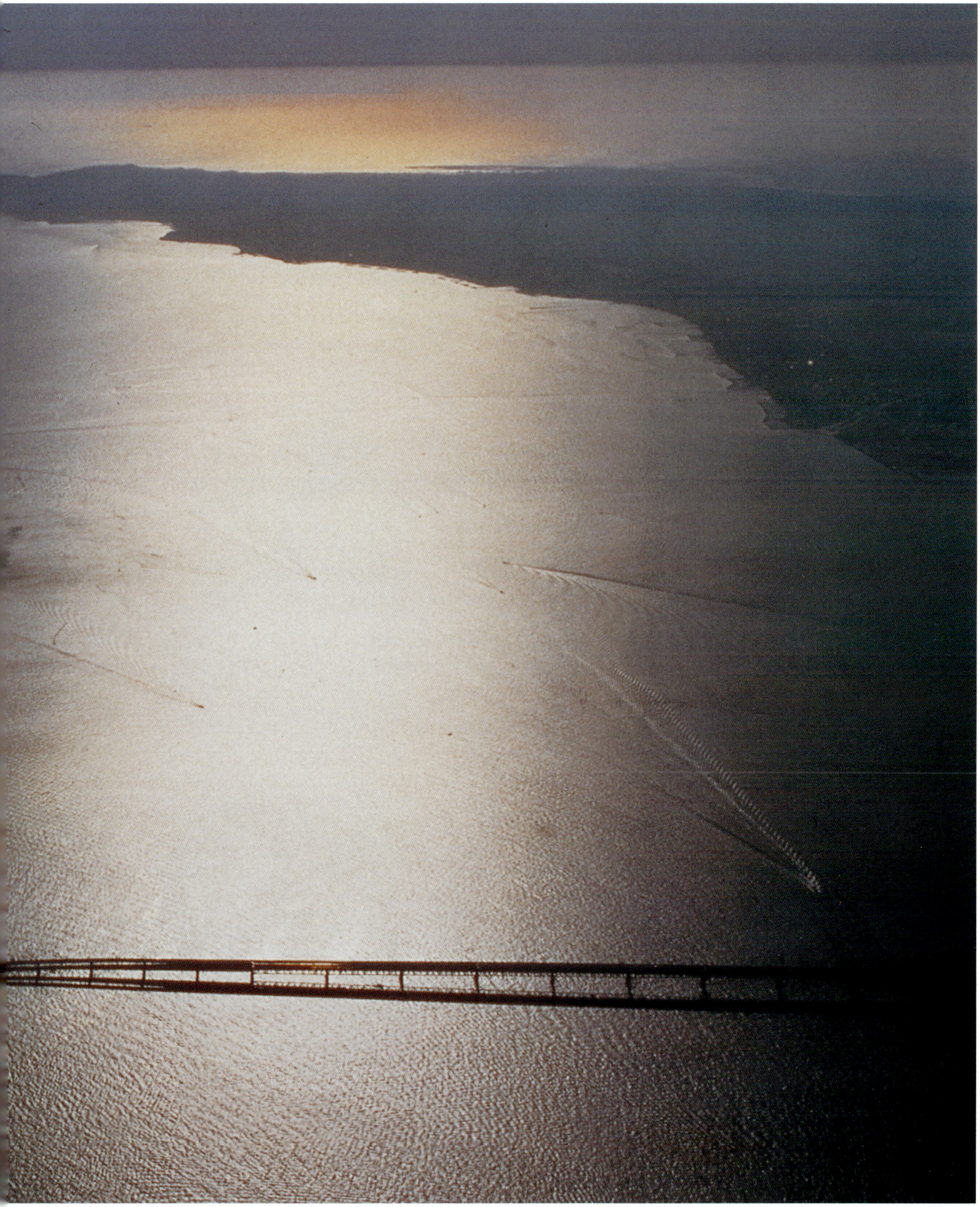

The air movement inside the terminal is controlled by a "scoop" that pushes the air across the curvature of the roof at thirty meters per second. While the curve itself was initially determined by the architect, the form of the scoop and the internal aerodynamics were worked out with engineers. When executing a project of this complexity, it is very difficult to separate the creation of architectural form and the application of structural technique, ergonomics, orientation, spatial organization, and, above all, human behavior. In a work of this scale all of these factors must be integrated.

It is important to note that one cannot perceive the end of the terminal building, because it is approximately eight hundred meters in length. The curve of the roof increases the sense of distance and the impression that the enclosed volume is infinite. It's like being inside a whale or a cathedral that never ends. The curve lends a very strong sense of orientation as one traverses the length of the terminal via the people mover that takes passengers directly to the plane.

Situated between New Zealand and Australia, New Caledonia is a beautiful island, so unspoiled that at first I felt we ought to do nothing there. However, we are now in the process of building a cultural center for the Kanaki peoples. Like the aboriginal Maori culture, this is one of the most interesting indigenous cultures in the Pacific area. The building, designed to shield itself from monsoons, is closed on one side and open on the other toward the south, abutting a continuous covered concourse. This concourse faces out over the lagoon. The back of the building is composed of some ten timber "cases" constructed like enormous huts. The project was designed in collaboration with an anthropologist. We tested the prototypical cases in a wind tunnel, exposing them to air currents of different direction and speed. From a functional point of view they serve to ventilate the building by means of the venturi effect. In this part of the world, there is typically no air-conditioning, so one has to rely on natural ventilation. All the material in these cases is of wood with heights ranging from sixteen to twenty-eight meters. Typically, we constructed a mock-up of one of these cases in our workshop in accord with our working method of passing from drawing, to sketching, to computer drafting, to calculation, to modeling, to making mock-ups at 1:1 scale, and then returning to the drawing board in a constant cyclical process of design and redesign. We constantly confer about everything with clients, engineers, and other specialists. It is a continuous feedback loop from different parts of the project.

After the fall of the Berlin wall, we won a 1992 competition for the reconstruction of the Potsdamer Platz area. The site, bounded in part by the Landwehrkanal, lies close to Mies van der Rohe's National Gallery and the Philharmonie and Stadtsbibliothek of Hans Scharoun. This project is difficult because we are not just designing a single building, but rather shaping a sector of the city. The entire scheme is made up of fifteen separate structures, as well as a system of access streets. We are responsible for the master plan and for designing the infrastructure in detail: the streets, the piazza and the paving. We will also take on the design of eight of the fifteen buildings. Among the architects working with us on this site are

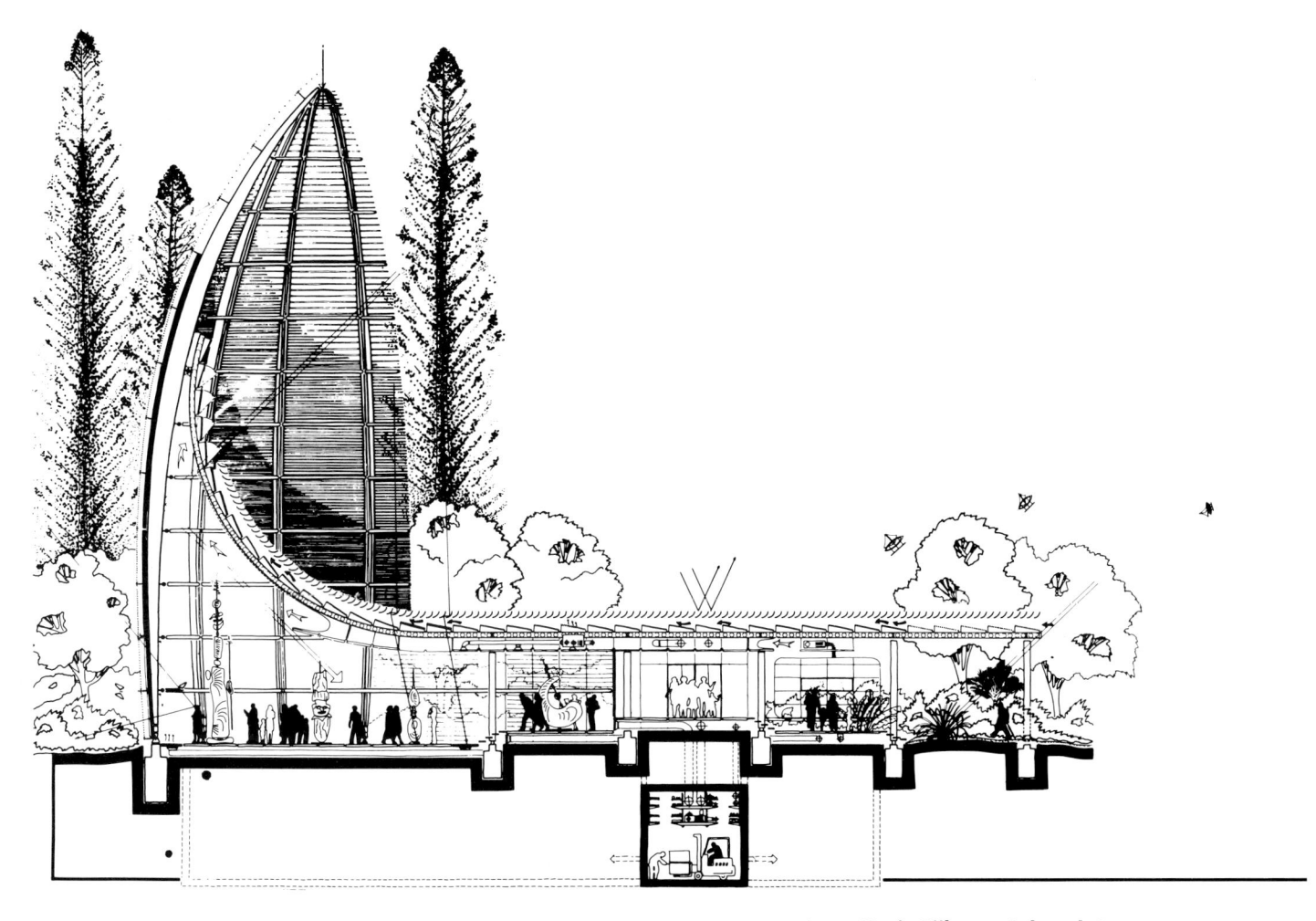

Jean Marie Tjibaou Cultural Center
Nouméa, New Caledonia, 1993–

Arata Isozaki, Rafael Moneo, Hans Kolhoff, Richard Rogers, Ulrike Lauber, and Wolfram Wohr. The total complex comprises a theater, a casino, a hotel, a cinema, some housing, offices, and a commercial center. However, large-scale work like this does not derive solely from the overall concept. From the very beginning, one must also develop the buildings in detail. Typical of this are the environmental studies for our Potsdamer Platz office building for Daimler Benz, where we developed a complex double-layered curtain wall system in which the membrane is allowed to breathe. There is generous air-space between the external skin of ceramic and glass and the internal glass skin. This is a kind of winter garden brought into being by two separate planes of glass set ninety centimeters apart.

I am the son of a builder, and I found building sites miraculous when I was a young boy watching raw material being transformed into built form. When I told my father that I wanted to become an architect, he reacted as though I were a mutation in the evolutionary process. He considered it a silly idea and told me: "But you can be a builder, why would you want to be just an architect?" He was correct in a way, because building, constructing things, is a fantastic endeavor; in it, the fundamental elements of revelation and creativity persist. Architecture is a great art, but it is also a contaminated art, an art contaminated by life. It is life that makes architecture imperfect insofar as it has to be able to accept evolution, modification, and adaptation to changing conditions.

There are many contradictions in architecture. One is surely the interaction

Jean Marie Tjibaou Cultural Center
Nouméa, New Caledonia, 1993–

131

between technology and place. Technology today is universal, and if you are not careful, you may easily destroy the spirit of a place. On the other hand, the place is by definition local, and local traditions or other constraints may inhibit the fantastic potential of technology. Equally mystifying, for me, is opposition between discipline and freedom. Many people believe that to be creative you must be totally free. I know now, after thirty years, that the opposite is true: to be creative you need discipline, you need rules and an obligation. Take the requirement to build with stone in Jerusalem. Many find this too restrictive; to me, this objection makes no sense, because the issue is not the stone. When you have a requirement, you simply have to work creatively within it. Nobody can find anything by searching everywhere. If you want to find something, you have to search in one precise direction. In architecture an obligation is a very important point of departure.

Another dilemma is the seeming conflict between art and science. People persist in believing that an artistic gesture is the opposite of a technical gesture. The art of making things, the *technē*, is neither the one nor the other; it is both. I consider myself fortunate to count among my good friends the great pianist Maurizio Pollini. Sitting beside him as he plays, I realize that he has mastered the *technē* so completely that he can forget about it. He closes his eyes and he plays, but only because he has mastered the technique so well that he may perform the miracle of forgetting.

Tradition versus modernity is another counterpoint. The sense of memory and the desire for innovation appear to be dissonant. Against this we may set the words of the poet Jorge Luis Borges, when he tells us that in a creative work, something lies suspended between things remembered and things forgotten. This simply means that nothing is totally original. You play all the time between something that is already in the world, in your spirit, your memory, or your experience, and something that is new. But these things go together. There is no modernity without love for tradition and a memory of the past.

There is no contradiction between technology and place, because technology is not what it was. Building technique has been transformed in the last thirty to forty years. There are completely new materials and innovative processes. Today, even the old materials may be revisited and transformed by modern techniques. Now we have composite chemical processes. If the last century was about welding, this century is about gluing. We are witness to a tremendous new potential, for the materials and the processes are changing along with the tools. When I was young, everybody told me that to make an economical structure, you had to use standard pieces. This is no longer the case. In the structure of Kansai Airport every rib is different, and this is the result of a relatively simple procedure. You input the tool with a program, and the computer cuts each piece differently or stamps out any number of different pieces. If you have programmed the machine correctly, everything is perfect.

The other big productive revolution is related to modern transportation. Many of my works were constructed in more than one place. For example, Kansai Airport was built on four continents. Even the small building in New Caledonia is being built in different countries. You may now

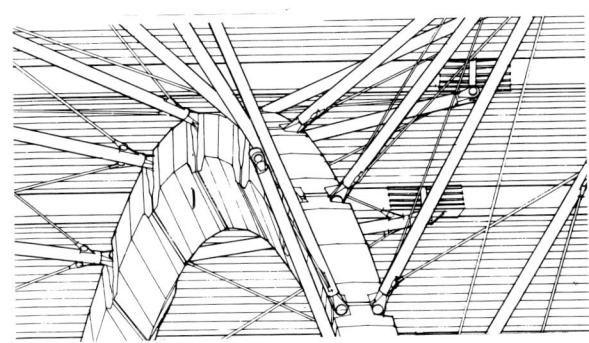

Padre Pio Pilgrimage Church
San Giovanni Rotondo (Foggia), Italy, 1995–

fabricate a piece of a building here and install it over there. However, I fail to see how this new capacity contradicts the deep feeling I have for place. Before starting a job, I spend hours in a place, just trying to capture the genius loci. There is always a small genius, even at an abstract site like the Kansai International Airport, where there was no site, no island, nothing at all. Nonetheless, we spent an afternoon in a boat with Peter Rice, thinking about metaphors, about the profile of the island and about the scale of the building. Such a topographic approach involves the land-form as much as the building. When everything is brought together, the sense of place is fundamental, but this does not contradict the impact of technology. The two factors must be brought to coexist.

I have my own approach to the conjunction of technology and place, namely, that the primary structure itself constitutes the place; it is sculpted in position, as it were, like a bas relief. This part is normally massive, opaque, and heavy. Then you craft a light, transparent, and even temporary piece of architecture, which is poised on top of it. In such a combination, the heavy is permanent and the light is temporary. I believe that it is possible to create a tension between these two aspects, the place and the building, or rather the place and the crafted fabric. They are of two different worlds, but they may certainly coexist.

When I reflect on these oppositions, discipline versus freedom, art versus science, tradition versus modernity, memory versus invention, technology versus place, they all tell the same story in different ways. It is the story of complexity, ambiguity, and complication. But what is wrong with ambiguity? It is a source of richness. If refusing to cut the knot of complexity means being ambiguous, then so be it. Indeed, I wear the label proudly. For duplicity in this sense has great dignity.

I believe that the architect must lead a double life. On the one hand is a taste for exploration, for being on the edge, an unwillingness to accept things for what they appear to be: a disobedient, transgressive, even rather insolent approach. On the other hand is a genuine, and not merely formal, gratitude to history and nature: the two contexts in which architecture has its roots. Perhaps this double life is the essence of the only humanistic approach possible today.

DISCUSSION
Renzo Piano
Arie Rahamimoff

Arie Rahamimoff: *Your work displays qualities summarized by Italo Calvino in his book* Six Memos for the Next Millennium: *lightness, quickness, exactitude, visibility, multiplicity, and consistency. Could you characterize your approach?*

Renzo Piano: My very first experiments with materials and structures were made some thirty years ago, and in this regard, I would like to emphasize that my early work as an independent architect derived from a pleasure in making things rather than from interest in technology as an end in itself. From my very first attempts, I was always searching for structures that were elegant, light, and simple. I began with various forms of prefabrication, shell, space-frame, and folded-plate structures in which I was particularly interested at the time.

In 1978, following the same experimental line, we created a workshop for UNESCO in Otranto in southern Italy. This workshop was about participation and research into the process of rehabilitating an old historical core without compelling the people to leave the center. It was my first exercise in participation, and I would like to stress these two aspects, technology and participation, rather than focus on technology alone.

Some people believe that when you are an architect you begin with a great idea, and then you design and somebody else takes care of the details. Unfortunately, this is indeed what often happens. But this is not the way we work. I never start solely from the general outlook. I start from detail, and go from there to the general. Gradually the two things come together to create the work. It does not arise out of an a priori adoption of a particular form or style. Style is like a golden cage in which architects enclose themselves. It destroys any possibility for exploration and experimentation. It is rather negative, a commercial obligation adopted in order to make yourself recognizable. However, there is another approach that is more anthropological. I refer to the capital of "know how" you build up in your professional life from working together with a particular group of people. In this context, style arises from the way of working. Today there is more and more of what I call the technological blackmail of feasibility. You go to the builder and he tells you that such a proposition is impossible. Then what you have to do is to work it out and show the builder how to do it. This procedure is what I prefer to call style, although perhaps we should call it lifestyle. In the end, a particular kind of form emerges from your way of working, and this in fact finally becomes recognizable as a house style.

Audience: *Could you explain the point of using large-span arches in stone as opposed to achieving a similar span in concrete? As you know, there is a regulation in Jerusalem which stipulates that all buildings must be built of stone. Over the years, this stone has become stone facing on top of a concrete superstructure. Since you recently designed the Padre Pio Pilgrimage Church in Italy, a long-span arched construction in stone, I was wondering if you could imagine a multi-cellular structure in Jerusalem made entirely out of load-bearing stone. Would this make any kind of economic sense?*

Piano: The structure you refer to is not a pre-compressed arch, it is simply an arch made of stone, with each stone touching the next. Each stone is precisely cut according to a perfect geometry, and this precision creates a continuous flow of forces. The difficulty arises when you introduce horizontal forces in a seismic situation. At this point the pre-compression comes into play. The cable inside goes to work as soon as the arches depart from the line of thrust. Under normal conditions, however, the stone assembly works as a simple arch. I am, of course, referring to real stones, not to a veneer of stone. I decided not to use a concrete arch, simply because this is a church and I felt that genuine stone was more in the spirit of a church. You might like to know that the money for this church came in large measure from the people themselves, and they were happy to pay for it. Each contributor is commemorated by having his or her name inscribed onto a particular piece of stone.

I am aware that this country has a regulation about using stone and I don't see anything wrong with that. One of the reasons why I find Jerusalem so fantastic is because there's this wonderful unity coming from the fact that everything is done in stone, and the stone is of good quality. I think mechanical uniformity is undesirable, but the unity of the material is positive. I don't agree that this regulation must be rescinded to ensure the creative freedom of architects. A creative architect has never been defeated by regulations. My theory is that rules and obligations actually help creativity. Bad architects use the alibi that they failed because they were obliged to be mediocre. But this is not true. Of course, I don't know enough about the regulation to comment in detail, but I think it should survive because it ensures unity. It is certainly possible to try to invent a new way of using stone. I've not done that, to be honest, but in Berlin, we have tried to find a new way of using terra cotta in order to create a double-layered, ventilated wall from this material. Siena is a city that I love, one in which every building is made of the same stone. Does that make it a bad city? I don't believe so. It was not dictated by regulations; the architects and builders were just going to the same quarry for their stone and then making fantastic buildings out of it, one slightly different from the next. At that time all the buildings were made of load-bearing stone.

Audience: *Why is it that in so many buildings today there is no relation whatsoever between architecture and construction?*

Piano: I believe that in architecture where construction is not visible, it is not understandable. The brilliant engineer Peter Rice, my late friend and colleague, used to talk about the trace of the hand in building, which is what you see when you look at a good old building of course. If you make a modern building with love and quality you still can see such a trace, even if there is no actual hand involved but rather the sensitive use of a tool. Thirty years ago when I was at school, we learned that, with standardization and modular coordination, you could not modify a single element, because if you did everything would become too expensive.

Today, we live in a different world, in which the computer permits all sorts of modifications. In the main terminal of Kansai airport, each truss is different from the next, because they make up a varying shell structure and so they have to be different. All the drawings were done by computer, and now these are made in such a way that you can transmit the memory of the computer into the tool. Thus, the machine cuts each piece differently. To have an intelligent sense of structural unity today you no longer have to make each piece identical. Everything has changed today, including the concept of standardization. But irrespective of all this, the sense of quality in construction comes from the love and attention that is lavished on the work.

Audience: *Did you ever change your plans because of engineering considerations, or is it that we have to train better engineers in order to do this kind of work? When you go from the details to the whole do you ever consider something that is not contained in the parts?*

Piano: Of course we must be better engineers but we must also be better architects. Making architecture is a circular process. It is not at all linear, it's not a unidirectional flow from the architect to the engineer or from the engineer to the builder. It involves a continuous feedback process. We work with a team of architects and engineers, and the important thing about this approach is that in the end, nobody can say from where a given concept came into being.

I have perhaps overemphasized our reactivation of traditional materials like stone or terra cotta. We also use modern materials, of course, like stainless steel, aluminum, or even plastic, although not very often. We did, however, build a traveling pavilion for IBM out of polycarbonate. I have always liked the idea of the skin of the building also serving as a structural element and polycarbonate is a good material for this. However, the great technical revolution of the end of this century has been gluing by means of chemical bonding. All of this finally means for us that the art of making is inseparable from the art of thinking. This is why I sometimes refer to using the computer and the hammer together.

Audience: *Could you say something about the way you work with builders and other associate architects? I mean the world may be shrinking, but your practice is also expanding. How can you cope with all the traveling around and working in different places, Japan, Germany, Italy, etc.?*

Piano: It's a difficult question which I have to answer every day. When you talk about big firms today, you're talking in the range of one thousand people. In comparison, our firm is not extremely large. We employ around one hundred people between our two main offices in Paris and Genoa. Despite this size we have to refuse a lot of work. We have established the maximum size at a hundred, since otherwise we would lose control. We have very good, experienced people in the office, and we communicate rapidly. It's like an old marriage, you watch each other and you understand immediately what is happening and perhaps even what is going to happen. The firm is divided up among people who have different approaches and who are each able to contribute unique abilities. We have about ten nationalities represented in the two offices, not because we love a multi-national approach, but because we find that it works better with respect to our international practice. Each person brings a different culture and thus a different attitude to the resolution of the work.

For twenty-five years, we have worked with the same team of exceptional engineers, Ove Arup and Partners of London, a firm in which Peter Rice was a crucial partner. I have to say that the loss of Rice was terribly tragic, not only in human terms because he was a great friend, but also creatively, because he was a man who combined scientific and humanist approaches, one with whom you could talk about everything.

It is hardly an accident that my firm is called "Building Workshop," because I have always felt a little guilty about having abandoned the métier of my father. Somehow or other, working as a team, as a workshop, we have managed to keep things under control. For the Kansai airport, we had to produce some fifteen thousand drawings, which is a colossal number when one considers that, for a building of average size like our Rome auditorium, we went out to the tender with 3,200 drawings. However, this is the kind of information you have to be able to handle; otherwise you lose control on the job. It's not that one doesn't trust the builders, but they are becoming increasingly lazy and they prefer to do only what they have already done. So they tell you all the time that this and that is impossible. However, with us, after a while they don't protest anymore and everything moves much faster.

Rahamimoff: *When asked about urbanism, Jean Nouvel said that authors write books, they do not write libraries. I think urbanism is in many ways at the scale of a library. It's a composite effort at dealing with the environment. Can you say something about this with reference to your urban scheme in Berlin?*

Piano: Making a scheme for Berlin is an impossible job, although I would never say this in front of my clients. A civilized person is called urbane, even in English, and when we refer to this term, we immediately think about all the beautiful cities that have ever been. We know, however, that they were not designed. They were and still are a product of organic growth. When you walk around these cities, what is beautiful is the very fact that what you are looking at has not been designed. Instead it represents the materialization of the millions of life stories that have been enacted within their respective walls across centuries.

When you are asked to design a piece of a city, even as little as fifteen buildings, it is really difficult, because you don't have the time to do such a thing. However, being an architect you still accept the challenge to do it. Then you begin to think of those elements from which a traditional city is composed: different kinds of streets and squares. You think about mixing the different functions. Above all, you have to make sure that in any one piece of the city you don't have just commercial or residential uses. You have to be sure that everything is there, operating twenty-four hours a day, the sacred and the profane. You need to have people walking, or shopping, or going to cultural activities like the theater. It is for all these reasons that in our Potsdamer Platz scheme we have juxtaposed a library, a casino, a hotel, residential buildings, and a commercial center. This is the urban tradition, and it is precisely this integration that is fundamental. Today, we are told that to be modern you have to forget all this, that you have to break completely with the past. Personally, I find such an attitude quite mad, because being modern does not necessitate abandoning humanist principles. Being modern entails something else; it's more subtle and less arrogant. Being an architect, especially when you are asked to design a piece of a city, is like being an acrobat. However, if you have grown up in the European humanist atmosphere, you have a net beneath you.

LECTURE
Álvaro Siza

Housing
Quinta da Malagueira, Evora, Portugal, 1976–

The differences that animate the panorama of contemporary architecture afford an opportunity for cultural cross-fertilization. Such interaction is a pre-condition for the formation of identity. However, architects today are often unduly preoccupied with being different, which paradoxically results in monotony in our towns, especially on the urban periphery.

In recent years, I have designed a number of chairs, always trying to produce a chair that looks like a chair—a rather uncommon phenomenon. They are all made of wood, fabricated by skilled artisans who still exist in Portugal today, and surprisingly enough, in other places as well, such as the Ticino in Switzerland, where there are still cabinetmakers whose work is quite brilliant, and also in the United States, where some of my chairs will now be produced.

When I design a house, I aim to realize a house that looks like a house, like those I designed for Malagueira, Évora, in southern Portugal. For me, the design of a house has to be capable of being easily repeated. The architecture of any town of quality derives from this capacity for repetition. A normative unit, such as a house, makes up the tissue of a town, against which the occasional monument may be read as a major institutional structure.

I first began to work in Évora in 1976. Flying over Portugal from north to south, we cross mountainous country until we reach the River Tejo, the river that eventually leads to Lisbon. After we pass over the river valley, there is a plain that extends to the south. Évora is situated in a rather poor region divided into large properties (*latifundia*). It has a population of forty thousand and remains encircled by a medieval wall. From the traditional boundary of the town, roads extend to the north, south, east, and west. The surrounding area is almost entirely unbuilt—or rather, it was so when I first arrived. The government commissioned me to realize some twelve hundred houses in this open area. On my first visit, I was only conscious of the profile of the town, with its Gothic cathedral and theater. After two or three visits, a number of things seemed to disrupt the landscape: trees and rocks, but more importantly, two unofficial, spontaneous housing settlements. Most of this "squatter" housing consisted of one- and two-story buildings together with necessary access roads. An east-west road crossing a small stream served to connect the two squatter housing quarters. These self-built houses were mostly painted white with some color used on the ground floor. The windows were small because the light is strong. Before the Portuguese Spring of 1974, an official housing scheme based on seven-story slab blocks was proposed which would have played havoc with the landscape profile of Évora. I was asked to adopt a more sensitive approach. The task was to introduce a new housing typology into the existing fabric, together with some small public facilities.

One of our initial decisions in planning the new quarter was to build only one kind of house. This led us to develop a typical patio house occupying an eight-by-twelve-meter lot. Our intervention presents a street facade that is apparently continuous, but behind this facade, each house, with its own patio, is a distinct unit with potential for individual customization.

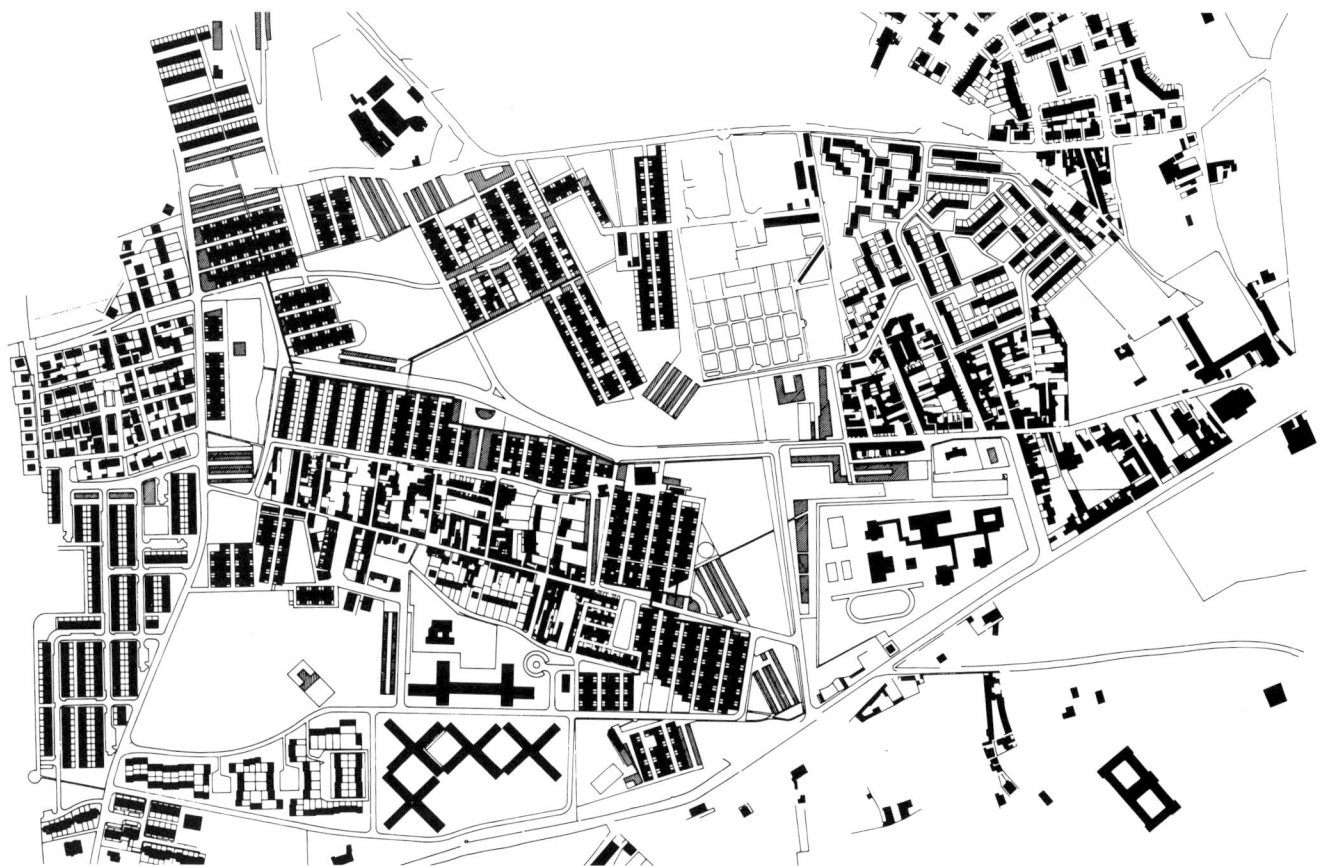

Site plan

The owners eventually paint the walls of these patios in natural colors; they install pergolas and cover these with climbing plants to create shade. Each L-shaped house was designed to be built on one level, but it can also be allowed to expand upward at a later date. The uniformity, combined with a possibility for varying the living space, exemplifies my belief that the architect must provide a fabric which the inhabitants can adapt to their own houses so as to make the town their own.

Running through our new quarter, parallel to the east-west road, we installed an elevated infrastructural duct, carrying electricity and other services. The particular form of this duct raised on piers was suggested by a nearby Roman aqueduct to which it makes an obvious reference. The ancient aqueduct crosses the land, penetrates the city wall and proceeds to the center of the town, where originally the palace of the king was located. The ruined arches of the Roman aqueduct have been used at times as shells for squatters' houses. The vernacular appearing here is very similar to that of many unofficial settlements elsewhere, but in this case, it maintains the same ancient stone construction technology found throughout the region.

Most of the houses were designated for cooperative ownership. This led to difficult discussions with future residents and other people of the town who objected to the initial designs, which they regarded as too uniform. They made the usual request for some kind of visual variation. I tried to show them how the houses were in fact variations on the same design, with a variable number of rooms and other elements that, over time, would give rise to further individualization. The discussion was long, and in the end, I had to redesign the house, retaining the back-to-back patio organization. During the discussions, people compared the design to the traditional house form, a suggestion I rejected as the populist use of the vernacular form.

One of the main justifications for adopting this type of house was the limited budget. We did not have enough money for special thermal insulation, nor for sun protection with fixed louvers or sun blinds. The patio, with its microclimate serving as a transitional area, was partial compensation for this lack. The patio also provided a space for outdoor living, which was crucial given the extreme climate of the south. Of course, there were cultural reasons for the design as well. In a context of deep changes, the tradition of family activity in the open air is maintained.

The new tissue of my Malagueira housing is slowly becoming integrated into the entire fabric of Évora. We recently added a small open-air theater, which people are beginning to frequent. We also introduced a small bridge over an existing water course, so that people can either cross the river and enter the town or come down and enter the lower area with its lake, water channel, and descending stair. In general, I tried to maintain the existing pathways that played an important part in the lives of people long before my arrival. I always try to preserve the habitual patterns of human movement. It is obvious that traditional pathways come into being organically, which accounts for the degree to which they have been consolidated over time. This is as true of Évora as it is of other places in which I have worked. In Évora, something slowly but surely is being created, and the relationship between the landscape, the planning, the buildings, the walls, and the people is gradually being articulated in all of its subtlety.

It is hard to imagine a greater contrast to Évora than the residential block I built in the Kreuzberg district of Berlin. Kreuzberg is composed of big six-story blocks with the consistent 110-by-90-centimeter window rhythm throughout. From time to time, this rhythm is broken by disruptive architectural incidents, such as cantilevered bay windows. When I started to work there, this district was largely characterized by degraded urban stock in the process of restoration. Nobody thought in terms of demolition or of introducing new architecture merely for its own sake. Our intervention was, however, partially a new building. It was a *bâtiment d'angle*, a corner building harmonizing with the character of the local urban fabric while providing improved residential amenities within the constraints of the existing regulations. Despite this, the popular reaction was generally negative. The building was thought to be too somber, there was no brilliant color, there was no traditional yellow ochre, and so on. When one goes through the street, the building appears to be a very strong volume having its own decisive personality. From other viewpoints, it disappears in the continuity of the surrounding texture. Sometimes it is invaded by light and sometimes it is in shadow.

Overleaf
Housing
Quinta da Malagueira, Évora, Portugal, 1976–

There are a number of my projects that have consistently provoked strong objections largely because of the seeming monotony of the work. In 1985, I proposed a plan for the Giudecca in Venice. It is not the heroic, brilliant Venice of the Piazza San Marco and other places in the town. It has its own proportional character and consistency. As in Évora, there has to be a balance between the repetitive fabric and the important institutional structures—the one being complementary to the other. It is important that the repetitive housing of a town maintain a certain discretion to ensure that the public buildings may claim their distinctive character and assert their monumentality.

In 1985 and again in 1989, I was asked to build some housing units in The Hague in the Netherlands, where the traditional material is brick. Once again, this was social housing to be built by cooperatives. The Dutch, strangely enough, do not demand variety; they always favor the repetition of the same thing. So brick is commonly selected, as much for its conformity as for its easy maintenance and its guarantee as a material. I was glad to use it on this occasion, as it adapted well to the area slated for preservation.

However, many Dutch architects react strongly against the use of brick, regarding white stucco as the touchstone of modernity and seeing other materials, like brick, as reactionary. It is as if we were back in the 1930s, when the struggle between Nazi architecture and the avant-garde first emerged. Perhaps for this reason, I was tempted to indulge in a more expressive configuration comprising a free-standing piece composed of a cluster of three duplexes and a shop. Here I played with two contrasting languages. One building is rendered in brown brick, while the other is

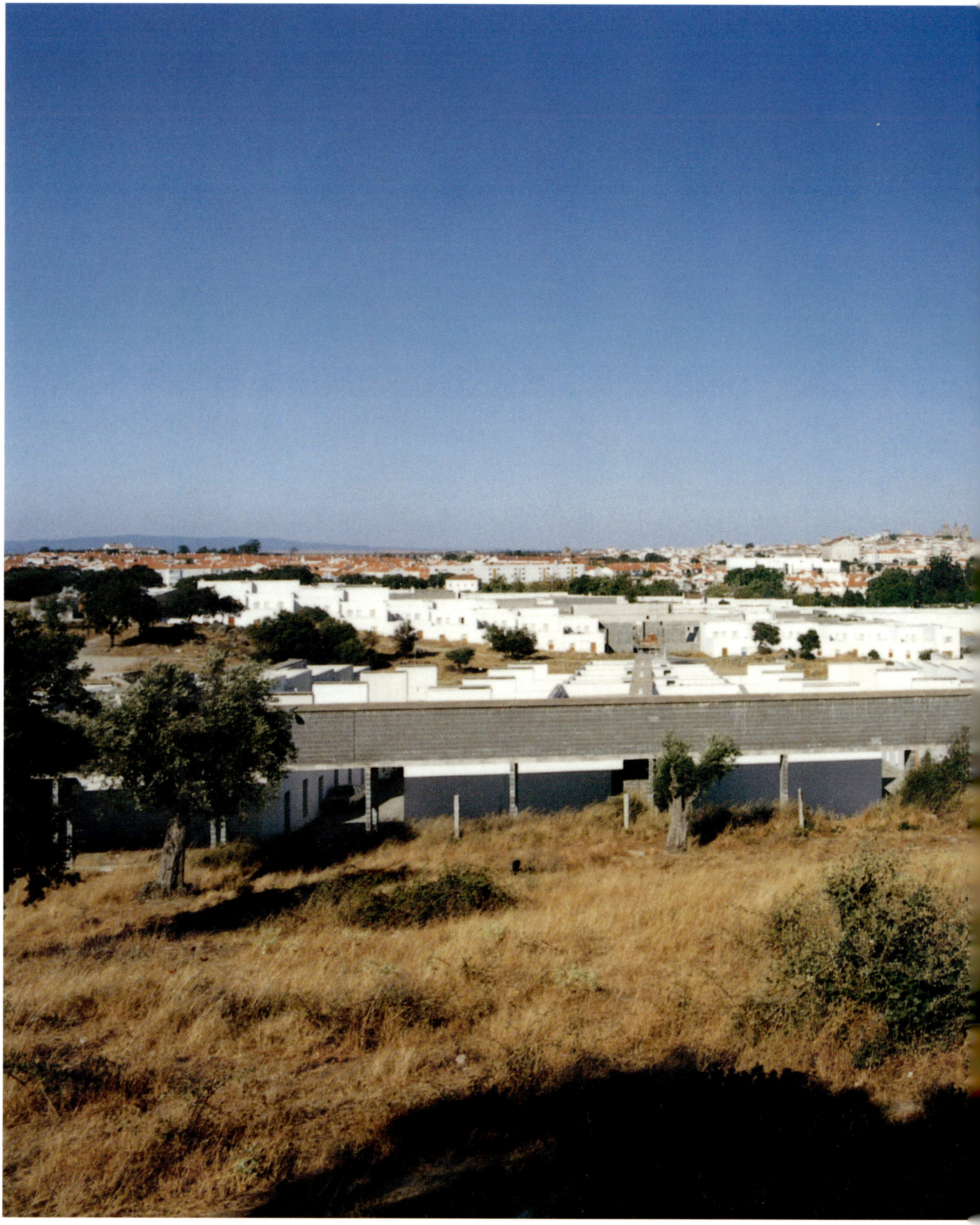

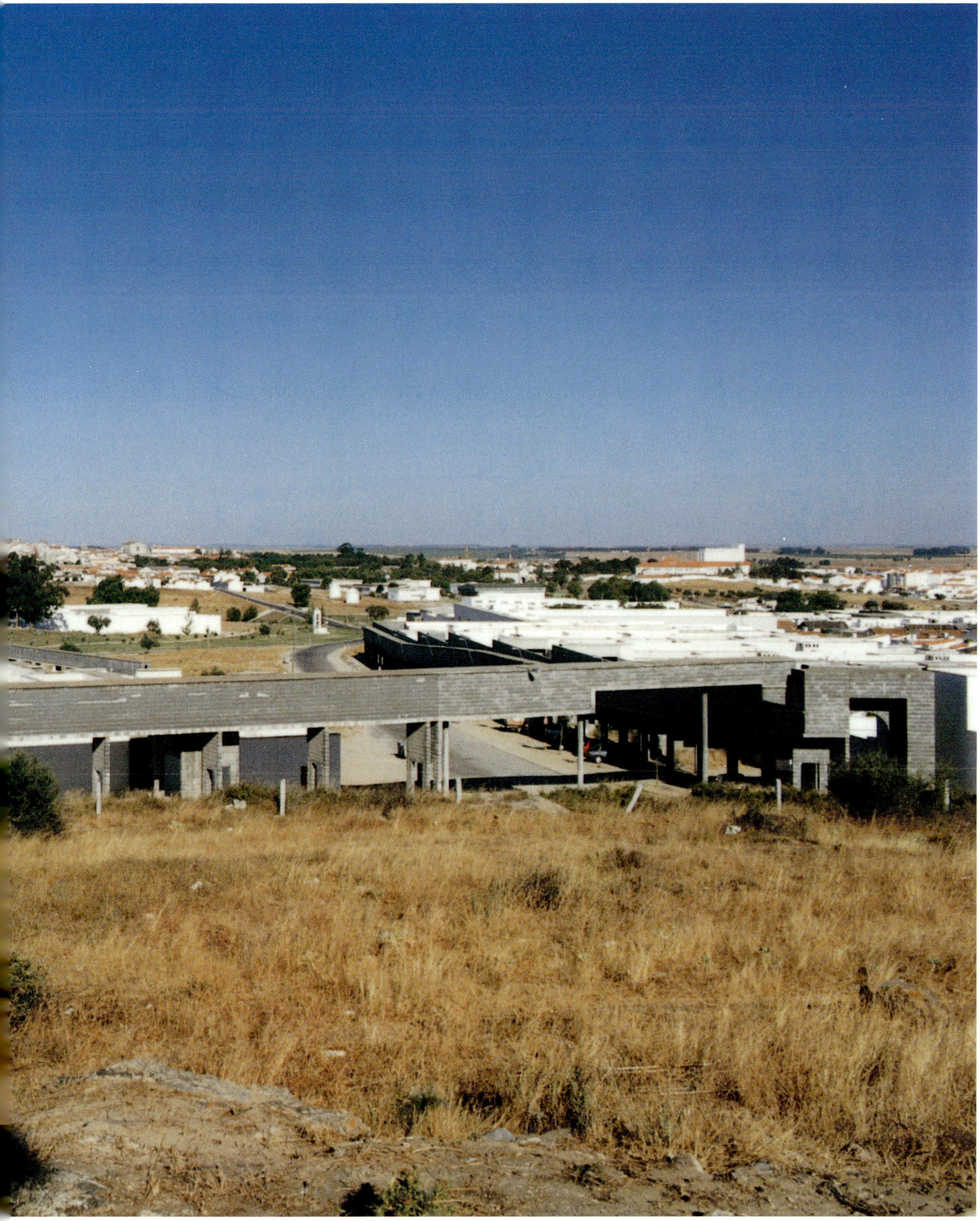

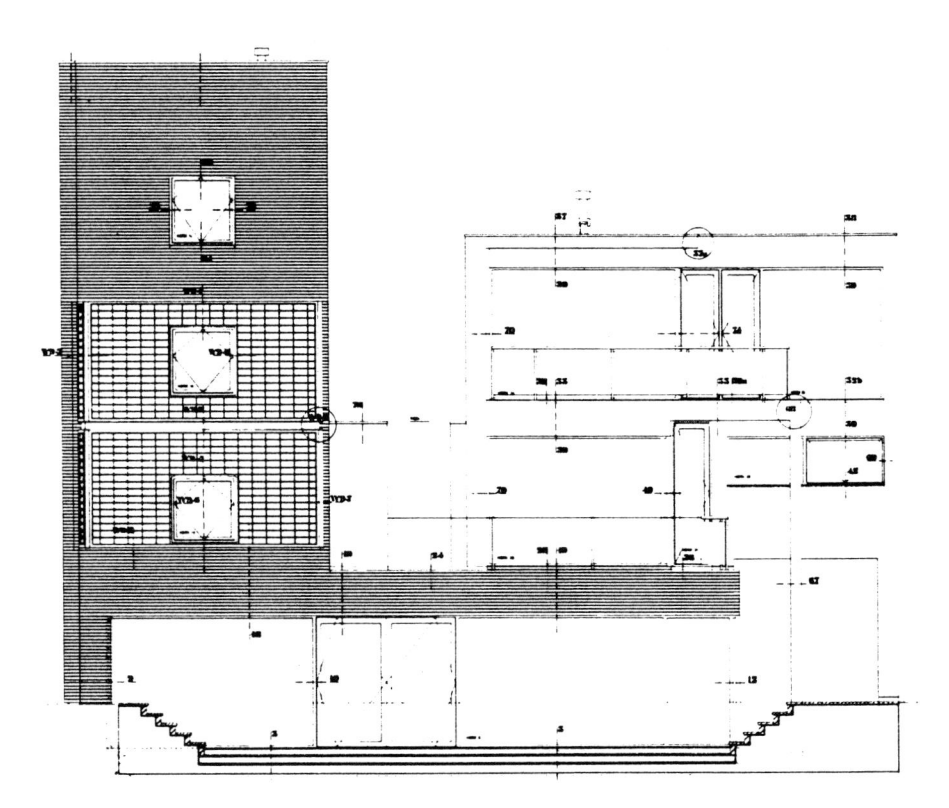

Right and facing page
House in The Hague
The Netherlands, 1984–1988

Southwest elevation

in white stucco. One is equipped with large windows, while the other has small ones. It remains nonetheless a single autonomous structure.

In 1988, I was charged with the restoration of Chiado, an important historic district in Lisbon, after its destruction by fire. Chiado is a transitional area between the center and other parts of the town. It was destroyed by an earthquake at the end of the eighteenth century, and then rebuilt according to a unified plan with identical facades constructed out of prefabricated parts. In some respects, it is a single prefabricated building. The fact that eighteen of the houses burned down was sufficient incentive for some people to propose filling the vacant site with modern structures with little or no regard for the preexisting context. Since in the main the exterior shells were still standing, I argued that these should be preserved and the gutted interiors totally restored. The buildings had originally been constructed from a flexible wooden framework. This system of anti-seismic construction known as *gaoia* was designed to move with the tremor. The outside walls were of stone, loosely connected to the structure. The theory was that, in the event of an earthquake, only the outside walls would collapse, leaving the structure intact. The streets have the same width as the general height of the residential buildings, so that in the event of a facade's collapse, collateral damage to facing structures would be minimized.

My basic strategy was simply to construct another *gaoia,* only this time, the inside would be of reinforced concrete rather than wood. Some people dismissed this approach as a kind of pastiche, but it is simply a

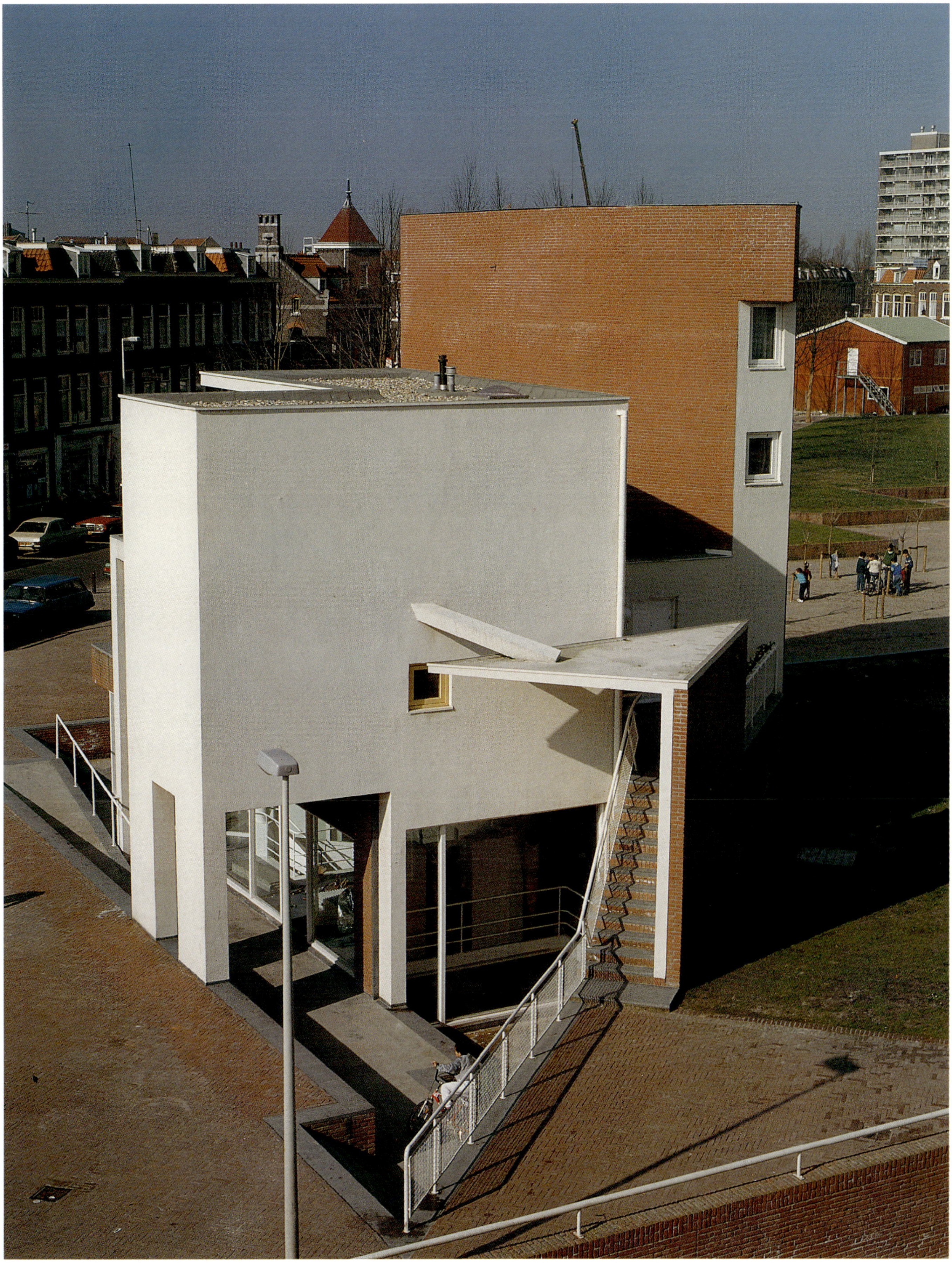

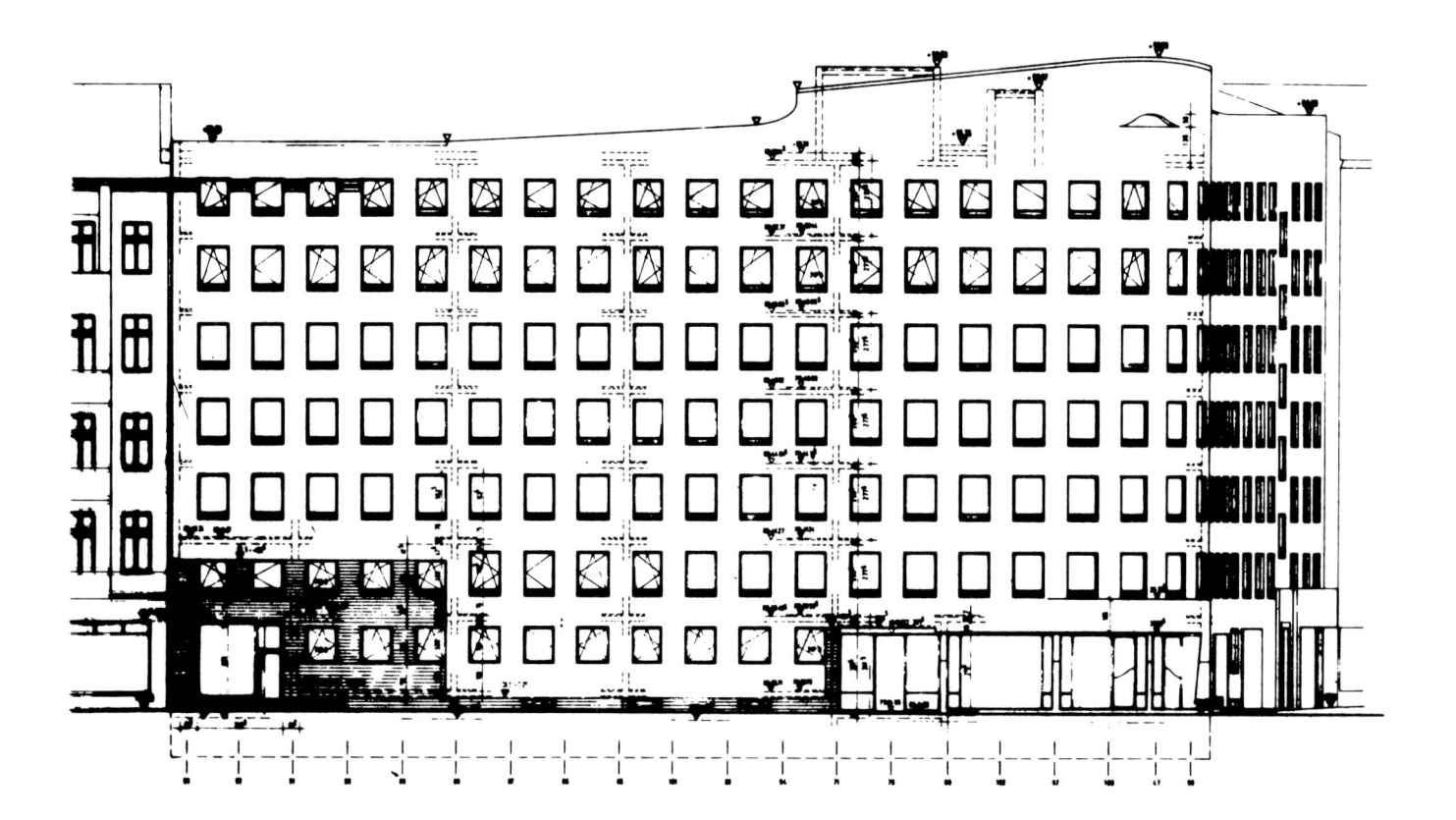

Above
Schlessisches Tor Housing, "Bonjour Tristesse,"
Kreuzberg, Berlin, 1980–1984

Facing page
Galician Center for Contemporary Art
Santiago de Compostela, Spain, 1988–1994

reconstruction of the same structural system, as the programmatic requirements for the whole area remained the same. However, totally new aspects are emerging. A new metro station will be integrated into the area. A large arch was introduced to allow people to pass through the buildings in one of the blocks, affording a link to the interior of the block, and by way of ramps, to the famous steel-framed elevator. In these specific new elements, the design interrupts the *"pombalino"* character of the architecture, the neoclassical style associated with the Marques de Pombal, who rebuilt Lisbon after the devastating earthquake of 1755.

From 1988 to 1994, I added an art museum to the old monastery of Santiago de Compostela in Spain. The challenge was to insert a museum within the garden of the monastery. At the same time, I wanted to bring the building forward to face the street, thereby lining it up with the monastery while creating a sort of portico. By putting the museum on the street I was able to restructure an area that had been disrupted by the willful introduction of a new street in the 1950s, as well as by the construction of some buildings at variance with the general urban profile.

The building is faced in stone, and one of the problems was how to deal with the stone's skin-like character. I elected to use the stone by setting it onto steel profiles; each stone being secured at the back to a secondary structure. The angled corner stones are L-shaped, so there is no joint in the angle, a vulnerable point which is invariably exposed to fracture. An arrangement that stresses the horizontal course as opposed to the vertical

Site plan

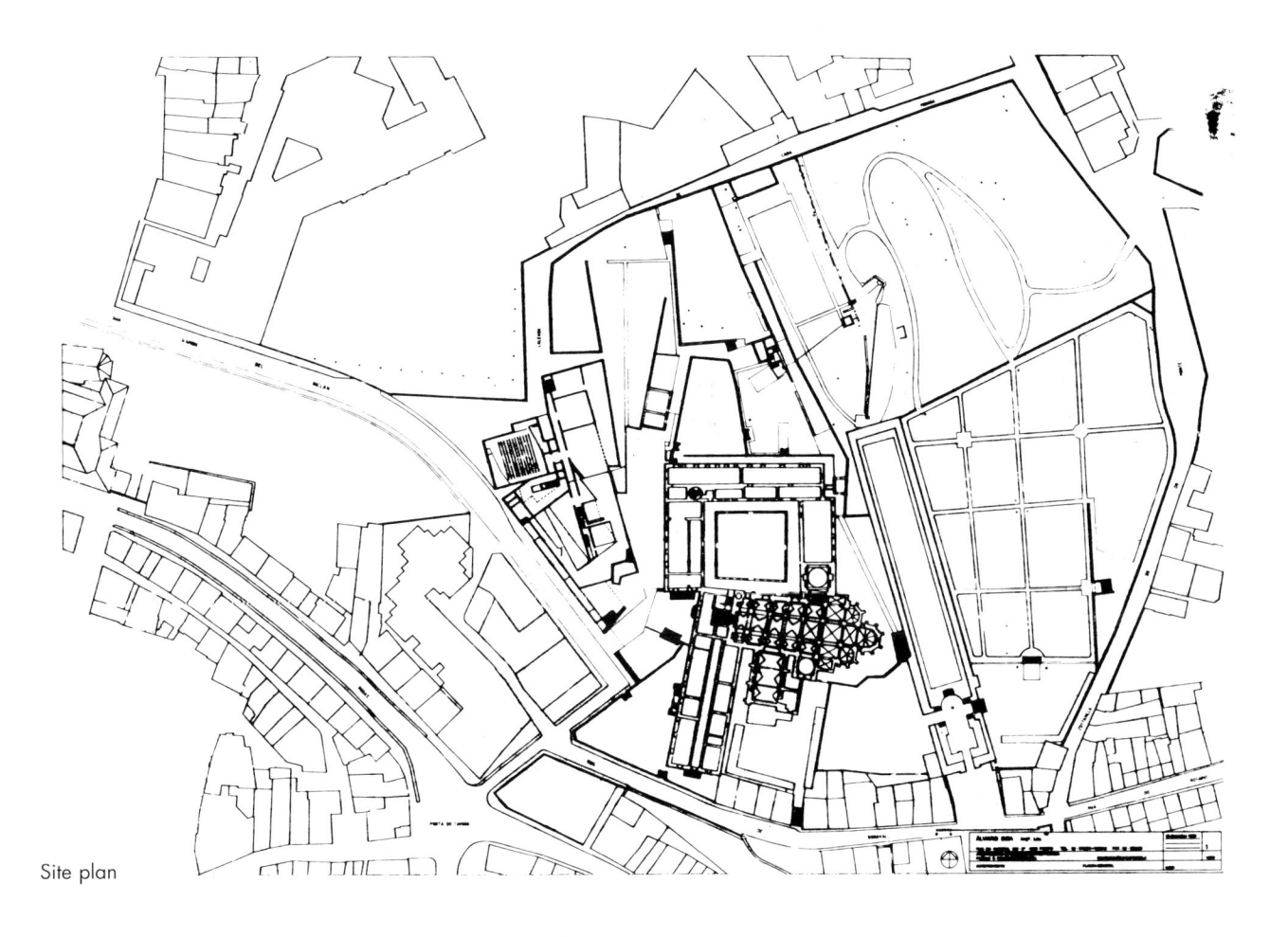

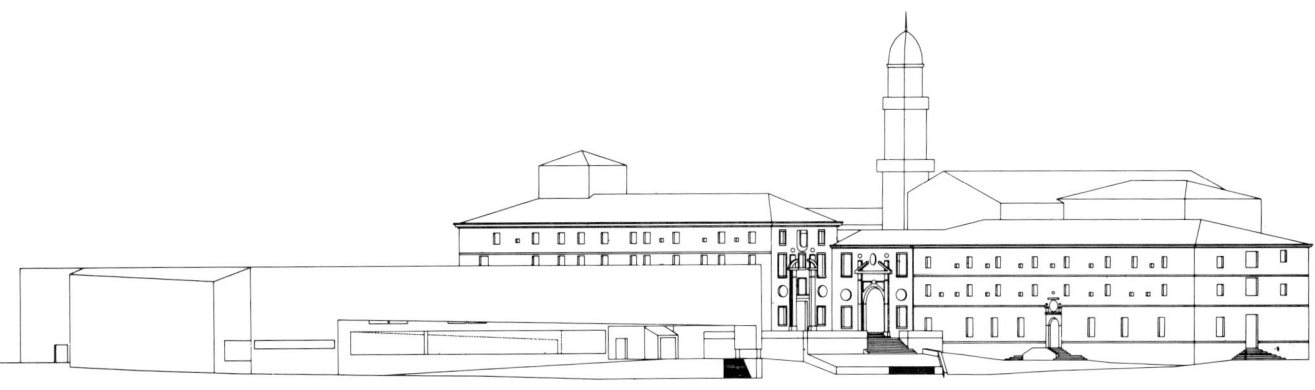

Elevation

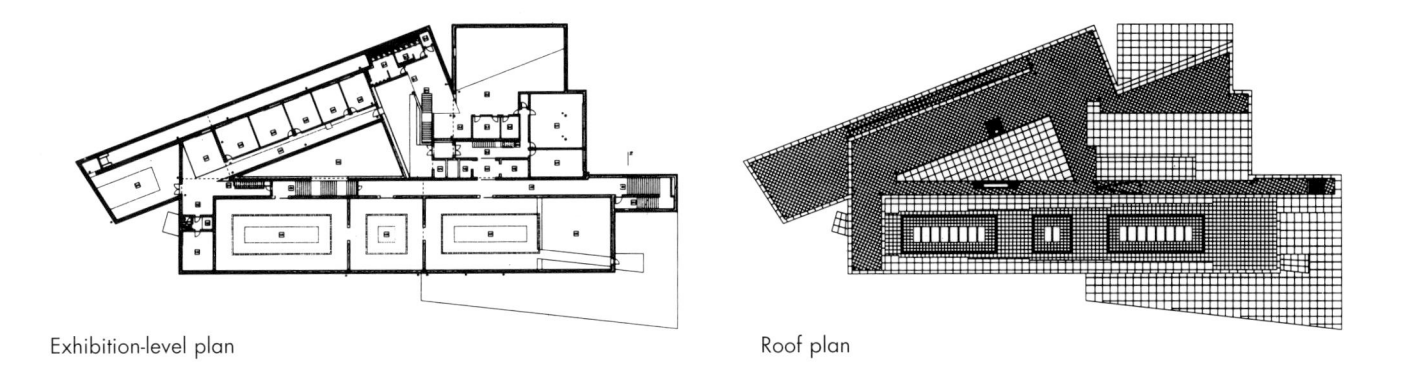

Exhibition-level plan

Roof plan

147

Aveiro University Library
Aveiro, Portugal, 1988–1994

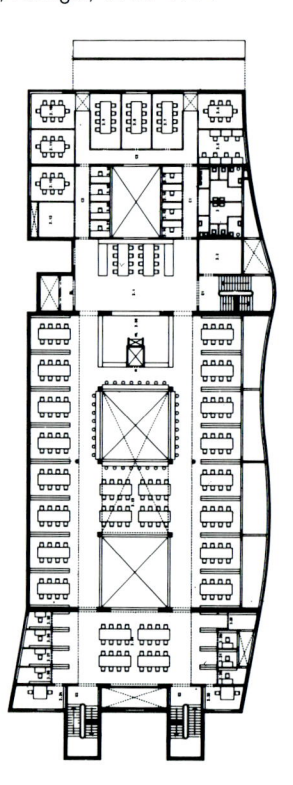

First floor plan

joint leads us to recognize, in a tectonic sense, the new way in which the material is being used. Yet there remains an ambivalence that is related to doubts that always arise when one uses traditional materials in a different way.

The portico of the building is the start of a zig-zagging route that climbs up the garden terraces flanking the monastery to culminate in the now disused cemeteries at the top of the hill. The organization of the interior of the museum follows a similar labyrinthine itinerary to echo the switch-back movement of the garden terraces and to terminate them with the building. The inner core of the museum is a double-height pyramidal space that reconciles the two lines of angled orthogonal galleries situated to either side.

While reworking the garden, we discovered a system of underground water channels that had been used to carry water from the fountains of the upper terraces down to the lower terraces. We refurbished some sections of this system and reintegrated it into a whole new irrigation system. The water course ends in a small pool belonging to the new building.

To varying degrees, all these works have taken the preexisting fabric as their point of departure, the character of the place depending in many respects on the further articulation and elaboration of these traces. In this sense, architects are always engaged in transforming the existing reality in light of the available technology, irrespective of whether these techniques happen to be new or old.

School of Architecture
Porto, Portugal, 1986–1995

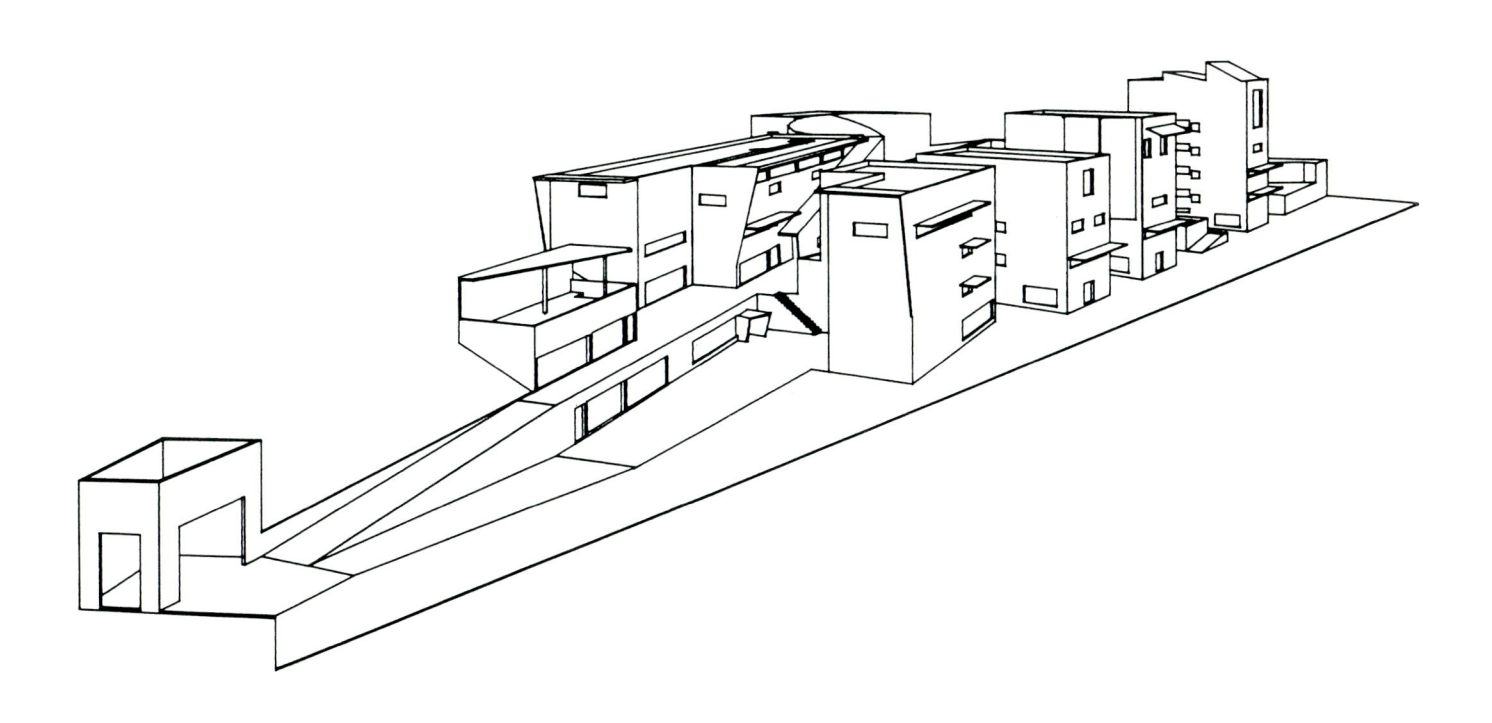

DISCUSSION
Álvaro Siza
Pe'era Goldman

Pe'era Goldman: *Would you comment on the difference between designing buildings when you were young and designing them as you do now? What has maturity brought to the process and what has been lost along the way?*

Álvaro Siza: The thing I missed most when I was young was being able to travel abroad and see architecture in other countries, because Portugal was then an isolated country. Students were not usually allowed to travel outside the country, except to Spain; travel beyond Iberia was out of the question. I made my first architecture study trip in 1968 when I was already thirty-five. I used to tell my students that we can learn more in one week's travel than in one year at school.

Goldman: *Where did you travel in 1968?*

Siza: We went to Holland, Sweden, and Finland. The place we spent the most time was Finland, in order to study the work of Alvar Aalto. We went as a group of students and teachers, visiting many of Aalto's works because he had become very important in Iberia. Our knowledge of the outside world came largely through Italy via Spain. We had annual contact with Barcelona and I was very influenced by what was happening there. At the same time, we were engaged in an extensive survey of Portuguese vernacular architecture. This was a marvelous project painstakingly assembled by teachers and students who traveled all over the country making precise drawings of then still-existing agrarian buildings. These records were published in a compendium subsidized by the government, and I was profoundly affected by it. The architects and students undertook this survey to demonstrate the architectural diversity of the country: north versus south, interior versus seaside. There is a North African, Arabic influence in the south of Portugal for example. The native materials are also different in the various parts of the country. In the north, there is a predominance of granite, while white stone and chalk prevail in the south. The two regions are clearly distinct, even if both are Portuguese. The architects who participated in the survey were able to demystify the notion of a "national" style. Aalto was important in this context, because he had made extensive use of traditional materials and he was one of the few architects who did so while participating in the debate about contemporary architecture.

Goldman: *Who was an important influence on you when you were a student?*

Siza: When I attended the architectural school in Porto, it was small, with only around one hundred students. Almost all the senior professors were on the verge of retirement, so a new faculty was being hired. Carlos Ramos, an architect who had been rejected by the School of Lisbon, was appointed director of the Porto school. Ramos, an admirer of Bauhaus and northern European architecture, had been in Holland and Belgium during the 1920s and the 1930s. Extremely intelligent and well-informed, he brought the ideas of the Bauhaus to the Porto school. He was very adept at selecting faculty. When it was politically difficult to hire a particular teacher whom he wanted, he would play the diplomat. Although he was not a fascist, he had very good relations with the power elite. He used irony to get what he wanted. He would go to the Minister of Education, a friend of his, offer to take responsibility for someone who had been a political prisoner and get an agreement establishing the terms of that responsibility. So he could call on the best. Some had just finished school themselves. I don't know how he acquired all his information. Much also depended on his social standing in the town of Porto. He was able to attract applicants from families who had given a good education to their children, thereby assembling a fine group of students. When I entered, I was surrounded by these top-notch teachers and students. One of them, Fernando Tavora, was indubitably the most important, not only for the Porto school but also for Portuguese architecture in general.

Goldman: *I would like to let the audience know that when Álvaro Siza was the Kenzo Tange Professor at Harvard in 1988, he invited Fernando Tavora to his final review. May I call him your mentor to some degree?*

Siza: Yes. For me it was important to have Tavora in the school, not only for his friendship, but also because he had contacts with the outside world. He was a member of CIAM [Congrès Internationaux d'Architecture Moderne] and a close friend of Aldo van Eyck, who claimed he was of Portuguese Jewish origin. I met him through Tavora. Tavora had a modest following, but he never wanted to publish anything or to make himself famous. In the early 1950s, architects felt that to publish something in a magazine was ethically unacceptable. They shied away from it as a form of self-promotion. They were ashamed to be involved in such activities. When I first published in a Spanish magazine, I was accused of trying too hard to influence those Spaniards with whom it was politically advantageous to have relations. My writing was not well received and I continually tried to get other people to publish because I thought it was important for us, for the profession, and also because I did not want to remain the only one with everybody accusing me and saying, "He published, he published." It was difficult. Only in April of 1974, after the revolution, was there an explosion of information. Then architects lost their inhibitions because they all wanted their work to be influential. Also, many distinguished visitors from outside Portugal—including architects—came to observe a revolution in progress. With the transformation of Portugal, it became normal to publish, even too normal.

Goldman: *In later years you met Hassan Fathy. Can you elaborate on the significance that you found in his architecture?*

Siza: I met Hassan Fathy in Corsica, in the late 1970s. I was very impressed by him, above all as a person. He was a gentleman of the kind that no longer exists. I remember we were at a seminar that was about participation. Corsican workers attended, as did a French historian of music who owned an old convent that was worth visiting. The atmosphere was one of revolution, evidence of the permanent fight for Corsican independence. I was included in this political fight, which I didn't understand very well, but I assumed that I had been invited because I was an architect who had been involved in participation. With the support of UNESCO, Hassan Fathy had started this movement in order to help the people of the Third World build for themselves. We were there to learn about the methods and techniques he had employed. Fathy always wore a faint smile, only becoming angry when someone mentioned air-conditioning. The subject made him furious, because someone had designed a university building in Cairo in which the air-conditioning did not work. After some time, they had to close it. For him it was inexcusable that they had not used traditional ventilation. But I have digressed from your question.

Goldman: *I was asking about your youth.*

Siza: What I remember best from when I was young was our constant enthusiasm and our strong love for architecture. I do not recall ever being annoyed about something connected to my work as an architect. It was more important than anything; it was present in every aspect of my personal life. That is not the same today, I must say. Maybe it's only fatigue—all these years working so hard. But I don't think it is simply that. I think that everywhere, but probably more so in Europe, there is a dearth of excitement. There is disappointment at the state of the towns, and in many cases, of the countryside as well. In part, the disappointment stems from the preservation movement and from our failure as a society to maintain a balance between old and new. Architects are prevented from doing anything in old towns, thereby totally arresting their cultural evolution.

We lack clients with enthusiasm. There can be no passion for architecture if there are not clients or promoters with enthusiasm. This is what I miss. Instead one has to accept conditions that are very disagreeable.

Let give you an example. Lisbon is in the process of organizing a universal exhibition for the year 1998, and I am designing the national pavilion. We have to finish all the details in thirteen weeks. This is typical of the contemporary situation: when we do get the work, we have to do it fast. We do not have time to think. We must produce the design as quickly as possible. Furthermore, often we receive a program that is so strict that we are only left with the task of designing the windows or detailing the stone cladding. Nobody wants us for what we can really provide. They just want us to supply decoration. That, more often than not, is how it happens. Of my youth, I miss my earlier capacity to engage myself with enthusiasm.

Goldman: *Could you tell us how you go about starting a new project? What sets you off? Is it the first impressions of the place, or a preconceived idea that you want to try out, or is it a particular request of the client?*

Siza: All of those, but the order varies according to the situation. For instance, I sometimes receive a commission for a place I have imagined, but which I didn't know previously. I have some photos, a map, or something; or I have an idea of the place from literature. After I receive the brief, and during the trip to the site, I can make sketches with these preconceived ideas. Then I arrive, and it is either quite different or not, as the case may be. I always make a certain genre of sketches before receiving too much information, because it is crucial to have a solid point of departure. If I establish this, then I can always find a way to understand the situation more fully.

The process is one of gradual augmentation of information, allowing oneself to learn about the program in an open way. It is not enough to know only what the client wants. In order to enlarge one's perception it is better to understand the specific wishes of everyone affected by the situation. Whether I am in Portugal or any other country, I need to immerse myself in the ambience and integrate my reactions into the slow process of realizing a building.

Goldman: *Your sketches are always enriched with human figures. Do you draw them to spur your thinking?*

Siza: I like to draw because I am a frustrated sculptor. When I began studying architecture, my original idea was to become a sculptor. This didn't suit my family, because in those days a sculptor was considered Bohemian and therefore a somewhat crazy person. Instead of forbidding me to pursue such a career, my father, who was an engineer and a very kind man, said I had better go to a school. At that time painting, sculpture, and architecture were combined in one school. I went there to study architecture, thinking that I would gradually change over to sculpture. Once I entered the school, however, I became captivated by this profession. The professors were very young, they were beginning the fight for changes in Portugal, and we students rapidly became their friends. We were soon working in the offices of the professors or independently. It was a small, highly conscious group. We were constantly discussing things and involved in relationships and marriages, love affairs and all kinds of things. It was a very tight circle, and even if it didn't realize many projects, the work was intense.

Goldman: *In a recent interview, Gabriel Garcia Marquez mentioned that he had a small group of friends, two or three, who were not writers, whom he often* *consulted about his writing problems. Is there a close friend with whom you can discuss an idea? Is he or she an architect?*

Siza: After the revolution, we were working for the residents of Porto, fighting to maintain their houses. We were engaged in a number of important projects, and we functioned as a group, discussing everything together. But life goes on, people change, and new ways of communication appear. A small part of this group maintained permanent relations with one another. Just now I'm in the process of realizing a new office building that will house both my office and that of Eduardo Souto da Moura. This testifies to a close, long-standing relationship. On the other hand, some of my former associates from the original group have even become opponents. One person who helped me very much in the beginning was my wife, who was not only a painter but also a very good critic of architecture. She could arrive at a building under construction, glance at it and say, "That's ridiculous." Maybe as a painter she had the capacity to see this clearly. We architects can become so involved in so many things that we no longer see anything.

Goldman: *Your projects are always rather unmonumental.*

Siza: Well, there are not so many opportunities to create monuments. These arise out of certain moments of history, according to a specific program. A monument used to be something that served everybody; it was, as it were, the keystone of the town. Public buildings constructed today can still be important, and acquire symbolic meaning in the town, but not often. It so happens that I worked on the competition for the Grand Bibliothèque de France. I designed this project in collaboration with Wilfried Wang. We spent one week in Paris making the initial sketches and then we developed the project with a team in London. Later we returned to Paris for a short period of intense work. Time was severely limited. We thought that such an institution should be seen as the catalytic core for developing the whole area. We had the garden in the library opening onto the Seine. We proposed a very strong, one might even say a severe, classical building. The critics saw it as the most conventional building submitted for the competition. The truth is we could not arrive at an appropriate architecture for a national library in two months. I simply could not do as the winner did, which was to take a preconceived concept and apply it. This solution, as you know, was realized, but not in a way that will enable it to act as a catalyst for the development of the entire area.

Goldman: *Is the technology you employ the result of the material culture and the building tradition in Portugal, or is it your choice?*

Siza: The first thing for me is to decide what is the most economical method of building. However, I sometimes choose the overall approach, the material, and so on for aesthetic reasons, particularly when the building is in the center of a historical town. Usually one tries to harmonize with the context, but sometimes it's better to make a work in contrast with what exists. Much depends on the program, the specific site, or the area where the building is to be situated. The question is: what can I make well in a particular place? To give an example, three years after the revolution, there was a construction boom in Portugal. As a result, there was a tremendous scarcity of brick and tiles. We took over a small local factory, and with the help of government subsidy, produced cement blocks. Given that the well-known contractors were occupied in Lisbon and other parts of Portugal, we helped organize a building cooperative where we trained workers from scratch. I would arrive on site and find myself involved in masonry work. The next instant I would be discussing carpentry. I had to inspect the quality of the work.

Goldman: *When you first received commissions outside of Portugal, it meant moving from one cultural context to another. Was that transition problematic in other ways, besides communicating with the contractors?*

Siza: At first it was very stimulating to practice outside the country. I liked it very much. When I went to work in Berlin—first on competitions and then on actual projects—I felt my enthusiasm coming back. I didn't know Berlin, this extraordinary city where you can study the beginnings of the modern movement firsthand. I saw all these buildings and it was very exciting. I had an extensive support network, which was essential, because when working in another town or country, you need people to help you, people with whom you can associate. You also have to learn very quickly, but this too is more interesting when the appetite is stimulated, because you are entering a new phase of life. Working outside lends a new perspective from which to criticize what is going on in your own country where you have the most direct contacts.

Goldman: *I sense a certain logical process in your work. In addition to the sculptural quality and aesthetic principle, can you say something about the role of logical procedure in relation to the artistic idea?*

Siza: Architecture is a logical process. Developing a project means making the logic absolutely clear and understandable. The logic has to be communicated to others even if it is a process that sometimes begins in an intuitive way. The process of designing a work is a critical procedure, a complex process whose duration cannot be stinted. The project, from the beginning, is always in a state of flux: a cluster of ideas, of possibilities, of different conditions in a state of becoming which we have to nurture, like working on a piece of sculpture.

Goldman: *In the new school of architecture in Porto, you broke the building down into small units. Is this related to your view as to how a school of architecture works?*

Siza: The design of the school of architecture was determined in large measure by the site. In addition, the program called for the accommodation of five hundred students. The specifications had been very tightly defined by the state and I could use only twenty percent of the space for circulation. Every architect knows that the halls and the corridors play an important role in the life of a school, because this is where people encounter each other freely and spontaneously form groups. With such a restricted distribution of space it is difficult to make this happen. This was one of the reasons why the project was broken down into a series of pavilions. I needed less space for circulation in each pavilion because by reducing floor area given over to the vertical core, I was able to redistribute the surplus, thereby attaining twenty-five percent in other parts of the building. The pavilions are organized about a patio from which one can look over the river. This was another advantage to the approach: it enabled me to maintain views over the river from different parts of the site. At a certain stage, the building had been conceived as a large and compact block with a central court. With such a form, modeled after the eighteenth-century bishop's palazzo in Porto, I could retain a land fall running down to the river. I was in favor of using such a strong structure and leaving the residual space free, but then I found it impossible to continue with this idea. The palazzo typology was out of scale with the neighboring buildings, and a school does not have enough urban protagonism to justify that. So I decided I had to go in another direction. I took the program and broke it up, realizing that one would now be able to see the river from the studios. Then I understood that I could save and redistribute the restricted circulation space. I began to see the pavilions as a series of towers, and to establish a flexible interrelationship between one tower and the next. When I finished all this, along came another architect and placed a big building behind the school, just like that.

Goldman: *What is essential for the education of the young architect, and what is merely a changing response to the demands of fashion? Is it important to learn to draw? And how important is it to think in terms of images?*

Siza: Prior to the 1974 revolution in Portugal, the climate in the universities was one in which we fought against the fascist regime. As a punishment, many students were sent to fight the colonial war in Africa after they finished their studies. If they were exceptionally militant, they might be sent in their second year, particularly if they had collaborated in demonstrations against the government. Thus, within the army there arose a nucleus of very brave and intelligent people who eventually made the revolution. However, in the architecture school at the time of the revolution, designing was considered a reactionary crime. Everything was up for discussion, for participation in a very general sense. The traditional curriculum was supplanted by social science disciplines, sociology, psychology, and so on. For a short while, each of them in turn would become the nucleus of the curriculum. Everything was then pursued in terms of the central element or discipline. Then this would disappear and along would come another one, geography, or something of the sort. When the revolution came, the School of Porto participated in the recuperation of the center of the city for working families. The people were invited to discuss these projects, and there were those who even claimed that we should not make projects until the people had invented a new architecture, the architecture of the revolution. Then the workers began to say, "You *talk* too much *about* houses. Please *make* projects, and we'll talk about them later." While some students still resisted returning to design, others went back to school and, realizing that they could not even detail a window, began to ask their teachers how it should be done. Things began to change, and among those who had resisted design, there were some who were very good, intelligent, and they took over the teaching. There followed a period during which the curriculum was discussed in depth. I emphasized drawing because it is essential that an architect learn to see and to understand, and drawing is a very important discipline by which to develop this capacity. The eventual outcome was a concentration on four disciplines: history, drawing, project development, and construction. It was a reduced curriculum, and the school was still small and rather open.

We developed the idea that the architect is a specialist in nonspecialization. Building involves so many elements, so many techniques, and such different kinds of problems, that it is impossible to command all the requisite knowledge. What is required is an ability to interrelate diverse elements and disciplines. Because architects have a broad overview and not constrained by concrete knowledge, they are able to connect various factors and maintain the synthesizing capacity of nonspecialization. In this sense the architect is ignorant, but he is able to work with many people and coordinate the integration of a vast number of particulars. These are skills one can acquire only through experience. With them, we are able to face the new situations that accompany each project.

I think that it was an unfortunate compromise when architecture was incorporated into the university. I say that the architect is ignorant, but the academy cannot accept this, even as an irony. If, within the array of respectable and traditional disciplines, one department is a maverick, it threatens the entire structure of university.

Audience: *I remember being deeply touched by your book, published in Italian and English as* Professione Poetica *or* Poetic Profession *(1986). In your presentation, we heard a lot about humanity, about your love for people. But I still recall the title of the book. What do you think today about architecture and poetry, and how is this reflected in your approach?*

Siza: We may be commissioned with a prestigious project by a client who loves architecture and expects a certain quality of work from the architect. But even in such a case, I feel that architecture irritates people, or rather what I conceive of as architecture does. To speak of architecture is not only to refer to functional and material issues. For me, architecture exists when someone goes beyond functionality and enters into the antechamber of poetry. Actually the response to functional issues can only be rigorous if this poetic point is attained. The process of projecting is a way of overcoming the constraints imposed by utility and by material. Most people are insensitive to the poetic of the architectural plan and the source of irritation resides in this singular fact. It's like the story of the fools: if everybody is foolish, then the one who is not is the fool. I should hasten to add that I am not the author of the title of the book. I would never write that the architectural profession is poetic, because I am not concerned with creating poetry. However I am convinced that there are moments when we may justifiably associate architecture and poetry. I remember the sensation I felt when I first entered a Frank Lloyd Wright building. I sensed the atmosphere, the density of the space. You cannot easily explain why when you enter some buildings you feel the presence of the building in its entirety. I am thinking of certain large eighteenth-century houses in the north of Portugal, with a chapel, within the confines of a farm, built for people who made a lot of money from agriculture. You enter these houses and have that sensation of what we may call poetic presence.

Audience: *We may regard the design process as a problem-solving procedure. There is an assumption that in the early phases of this process, the architect produces a lot of sketches as a form of inner dialogue between the architect's thoughts and reality. In this process are you aware of external images that influence your creative process?*

Siza: There is a beautiful text by Aalto in which we learn that when he found himself blocked in the design process he would take paper and make a drawing or a painting. Sometimes after such free artistic activity the solution would emerge of its own accord. Then he returned to the table and continued to design. We seem to have a need for such images, many of them coming from the other arts.

Audience: *It seems to me that your buildings are like bodies. I have the sense that they can move, that they are not wholly static. Can you expound upon this?*

Siza: This dynamic character of some buildings arises out of an intention to relate the building to its context. If there is a strong relation to the landscape, a building invariably possesses this dynamism. As to the literal configuration of the body in architecture, it's enough to go to Venice to see how many faces there are in a typical Palladio palazzo, eyes, mouths, etc. I think that architects need help from existing things, from the organic aspects of the body, in order to arrive at good proportions and interrelationships. When the project drifts toward becoming an animal, a monster, however, one has to react. The symmetry of the human body helps to control this tendency toward monstrosity, to control and domesticate it. I think we may make a comparison to literature. In the process of writing a long novel, some writers mention how in a particular instant the characters escape them and they have to try and control them or the novel is ruined. One uses the image of the body as a way of controlling a certain decadence that can arise in a design. Sculptures also have this referential corporeal aspect and help to structure the work. Artistic caprice constantly looks for some basis of proportion and solidity in form.

Audience: *This brings up a delicate issue, namely, the balance between the building as a body and the place of the body in the building. There is a need to* *distinguish between building as large sculpture and building that has sculptural aspects but is still within the tradition of construction.*

Siza: This is what I meant when I referred to a building becoming a monster. When a building approaches zoomorphic form and escapes our control, then it becomes a monster. While all the arts are influential in the development of a project, there is always a problem when one of the aspects becomes dominant. One way I overcome the sculptural temptation, whereby the work may become monstrous (perhaps due to my initial ambition to be a sculptor), is to take myself on a tour of the building. I mentally sketch the sequence of what it feels like to enter the hall, pass through the corridor, enter the living room, etc. I try to get a sense of how the fireplace is positioned, where one can or cannot place the television set—all of those things in the program that directly affect our experience of the space. I have to be the lady of the house, the man of the house, the child, the person who comes to work in the kitchen. As far as the interiority of architecture is concerned, I remain a confirmed functionalist, and I find that such a self-conscious technique may be used effectively as means for overcoming the tendency for architecture to devolve into a sculptural form.

LECTURE
Peter Walker

Landscape architects tend to look at technology with, at best, mixed emotions. We fear that the unremitting expansion of technology imposes threats to the natural systems on which we are dependent. We are well aware of the ecological warnings of Ian McHarg, the land-use ethics of Donald Judd, and the larger political movement that we now call environmentalism. However, I would like to focus on the somewhat narrower urban or suburban scale at which most landscape designers practice.

American landscape projects are invariably commissioned by architects. This is due, in part, to the way our society allocates funds, but it also stems from the Beaux-Arts tradition going back to the middle of the nineteenth century. Compared to the late nineteenth and early twentieth centuries, however, the contemporary design of public open space has changed radically. Today, instead of formal building compositions, elegant courts, plazas, boulevards, and parks, we have what we euphemistically term "infrastructure," an endless system of low-grade roads, freeways, parking lots, and tracks on the surface, and a forest of pipes, wires, vaults, and tunnels underground. There isn't much ground left for the landscape architect. These networks squeeze the pedestrian into a series of narrow, often fragmentary, spaces that have little human scale relative to the large modern buildings served by the infrastructure. Buildings are almost invariably conceived as freestanding objects, often incorporating public open spaces and amenities such as shops and cafes and fed by mechanical elevators and escalators. These functional and profit-driven assemblies attract a constellation of poorly-related open spaces built at different times and by different authors of varying ability. The exteriors rarely aggregate into well-organized open spaces suitable for pedestrian use. Under such conditions, the achievement of a continuous and well-scaled public realm is practically impossible. Over the years, our office has employed a series of strategies to overcome this situation.

An example of suitably conditioned exterior space is the Upjohn Corporation World Headquarters, which sits on a one-hundred-acre campus in Kalamazoo, Michigan. The centerpiece is an administrative building by Bruce Graham of Skidmore, Owings & Merrill (SOM). The original site was a flat, undistinguished Michigan field, an open tract that had to be completely graded, reshaped, and transformed. It was organized and planted as a landscape so as to provide a slightly different perspective from each office. Another SOM project, with Chuck Basset as architect, was designed for the Weyerhaeuser Corporation on a large site located between Seattle and Tacoma, Washington. Here we were able to restructure a largely natural landscape with a lake on one side and a large meadow on the other, drawing the landscape through the building so as to connect these two realms.

As I have already indicated, handling infrastructure is always difficult and never more so than in the case of Crocker Plaza, San Francisco, where we designed a terraced subway entrance in collaboration with Welton Beckett. The garden begins at the street level, with the plaza and the trees stepping down into a courtyard as you enter the subway. In this instance, all of the trees were planted in boxes slung between the tunnels

Upjohn Corporation World Headquarters
Kalamazoo, Michigan, 1957–1961

Weyerhaeuser Corporate Headquarters
Tacoma, Washington, 1974

160 PETER WALKER 1996

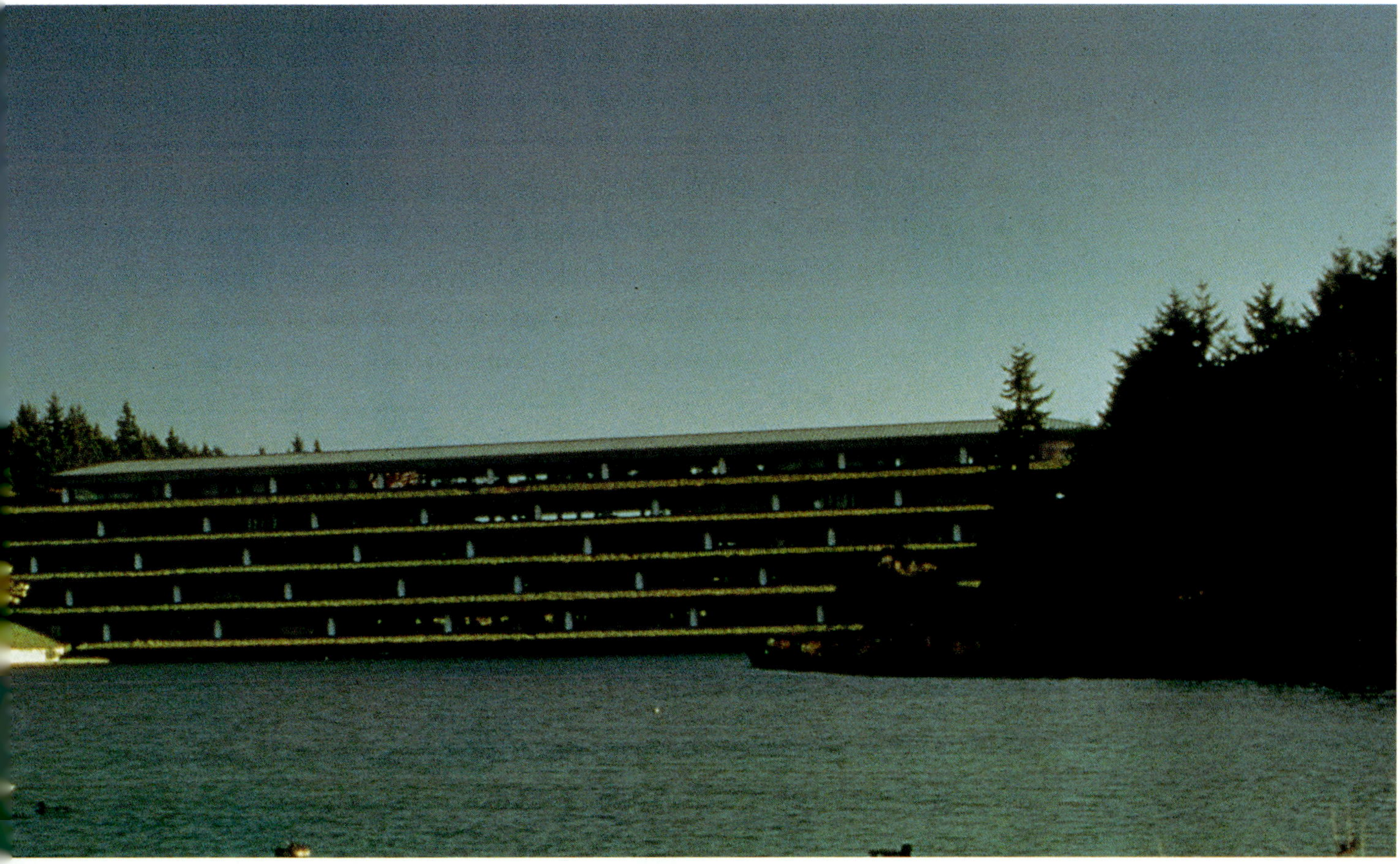

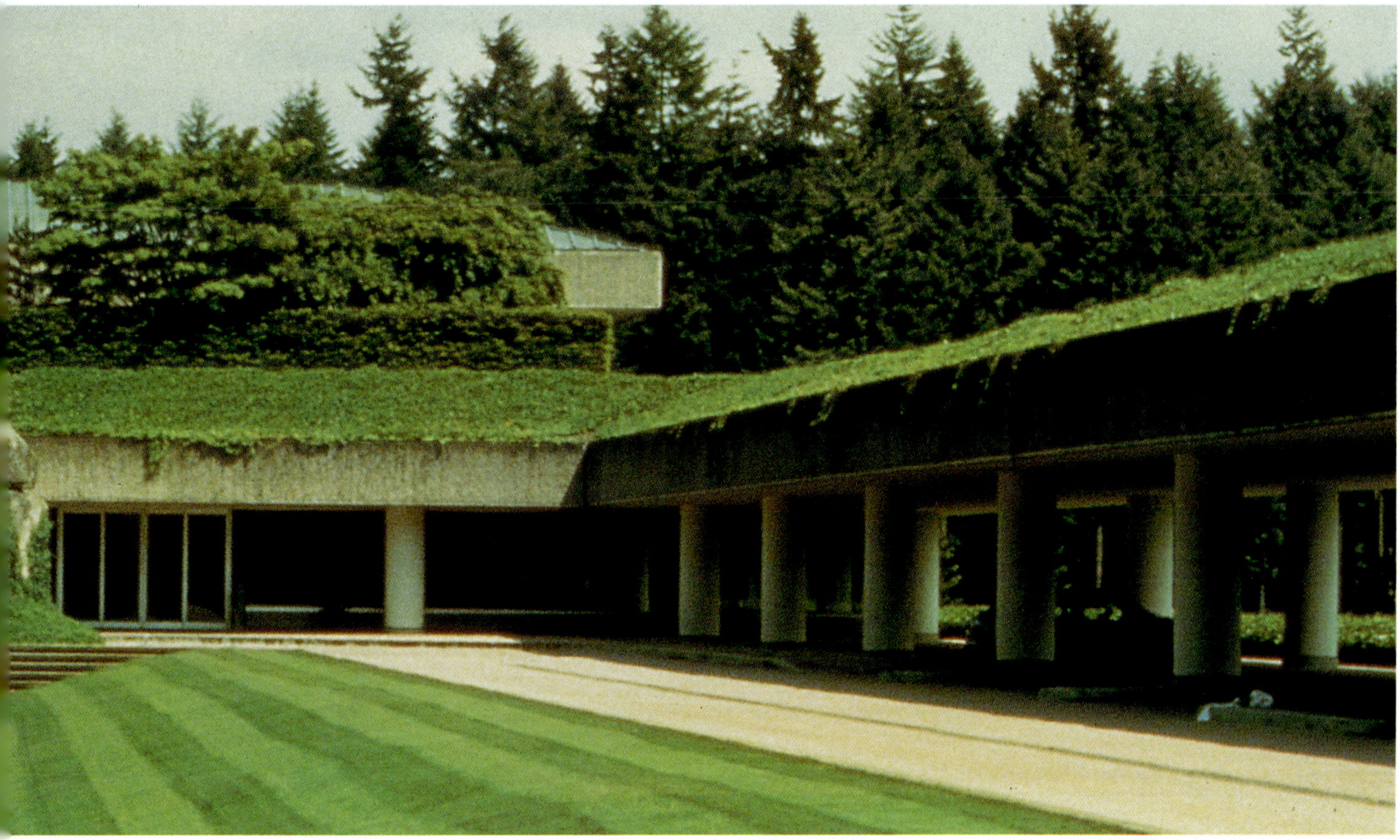

Facing page, top
Burnett Park
Fort Worth, Texas, 1983

Facing page, bottom
Plaza Tower
Costa Mesa, California, 1991, reflecting pool

and pipes that make up a typical undercroft in the San Francisco street system. Occasionally we will find a more sympathetic infrastructure, as in the case of Marina Linear Park in San Diego, where we had to integrate an existing rail line—complete with a little red trolley running along the tracks from San Diego to Mexico. To exploit this feature we devised a linear park planted with flowers and shrubs. We even incorporated the large highway that runs parallel to the tracks. From within the park, one sees rows of trees that lie outside of it, essentially subverting the parallel infrastructure in order to make it part of the park. The park designates separate lanes for pedestrians, joggers, and bicyclists; these are modulated by side alcoves where one can sit and watch the constant movement.

Burnett Park was redesigned for The Anne Burnett and Charles Tandy Foundation (one of the benefactors of the Kimbell Art Museum in Fort Worth, Texas) in honor of Anne Burnett's mother and her grandfather, Burk Burnett, who built the original park in 1936. In the 1930s this area was still a suburb of Forth Worth, but in recent years, it had become hemmed in by tall buildings and very run down. The only thing that remained in good stead was a beautiful stand of magnolias and crape myrtle, around which we redesigned the park. Since the buildings around the perimeter were no longer strictly residential, we reconstructed the park as half plaza and half green space. The idea was to make these two halves, the hard half and the soft half, ambiguous and almost equal. We achieved this by pressing the green area down below the paved level dedicated to pedestrian movement, so the grass is six inches lower and the water six inches lower still. In effect, the entire park is operating below the level of the plaza, although you can move across in any direction. Fort Worth has a very difficult climate: it can change forty degrees in a single day, and it can snow one day and be hot the next. The constant winds make it a landscape architect's nightmare since conventional fountains blow water all over the place, thereby saturating the park. For this reason, we introduced stainless steel wands, illuminating them with fiber optic lights which just touch the tops of the water jets so they dance like candles at night.

Another strategy that we have occasionally adopted is to incorporate collective memory into the design of public space. An anonymous benefactor wanted to give Harvard University a fountain. President Derek Bok insisted that we come up with a fountain design that would invoke the traditional image of New England yet not suffer the typical fountain's fate: fountains are hard to maintain and clean, and thus they are eventually filled with dirt and planted with tulips. We proposed a low podium sixty feet in diameter of New England stone, with no particular pattern except on its outside edge. We buried the stones in Japanese fashion so they were all almost the same height and made them smooth enough so they were easy to stand or sit on. As this stone circle approaches the center it becomes denser, and a mist fountain arises and dematerializes the stones at the center. This is a very simple yet unconventional fountain. We did not situate it at the center of axial paths. Instead we ran the stones across the lawn, across the asphalt, just wherever they landed, even containing a tree within the perimeter. The fountain assumes a different aspect in each season. It has a wonderful cooling quality in the

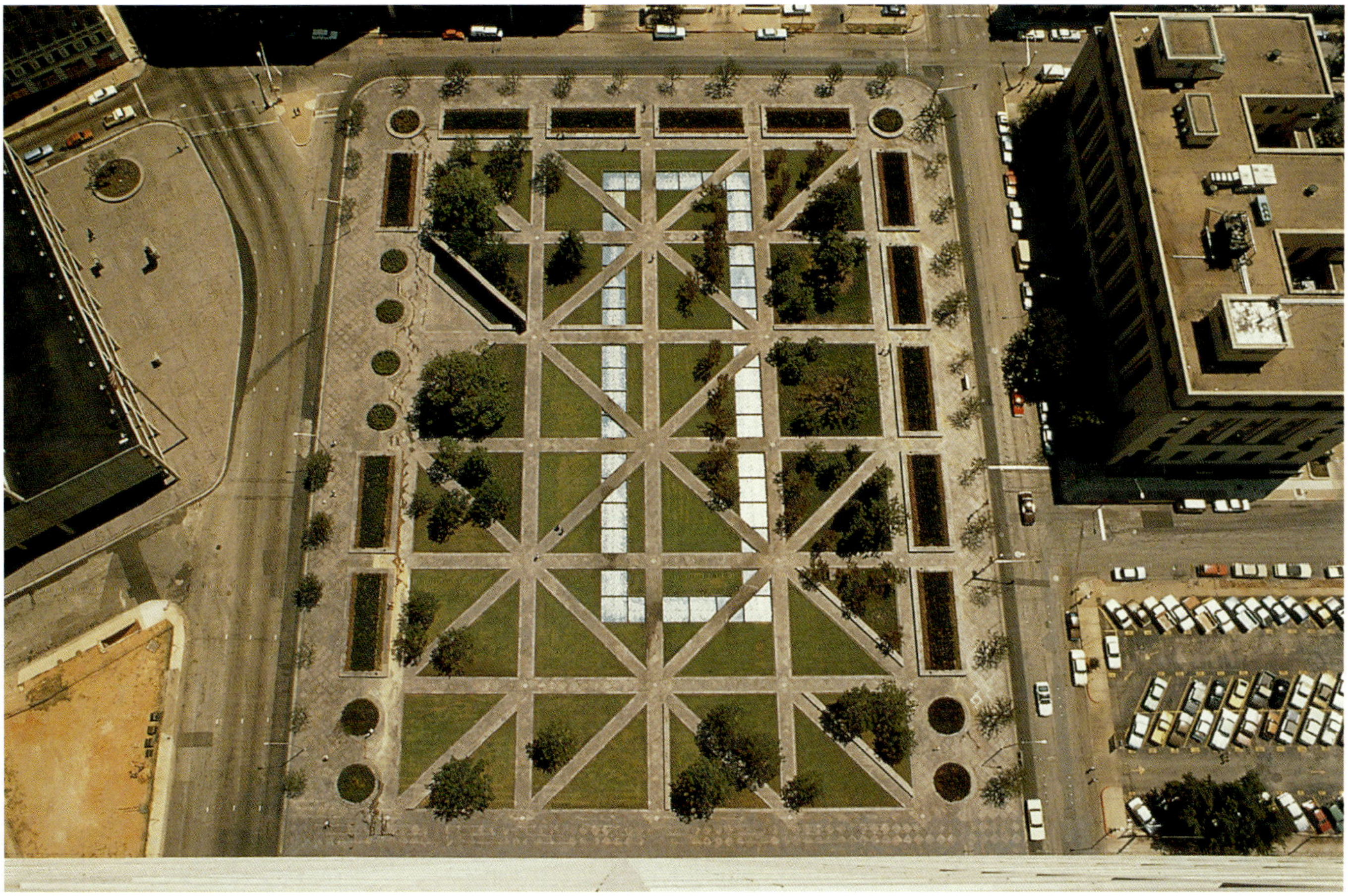

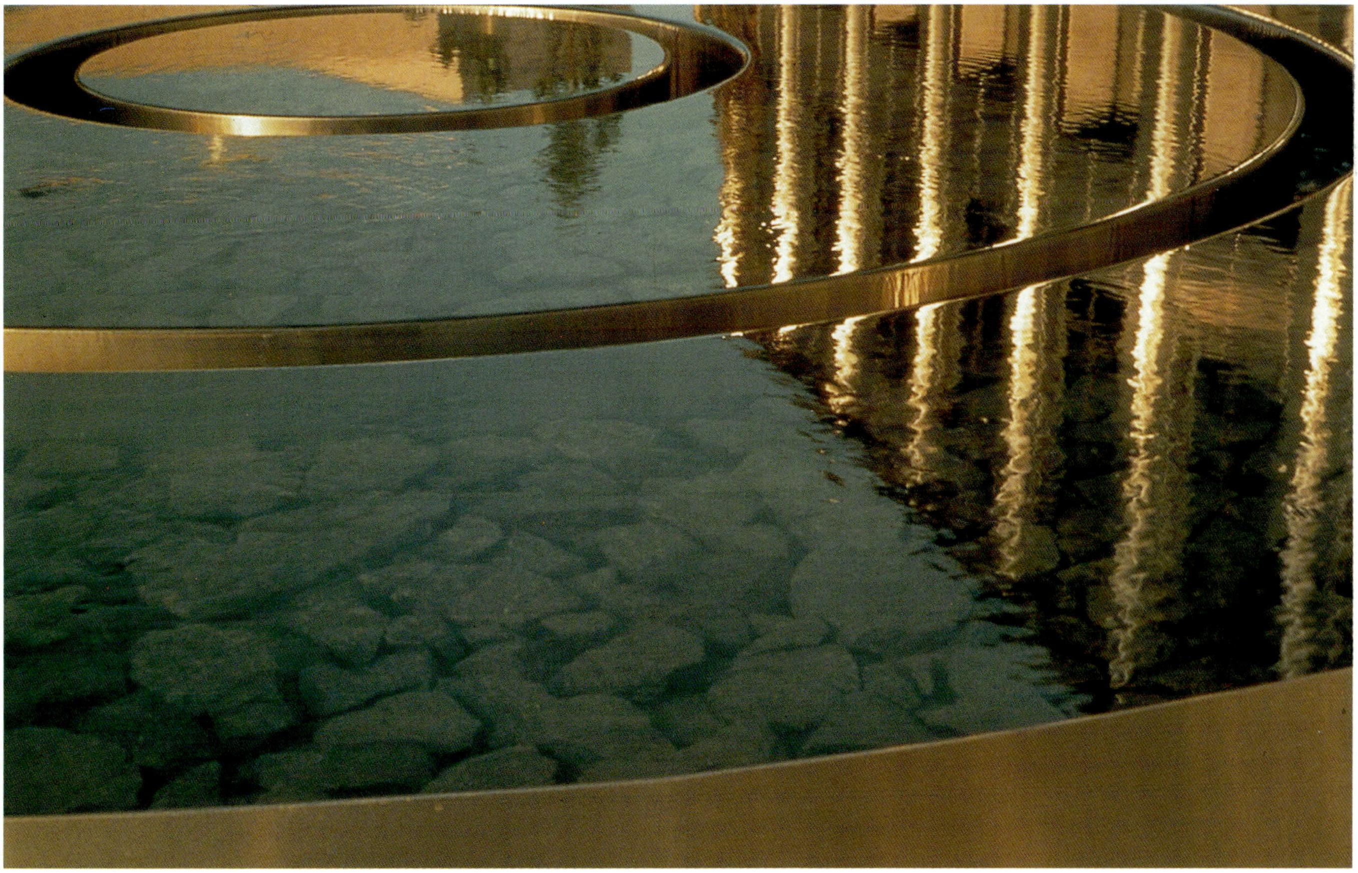

Marina Linear Park
San Diego, California, 1988–present

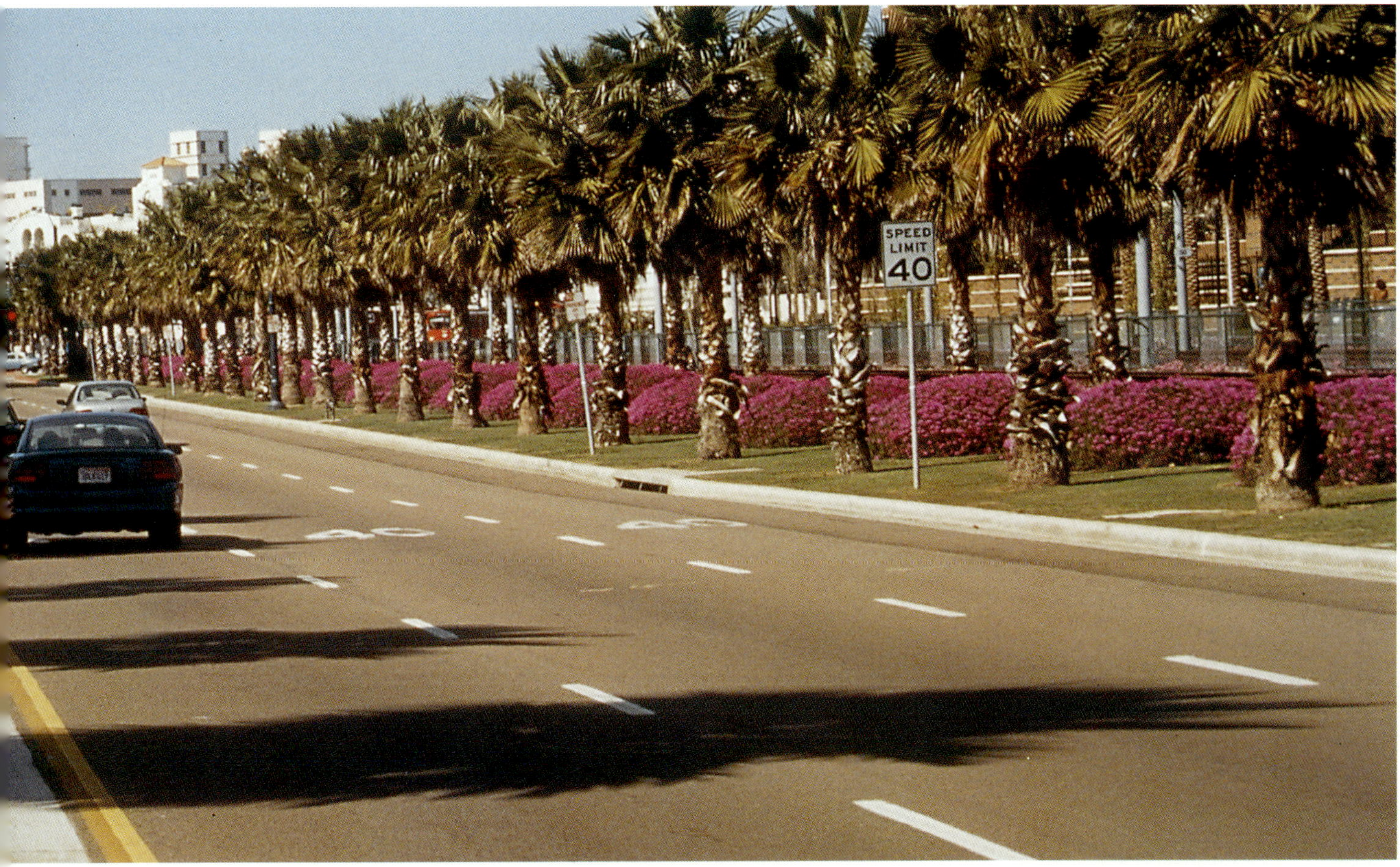
SPEED
LIMIT
40

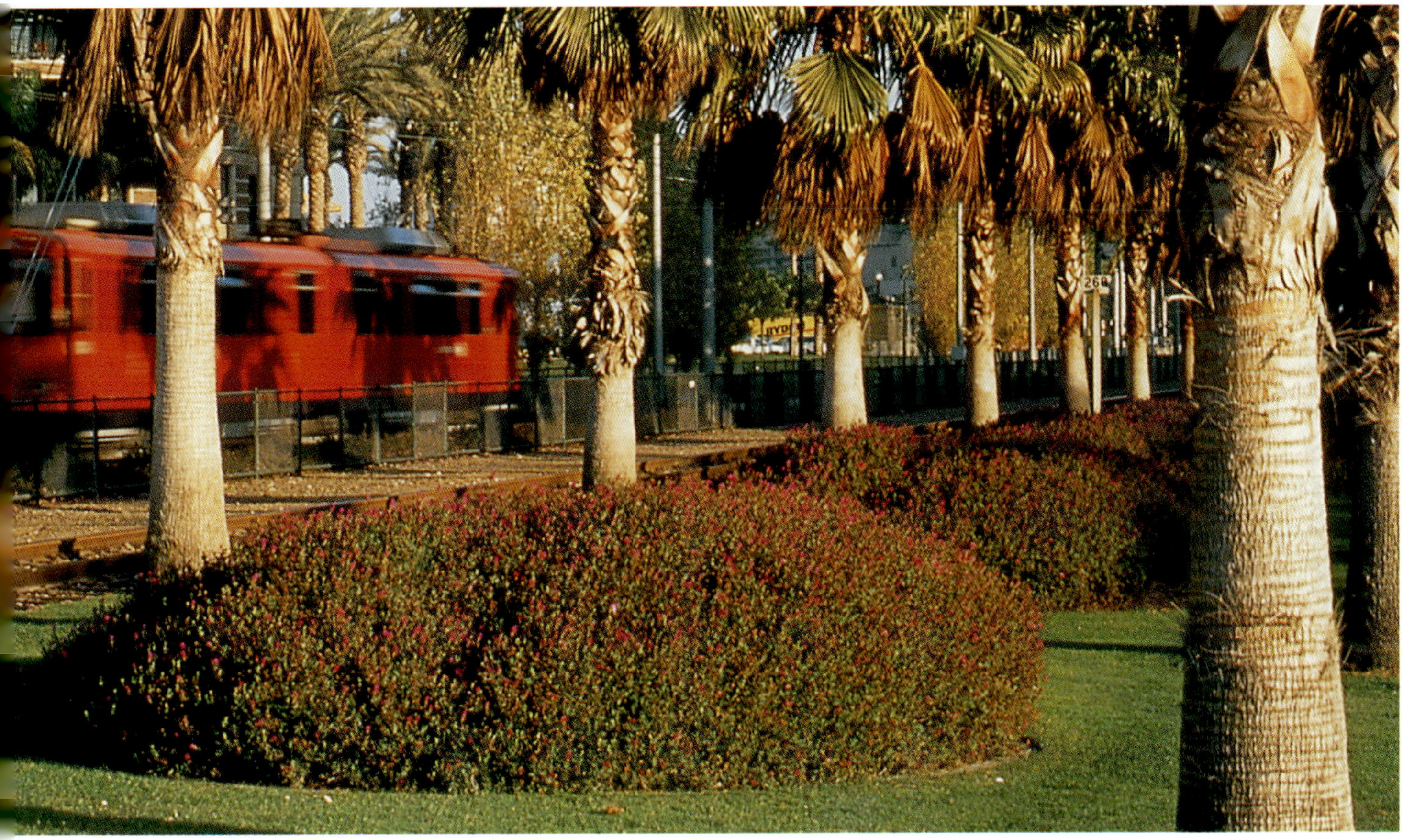

Facing page, top
Center for Advanced Science and Technology (CAST)
Harima Science Garden City, Hyogo Prefecture, Japan, 1993

Facing page, below
IBM Japan Makuhari Building
Makuhari, Chiba Prefecture, Japan, 1991

hot summer, and freshness to match the spring. It has a nice soothing quality in the autumn. In winter, we pump steam through so one doesn't forget that the fountain is there, creating a hot fountain to correspond to the cool fountain of summer. One may illuminate the mist in the evening so it resembles a theatrical scrim. When you walk through the campus and come out of the old yard, this is the first thing you see. Under certain conditions it is covered by a rainbow in the mist because of the fractionalization of the water.

Arata Isozaki asked us to work with him on the design of the Harima Science Garden City and Town Park, a small community being built around a super-collider for research in high-energy particle physics. Isozaki wanted me to design a Japanese garden, something everyone else in Japan had told me we should avoid. In the end we used modern technology as a way of reinterpreting the local tradition. We designed the garden in homage to all the mountains that had been leveled to make room for this project. The key elements in the garden were two mountains, intentionally larger in scale than the *ryokan* itself. Then came a series of small mountains which may be read as an analogy to a volcanic system. One of our big mountains was of stone; the other was of moss. Across the bottom of the garden was a series of stone lines, some polished, some rough. These extended right into the lobbies of the buildings. We added a mist fountain emerging out of a bamboo grove, filling up the entire lower portion of the garden. When the mist fountain is active, all the low stone elements disappear. Only the mountains remain, rising above the mist. When the fountain is turned off, the mist dissipates and the ground plane reappears. We even went so far as to crown each of our small volcanoes with a cypress tree, serving as an analogy for the plume of the volcano, complete with a little red light on the top of each tree. In effect, we have designed a light which will rise higher and higher as the tree matures.

The Boeing company, the largest employer in Seattle, bought a race track dating from 1936 in Renton, a place situated halfway between Tacoma and Seattle. Boeing thought nobody would mind if they reused this site as a new headquarters for the company, and thus planned to construct a series of office buildings and training facilities. However, in the United States, there are complex environmental laws and it turned out that the race track qualified as a protected wetland. This led to Boeing's request that we organize the site as both an administrative campus and a wetland. In wetlands, water doesn't move on the surface, but actually permeates the soil and flows underground, thus allowing a varied number of species to grow. In a riparian area, certain plants are found virtually under water. Meanwhile, all the trees are generally located on slightly higher ground. Instead of trying to recreate the diversity and complexity of a native forest, we planted the area as would a nurseryman or a forester. Ecologists provided a list of trees found in local forests. Following their recommendations, we planted these trees in a series of rows, in the same proportions as those growing in a historic forest. The streams and wetlands follow a more natural curvilinear pattern, in contrast to the geometric order of the new forest. We aligned the trees toward Mt. Rainier. This project realized a very complex landscape by operating across an enormous distance both spatially and temporally.

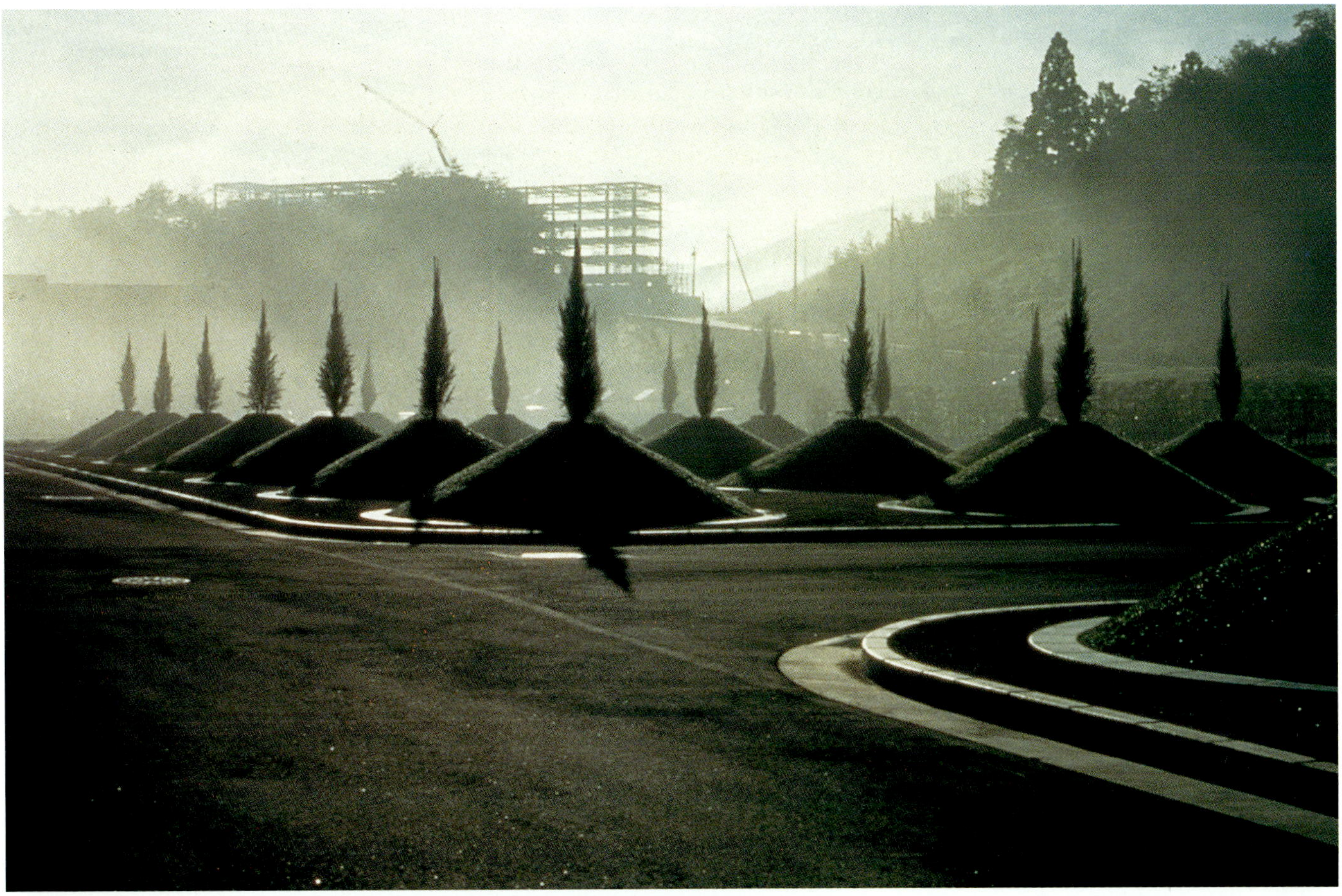

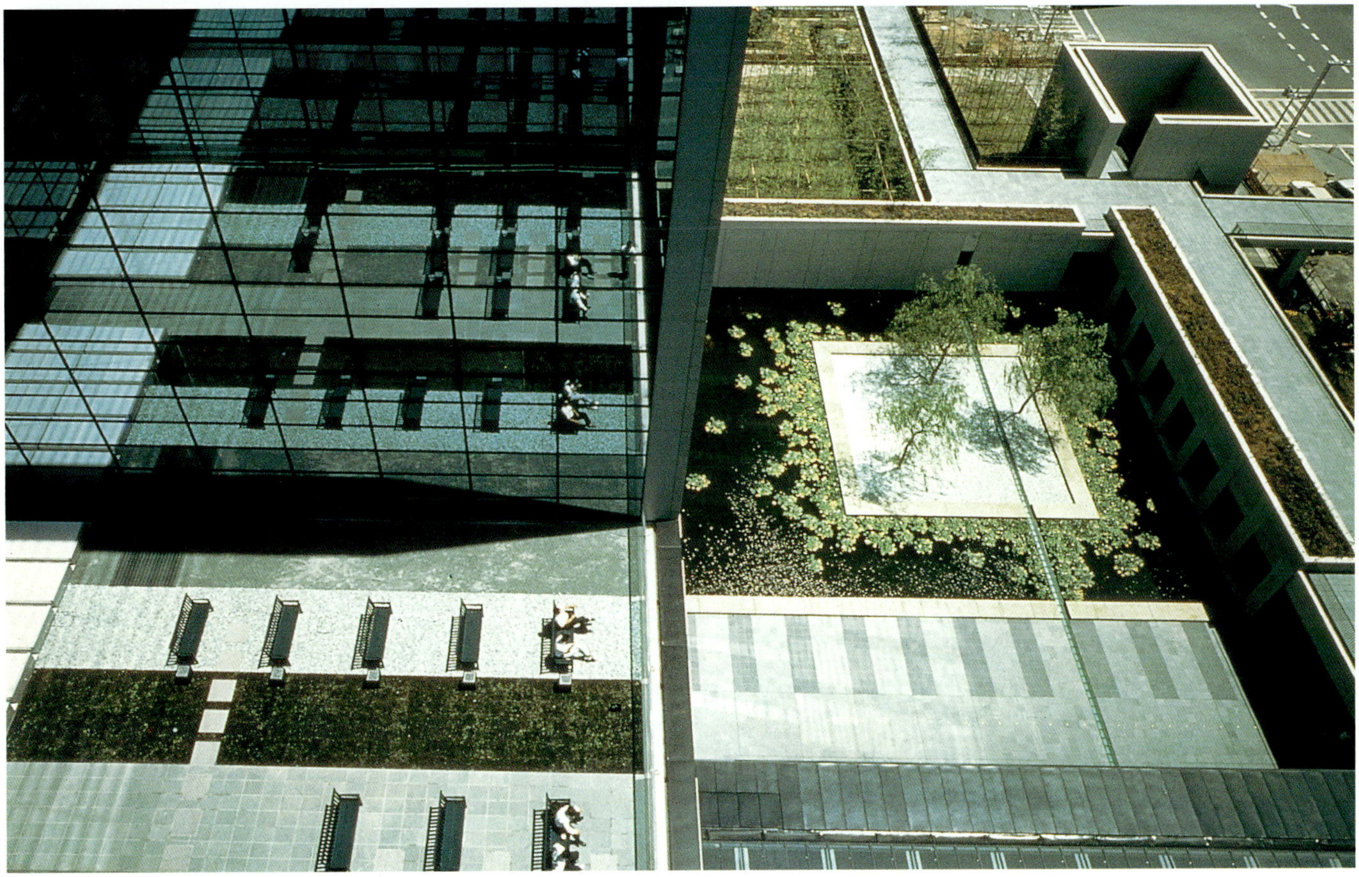

Occasionally we get a chance to intervene in a polemical way at the level of the infrastructure. We were asked by the architects RTKL, Pierre Lesage and Sandy Anderson, to formulate a proposal for the extension of the Grand Axis through La Défense, across western Paris, and out through Nanterre. All the technological infrastructure you can imagine was packed into this linear band: highways, trains, services, and tunnels of all kinds. We projected a two-hundred-foot-wide strip meadow, which would run from the base of La Grande Arche, up onto the podium of La Défense, and across the Seine out into the countryside for three kilometers. The aim was to connect modern Paris and the original agrarian landscape. We planned a series of bosquets on either side of this band, which would accommodate markets, cafes, etc. There would be a helix running through the meadow between the two sides. We had the intention of embedding millions of tiny lights into the sixty-grass meadow, sown with a mixture designed to survive and flower all year long. Conceptually it was the horizontal equivalent of Jean Nouvel's Tour Sans Fin, his vertical monument for La Défense. During our presentation, we were asked if we were prepared to construct half the plan. We refused, insisting that to build less than the entire project would miss the point. We did not get the commission.

The last project I want to discuss is Solana, commissioned by the IBM Corporation and Maguire Thomas Partnership. Situated between Dallas and Fort Worth, Solana actually straddles two counties, Southlake and Westlake, with a highway passing between. When we began work on the project, it stood at about eight hundred acres; now it's grown to almost nine hundred. The commission was to situate seven million square feet of office space in open countryside. They wanted to achieve this in a new, sensitive manner. I find it essential to educate the client if one is going to successfully realize imaginative and responsible works of this scale. For this reason, we begin a project like this with a very intense period of research, during which we prepare an exhaustive physical assessment of the site. In this case, we made a geological, geographic, ecological, and hydraulic analysis of the entire area. We assembled a history of each plant or species found there. This analysis was put together in such a way that, at the end of the three- or four-week assessment period, everyone on my team, Romaldo Giurgola, Ricardo Legorreta, Barton Myers, and the various engineers, was thoroughly informed about the site. Everybody was thinking about how best to place buildings on this site rather than turning first to the actual building program. It was an interesting experience, with the design process taking about three months altogether. During this time, we established ground rules: the restrictions governing building height, placement, and parking strategies. We decided to preserve the older trees in large areas of the site, in the meantime forming a "bowl" of ample size, with the buildings being placed either inside or outside of this bowl according to their dimension.

The buildings and the landscape are largely organized according to lines of sight. Typically these lines of sight turn from a single point in two directions. In this manner, we tried to connect urban areas to the natural areas and to construct a sequence of spaces with a network of visual links to be perceived as you walk or drive through the project. We

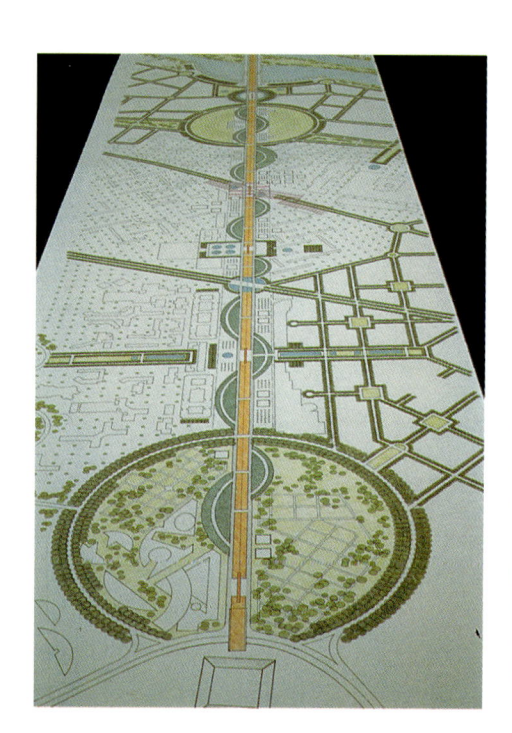

Grand Axe Competition Entry
La Défense (Paris), 1991

Solana
Westlake and Southlake (Dallas),
Texas, 1985–1991

encountered the usual prejudices among the users of the buildings, with the people on the courtyard side regarding themselves as superior to those on the meadow side.

We tried to keep the landscape very flat, because that is its nature. It naturally comprises a series of lifts between large, flat plains, while beyond this layered plateau lies the meadow itself. Some parts of this land are grazed, and in some places the site is so flat that a stream can do no more than meander its way through it. We planted the banks of such streams very heavily, which is typical of waterways in this region. People can come here to find shade, walk down the stream, and then move through a tube of green, even on the hottest days.

From the center of the conference center and cafeteria complex designed by Giurgola, you can look out past the office buildings and down the waterway. In the other direction lies the meadow, where the few existing trees have been left and other parts have been reforested. Coming into this complex, you pass a series of fountains announcing the entrance to a group of parking areas and garages brilliantly arranged by Giurgola. In the center of the complex is the village, which is actually a shopping center plus two office buildings and a hotel. Legorreta spun the shopping center into a circle. We surrounded this form with differentiated parking lots so there is no sense that this is a strip shopping center. Because we were missing buildings, like missing teeth, we introduced temporary gardens in areas which will later receive buildings. We pursued the same flexible strategy in certain other areas, because we couldn't predict exactly what would be built.

Although small and functionally insignificant, the village rises higher than the rest of the development, thus forming the center of the complex. The village took the form of a more dramatic, vertical architecture, whereas almost all of the rest was horizontal and low. In the temporary gardens, the paths are made of grass and everything else is gravel in an inversion of the conventional relationship. We don't want people to like these too much, because eventually there will be buildings on these sites.

Legorreta was a lot of fun to work with because he uses color flamboyantly, yet skillfully. We always tried to find a relationship between his colors and the landscape, one that you wouldn't exactly expect; like setting green against blue. I spent a lot of time trying to come up with plants that would provide just the right color. Landscapes operate throughout the year, and they have to be beautiful in every season. To achieve this, we have to exploit seasonal changes, something architecture can barely do and landscape architects tend not to do enough. Following Legorreta's cue of building walls and then punching holes in them, we built a hard ground plane, punched holes in it, and filled them with water. We attempted to find an extension of the kinds of ideas he works with, using the materials of landscape architecture.

Between the hotel and the office buildings in the village, we built a fountain out of stone. It's similar to the Harvard fountain in that even though it is constructed of densely laid stones, when the mist rises, it virtually

Facing page
Solana
Village Center, Westlake and Southlake (Dallas), Texas, 1985–1991

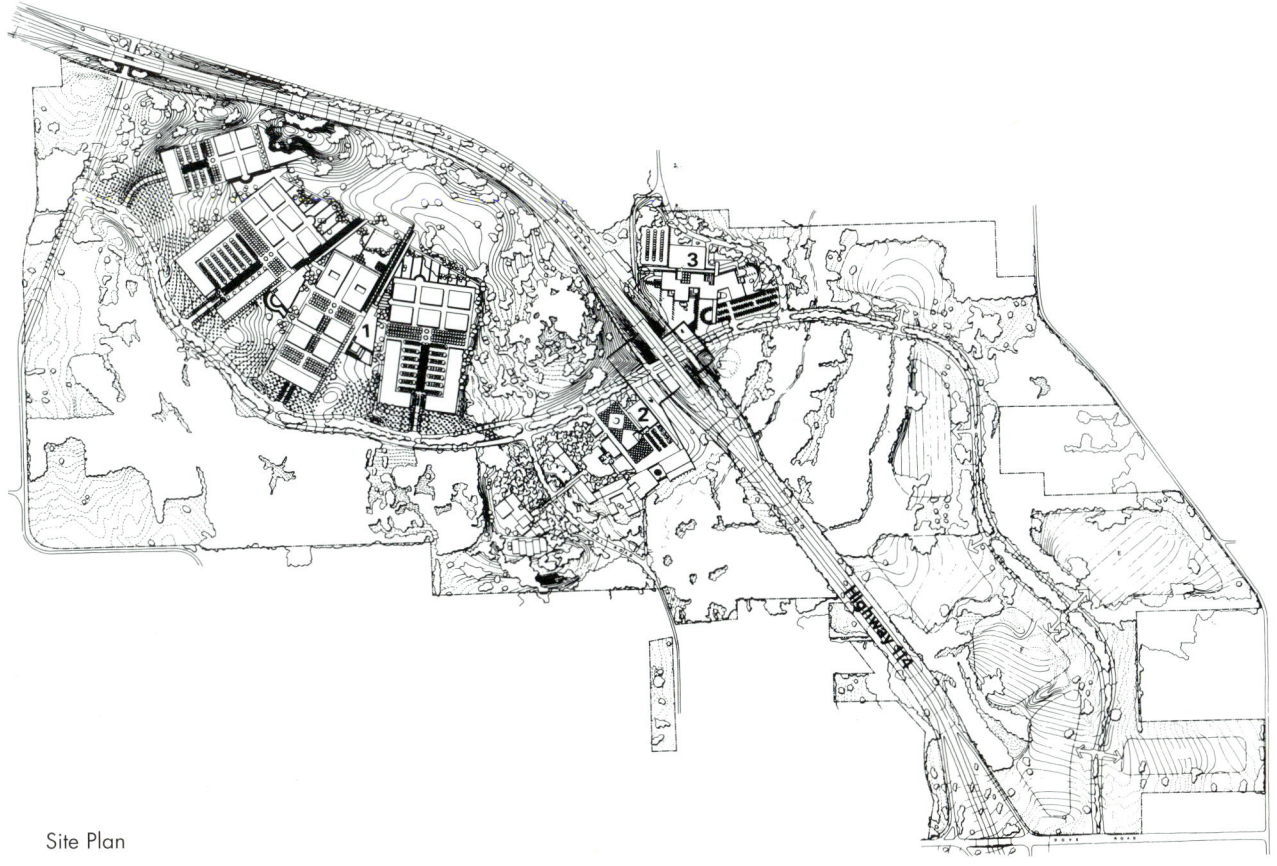

Site Plan

Above
Solana
Westlake and Southlake (Dallas),
Texas, 1985–1991

Right
IBM Japan Makuhari Building
Makuhari, Chiba Prefecture, Japan, 1991

Solana
Westlake and Southlake (Dallas), Texas, 1985–1991

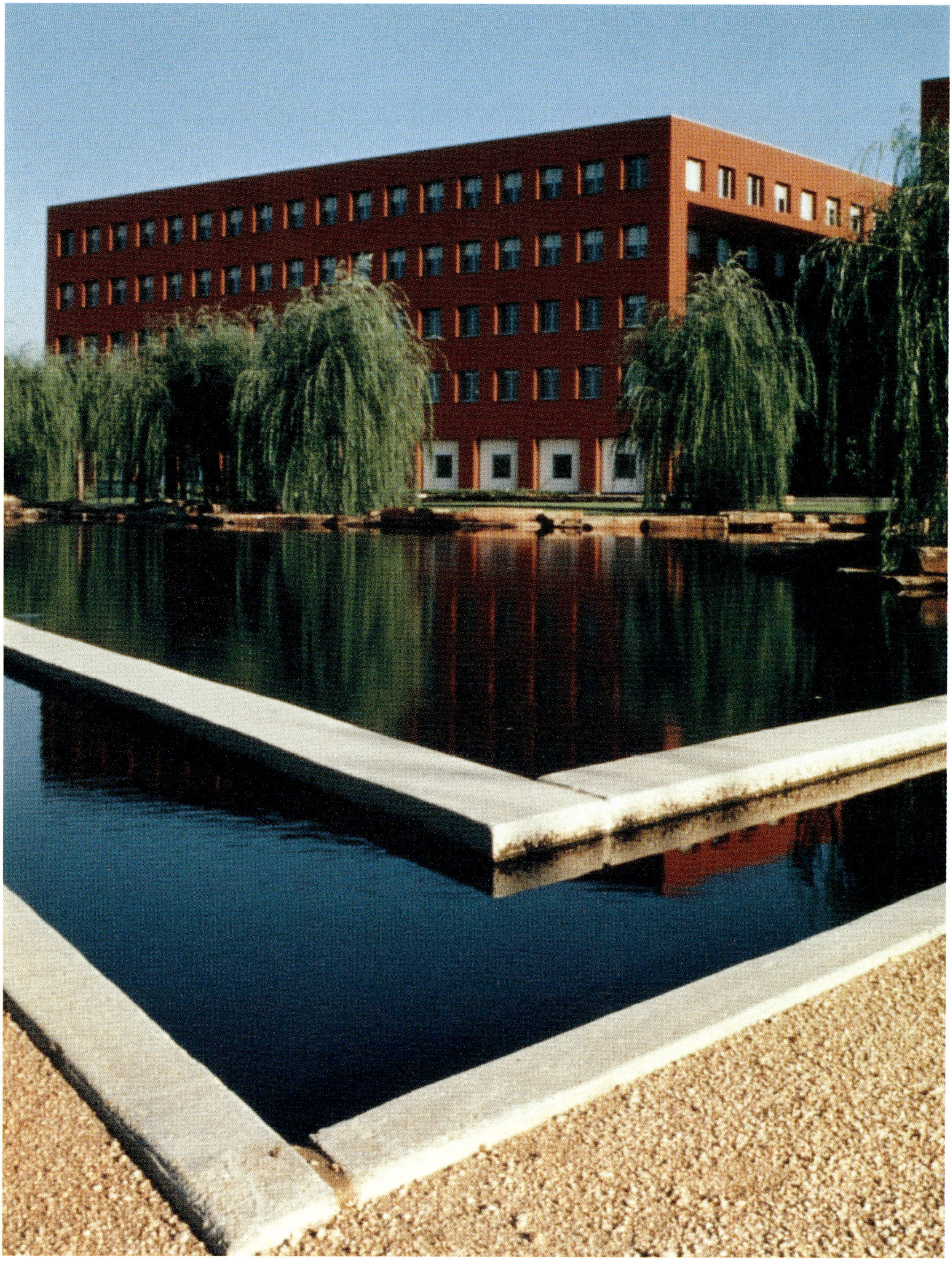

Detail of site plan

Above and facing page
Solana
Westlake and Southlake (Dallas),
Texas, 1985–1991

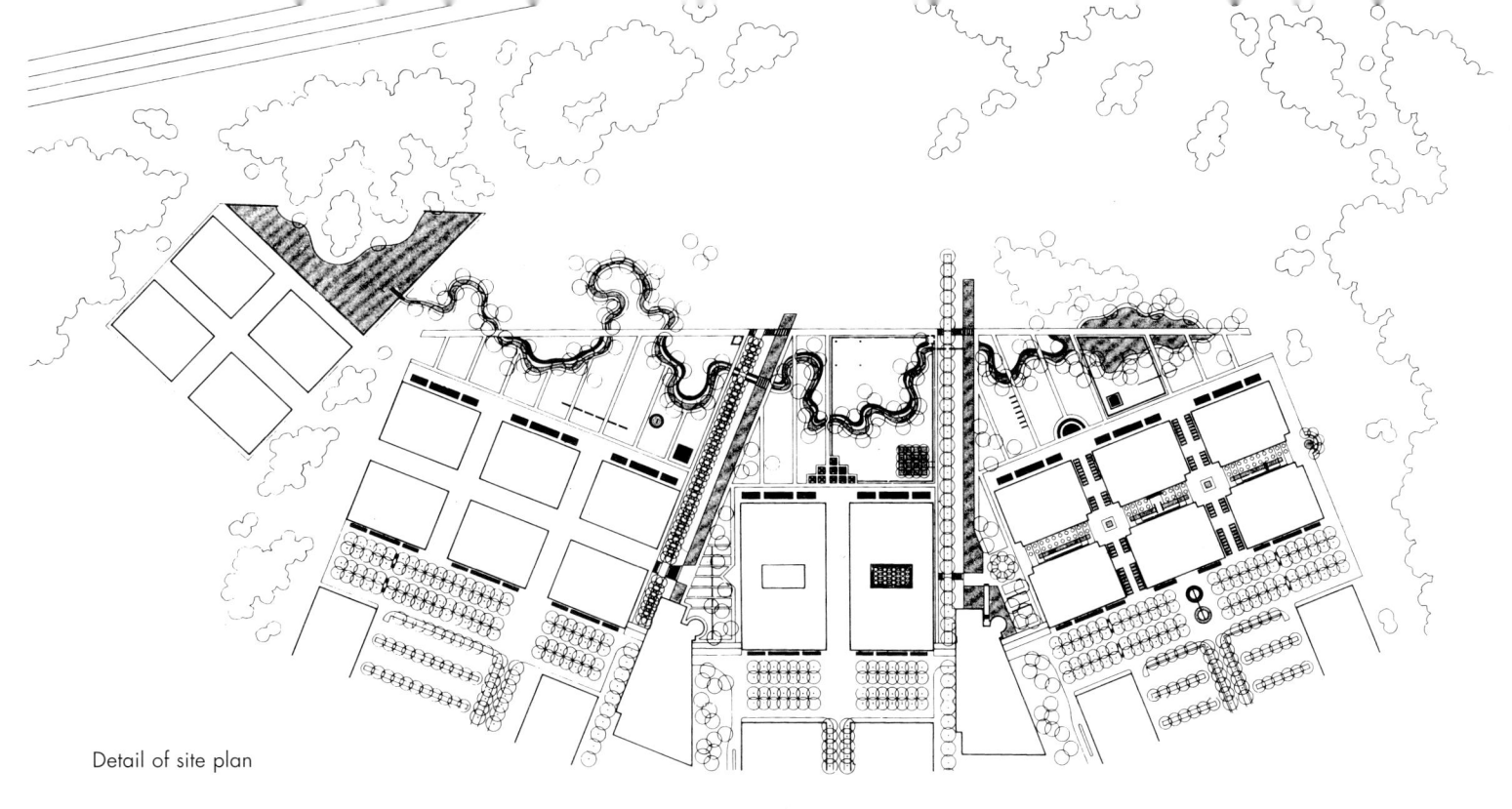

disappears. At Solana, the fountain represents not only Native American structures, but also Native American attitudes. It alludes to the prehistory of the site. The only problem is that many people in Texas drive trucks, and, occasionally, when the fountain is completely enshrouded in mist, people run their trucks right into it.

Within the almost nine hundred acres of the project, we have some four hundred acres of preserve, with about 325 of those devoted to a meadow. When we found the site, it was not a particularly rich meadow. It had been grazed very heavily and over half of the topsoil had been lost. There were a few handsome trees that stood up to the grazing and somehow survived, but they were almost the only feature of this meadow that we found in good condition. To repair the rest of it, we took the topsoil off of every single road, building, or parking lot site, stockpiled it, and put it on the meadow, thereby doubling the amount of topsoil. An ecologist told us that when the German settlers first rode into this area on horseback, the grasses were as high as their saddles, which would probably be about four and a half feet. It must have been magnificent to come across these meadows then. It probably took about a sixty-seed mix to produce so much tall grass, but despite Ladybird Johnson's efforts to replant the meadows in Texas and in the Southwest generally, we could find only a forty-seed mix. At the end of the first year, there was a ruddy looking mix of flowers and grasses with a very complex structure. The reason all of this takes some time is that you have to go through not just one year, but also the drought cycle, which sometimes lasts five or even seven years. The complexity of the seed mix has to be protected throughout that long period. Grazing does the opposite; it reduces the number of seeds, and then the droughts take their toll. This meadow has been in place for about four years and it is becoming much richer. I think about all the people sitting up in their boxes: IBMers, staring at their computers. I hope I have succeeded in enticing them to look out of their square holes from time to time to watch what is happening in the meadow.

DISCUSSION

Peter Walker
Shlomo Aronson

Shlomo Aronson: *When one looks at your curriculum vitae, one can't stop thinking about the diversity and the different paths you have elected to take. There are many examples of promising architects who reach their peak and a few years later their production deteriorates. With you, it's new things all the time.*

Walker: This may be due in part to the fact that I've lived in a very turbulent time. Forty years ago, in the 1950s, we started at the very end of the modern movement. Gropius, Le Corbusier, and Mies had virtually stopped practicing by the time I got out of school. My teacher and subsequent partner Hideo Sasaki was a brilliant organizer, and he inspired many of us. In some ways, he was a modernist in that he aspired to the kind of modernism represented by the great American corporate architectural offices, such as The Architects Collaborative (TAC) and Skidmore, Owings & Merrill (SOM). When I first got out of school, there were one or two landscape architects, among them Dan Kiley and Lawrence Halprin, who had started to work at a very large scale. They hadn't the slightest idea how to execute work of vast dimensions, because these were the first commissions on this scale since the 1920s. There had of course been large projects in the first part of the twentieth century, but because of the Depression and World War II, there had been a hiatus of almost thirty years. There were few firms where one might gain initial experience with the exception of Thomas Church. In the main, we just started from scratch. Kiley and Sasaki started their offices without any real experience. Over the next ten or fifteen years, however, we began to assemble huge firms that ended up with hundreds of people in them. Sasaki's office now has I think six or seven hundred people. SWA, my branch of the office, has another two hundred or so. Unwittingly building up these huge offices, we knew what we were supposed to be trying to do, but we didn't know where we were heading. We certainly didn't know what the future had in store.

In the mid-1970s, the world suddenly changed. While we had developed managerial and technical skills of an order that hadn't existed since the 1920s, there was a sudden shift in the economic climate and the social purpose of the United States. In particular, everything became privatized. At the same time I personally became tremendously confused about my direction, and questioned a lot of assumptions I had held since graduation. Consequently, I went back to school to rethink what we were all supposed to be about—only this time as a faculty member. There seemed to be an enormous discrepancy between the work we were doing at that moment and the ideals we had learned in school, the dreams that had been imparted to us. By the mid-1970s, we had gone through the environmental revolution. Things were becoming regional in context. All the natural sciences were being brought in, and that was really changing the complexion of things. When I returned to Cambridge, I realized that we had moved away from design and into management. The scale of our operations and the scope of our work had transformed us from what Thomas Church and Lawrence Halprin had been doing in the 1950s into the operators of very large managerial systems. The leaders of these large offices were now managers rather than designers. So, I decided to start an atelier. It was nothing very fancy. We were just going to start a small office with advanced students, which is what an atelier is. It's young people and one senior person. I started practicing as a teacher with two or three young people. And again, I don't think the ideas really came from me, they came from the situation, from the changed viewpoint. Now again, another ten or fifteen years have passed, and the little ateliers have become larger. Now you have Martha Schwartz and George Hargreaves, a completely new generation of individuals who are analogous to Halprin and Church. Of the older generation, only Kiley has maintained an atelier throughout, and this is surely one of the reasons he does such beautiful work.

Aronson: *During the late 1970s, you became interested in art and you started to introduce artistic concepts into projects. How did this happen?*

Walker: When I went back to school, I gave a course that focused on the relationship of the earlier generation—Garrett Eckbo, Church, Halprin, and Kiley—to the art of their time. We explored the connections between the designs they had done and the cultural and artistic ideas of the time. It took us two or three years to get this research seminar working, and there were a lot of things that came out of the course which changed my life. Above all, I began to see the discrepancy between my rather picturesque approach to landscape at that time and the kind of art that was being produced by artists like Carl Andre and Donald Judd.

I became increasingly involved with minimalist paintings and sculpture. I began to wonder how you could make a landscape out of squares of metal, or boxes, or something like that. And I remember going with Bill Johnson, my present partner, and a group of students to France one year. We started in Tours, and we went up the Loire and saw practically all of the châteaux, looking at them fairly carefully. We were spending days on them, rather than just taking a quick tour. By the time we got to Vaux-le-Vicomte and Versailles, I had started to figure out how you could do minimal sculpture and make landscapes, because André le Nôtre had been doing just that.

As time went on, I derived less from the art itself and more from the attitude of minimal artists toward their work. In landscape architecture, you never have an adequate budget. If you look at something minimally, however, you can do much more with much less.

Aronson: *But you do find quite a lot of environmental art coming from artists today, rather than from landscape architects. Would you agree that dealing with the environment as a work of art is more an artistic concern than a topic for landscape architecture?*

Walker: I also think landscape architects carry an exaggerated view of how much they can actually accomplish at a high level. Politically speaking, we take ourselves much too seriously, while culturally we don't take ourselves seriously enough; that is to say, our artistic ambitions are probably not high enough. One of the problems with the environmental revolution was not its high-mindedness, but its normative nature, where you try to take huge areas and fix them as opposed to taking smaller areas and making them magnificent. I think that we need to do both; but, more importantly, we need to honor both activities. They're both necessary. Many landscape architects are actually doing both, and they have to realize that the terms change from the larger scale to the smaller scale, the artistic demands being greater in the case of the latter.

As for artists, in the mid-1970s, the National Endowment for the Arts put together a series of programs patronizing design and the visual arts. Special funds were allocated to cities in order to further collaborations between designers and visual artists. At the time, many designers and artists responded to this idea. By the 1990s, however, artists began to realize that the public realm is not necessarily conducive to creating art. There are public meetings where you present your art work and they chew it to pieces. Artists don't like that any more than we do. So a lot of them have withdrawn from the environmental scene. But there are artists like Mary Miss and Richard Fleischner who have persisted and crossed over.

We landscape architects do have wonderful tools and tremendous skills. The culture in general doesn't appreciate this, not even architects. I once had an exchange with Frank Gehry when he was in the process of designing a lopsided structure. I said, "Frank, if I plant a eucalyptus tree next to this little box you've tipped and crunched, it's going to dwarf this thing, it's going to make it unimportant." He looked at me and said: "That's ridiculous. This thing is a piece of sculpture; this is more important." So I went over to the model and I just made a pile of sponge next to the thing, and of course it wiped it out. It is perhaps no coincidence that I rarely work with him anymore.

Aronson: *On the way here we were talking about Isamu Noguchi. Would you mind repeating our discussion?*

Walker: Well, we went to the Noguchi garden this morning. I have been looking at that in photographs all my mature life. I didn't know Noguchi terribly well, but I'd worked with him a couple of times, and we had close mutual friends. I have been to his place in Takamatsu, and I've written about his work. But one of the things that surprised me this morning was how different the outdoor museum is from the impression I hitherto had of it from photography. This is a lesson to us all. We all come and give these slide shows, but neither as students nor as practitioners should we take any of it at face value. You have to see the stuff because it's different in reality. Sometimes it's better and sometimes it's worse; but in any event, it's different. I was really surprised, because there are a number of moves that he made, like those great rolling plains that move up to the external prospect, which don't photograph. I had never seen the rolling plains until this morning, and they were by far the most impressive thing in the garden. I think Noguchi often made the mistake of being first a sculptor and second a landscape architect. He could just as easily have worked the other way round. He had a tendency to abandon the spatial element. He would move along in a certain direction with a spatial concept and then suddenly he would switch and become objective. I don't think he was aware that he was doing that. Landscape architects have to resist that if they want the landscape to hold. The objective move is so powerful, that you have to be careful not to destroy the space with that one gesture.

Aronson: *Do you feel that the landscape profession lacks critical capacity? People like J. B. Jackson for instance, people who are not just practitioners, but who look at the landscape and try to place it in a context?*

Walker: The modern movement has been plagued by two failings. One is the modernist dictum that history is dead, which isn't true, and has never been true. You see French gardens today and you know that history is not dead. It's just as alive today as it ever was. These are remarkable works of art, great works of landscape. By any standard, they are incredible works. You see Japanese gardens, and it's the same thing. The idea that modernism has no interest in history and has nothing to gain from it is the one great failing of our profession and of modernism generally. The other thing is the failure of criticism. I think a profession without criticism is simply going nowhere, because no critical feedback comes into the profession. The other thing that critics can do is to serve as a bridge between the profession and the culture as a whole. We don't have nearly as much writing about the field as we need, be it descriptive, historical, or critical. I used to have a colleague at Harvard, Al Fine, who would say when he started his classes, "If you want to be famous, learn to write. Your gardens are going to be remote; very remote from your audience." We now have three or four professional critics in the United States, and I've been participating in a movement that is now trying to give them larger currency. I have in mind such writers as Beth Meyer, Marc Treib, and James Corner. Unfortunately, most of their work goes into the landscape journal that is read by perhaps forty people, and this is not enough. It is not even widely read in the profession. It's read mostly by academics, and I think that's much too narrow an audience for the quality of today's critical writing.

Aronson: *Many people, particularly in Europe, have advanced ecology as a saving device instead of getting to the roots of landscape architecture. Don't you think they use ecology as an escape, as a means of trying to find a quantitative—instead of a qualitative—way of describing things?*

Walker: It is virtually impossible for someone who's a landscape architect and who has had some natural science not to care about natural systems. Whether you take a Cartesian, romantic, or Presbyterian view, as Ian McHarg does, I think it's impossible for someone who cares about nature and the out-of-doors not to be interested in these subjects. But I think that the ecology movement has become normative. A generation and a half of the brightest American landscape architects moved away from design and became environmentalists. They were among the most gifted, so we have almost no one of that age practicing in the United States. I know almost no practitioners from Penn, which, given the presence of McHarg, was the center of environmentalism in the United States. My critique is cultural rather than anti-environmental. The last point that I would make is that most environmental action is going to be just as restrictive as planning legislation. You write a series of rules and put them into restrictive law. I don't think that restriction is a bad thing, but it's only half of the picture. Architects, landscape architects, and many planners are initiators. They are people who create solutions to problems. I don't think that these two opposing methodologies are necessarily ideologies, but we have tended to frame the conflict in ideological terms, and I don't think we are going to develop until we rid ourselves of this confusion.

Aronson: *Last night, Jean Nouvel presented the elusive part of architecture, showing how things suddenly disappear, how they merge, how they are not so concrete. Well, here we are in a city that is built with stone, with very durable material, and with trees, both of which are supposed to last for a long time. These are two totally different approaches to design. How do you feel about these two rather antithetical approaches?*

Walker: I was very moved by what Nouvel was saying about the visual realm, and about the degree to which he is able to accomplish his vision. Clearly he's also an artist, and I'm fascinated with artists. When I first started to practice on my own, I was with a group of architects who were classical modernists. They were operating along Miesian lines. They were people from SOM and from Saarinen's office who were interested in classical issues. They were also very interested in the landscape, particularly those from the Saarinen school. However, they all were interested in rows of streets that were perfectly straight and in trees where each one was identical to the next. In other words, they had an architectural view of how trees should be, and so forth, and I was supposed to make these perfectly straight lines of trees. Well, I totally failed, since I didn't know enough about the technology of landscape; I didn't realize then how such "classical" planting demands constant care in terms of both maintenance and drainage.

One day I was in a Thomas Church garden where he had planted a row of poplars. It was some twenty-five years old. The trees had been reasonably well cared for in their earlier years. They had been trimmed so that they didn't have two leaders, and they were coming out of the ground in a fairly orderly way. He had gravel around them so that the roots were not invasive and the water was going down. He had taken care of a lot of things. By then I knew something about this, and I was appreciative of those techniques. But they weren't straight. And they weren't coming out of the ground like pieces of metal. They were actually moving around. They were very beautiful. I started watching how these things were twisting, slightly moving. And it was much more interesting than a line of poles. Certainly much more interesting than most sculptures that are done that way. It suddenly dawned on me that I had been on the wrong track. It was a little epiphany of discovery. I guess I was on my way. Since then, I've been planning straight lines all over the place and just waiting for them to twist up and do all this kind of strange stuff.

Audience: *I find myself getting more and more involved with landscape. It seems to be inseparable from architecture. It's impossible to deal with architecture with one half of the brain and bring in landscape architecture with the other half. Do you find this division between the two natural or not? That's one question. The other turns on the fact that, in landscape architecture, there is often no program. How do you deal with a field in which there is no program?*

Walker: Well, let me take your first issue, the differences between the two. I went to the Bauhausian graduate school at Harvard, and the myth of the Bauhaus as it was filtered through Harvard was that we were all the same, that we were simply working at different scales. The planners working at the largest scale, the architects working at the next largest scale, the landscape architects at the next, and so forth. That's pretty much nonsense, mainly because we all work with elements at the large scale and at the small scale. But the really dangerous idea in there is that we're all the same. I think they could get away with that concept because they denied the importance of history. The history of landscape architecture, at least in the United States, is drastically different from that of architecture. It comes from a different root and is a consequence of different interests. Architecture grew out of craft and the concept of building, while landscape architecture grew out of Olmsted, Andrew Jackson Downing, and the English landscape garden tradition.

I find it strange that people drift in and out of the two fields or that they would share or combine them. I do my best work with architects who are quite different from me, and who have distinctly different views, and yet with whom I share a mutual respect and an interest in accomplishing something in common through our various methods and different viewpoints. That is probably a more healthy attitude than the idea that we're all peas in a pod.

The lack of program is one of the joys of landscape architecture. It's a field that is constantly in a state of being redefined. Each generation, depending on its approach, redefines the field. It's a little like democracy. It's not supposed to be defined; it's supposed to be worked at. Sometimes you do have a program, and while it's fun to invent, it's also important to have a purpose, although I don't think this has to be functional, it can also be commemorative.

Audience: *As architecture gets more and more international, do you think landscaping will also become international?*

Walker: I think there's an element of internationalism which is bound to appear since a great deal of modern culture is becoming international. However, you can't successfully violate the natural ecological basis of the place. There's either water or there isn't, there's either too much of it or just about enough. You have to deal with those things or the garden fails. I think we have an exaggerated notion of what internationalism is, not just in terms of what is appropriate, but also in terms of what is possible. The first thing I do when I go to a site, even in the United States, is to get in touch with the local farmer or nurseryman and try to find out what's going on. It is important to have this kind of information at the outset. There are local rules that you have to observe.

Audience: *Given the commodity culture in which we live and the proliferation of materials, it seems to me that plants are becoming less important.*

Walker: One of the reasons for this is that we're into a totally urbanized culture that does not want to take care of plants. A crucial issue in all this is water and how it is used, together with the kinds of plants and maintenance that one can expect. The final difference between contemporary and historic gardens can be summed up in one word: maintenance. The reason that I don't plant as much as I would like to is that, if you base the structure of a garden on its plants, you can't count on them surviving. The first thing that most clients tell me is that they want low maintenance, and clearly, a rock is reasonably low on maintenance.

Unfortunately, this is the trend in contemporary culture. It's certainly the case in the United States, if less so in Japan. I use more plants in Japan, and I use them more at higher risk, but I count on the client maintaining them. Most Japanese gardens could not be made in the States today. They wouldn't live through the first three or four years. Through lack of maintenance most early gardens have not survived. As far as maintenance is concerned, universities are notorious and cities are even worse, because when there is a drought, politicians simply stop watering, and they never ask you which things they can stop watering. I've never had a client that I haven't harangued about maintenance, and I don't have much success.

Aronson: *I would like to ask you one last question. What do you see as the future of this profession?*

Walker: Well let me just mention three things. One is that I think the students in the schools are brighter today than we were. So on these grounds, I'm very enthusiastic. They're coming from backgrounds that are more diverse, and more interesting, and I think the three-year programs are better than the five-year or four-year programs—all of which is going to bring a lot of life to the profession. The second thing is that, in the United States, Germany, and France, a number of small offices have come into being, and although I don't think it's the only way to practice, I think it's a good sign for the general creative level. Finally, I do see the beginning of ecumenical exchange between the factions of environmentalism and activism. The wiser people on both sides of this fence are starting to synthesize the two approaches. For all of these reasons, I think it is probable that we are going to see a fertile period over the next ten or fifteen years.

COMMENTARY

Stanford Anderson

Technological Euphoria
vs. Critical Practice

Città Nova
(City for Year 2000),
Antonio Sant'Elia, 1913–1914

The technologies which most threaten place and the city today are not those of a new material tectonic, but rather those of the new electronic technology. Our personal and social lives have already been transformed by the telephone and the automobile. Television, among other things, killed small town cinema and greatly altered its role in cities. Television also significantly changed reading habits. Who can deny that electronic networking will not exert its influence on us and on place and urban form? It is worth recalling in this context the fifth thesis of the Manifesto of Futurist Architecture, written in 1914 by Antonio Sant'Elia and Filippo Tommaso Marinetti:

> Just as the ancients drew the inspiration for their art from the elements of nature, so we—being materially and spiritually artificial—must find this inspiration in the elements of the immensely new mechanical world which we have created, of which architecture must be the finest expression, the most complete synthesis, the most efficacious artistic integration.[1]

That Sant'Elia and Marinetti thought of themselves and their world as being "materially and spiritually artificial" might prompt the retrospective assessment that they were still marked by the fantasies of Jugendstil decadence, or alternatively, that they were stunningly in advance of their time. Immersed as we are in the radical artificiality of rapidly intensifying cyberspace, we may look back on the Futurist's sense of artificiality as "quaint." In this regard, it is revealing to compare the architectural Futurism of 1914 to the recent book *City of Bits* by the dean of the School of Architecture at the Massachusetts Institute of Technology, William J. Mitchell. He adopts a rather Futurist attitude toward the advent of cyberspace, claiming eighty years after Sant'Elia and Marinetti that classical architectural unities have been shattered. As he puts it, "We are all cyborgs now." He continues:

> We will all become mighty morphing cyborgs capable of reconfiguring ourselves by the minute—of renting extended nervous tissue and organ capacity and of redeploying our extensions in space as our needs change and as our resources allow. Think of yourself on some evening in the not-so-distant future, when wearable, fitted, and implanted electronic organs connected by bodynets are as commonplace as cotton. Your intimate infrastructure connects you seamlessly to a planetful of bits.[2]

What architectural implications does Mitchell see in this? He follows a conventional functionalist line in analyzing a series of building types: libraries, prisons, museums, schools, banks, and private homes. Throughout, he finds that the events taking place within these institutions, their locations, and their organization will become increasingly ephemeral. The rationales for their specific location and for their on-site programmatic articulation mutually evaporate as their former service functions are absorbed into cyberspace and they become accessible from anywhere. With the traditional link between architectural space and experience broken, and with the growing capability of rendering so many different services from anywhere, architectural realization comes to be marginalized or totally eclipsed.

Contrast this with Sant'Elia, who for all his radicality, still affirmed that architecture must be the finest expression, the most complete synthesis, the most efficacious artistic integration of a new mechanical world. He was as ambitious for architecture as ever. His call was to take architecture away from its historicizing play with styles and to bring it to engage with the emerging technological forces of the time.

The promised cybernetic future seemingly fulfills what Melvin Webber long ago extolled, namely, "community without propinquity." In the cybernetic version, this prospect is almost universally presented as a satisfaction of individual desire. The individualization of learning, tailored to the child, and the envisioned automatic scanning of databases to compile a highly selective individualized newspaper for each person, are cases in point. The traditional newspaper, even if less than brilliantly or fairly edited, selects information in tacit accord with a proposition about the larger general spectrum a community might come to share. The readership can hold different opinions, accept or contest the editorial program. Their collective readership or lack thereof influences what is to be taken as common knowledge. Through it all, a medium like the traditional newspaper is a force for shared communal knowledge and action. In the newspaper, we gain serendipitous encounter with information we would not necessarily have preselected for ourselves. I would argue that social well-being surely relies on some minimal level of commonality as engendered by institutions like schools and newspapers, along with those aspects of other media that are not individualized.

I see no reason why we as individuals or as architects should participate in the possible, but not inevitable, exploitation of new media solely for the often narrow and selfish individualization of society or the ephemeralization of the environment. Architecture can be more than minimal shelter to the still physically and psychologically vulnerable organism who is otherwise designated as a cyborg. It should still be possible to go beyond shelter to the tectonically invented realm of architecture itself, and this in the service of evolving, but not rootless, communal goals that remain the imperatives of social life.

I would like to shift from the Futurist prospects of cybernetic technology to the more immediate tasks confronting architects. I want to contemplate the material conditions and techniques intimately bound up with the act of building and to reveal at the same time the relativity of historiographic interpretation. To explore these issues, we may consider the career of Adolf Loos, a noted architect of the early twentieth century. Since I don't consider myself a Futurist in the sense of either Marinetti or Mitchell, I elect to align myself more with the work of Loos and with Loos's concern for a changing and ambiguous present that can and should inform architecture. For these purposes, we may begin with two early works by Loos: the Goldmann and Salatch Store, realized in Vienna from 1898; and the Steiner House, also in Vienna, of 1910. The garden front of the Steiner House is the image most frequently associated with Loos. In his book *Pioneers of Modern Design* of 1949, Nikolaus Pevsner viewed this elevation as anticipating the white architecture of the 1920s. He regarded Loos as one of the pioneers who came

> . . . to admire the machine and to understand its essential character and its consequences on the relation of architecture and design to ornamentation.[3]

Goldman & Salatsch Store
Adolf Loos, Vienna, 1910–1911

Steiner House
Adolf Loos, Vienna, 1910

Behrens House
Peter Behrens, Darmstadt Künsterkolonie, Germany, 1900–1901

Arc lamp
Peter Behrens, 1907

Pevsner went on to compare Loos to Otto Wagner, Louis Sullivan, Frank Lloyd Wright, and Henry Van de Velde, indicating that he was not so narrow in his view of Loos. And yet, placing Loos in such company and according him this posture with regard to ornamentation suggests a questionable interpretation of Loos's position. Pevsner contrasts Loos's work to Josef Hoffmann's, and observes that in Loos's Goldmann and Salatch Store, there is ". . . nothing that can, strictly speaking, be called ornament. The value of this work depends entirely on the high quality of the materials used, and the dignity of the proportions."[4] Elsewhere, Pevsner sums up his interpretation of Loos's Steiner House in the following way:

> . . . he achieved the style of today completely and without any limitation. The unmitigated contrast of receding center and projecting wings, the unbroken line of the roofs, the small openings in the attic, the horizontal windows with their large undivided panes; who without being informed would not date this house about 1924–30, or even later?[5]

Pevsner's observations on Loos exemplify the use of historiography in support of a contemporary polemic. Pevsner believed in a historical determinism that was leading architecture along one particular route, embodied in the white architecture of the late 1920s and 1930s. With such a bias, he sought a particular historical trajectory culminating in this development even when it entailed a selective reading, such as the single view of the Steiner House. No other view of this house, internal or external, fits with Pevsner's reading. Even more to the point, the complex character of the Steiner House did not in any way conform to Pevsner's stylistic theory, since Loos was categorically opposed to any kind of *Gesamtkunstwerk* (total work of art) or unified style, be it "modern" or otherwise.

Loos's resistance to the willful superimposition of stylistic unity extended to those whose ambition was to burden architecture with the task of restoring a unified or harmonious culture. One of Loos's references to this totalizing project questioned which individualistic artist's vision of a new unified culture we should accept. Should it be Van de Velde or Hoffmann or Josef Maria Olbrich or Richard Riemerschmid?[6] However, Loos agreed with the first premise of the *Gesamtkunstwerk* argument, namely, that Europe no longer possessed a unified culture—the last moment of such a culture was perceived to have been the time of Goethe and of Biedermeier, the first years of the nineteenth century.

Loos's vision of overlapping disciplines and conventions, not fully coordinated and sometimes competing with one another, ruled out any holistic interpretation of society, as well as any demand for action based on the presumption of such a "whole." In his early resistance to Art Nouveau, Loos strenuously attacked its imposed formalisms. In such debates, he based his position on a distinction between art and craft, and on locating architecture within the general field of cultural production. As we have noted already, Loos was opposed to the Art Nouveau ideal of the *Gesamtkunstwerk* as pursued by the Darmstadt Künstlerkolonie under the creative leadership of such architects as Olbrich and Peter Behrens.

Once formulated, Loos's criticism of the *Gesamtkunstwerk* could be addressed not only to Art Nouveau, but even to an important movement developed in opposition to the Art Nouveau. Equally assertively, Loos argued against

Steiner House
Adolf Loos, Vienna, 1910

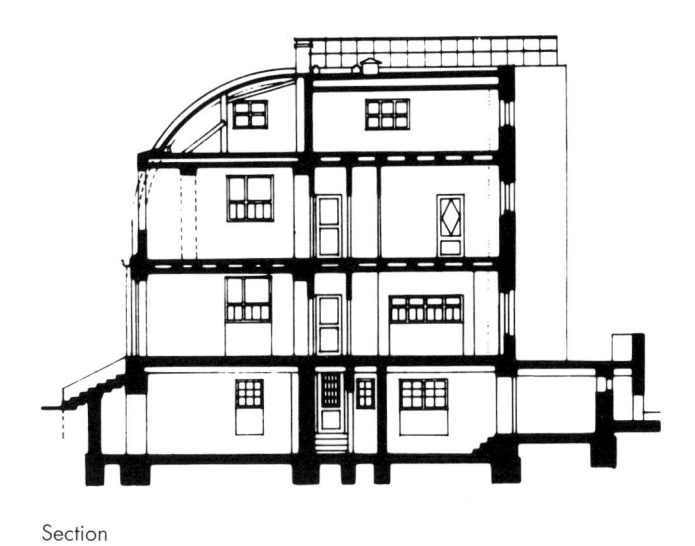

Section

Ground floor plan

the production aesthetic of the German *Werkbund* and its will to control industrial production according to a modern aesthetic as defined by elite artists and architects, such as we see in Behrens' designs of aestheticized arc lamps for the Allgemeine Elektricitäts Gesellschaft (AEG).[7]

If at the end of this century we now return to Loos's own work, we can appreciate his conception more concretely, and we can also recognize the rather perverse way in which his work would later be interpreted by Pevsner. When one looks at the street facade, the section, and the plan of Loos's Steiner House of 1910, one realizes the absolute partiality of Pevsner's cubic reading of the garden facade. The programmatic and labyrinthine character of Loos's so-called *Raumplan* or space-planning also confirms how far he was from Le Corbusier's "free plan" or other formal inventions of the "white" avant-garde architecture of the 1920s and 1930s. For the Steiner House, set in a suburban location, Loos designed an interior notable for its private, traditional characteristic, such as arts and crafts oak beams on the ceiling and the accommodation of English furniture in the dining room. At the same time, the plain exterior of the house was shocking and totally unprecedented.

It is instructive to compare the Steiner House to Loos's building on Michaelerplatz, also in Vienna, and built in the same year. This is a mixed-use structure with a retail establishment on the ground floor and mezzanine levels, and offices and apartments above. The Michaelerplatz

Left and facing page
Goldman & Salatsch Store
Adolf Loos, Vienna, 1910–1911

building is in the center of the city, directly opposite one of the entrances to the royal palace in Vienna, and in the midst of other monumental late-nineteenth-century historicizing buildings. Here, Loos worked with the continuous street lines. He aligned the parapet of his building with the cornice elevations of the surrounding buildings, adopting fine material and a very reduced kind of classical order in the facade. It was seen at the time as a radically abstract building, but certainly in comparison to the Steiner House, one can see that many concessions have been made to its placement within the city and the representational civic role that it had to play. At the same time, its interiors and the light well were much more abstract and radical than the interiors of the Steiner House. Thus, in the historic center of Vienna, contemporaneously with the Steiner House, Loos designed a modern and formally inventive shop interior, while the exterior reflected the traditional, monumental context. At the same moment and in the same city, Loos not only differentiated his buildings one from another, but distinguished between the interiors and exteriors of the same building. How should one account for such diversity?

The historiography of the modern movement sustained its interpretation of Loos as a proto-modern, by examining his works selectively. The building on Michaelerplatz was ignored because it employed a reduced form of classical order. The Steiner House was shown from the exterior, usually in an axial view of the garden facade, for this was the view that seemed to anticipate most closely the new architecture of the 1920s. If we can bring ourselves to understand how Loos was able to produce such diversity in 1910, we may also begin to understand what alternative he was offering.

In the sitting room of the Steiner House, as in the dining room, one observes the accommodation of certain received objects that were not uncommon in the bourgeois homes of the time—the Oriental carpets and the lamp, for example. At the same time, with the help of the furniture-maker Josef Veillich, Loos invented a version of the so-called Thebes stool, based on stools that had been found in the recently unearthed tomb of Tutankhamen.[8] Loos argued that these stools were still the best stools known. Their legs spread out to give stability, their seats were shaped to the human form. For Loos, there was no reason to forcibly conceive a modern stool, as the ancient Egyptian model would continue to be modern until a superior design could be conceived. Loos claimed that it was preferable to be closer to an ancient truth than to a lie that happened to walk beside us.

Steiner House
Adolf Loos, Vienna, 1910

I have emphasized Loos's acceptance of the past and the present with regard to various forms of production as these came about through agents other than the architect himself. Nonetheless, even in the seemingly reticent interiors of the Steiner House, Loos reveals his critique of Viennese bourgeois culture and his readiness to innovate. The intimate nook of the sitting area, the fireplace, and the general air of Anglo-American domesticity: all these reject Viennese bourgeois pomp, and reveal an openness to other cultures. The Liberty fabric of the benches proves that Loos could even accept an element tinged with the sensibility of Art Nouveau if it was of excellent quality and if it was not allowed to dominate. For Loos, the interiors of a house were private places most intimately tied to the individual and the family. They were to be in accord with the idiosyncrasies of individuals and with the remarkably diverse demands made on the home throughout the cycles of the day, the year, and even the lives of its inhabitants. At the same time the abstract simplicity of the exterior of the house did not result from an abstract aesthetic. The fact that it was relatively mute was a matter of decorum, for while the house must protect the privacy of its occupants it must also refrain from projecting individual taste into the public realm. Thus, the interior and exterior have different roles to play—the one supporting the conventions and peculiarities of domestic life, the other concealing these intimacies. The disparity of Loos's interiors and exteriors is not a failure of a single, synthetic, formal sensibility, but a demonstration of the proper relationship between architecture and life.

Loos respected tradition in whatever was tenable from the past. He was mistrustful of an "invented" future, although he was keen to recognize modern innovations that are practical improvements. Loos was moved by the monumental civic structure in its appropriate place, and he was appreciative of the vernacular of the countryside. He sought to honor both art and craft. Art was a high calling that transcended industrial values. Artists, however, should not seek to dictate forms to either craftsmen or industrialists. Loos incorporated what are often taken to be polar opposites between which one is required to choose. In Loos's work, these poles are envisioned as the ends of strands and are woven into one another and deployed in what we might visualize as a field. Within this cultural field, Loos did not seek to define one correct place for man to inhabit—not even one place for modern man, or even one place for himself as a secular architect of Vienna at the turn of the century. Rather, he thought that every task demanded a considered decision about where one should locate the work within the cultural spectrum. The cultural critic Karl Kraus, in celebration of Loos's 60th birthday, sought to explain what both of them had contributed. He wrote:

> Adolf Loos and I . . . have done nothing more than to show that there is a difference between a [funerary] urn and a chamber pot. It is in this difference that culture is given the space to play itself out. The others, those with [claims to] positive knowledge, however, divide themselves between those who would use the urn as a chamber pot and those who would use the chamber pot as an urn.[9]

Kraus was criticizing both the historicizing work of the late nineteenth century and the abstract work of modernists. Both were distorting the relationship of everyday objects to ceremonial objects. Within the cultural field that I have evoked, Loos would see the urn as closer to the monument, art, and tradition, and the chamber pot as closer to the vernacular, privacy, and craft. It is correct to give each its place within the cultural field, and thus also to determine who should design it and make it. For Loos, architecture was a discipline that is closer to craft than to art. But architecture covers a certain range within the overall cultural field. A funerary monument approached art; a country house approached the vernacular.

In my view, Loos offers a general proposition on the discipline of architecture which still continues to be viable. He spoke of the three-dimensional character of architecture, pointing to the autonomy of the discipline, while demanding that "the inhabitants of a building should be able to live the cultural life of their generation successfully."[10] For Loos, architecture has relative autonomy. On the one hand, the autonomy of the space plan, *Raumplan*; on the other, the thesis that architecture exists to serve the cultural life of a generation. Society must be able to appropriate the work, but not solely in a utilitarian manner. Loos directs us to the demands of the present, temporarily, selectively, and critically located, devoid of revivalism, traditionalism, or Futurism. He would rather celebrate the ambivalence of modern society, not with irony or despair, but as the most rational and liberating avenue available to us. Loos's endorsement of the classical in general, and especially of the work of Karl Friedrich Schinkel, recognized the then weak but enduring thread of the Western tradition. It also offered a typology that inhibited individualistic imposition and the consumption of arbitrary forms. His work was crucial in its resistance to what he saw as a false modernism. It was critical, too, in its assessment of what could be selectively affirmed in both the past and the present. What he would not tolerate was a false unification of this complexity under an imposed aesthetic. It is just this critical professionalism that sets Loos apart from the architects of his time, and in my view may still well serve as a model for the critical practice of architecture in our time.

Notes

The section of this essay pertaining to Adolf Loos relies in part on an earlier essay by the author: "Architecture in a Cultural Field," in Taisto H. Mäkelä and Wallis Miller, eds., *Architecture and Modernity: Wars of Classification* (New York: Princeton Architectural Press, 1991), 8–35.

1. Thesis 5, from Antonio Sant'Elia/Filippo Tommaso Marinetti, *Manifesto of Futurist Architecture* (1914), in Ulrich Conrads, ed., *Programs and Manifestoes on 20th-century Architecture*, trans. Ulrich Conrads (Cambridge, MA: The MIT Press, 1964).

2. William J. Mitchell, *City of Bits: Space, Place, and the Infobahn* (Cambridge, MA: The MIT Press, 1995), 31.

3. Nikolaus Pevsner, *Pioneers of Modern Design*, 2nd ed. (New York: Museum of Modern Art, 1949), 12.

4. Idem., 123–24.

5. Ibid., 124.

6. Adolf Loos, "Die Überflüssigen" ("Deutscher Werkbund") (1908), in *Trotzdem 1900–1930* (Vienna: G. Prachner, 1982, reprint), 71–73; 1st ed. (Innsbruck: Brenner, 1931).

7. Ibid.

8. Liberty in England produced a different four-legged version of a Thebes stool in 1888.

9. Peter Altenburg, et al., *Adolf Loos zum 60. Geburtstag am 10 Dezember 1930* (Vienna: R. Langi, 1930), 27 (my translation).

10. Loos, as paraphrased by Henry Kulka in "Adolf Loos," *Architects' Yearbook* 9 (1960), 10.

COMMENTARY

Robert M. Oxman

The Daemons of Place

> The contemporary place must form a crossroads, and the contemporary architect must have the talent to apprehend it as such. Place is not a ground, keeping faith with certain images; nor is it the strength of topography or of archeological memory. Place is, rather, a conjectural foundation, a ritual of and in time, capable of fixing a point of particular intensity in the universal chaos of our metropolitan civilization.[1]
> —Ignasi de Solà-Morales

In *Technology, Place and Architecture* a proposition was advanced that architecture's redemptive cultural function derives from its intrinsic ability to reify place. This suggests a position beyond the phenomenological content frequently attributed to the idea of place. The architectural achievement of a sense of place is projected as an ethical imperative. However, despite this theoretical precedence granted to place, there is also a contemporary problematic of place. It is not self-evident that the architectural act remains today a valid medium of local identity and phenomenological presence. If the postmodern condition is a legitimate interpretation of contemporary reality, does the concept of place remain a logical possibility; or can it also be, on the contrary, a retrograde formulation, a manifestation of cultural nostalgia?

The positing of this set of issues was implicit in the subject of the seminar, and in the presentations and open discussions with the public, a series of expert witnesses explored this intellectual territory. The thematic focus ultimately provided a mapping of the multiplicity of interpretations and the general complexity of *thinking place*. In foregrounding theoretical issues and exemplifying diverse strategies, the seminar also touched on contemporary questions of the artistic and cultural validity of an architecture of place.

In constructing these arguments the term *technology* held multiple and sometimes contradictory meanings. First of all building technology and the concept of place have a significant and positive space of conjunction. Kenneth Frampton has developed this thinking in his recent work on the "poetics of construction."[2] The built environment is seen in terms of the integral relationship between *topos* (site, context), *typos* (type), and the *tectonic* (the expressive potential of building). The material and tactile components of a building contribute to the bounding and definition of spatial qualities. Earthwork, as one of the significant realms of tectonic culture, contributes to the grounding, or situating, of the work in a physical and symbolic context.

However, there are also negative connotations to technology.[3] If materiality is significant to the transmission of cultural continuity, contemporary developments in building technology may be seen as abetting the undermining of materiality through the dematerialization of building. In the broader sense of "technological culture," modern technology and particularly the "consequences of regional urbanization" and a communications culture are seen as deleterious to cultural specificity, to local identity, to the authenticity of human experience. In a mediated world, the real and the virtual are often indistinguishable, and even the sense of place can be made a form of hyper-reality. The numerous visions of this possibility have become normative rather than marginal. Nowhere is everywhere.

If we are beginning to have a modern theory of tectonic culture, we lack a coherent theory of place. Though the marking and identification of place in land and built form are primordial phenomena, each period appears to have its own conception of place. Thus, there is a proliferation of meanings associated with the term. What is place? What are the possibilities for a modern theory of place? Are there uniquely modernist strategies of place making? Elucidating the state of theory and the theoretical problematic of place have been an implicit agenda here, particularly for the respondents to the plenary presentations.

The literature (architectural history and theory, geography, environmental psychology) is extensive. However, it is still difficult to define the territory because of the proliferation of concepts associated with the term *place*. Despite period distinctions, there are certain general classes of place concepts in built form. The first three as forms of *place-making* do not necessarily coexist with the fourth, a form of *place association*, and may even be contradictory to it.[4] Certain of these contradictions became apparent during the seminar.

Identification, or marking special (natural, frequently topographical, or geographical) characteristics through personification or some other form of symbolization of the genius loci. This is the symbolic enhancement of an indigenous quality. Among examples are the titular deities (daemons) associated with, and symbolically representing, unique natural places.

Transfiguration, or the making of a special entity through a physical act of formalization. This may be accomplished by the transfiguring, or emphasizing, of an inherent quality, or the construction of a new entity. It is frequently related to land forms, e.g., neolithic circles, or other markings of topographical entities.

Articulation, or bounding. This is place-making through the creation of a spatial entity by means of "bounding," or otherwise making a spatial entity, formal qualities, or relationships palpable to experience, e.g., the *temenos,* or sacred enclosure as a set of boundings. Though achieved through spatial articulation, it does not necessitate physically bounded space. For example, it may be a presencing through the sequencing of built and landscape elements.

Association, or localization through the experience of, or response to, common shared characteristics. The building of a sense of association with place through the response to, or emulation of, the components of the genius loci is significant in the sharing of community, as in regionalism. Contextualism is also a form of association in which the new responds to some existing phenomena of place. While place-making and place-association are historically well-known phenomena, it is their specific architectural strategies—how place is actually realized—that may today be problematic. Strategies frequently have ideological foundations. For example, modernist dematerialization, or "flowing space" in the words of Giedion, presented certain problems for spatial bounding. Architects and of broadening the semantics of bounding. A similar phenomenon has occurred in landscape architecture. *Criticality* in regionalism deals with contemporary aesthetic strategies for engaging the *cultural problematic of association*.

Israel as a cultural crossroads is an important venue for case studies in place. An amalgam of influences created an Israeli modernism rich in the substance as well as the intellectual problematic of the phenomena. The early eclectic period, with its diverse attempts at a neo-Palestinian style, produced a vocabulary of innovative formal strategies despite its essentially eclectic iconic predisposition. However, the spatialization of place, or the engagement of a regional topos of spatial relationships, emerged even in neo-eclecticism. The Joseph Berlin House (1924) in Tel Aviv, with its screen walls and spatial transitions, is a case in point. The problematic of a visual and iconic approach to association as a class of place-theory certainly was endemic in Mandate architecture and its philosophy of empire. Austen Harrison's well-known Archaeological Museum (1937) in Jerusalem is again rich in formal strategies and typological suggestivity that coexist with eclectic motifs.

These examples illustrate certain of the *dilemmas of association*. Prominent among these is the problem of formal stereotypes. However, the works also collectively demonstrate the regional significance of the *formal capacity to spatialize place*, particularly of strategies to spatialize *typos,* or regional typologies.

As rapid development, the automobile, and commercialism coincide with local conditions such as the absence of an environmental vision, a strong cultural framework for environmental design, or a cohesive and supportive professional community, we observe and participate in the deterioration of the Israeli environment. As this process accelerates, the cultural necessity of place becomes, ironically, both more immediate and harder to defend. There is a growing awareness and revival of interest in Israeli place, particularly in the restoration, preservation, and development of rural, seaside, and agricultural sites. But in these sites (Jaffa, Carmel Park, Rosh Pina, etc.), localization, or the gentrification of place, makes an easy alliance with commercial sponsors. A creative and *situated modernism*[6] is possible, but difficult to achieve and consequently rare.

It is in this general framework of an absent, but hopefully incipient, theory, and of the local vicissitudes of place that the third Jerusalem Seminar has had a special poignancy. The city with its multiple presence and its endemic conflict of memory and modernization was an appropriate venue for the daemons of place. The seminar illuminated the idea of a place as a "conjectural foundation,"[7] and the presentations began to trace a discourse of place as certain principles and strategies, issues, and contradictions emerged. All of this was well-wrought, and in certain cases, even delivered with degrees of magisterial presence.

These *traces for a theory of place* demonstrated some of the complexity of thinking and designing place. Here, I can mention only a few points in passing, particularly those that suggest the breadth of architectural strategies of place.

Glenn Murcutt represents one articulate pole of the complexity of place. His work expresses certain of the distinctions between place and the culture-specific. The significance of responsiveness to climate, particularly wind, as a formal generator, anchors creative reactions to traditional culture and is a pillar of critical regionalism. His own critical exploration of a modernist interpretation of the bungalow type is one aspect of his commitment to buildings as a part of their setting. That the bungalow is generally on the land rather than of it, that his characteristic plan form is open to the exterior (e.g., in circulation) rather than "rooted," that the building fabric suggests advanced as well as traditional technology are characteristics of the semantic complexity and oppositions of much of the work shown.

Another, differing set of poles, both of which *dissemble traditional presencing*, begin to address problems of contemporary aesthetic strategies of place. These were exemplified by aspects of the work of both Patricia Patkau and Enric Miralles. Patkau's essays on the "concretization of local reality" are based on strategies of heterogeneity of architectural media (light, materials, structural expression, etc.). They combine formal motifs (layering, rotation), complex building geometries, and generic and particular spatial structures in a heterotopic manner. Works are site-specific and site-enhancing. Miralles shares with Patkau the ability to create presence through *particularization* par excellence, the contemporary strategy of place. His challenging vocabulary of formal strategies synthesizes the linearity and dynamism of Catalan modernism, and constructivist tendencies, with a Mediterranean sensibility and a remarkable ability to make manifest the metaphysical qualities of landscapes and built environments. As Frampton pointed out and Peter Walker and Miralles demonstrated, the practice of landscape architecture, and particularly of urban landscape design, has a special contemporary function in the evolution of the design thinking and practice of place.

In presenting this work undogmatically as a set of essays, the seminar achieved an eloquent statement. The most profound possibilities for the reconciliation of modernism with the culture of place were suggested through the various presentations and discussions. It is important to be aware that these possibilities challenge the validity of a simply oppositional architecture. In place of an architecture of tradition *and* innovation we are offered a "conjectural foundation," and contemporary strategies for creating by design "points of particular intensity." It was shown to be possible to presence place through particularization without iconic reference to localization and to achieve continuity with context without qualification of contemporary sensibility. Though we must await a comprehensive theory of place, we were presented with evidence of the potential of these ideas, ideas that are beginning to configure both the praxis and the poetics of place.

Notes

1. Ignasi de Solà-Morales, "Place: Permanence or Production," *Differences: Topographies of Contemporary Architecture*, trans. Graham Thompson (Cambridge: The MIT Press, 1996), 104.

2. The term *poetics* is employed in the Aristotelian sense of the comprehensive explication of a field of endeavor that can serve as a theoretical basis for praxis. Kenneth Frampton's recent *Studies in Tectonic Culture: The Poetics of Construction in 19th and 20th Century Architecture* (Cambridge, The MIT Press, 1995) attempts to provide such for building technology. In this piece I suggest that a comparable "poetics of place" is lacking and is a necessary theoretical ingredient for contemporary architectural culture.

3. Arguments regarding the deleterious influence of technological culture and regional urbanization are brought forward in the introduction by Kenneth Frampton to the seminar brochure, *Third Jerusalem Seminar in Architecture: Technology, Place & Architecture* (June 1996, 8–12). These ideas were further expanded in his introductory lecture to the seminar.

4. This distinction between two related phenomena, the construction of identifiable place and the strengthening of associations with the characteristics of particular places, appears important. There is a subtle historical process of interaction between these ideas from the 1950s. These include on the one hand, the strengthening of place through the configurative content of structured space, and on the other hand, theories of regionalism and *genius loci*.

5. See for example, Terence Riley's introductory essay to the catalog for the exhibition *Light Construction*, Museum of Modern Art, 21 September 1995–2 January 1996 (New York: The Museum of Modern Art, 1995), 7–32.

6. I propose that the term *situated modernism* connotes an architecture that is simultaneously reflective of its own time and cognizant of the culture of place. It appears to me that this terminological juxtaposition avoids some of the theoretical difficulties of *localism, radical eclecticism*, and even *critical regionalism*.

7. Solà-Morales presents a rather unique theoretical construction for an equivalence of place in the transfigured experience of an aesthetic event: "the value of places produced out of the meeting of present energies, resulting from the force of projective mechanisms capable of promoting, intense productive shock," "Place: Permanence or Production," 104.

COMMENTARY

Kaarin Taipale

Technological Change
and the Fate
of the Public Realm

Facing page, top
Helsinki, Finland
Aerial view of urban core and traditional public space

Facing page, bottom
Piazza San Marco
Venice, Italy
Public space appropriated by advertising

The subject of my presentation is technological change, how it affects our urban environment, how, as a consequence, the concepts of public and private space are redefined. My message can be condensed into two points: in order to keep our cities livable, we have to be the advocates of civic space, and the only way to make our urban environments sustainable is understanding and applying contemporary technology. My everyday practice consists of moderating a continuous debate between legislators, land-owners, builders, politicians, citizens, and the press. It may seem that this isn't the proper work of an architect, but I think there ought to be more architects working in this way, in the no-man's-land that we call "the real world."

Today in our cities, the primary juxtaposition is between public and commercial space rather than between public and private space. In the Nordic countries, we have developed the welfare state to such an extreme that we find we can no longer afford it. Technological change is to a large extent responsible for this development. Formerly, labor-intensive smokestack industry charged the city with manpower, while the so-called public sector redistributed taxes so as to take care of health, housing, education, and transportation, all services that were essential to the maintenance of the labor force. Computer-controlled manufacturing technology has greatly reduced the industrial labor force with an accompanying decline in the tax base. The welfare state is left empty-handed, with insufficient tax revenues but with more demands to fulfill. Incurable unemployment and the risk of polarization are the biggest problems facing the public sector in the management of urban environment. Moreover, this seems to be the case all over the industrialized world. Obsolete industries die, local unemployment reaches unforeseen proportions, entire sectors of the city are evacuated, and city planning has to find ways of reusing former harbor, warehouse, and smokestack industrial facilities.

Terms that have had a civic history, such as "main street," are now co-opted by commercial usage. I become skeptical whenever I hear such expressions as "The main street of the shopping mall" or "a winter city." They are not real streets in real cities, they are merely look-alikes. One does not organize a political demonstration, public celebration, or commemorative event in a shopping mall. Even today, true public spaces may acquire an air of sanctity: witness the arena surrounding Álvaro Siza's swimming pool in Matosinhos, near Porto. A sacred space is a public space, since the celebration of religion is also a communal activity.

Democracy cannot exist without public space. The public realm is open to everyone; it doesn't require a keycard or an entrance fee. Think of Greek culture and the birth of democracy, free men meeting in the agora; at the other extreme is the curfew of a dictatorship. Ultimately, public space exists so you and I can stand there, see ourselves reflected in each other, and love each other. Without love, nothing has any meaning. But what and where are our public buildings and spaces now? Do public-private joint ventures produce civic architecture? Earlier, the concept of a public building was quite clear. It meant a post office, a school, a city hall, institutions that even the wealthiest states seem to be unable to afford today. Everything has to be sponsored, like our television channels where

195

Rome, Italy
Automobiles increasingly occupy space in the city, vitiating the public realm.

soap operas are enacted in order to sell soap. What used to be public buildings are mostly public-private initiatives today. There are office buildings with public health centers and sports arenas supported by the money that comes from selling beer.

If very few new buildings are public in the traditional sense, urban space still remains public. Unfortunately, most of our squares and green areas are dealt with today as if they were leftover space, perfect for storing cars, garbage, technical equipment, and advertising kiosks.

Squares and parks are spaces where the unexpected may happen. Squares and parks are traditionally the bearers of collective and private memories. One recalls the great events that took place in an urban square. The sweetest private memories may be connected with lazy walks through mysteriously scented quiet parks. Flâneurs, those lazy strollers, consummate the city. Without the street and the pedestrian there is no urban culture.

It is no surprise that today, roadsides are much more crowded with advertisements than are subway stations. Advertisers are more interested in people who drive cars since they have more money than people who take the subway. For the same reason, shopowners, too, are interested in facilitating car access. That is why they fight for more parking garages and tunnels, and that is why we have to fight for public transport that works. The street is the essence of urbanity, but nothing has ruined our cities more than the private car. Traffic areas create huge no-man's-lands that cut up the city, not to mention the pollution and noise that result from maximized automobile usage.

Public art has meant monuments, common symbols of common values. Today, only dictators erect statues of themselves. There are no more common values. The task of today's urban art is to give the place an identity. It grows from the place; it is not a piece sculpted in the artist's atelier and moved to an empty spot. The task of environmental art is not to make a place more beautiful, but to reveal something about the place and the time to the passerby. If we don't fight against the invasion of non-art in

Las Vegas, Nevada
The Strip exhibits a kinetic continuity, with the driver as consumer and the street as a continuous billboard.

the name of art, we lose the urban space square inch by square inch. "Art" becomes street furniture.

To appear in public no longer necessarily means that one has to deliver a speech in a civic space. Today it is sufficient if he or she makes an announcement on television. At this juncture, public space and television overlap. Someone gives an interview on the lawn of the White House or from Red Square: televising it makes it truly public. In general, only mass media can make something fully public by today's standards. Shared information creates new communities. All over the world, we read the same news every morning. Our lives have become globally simultaneous. We all watch the same football match at the same time. What we used to hear as stories from neighbors or read in the newspapers days or weeks after the fact has become instant information.

The information superhighway, the cellular phone, the World Wide Web are all key elements in the second industrial revolution of the twentieth century. Information and knowledge can now be shared by everyone who has access to the Internet. However, you have to be well educated in order to find the information you need. These new kinds of informational networks inevitably lead to new interpretations of what a community is and of what public space can mean. Virtual public space—networks— have the capacity to link up several collective identities simultaneously. Our paradoxical hope is that the new virtual space will make the physical immediacy of urban space and the intimacy of face to face human encounter all the more powerful. Meanwhile one of the tasks for new technology is to discover how the moving around of information could perhaps replace the moving around of material and waste. Already there is a system whereby a transmitter from a traffic satellite may provide instant feedback as to the most expedient route for an automobile to take.

It is equally clear that advanced technology may be immediately deployed so as to respond to the direct challenge of the ecological crisis. In his brilliant lecture series for the BBC, Richard Rogers argued that if the governments of the United Kingdom and the United States made a joint

Helsinki, Finland
Art reduced to "street furniture": corporate-sponsored sculpture is located arbitrarily in the street.

Exposition des Arts Décoratifs poster
Paris, 1925
Belching smokestacks were once perceived as a desirable symbol of modernity and industrial progress.

decision to buy nothing but electric or solar-powered cars, the orders would be big enough to spur the industry to develop such a car. The only reason we don't have electric cars yet is a lack of collective will. We should decide that we are not going to use the old technology anymore if it is harmful to the environment.

Despite the enormous potential for the application of advanced technology, very little has happened in the construction field. Granted, we now have computer-aided design and some computer-aided manufacture, and the computer is commonly used for the monitoring of time schedules. In Finland, especially in the housing field, prefabrication construction technology has become, it seems, as regional a phenomenon as log cabins used to be a century ago. However, by and large, prefabrication has no architectural aim whatsoever. Only now are architects starting to examine the architectural potential of prefabricated concrete. Until recently, prefabricated technology was exclusively instrumental. It facilitated the production of huge quantities of apartments in the 1960s and 1970s when a whole generation of people moved from the countryside to the cities in Finland. Prefabrication also made it possible to prolong the construction season from the short summer months to the whole year, because the casting of concrete could take place under controlled factory conditions. This was also connected to the labor unions' and the construction workers' demands for better working conditions. However, the technical results were not lasting and the current problem is how to renovate the first generation of prefabricated housing. Next to this issue, the prime concern is the regeneration of public space and the creation of new workplaces out of empty shopping malls. Other leading concerns are the social and health problems arising from long-term unemployment and the need to arrange for the elderly to live in their own homes as long as possible since society is not able to afford to build new institutions for the aged.

Seventy years ago, black smoke meant progress and development. Now it has come to signify the reverse. We hope that new technology will entail less pollution, although we also know that no new technology will prevail if it fails to increase the profit margin. Technology must use fewer resources, less energy, and less material, and produce less waste. It also has to produce sustainable products. New construction technology is not only about making harder concrete that is capable of weathering, but also about limiting toxic emissions, developing solar-power systems, and deploying adaptations of communication techniques so as to enable an elderly person to shop at home and maintain a savings account while still living in his or her own apartment. The challenge facing new building technology is to maintain an equilibrium between the building and its context.

Recently the French authorities organized an international competition for the design of an ecological house. This was won by the Finnish architect Kai Wartiainen, who argued through his design that architectural problems characteristically have three aspects: the ecological, the social, and the technical. The social organization is defined by human scale and human needs. The ecological system creates possibilities for natural resources to interact with the structure in a balanced way. The technical system maximizes the efficiency of the building. The house designed by Wartiainen has two main facades: the low-tech southern elevation, which catches the sun, and the high-tech northern facade, which contains the technical spaces. The house is connected to a LON-network (Local-Oriented Network), an American system created by Mike Markkula, one of the fathers of Apple. It is an interactive system that sends and receives information about almost anything. It is able to control the energy flow throughout the system. In social terms, the house is divided into a public and a private zone. Kai Wartiainen argues that eating is the most public function in a home, because it creates a community around the table.

What is the connection between reclaiming the public realm and the goals of a sustainable technology? We need a sophisticated form of urban planning that is capable of stimulating new industries and providing employment without creating waste and generating traffic congestion. We need more energy, efficient public transport, and fewer private cars in the inner urban area. Not only do materials have to be recycled, but land has to be reused. Urban areas given over to obsolete purposes must become new neighborhoods for housing and work. The identity of these new communities must be reinforced by their public spaces and by the introduction of nature. It is obvious that new technology makes the old industrial zoning strategy obsolete. There is no need today for the separation of housing, work, and leisure into places connected by traffic. Since high-technology workplaces and high-technology transport will not pollute the environment, housing, work, and traffic may be intertwined again. The sustainable city has to have its roots. People need to know where they come from, where they belong. In order to identify with our environment, we need memories, layers of time that become visible in the city. This is why now, more than ever, we need old squares, parks, and even ruins that embody the past.

Eco-Logis
Kai Wartiainen, project, 1996
Interactive network computer system controls energy feedback system throughout the house

1994

ARCHITECTURE, HISTORY & MEMORY

November 7–10
The Jerusalem Theater

Seminar Co-chairmen
Julian Beinart
Arthur Spector

Session Chairs
David Cassuto
Lou Gelehrter
Peter Keinan
Ulrik Plesner
David Reznik
Moshe Safdie

Presenters
Dimitris Antonakakis
A.J. Diamond
Balkrishna V. Doshi
James Ingo Freed
Arata Isozaki
Antoine Predock

Commentary
Stanford Anderson
Kenneth Frampton
Joseph Rykwert

Editor's Note
Texts on the following pages
are edited excerpts
from full-length
seminar presentations.

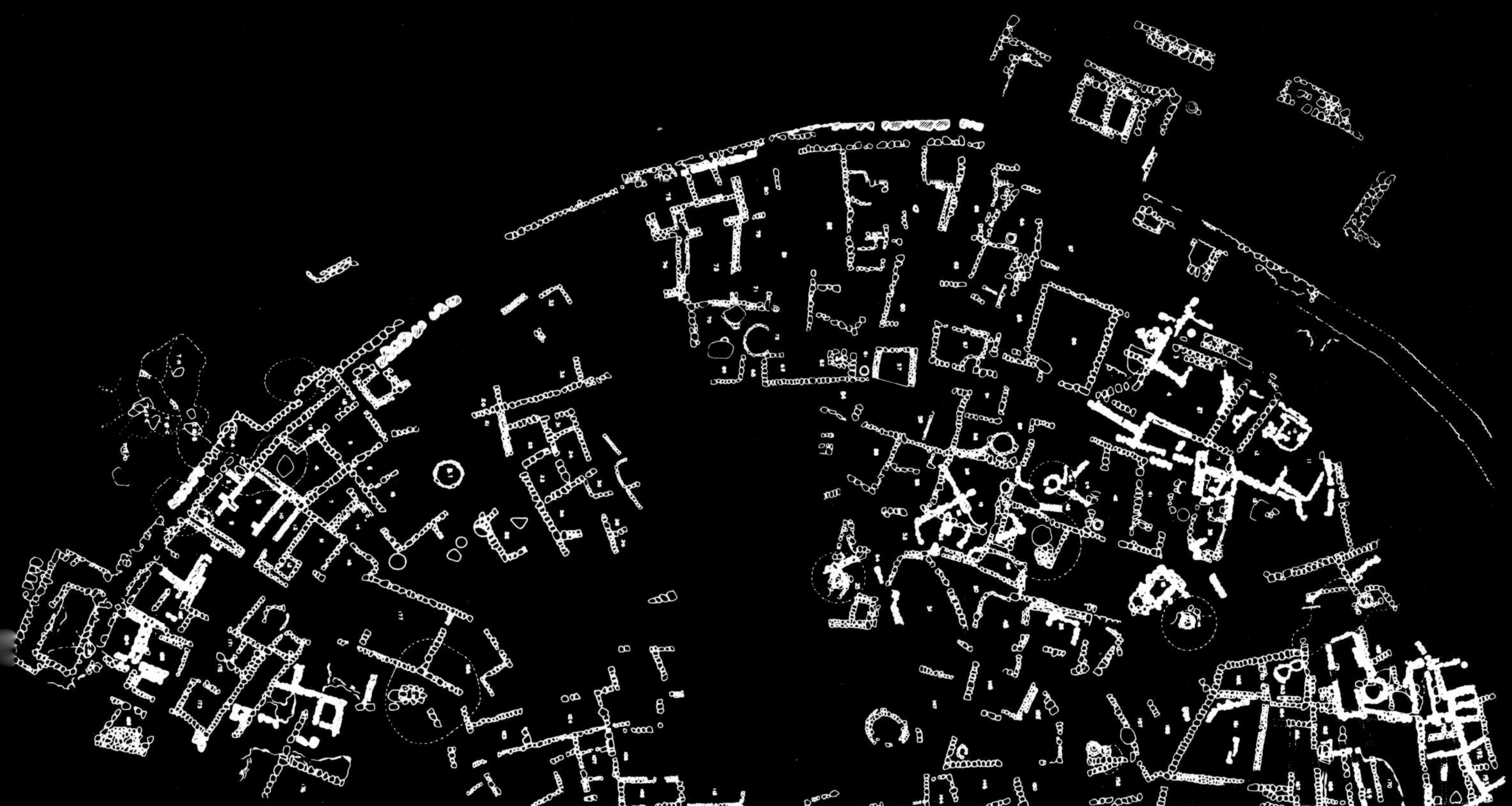

INTRODUCTION
Julian Beinart

The 1994 Jerusalem Seminar in Architecture, *Architecture, History and Memory*, invited architects and theorists to reflect on how contemporary architecture deals with the past, both as the accumulated building of the city and as inherited ideas about architecture.

Architecture comes about only in the context of existing places: buildings are restored, reconfigured, or replaced within already formed urban plans. Even isolated virgin sites possess a territorial heritage. Monuments, memorials, and museums are deliberate attempts to maintain memory, battles against the terror of forgetting. The artifacts of our cities give us biological equilibrium and cultural continuity by virtue of their stability. Since classical times, architecture has served to train individual memory; it is essential for our collective memory as well. "We may live without architecture, and worship without her, but we cannot remember without her," John Ruskin said.

The seminar speakers were encouraged to reflect on two methods of knowing the past, history and memory as interpreted in the following five comments:

> History exists only as long as an object is in use; that is, so long as a form relates to its original function. However, when form and function are severed, and only form remains vital, history shifts into the realm of memory. When history ends, memory begins. (Aldo Rossi)

> The collective memory is not the same as formal history. General history only starts when tradition ends and the social memory is fading or breaking up. So long as a remembrance continues to exist, it is useless to set it down in writing or otherwise fix it in memory. (Maurice Halbwachs)

> Memory and history are processes of insight; each involves components of the other, and their boundaries are shadowy. Yet memory and history are normally and justifiably distinguished: memory is inescapable and prima facie indubitable; history is contingent and empirically testable. (David Lowenthal)

> Memory is life, borne by living societies founded in its name. History, on the other hand, is the reconstruction, always problematic and incomplete, of what is no longer. Memory is absolute, while history can only conceive of the relative. History is perpetually suspicious of memory, and its true mission is to suppress and destroy it. (Pierre Nora)

> Memory, in sum, is not only authentic, and radiant, and poetic. It is also hurtful and fragile and, in a sense, untransmittable. Therefore, it needs the fortifyings of history; the connections, the comparisons, the conclusions. Memory is color, history is line. (Leon Wieseltier)

Most of the invited architects preferred not to speak directly to knowledge constructs of the past but presented their work so that it might be open to interpretation. James Ingo Freed, however, answered directly, saying that he preferred memory to history because he preferred its authenticity and rich detail to the abstraction and consistency of history. Architecture, he acknowledged, however, could not survive without both. The critic Joseph Rykwert took an opposing view. Memory, he argued, is generated involuntarily while history requires active thought. Consequently, only history allows the architect to reconstruct the past in an accessible and rational way.

The subject of Freed's presentation, the United States Holocaust Memorial Museum, is an attempt to preserve memory through architecture before memory of the Holocaust fades into history. But how to do this without using directly the physical environment in which the Holocaust took place? Freed's solution was through what he calls indirection and the discovery that the only way into a phenomenon as immense as the Holocaust was through both the tectonics of the Holocaust and the invention of a tectonics of his own.

To forget is as necessary as to remember. Stanford Anderson stressed the importance for oral societies of forgetting and even forgetting that one is forgetting. Rykwert described the current condition of Tiananmen Square in Beijing and Las Vegas in Nevada as places that—each in its own way—facilitate forgetting. Antoine Predock, on the other hand, in explaining a project of his in Las Vegas, saw the city in terms of its ability to inspire a kind of amnesia that allows an architect to forget specific context, and, as a result, to design a hotel that is purposely and extravagantly unforgettable.

Anderson introduced the idea of tradition in contrast to memory. Despite its often conservative use, he argued, tradition, unlike memory, points forward rather than backward and can more easily be turned to progressive uses. The architects Balkrishna Doshi and Arata Isozaki in particular often referred to their buildings in terms of bringing their past into the conflicted state of their present culture. Anderson also distinguished between memory *through* architecture, social memory, and memory *in* architecture, which he called disciplinary memory. Early architecture did not divide them: Anderson argued that the many copies of the Church of the Holy Sepulcher outside Jerusalem are examples of an undifferentiated social and disciplinary memory, in contrast to later emulations, such as those based on Palladian villas, where only disciplinary memory is at play. He concluded that most architecture, in particular, the great works of Le Corbusier, Aalto, Kahn, and others, is an exercise in the use of memory rather than of history. And that this is precisely why disciplinary memory should interest not just architects, but historians as well.

LECTURE
Dimitris Antonakakis

Below and facing page
Lyttos Hotel
Anissaras, Crete, 1977

Today, the mass media focus our attention on the spectacular in architecture—large public buildings, grand projects, freestanding buildings. This systematically diminishes our interest, not to mention the interest of the wider public, in the entity that forms cities, the residential building and in particular the unit of habitation.

The single housing unit, which with its multitude of combinations wove the close network of the urban fabric, once again must become the main subject of our architectural practice. This is something that everyone of us can address. This unit is complex and difficult, but also charmingly direct in its relationship with the inhabitant. The care for the small-scale is what establishes the correct relationship with public buildings and what creates the preconditions for their existence.

Tradition is a continuous line that reaches all the way up to yesterday, a line that supplies us with knowledge and experience, defining to some extent the way we see things. The great issue for us is the way in which all experience and knowledge are to be interpreted within a complex contemporary reality. Whether we design a large public work or a small house, we must discern to what extent the human environment allows itself to be appropriated, to become friendly, to mirror human care.

In Greece, we systematically attempt to combine open-air space with the built space, however small it may be. We insist on open-air space because the Greek climate, as in many other places around the Mediterranean, allows a comfortable outdoor life—covered or open, enclosed or free—for more than eight months of the year. The advantages are in part financial: the creation of economical open-air spaces multiplies the possibilities of the limited, indoor ones; open-air spaces also offer the potential of contact with nature and a certain general enrichment of life. This is especially necessary in the sterilized environment offered to us by the *prêt-à-porter* buildings that multiply at such an incredible rate.

The housing settlement in Distomon, a small Greek town, was commissioned by a mining company in the late 1960s. The commission was for eighty-five apartments divided into three buildings designated for workers, foremen and technical assistants, and engineers.

During the years we were engaged with this project (1968–1970), Greece was governed by a dictatorship. The social problems that arose from the organization of space were significant, and the idea of creating three buildings for three "classes" of working people was rather chilling, if not repulsive.

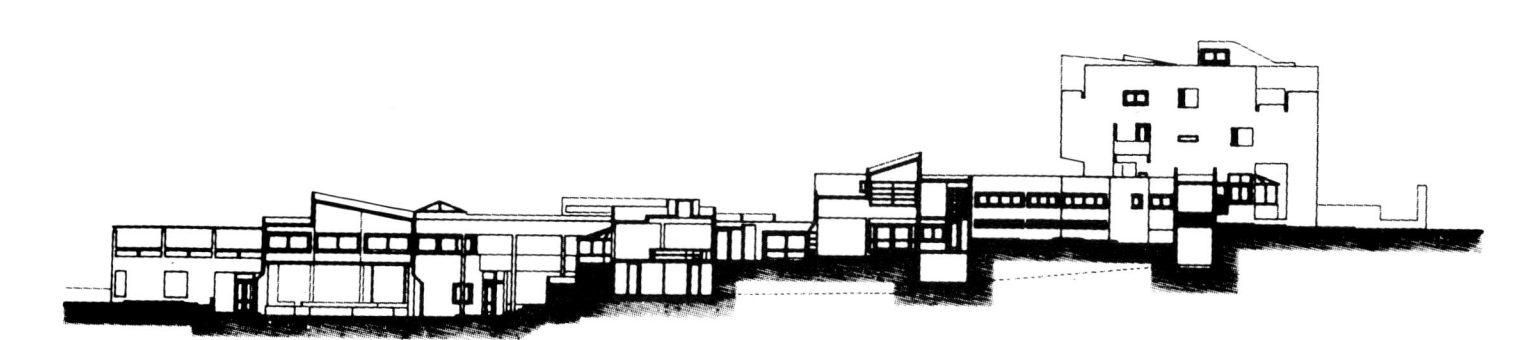

Longitudinal section

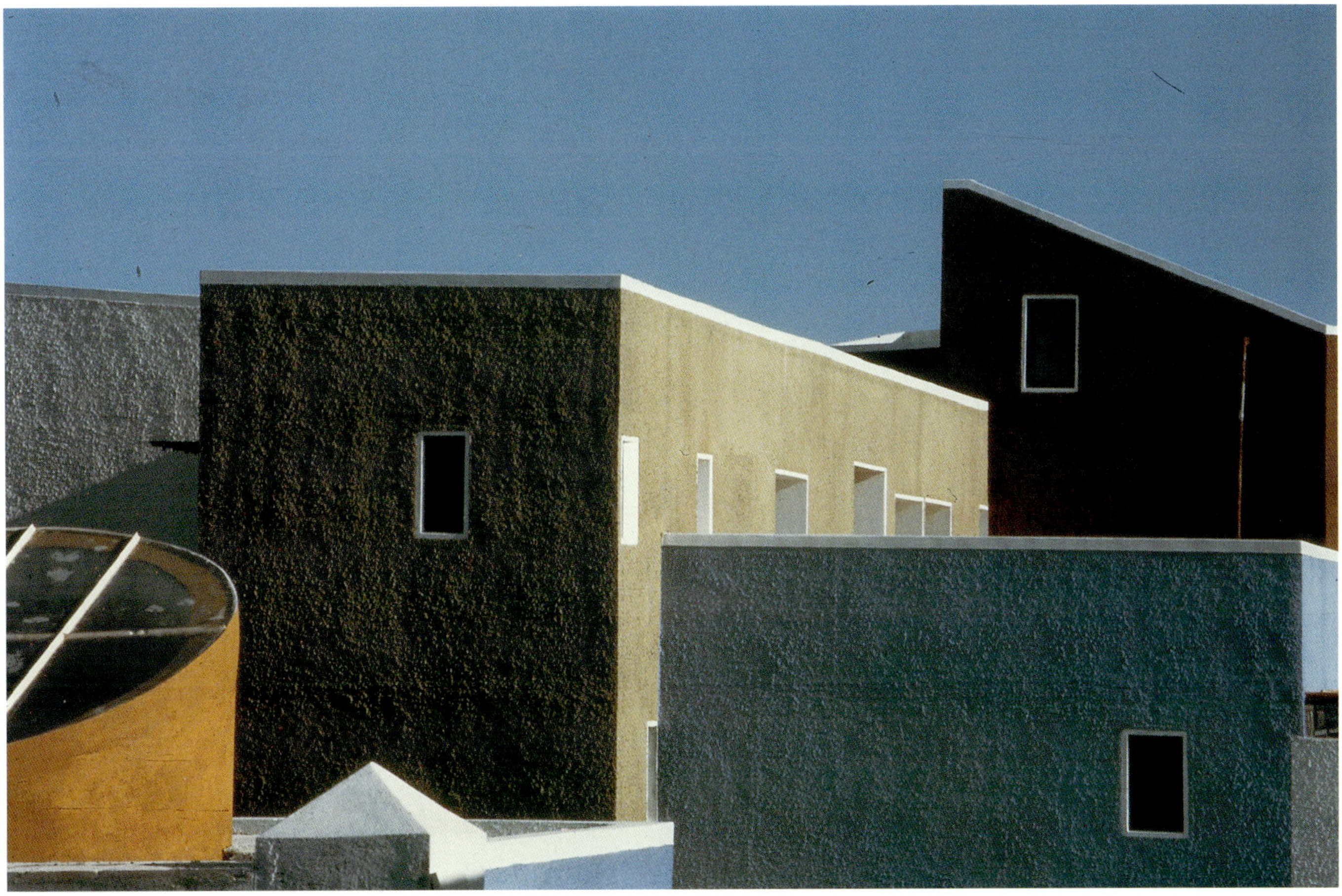

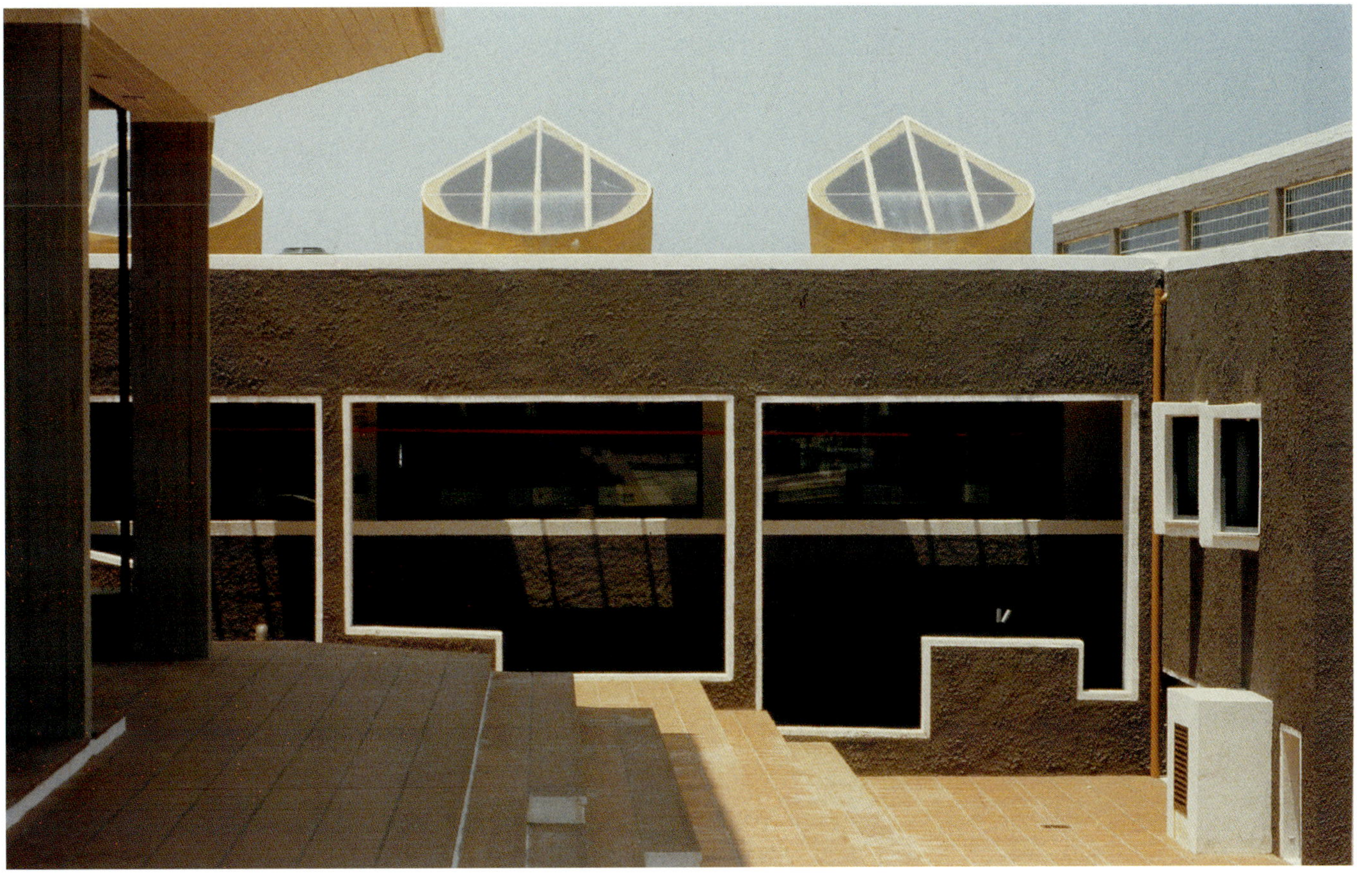

School of Humanities
University of Crete, Akrotiri, Crete, 1981

We tried to find an appropriate socio-cultural character for a workers' settlement, rather than simply produce the required number of units. This communal approach took into account that future tenants might be of a completely different background, and for us the social stability of the community was a top priority.

The entire complex was laid out in a "zone system" with open-air, semi-covered, and closed spaces integrated into a continuous whole. These zones descend the slope roughly parallel to the contour lines and contain a series of spaces of varying character, indoor and outdoor, private and public.

Smaller and larger patios enhance the walkways throughout the settlement. A variety of threshold or transitional areas were created so dwelling units could be entered from a varying set of identifiable places, which could be characterized as streets, squares, courtyards, or covered passages. We tried to assure privacy in the units while creating a hierarchy of public spaces that could contribute to the development of social life.

The Lyttos Hotel in Anissaras, Crete, is built on an almost flat site without any trees or rocks. This windswept site is situated next to a beach that extends for some distance with interruption. We articulated the circulation space of the hotel so as to clearly distinguish among the main entry, the reception hall, and the attendant path leading from the reception hall to the beach. We attempted to give specific identity to elevators and stairwells by opening them up to the surrounding landscape and unexpected views. We varied the rhythmic interpenetration of the indoor and outdoor space and the density of the natural light.

The reception hall is the heart of the hotel. It leads into three different passages at three distinct levels, while connecting to a number of public facilities such as the lounge, the vista restaurant, the bar, the nightclub, and the conference room.

Throughout the hotel, great attention was given to the differentiation of surfaces: smooth and brilliant, smooth and matte, etc. We used these different surface qualities to stress various volumetric and superficial relationships, and even, on occasion, to mark a route, correct a proportion, or simply emphasize idiosyncratic "sculptural" elements in the construction of the site. Our overall aim was to create a grid of differentiated open spaces running between the public and private domains, a network that would be capable of alternating the pattern of rest and movement toward the sea.

Technical University of Crete
Akrotiri, Crete, 1982

The campus of the Technical University of Crete at Akrotiri, near Chania, is situated in a relatively inhospitable, treeless area that slopes slightly from west to east. We won this commission by competition, and the brief demanded a building complex that would contain a variety of activities. We were asked to do a building and responded with a group of open-air spaces around a central piazza. Our first priority in designing the buildings that enclose the open-air spaces was to shape these enclosures; the buildings themselves were secondary. We proposed a set of variant, repeating elements where the repetition would work its effect without being obvious. A square serves as the central reception space.

Architecture cultivates, shapes, enriches, and perfects the building in the landscape. It is a primeval creation of individuals and of peoples. For centuries, humans have built works large and small that create complete worlds. There is no building that merits our scorn. All demand our careful consideration.

In this world, some works are distinguished, surpassing the rest in technical terms, importance, and meaning. They become standards, symbols, jewels for the world that encompasses them. But without that world they would not have any significance.

Architecture is not merely a technical art, a profession, or a business, although it is all of these. Its aim is not simply to fulfill human needs, but also to light up human existence in private and collective expression.

The language of architecture has the right and the duty to evolve and change following the development of technology and the transformation of human behavior. Let us seek the rules of this language that will facilitate free expression. Rules must remain flexible, responding to daily adjustments in the complex reality surrounding us and the larger transformations that life itself requires. The result should be a poetry of daily life that springs from the elements of space and from its thoughtful reckoning with sensitized contemporary human consciousness. Interpretation of this reality must respect the equivalent value of the general and the specific, the initial idea and its elaboration.

The work of architecture is never ending. It is always coming into perfection through the efforts of the architect and the inhabitant. As the snake said to Saint Exupery's Little Prince, "you have responsibility for the flower that grew in your hands."

LECTURE
A.J. Diamond

Below and facing page
York University Student Center
Toronto, Ontario, Canada, 1987

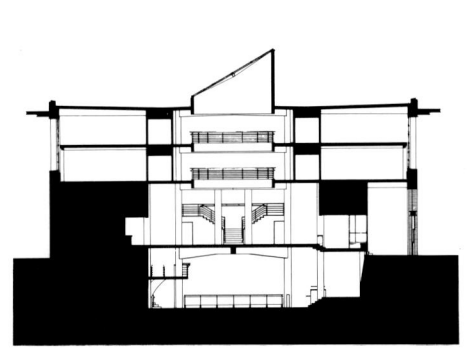

Cross section

A turning moment in my life was a lecture that I heard by Karlheinz Stockhausen, the composer. He advanced the theory that there is no such thing as progress in art. The organic model of birth, development, maturity, decay does not apply. Rather, there are polarities and the best art is the resolution of those polarities. Thus Stockhausen denied that the Parthenon is the best because it is at the apex of a process of refinement and that Paestum is not the worst because it is a crude beginning. Whether you look at an Egyptian hieroglyph or a modern work, it has a thrill in it, and a genius all its own.

Architecture is a discrete discipline. It is not reducible to art, philosophy, or science—it is architecture. Its central essential ingredient is space, space that houses people. Space is our medium. We must study how people live and work and then decide how they will inhabit and utilize space. To me, the resolution of the extremities of space is the essence of our task as architects.

The battle of the "isms"—deconstructivism, postmodernism, post-post-constructivism—is an absolutely sterile game to play. Language isn't the issue. I want to go beyond language, and I want to deal with architecture as an inclusive formula—not simply as surface, or as architecture for art's sake. Buildings have to stand outside in the rain and the cold, and they have to weather over time. You have to know how to build to keep the water out. You have to build so that people are content and happy with the results. When people like or dislike buildings, they don't always know why. The business of architects is to address what is intuitive to the layperson.

Classical space may be dressed up in many ways, but there are always corners and walls and doors and ceilings and floors. Weight is visibly distributed to the ground. It is possible, however, to undermine such fundamentals deliberately. There can be partitions that don't meet at corners, roofs that "float," and the kind of romantic notion that the outside is the inside. What nonsense! The outside is the outside, the inside is quite different. Its scale is different; its climate is different; its content is different. Where the inside and outside come together is a great event, one not to be obliterated.

Regardless of my opinion, however, two polarities do exist: well-defined rooms versus un-defined rooms; discrete space versus continuous, interpenetrated space; transparent buildings versus opaque, solid ones. The resolution of these two, the balance between the two, will make the best kind of architecture for our time. There is enough here to work on for a lifetime.

The YMCA of Toronto is the type of urban institution that provides a place for people to meet in a neutral and attractive manner. So the question is how do you meet? The YMCA provides the setting, and within it, the device I chose to facilitate meeting was the staircase. Czar Nicholas II used the staircase of the Opera House in St. Petersburg to receive his court, and classical staircases have something processional and quite wonderful about them. I used a wide staircase to bring light to the basement and link every space in the building. When you go up and down the staircase to your particular destination, you see the other activities and realize that they aren't quite as forbidding as you may have thought. They catch your interest and engage you. Socially, the landings are natural gathering places where people stop to observe adjacent activities and begin conversations commenting on how well someone is doing, or remarking about the equipment. The staircase is conducive to easy, comfortable social exchange.

Spaces within the York Student Center are narrated on the outside, so you understand and read the building. Natural light is the organizing instrument within.

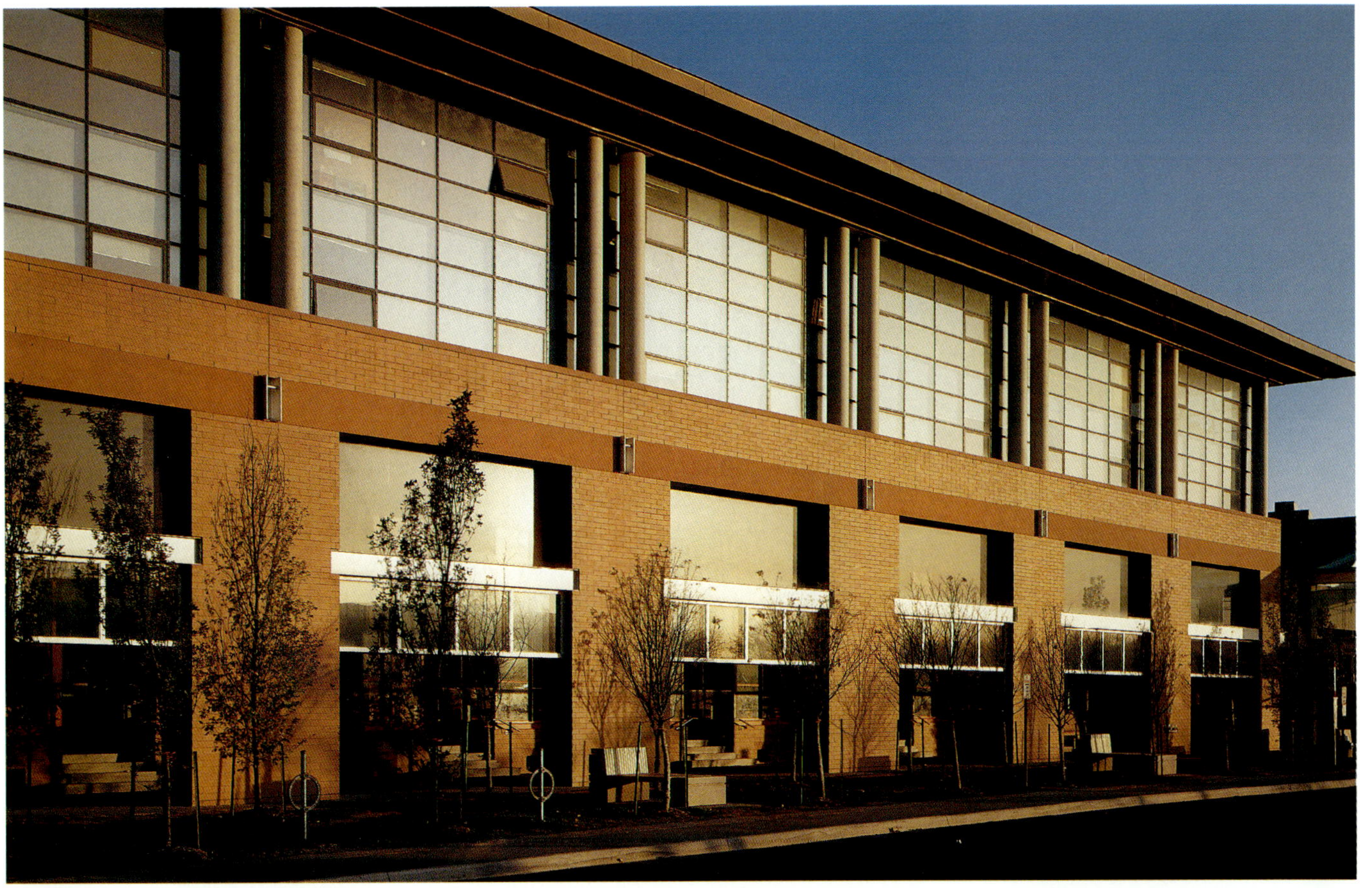

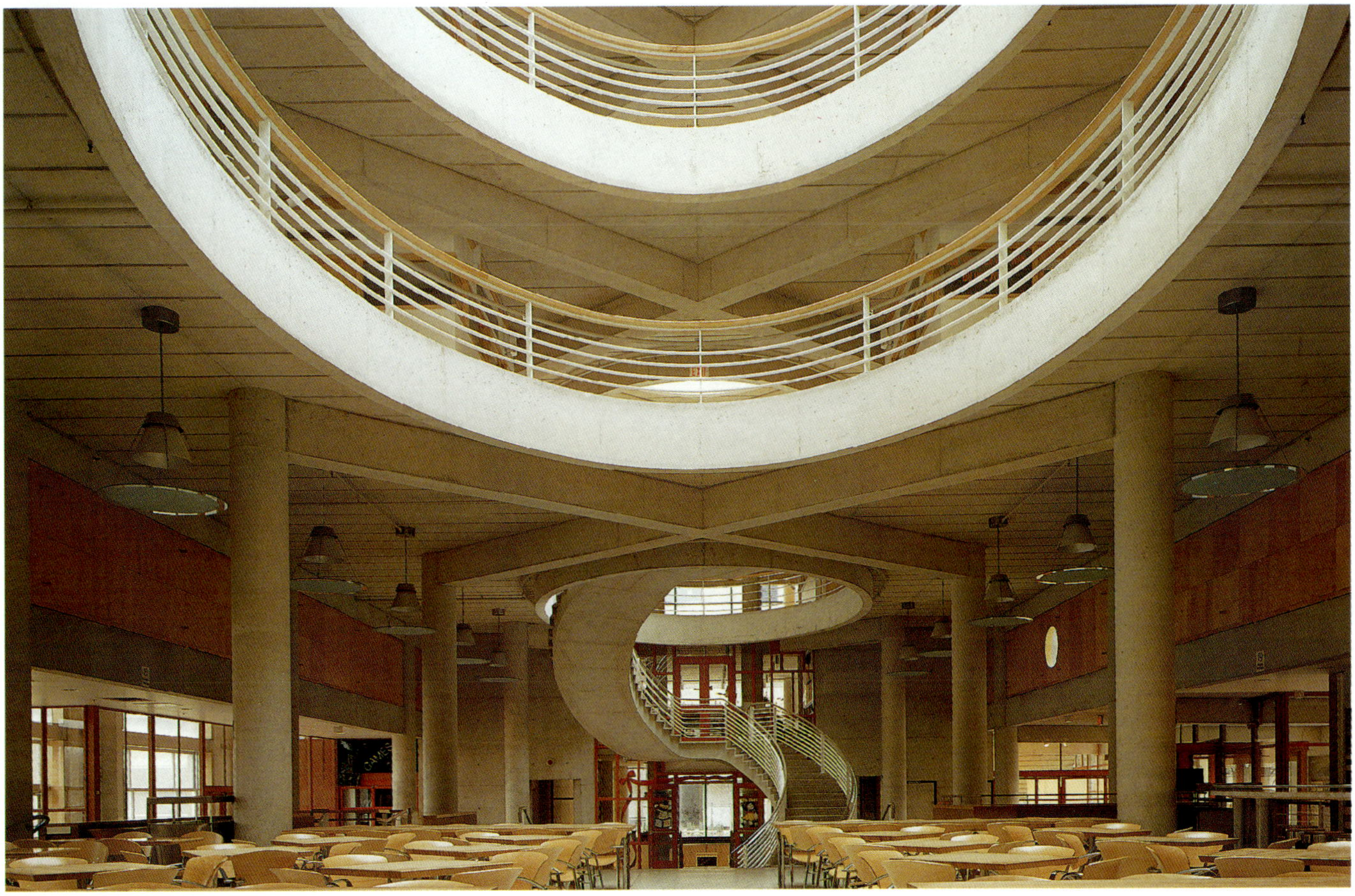

Three light wells are the main means of admitting light to the interior. These wells also provide good views from every position and vantage point all the way through the building.

One of the problems of libraries is that intense summer heat or even bright sunlight can destroy books, but good light is essential for reading. In the Richmond Hill Central Library our objective was to provide sufficient light for reading without admitting direct sunlight. So we had to design some control systems to make that work.

While walls, floors, and ceilings allow for strong definition of space, spatial division can be more subtly suggested by the positioning of structural elements, such as columns. A column can do more than simply support the weight of the building. It can calibrate a room, define a space, serve as a means of reflecting light. An order of columns can imply spaces and circulation routes as well as integrate the mechanical system in a comprehensive way. This is one way you begin to elevate *building* to *architecture*.

Most good public buildings in the northern hemisphere have a public space on the south side. It is no different in Jerusalem. Coming up the Ophel from the City of David to the Temple Mount, there is an open space before the edifice, whether it was Temple or Mosque. In planning the Jerusalem City Hall, this processional feature interested me. I also observed that there is access to the Temple Mount from many different directions, some by accident and some by careful calculation. We felt that if we could replicate the processional and the access experiences, even if we did it a tenth as well, we would have succeeded.

Left and facing page
Jerusalem City Hall
1993

The architecture of Jerusalem has walls and landscape. What is instructive is the way landscape is contained by walls, by man-made objects. The landscape plan of the City Hall is, in essence, this: there is a formal dry square in which there will be scheduled events. This contrasts with an informal green space that lies alongside, the Gan Daniel park. In attempting to integrate the civic complex into the city and not make it a "project," we framed views embracing the surrounding city.

Jerusalem's traditional architecture impressed me with its rich possibilities. In Jerusalem one should not make an enormous egotistic statement, but design buildings that blend and sit well within the landscape. A city hall, however, needs to have more presence than the surrounding buildings and so I began a series of studies to explore ways in which the City Hall might be designed. The Mamluk motif and the way it provides scale interested me very much. I began to study how to introduce what Turkish architecture teaches us. Many of the buildings in Jerusalem are simply stone buildings, without the relief of any delicate detailing, as the Turks used ironwork, or as early Arab architecture used lattice woodwork. The trick was to both enhance the stone and give it a lightness, as well as provide the kind of sunscreening and dappled light characteristic of Middle Eastern architecture.

LECTURE
Balkrishna V. Doshi

The essence of Hindu architecture is to bring life into a building. It must breathe and come alive. This happens through a dynamic harmony between spatial elements and their ability to associate and establish rapport with an onlooker through constant encoding and decoding of messages.

Memory is the mind's accumulated perception of action, image, and time. Present, past, and future have no independent existence beyond the mind. For a Hindu, notions are more important than reality. That is why a stone painted with saffron can become an idol and four banana leaves in a wedding ritual can create shelter encompassing the universe.

India has a long history, and there is a host of historical influences—regional, colonial, Islamic, Hindu, Christian. The effect is like that of blotting paper which over centuries has absorbed various inks. India has adopted new concepts, new cultures, new ideologies, and even diverse religious beliefs. Eventually, the virgin paper is not seen in its original color; each cultural absorption has imparted its own patina, which has become part of the overall cultural scene. Each is different, yet equally valid. This is the reality in which we live.

When one travels in India from North to South or from East to West, one sees all kinds of paradoxes; there is diversity, fantastic vitality, and unimaginable energy. Is it heterogeneous or homogeneous? Is it both? If it is both, how do they coexist simultaneously?

Time has different connotations to an Indian. For a Hindu, time is a cyclic phenomenon. We believe in reincarnation. We believe that there is always going to be a better day. Hope is constant. Forces create and destroy, but then they recreate, and the cycle of creation and destruction continues. This concept allows one to detach from the confines of time and to extend beyond the self to a larger world.

There is a continuity of traditions, rituals, and festivals; ways of life continue. Yet there is acceptance of change, room for discretion, tolerance of difference. In the streets of Ahmedabad, a city of three million people, elephants, cows, and cars stand side by side. What may appear to be an absence of rules, a lack of control, is really tolerance and generosity.

The design of Vidyadhar Nagar (the new city of Jaipur) was an attempt to merge the reformist urbanism of Le Corbusier with the traditions of old Jaipur—two powerful types drawing on different spiritual and intellectual traditions. Incorporating façades and gates, we constructed a set of open spaces of varying scale with an eye to defined functions as well as spontaneous festivities. These were based on the idea that the lifestyle of the people would determine the public space.

Context must and can be created. Memory can be linked to a set of associations from past, present, and future, from symbols, spaces, or situations. Apart from security, functionality, and the technology of a building, I fashion a context based on the sensibilities and the roots of the people for whom I build. People entering the Bharat Diamond Bourse in Mumbai want to feel that they are in a world of magic, an unusual place, a dreamland totally different from their everyday lives. The physical design of the Bourse grew out of the building program and the site itself, which might have been a quarry and trading center for precious stones in the ancient past. Connecting the present to the past, the general plan of the building is that of a many-faceted diamond. The jewel of the Bourse, the trading hall, appears to float. The ceiling is constructed of shiny metal sheets, punctured at selected spots to allow glimpses of the sky. These openings and the roof cover are made of special glass lenses, eliminating glare during the day and offering

Above
Sangath (Doshi Studio)
Ahmedabad, India, 1979–1981

Below
Vidyadhar Nagar (new Jaipur)
Jaipur, India, 1984–1986

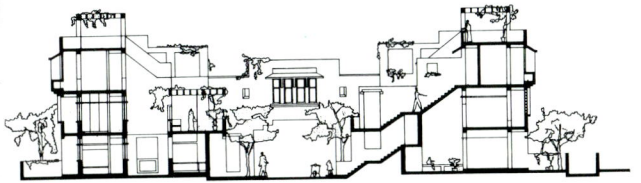

Cross section

Site plan

Right
Indian Institute of Management
Bangalore, India, 1977–1985

Above
**National Institute of
Fashion Technology**
New Delhi, India, 1988–1994

Middle right
Bahrat Diamond Bourse
Mumbai, India, 1992–1998

Right
Hussain-Doshi Gufa
Ahmedabad, India, 1992–1994

a clear view of the stars at night. The structure of the ceiling is totally concealed, making the roof of the trading hall a part of the sky.

I believe in avoiding confinement. There should always be choice, the potential for diversity. I designed the Indian Institute of Management in Bangalore to facilitate education free of constraints. Walking through corridors and courtyards you move through closed and open space, the defined alternating with the flexible, discipline combined with exploratory freedom.

In the Institute of Management, the idea is that the building almost disappears among the pathways, courtyards, and trees. Architecture should become self-effacing. What remains is the sensation of the space and the long "routes" which remind one of the temple, of the villages, of the city spaces. Multiple references convert the passage of truth, and memory is conjured.

Often we don't notice the natural elements unless they are imposing. It is when shadows are hard that shadow and sun are observed. Individual trees are ignored but in a park or a garden the trees become important. Such imposition is what I attempted in this project.

In India there are many juxtapositions: Hindu and Muslim buildings, a big palace and a hut, a temple and a school. They adjoin in such a way that it is impossible to discern what came first, what is intended to relate to what, or indeed what should or should not relate. The point is understanding that everything is coexistent, everything is possible. Relationships arise as a function of the perceiver's beliefs.

In The National Institute of Fashion Technology in New Delhi, my objective was to study light in order to create space which is inside and outside at the same time. Is it possible to move in an interior space, feel outside through visual images and memories, and yet be in balance?

My office in Sangath expresses my personal associations with my own house, Le Corbusier's studio, and more. But I have discovered that other people who come here find evocations of their own experiences in the building.

I strive for architecture that extends beyond one's own memory, activity, community, or message. Water, gardens, landscapes, birds, animals, people, celebrations: these are things people relate to, and they have become major components of my effort in architecture.

The Hussain-Doshi Gufa in Ahmedabad, an underground gallery for a noted artist and friend of mine, is a search for new idioms and interpretations in Indian architecture: architecture that touches psyche. Such a building seems to touch people because there is tremendous diversity, ambiguity, and admixture which the Indian people see every day in their lives. India is a changing, dynamic society with a long tradition: jets and bullock carts, computers and illiteracy, age-old songs and television stations. Indian architecture can be understood as a centuries-long process of absorption and layering. Hindu form was augmented by the Islamic, and the Islamic and the Hindu together have been assimilated to the colonial, and so on. Every period brings additional layers. The added layers have become part of our lives. There are no isolated canons. I believe in a homogeneous heterogeneity, just as I believe in paradoxes, and therefore, in an architecture where order and change are the basic strengths, and paradoxes continually redefine the rules only to break them again.

LECTURE
James Ingo Freed

Some people think memory comes after history, some that history comes after memory. I believe that, as time passes, history becomes a distillation of individual memory and experience distorted through the lens of the present. We constantly reinterpret the past to fit our model of the present.

Memory is a specialized form of history. History is, of necessity, more abstract, more condensed, seeking a cooler rather than a more passionate role. It can even be a merely recitative role. Memory stirs and moves individuals and is therefore vulnerable. History, on the other hand, compels our attention. When memory is institutionalized it becomes political.

I prefer memory to history because I prefer the authentic to the reconstructed. History erases detail at a painful cost. It gains consistency through abstraction and it yields a loss of the richness of life. As a physical artifact of a given time, place, and culture, architecture is an undistorted and unchanged thread of memory woven into the tapestry of history. Yet this thread is constantly strained by the ravages of nature and man.

The unique, freestanding object-building is rare, for buildings relate, even if unwillingly, to their context. There is always a potential conflict between context and invention. Inevitably, both are addressed by the architect. They need to be seen for what they are before the architecture can be read.

When reading, however, we must understand the significance of the text. An example: For some, the industrial architecture of the 1920s is merely a style—just a surface, a lake to fish in for architectural goodies. I find this architecture rather remarkable. That period was one of the few times in history when architects had to invent a new language to contend with new kinds of functions and activities and a completely different scale.

The Los Angeles Convention Center is a sunny, almost joyful building. It explodes outward. It invites you to look in—the opposite of the U.S. Holocaust Memorial Museum—you must look in, and you see it. It is an immense thing, almost a half-mile long. Yet, it has to live in the city and be part of the city. When you think of the city of Los Angeles, you don't think of a long, hallowed history; you don't think of rooted, venerated culture. But there is a culture of the freeway. The freeway is the theme that runs through the city; so we designed the center on the scale of the freeway. While the structure works as a representative of a sort of late iconic modernism, it also stands as a barrier for everything behind it.

Los Angeles Convention Center Expansion
Los Angeles, California, 1986–1993

Top and left
United States Holocaust Memorial Museum
Washington, D. C., 1986–1993

Above
Auschwitz Concentration Camp
Auschwitz, Poland
Entrance sign, ARBEIT MACHT FREI
("Work will make you free")

I was absolutely stunned when I got the commission to do the Holocaust Museum. I had nowhere to start. One of the things that is very difficult to deal with in architecture is the expression of emotion. I decided, after some thought and some unfruitful initial studies, that I would have to go to places where the Holocaust took place. We went to Poland and elsewhere and I was left with images of gates, of bridges that segregate people, of transparencies, lies, screens; images of pathways to death.

I was born in 1930 in Germany; I went through Kristallnacht. I got out very quickly in 1939 when I was nine years old. I remember Kristallnacht because my father took me down to see the synagogue burn. We had never been inside it before. When we saw it burn, he managed to get a little tessellated piece of decoration that he kept with him for a long time. Had I stayed there a year longer, I probably would not be here now; and that conclusion came to me as I walked through the gates of Auschwitz. The climax was coming face to face with the ovens. I walked in and saw an oven; a number of people had placed flowers or candles inside it, and I considered that indecent. I realized I couldn't work in this environment. Instead, I decided to do it by indirection, by moving another way, by looking at it out of the corner of my eye, by assessing what it was: a perfectly good piece of machinery.

The doors to the gas chambers were stamped with the logo of the producer, who wrote to his SS patrons—who were running a normal construction office, doing shop drawings, and the like—saying his firm had done such an efficient job that he wanted a bonus. Then he asked: Would you please send other work my way?

In the death camps ordinary machinery became, by use, evil. The nefarious function changed the design. Braces were added to keep the ovens from exploding from the gases generated and accumulated in them due to overuse. The oven company was required to manufacture a super-charged oven that let people be loaded from both front and back.

I looked at the ovens, and considered how we could organize a building that somehow would embody this. After about three months of thinking, I decided that the building did not pose the familiar problem of the contained and the container. This is a building wherein the contained works on the container; the container strains to suppress its contents. Nothing overtly connected with death could go into it, but somehow the spirit of the death machine had to move through it: a daunting spirit, a spirit that in many ways was difficult to contain, as the gases from the ovens were difficult to contain.

When I looked more carefully at some of the details of the death camps, I discovered that these were details that had been perfected by the late-modernist attitude toward structure. The architecture was really not so different from anything I had been previously looking at or doing.

I discovered that for me the only way into the Holocaust was through both the tectonics of the Holocaust and an invented tectonics of my own. There was an architecture of the Holocaust, with its own tectonics that surround the surfaces; and there was a raw structure that activated the spaces inside.

Consider that in some of the camps they utilized an English cross-bond applied to straps used as mullions on constructed walls. It is the most difficult bond to lay up, and this presents one of the many anomalies, great and small, of the Holocaust: Why use this difficult bond when you are only going to destroy it?

I believe that it was necessary to build this memorial museum because it could

United States Holocaust Memorial Museum
Washington, D. C., 1986–1993

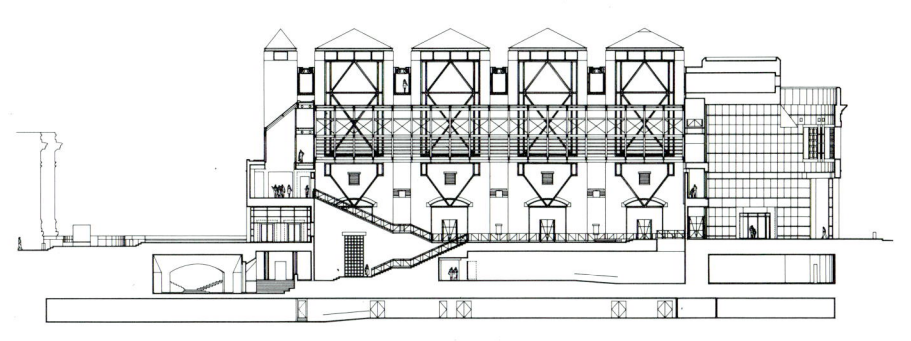

Longitudinal section

become an institution of learning in the United States, an institution of ongoing receptivity to all that becomes known of the Holocaust. Without it, the memory will soon change into history and disappear.

All the windows in the memorial are blocked up. One of them quotes Dwight D. Eisenhower saying: "Remember, they will try to change it. They will try to say it never happened. I want you to bear witness that it did."

When I was first invited to come to the seminar, I had six projects I wanted to discuss. The Holocaust Memorial was not one of them. I thought it would be very difficult to include it because the Holocaust Memorial in Washington is so different from Jerusalem's Yad Vashem; it has a different role to play. But finally, I thought: If not here, where? If not now, when?

LECTURE
Arata Isozaki

Facing page, top
Tateyama Museum of Toyama
Toyama, Japan, 1989–1991

Facing page, bottom
Team Disney Building
Orlando, Florida, 1987–1990

I think history is a fiction fabricated out of a view of the past. Everybody constructs a history of their own; I have my history, you have yours. As a construction of the facts and events of the past, history looks like a kind of a tissue, or weaving of tissues, in a chronological or topical pattern reflecting the beliefs of various nations and tribes. The tissues of past events are texts from our point of view.

Memory is a message from the past carried by members of a community or a civilization. But the carriers have their own messages as well. When designing, architects have to confront the entire constellation of messages which engenders the cultural context. They must decide what to continue, from what to disassociate, what to augment, and what to elaborate.

Japanese culture incorporates special practices intended to lead to a high level of understanding of life. Tea ceremonies and martial arts are not just hobbies, not just pleasure, but rituals which endow a kind of mental rigor and indicate a spiritual path.

The site of the Tateyama Museum of Toyama is one of the most sacred mountains in Japan where, until the mid-nineteenth century, people traditionally climbed in pilgrimage. The museum design attempts to reconstruct the spirit of this tradition and of the Buddhist temple that once stood on the site.

Inside we used the Japanese tatami-mat seating arrangement, above which are windows and, over them, three white panels. There are three large-scale screens and projections from the top of the walls. The screens are used to teach about the area, as the preachers used to sermonize in the days of pilgrimage. Then the screens are pushed up to the panels above the windows through which the sacred mountain is revealed. In this way, I tried to let memory enter in while facilitating simulation of what happened in the past.

Sometimes we have to build some completely blank enormous structure without history, without any memories. The Team Disney Building in Orlando, Florida, the office headquarters for the big theme park and Epcot Center, is such a project. When I took a flight in a helicopter to look at the site, I found there are almost no significant physical features such as a hill or a mountain. The only thing I saw was infinite flatness, damp grasses, trees, and forest. There were some bodies of water but nothing more. I thought that if we had to land some structure on this site without any context, the metaphor of an ocean liner might work. An ocean liner always moves around, but has to anchor at a port, and this could be a port. Thus, water surrounds this building.

The Disney Company's major business in Orlando is a theme park, so they always think in terms of themes. From the first presentation to Michael Eisner, we were required to have a theme for the building. Considering the very nice weather in Florida, and thinking about the way shadow is important as a design element, I realized that a sundial—the world's largest sundial—could be a part of the theme of this building. With the sundial as symbol, the theme of the building became time itself and the project was approved.

The most misunderstood project I ever did is the Tsukuba Center Building, completed in 1983. I started to design this building at the end of 1970 for the only postwar, large-scale, new town initiated by the Japanese government. Many laboratories and universities were moving out of Tokyo, but people did not want to follow them, because Tokyo had cultural attractions and offered convenient facilities. To encourage people to come to Tsukuba, the government decided first to build a hotel-shopping mall complex at its center. For me this was a difficult

221

Right and below
Tsukuba Center Building
Tsukuba Science City
Ibaragi, Japan, 1979–1983

Bottom
Art Tower Mito
Ibaragi, Japan, 1986–1990

project. I had to overcome profound ambivalence. I am part of the immediate post-war generation that saw itself as an avant-garde negating the traditional notions of government, which in our view had led to the fascism of the war period. How could I, an opponent of the idea of the nation-state, engage in a government-sponsored project celebrating the Japanese nation-state? Moreover, it was just at this time that the center of gravity in Japan's image was shifting from governmental-military power to private economic power, from samurai to salaryman. My response to both my own ambivalence about the traditional Japanese nation-state and the new ambivalence concerning the state's identity was to look exclusively to Western architecture for inspiration. This project was much criticized because I did not use any Japanese images.

Art Tower Mito in Ibaragi is a cultural center of museums, concert halls, theaters, conference rooms, and a tower. The tower is one hundred meters high and symbolizes the hundred-year anniversary of the city. The tetrahedrons are clustered and covered by titanium. The effect is an endless tower that provides a stage for one hundred years of past and a future of indeterminate length.

The museum building as a building type must have some connection to memories and the history of institutions. For thirty years I have studied, designed, and built museums, especially art museums, in Japan and abroad. I think their development over the last two centuries may be schematized in three stages. A first-generation museum exhibited traditional art, classic art, which was produced not for a gallery but for a temple, a palace, or church. Such art was torn out, usually stolen, from its intended venue, then gathered and collected by a king, an aristocrat, or

The Museum of Contemporary Art
Los Angeles, California, 1981–1986

a government representing a nation-state, and ultimately intended for exhibition in a museum open to the public. Such museums are a means by which nation-states define their own identity, and they are invariably important institutions within the cities where they are located. In such museums, all the objects have a frame or a base which means they are movable. This renders them a kind of commodity in a market.

The second stage of museum development was tied in with the modern art that appeared in the latter part of the nineteenth century. Impressionists, modernists, and various avant-garde artists opposed the state's idea of the museum. For them, art pieces were two-dimensional planes or three-dimensional bodies created independently of specific contexts. The modern art gallery is merely a convenient place to locate these art objects, which are displayed on their own terms. This is the basic idea of museums of modern art like MoMA in New York and others.

The Museum of Contemporary Art in Los Angeles is a third-stage museum, different from a traditional museum of modern art in that its collection combines the changed, new type of art with the traditional "frame and base" type.

When I designed The Museum of Contemporary Art I thought about the very beautiful sunshine of Southern California and about very strong contrasts of shadow and light. I also realized that this museum would be surrounded by large-scale, high-rise skyscrapers and condominiums. This induced me to make all the building elements smaller, like a village under the cliff of a mountain.

LECTURE
Antoine Predock

Above and facing page, top
Fuller House
Scottsdale, Arizona, 1987

Facing page, bottom
American Heritage Center and Art Museum
University of Wyoming at Laramie,
Laramie, Wyoming, 1993

There is a Jorge Luis Borges story called *"Funes el memorioso,"* translated as "Funes the Memorious." Funes had infinite memory. As an adult he remembered the fly that buzzed around his ear as a seven-year-old. He remembered the waft of the breeze across his face when he was twenty-one. His infinite memory was ultimately a cacophonous realm that entrapped him. He died confused and alone in a dark room where he had tried to limit his sensory input, to stop the memories from accumulating.

For all of us today there is too much memory, and we must be selective if we are to use our memories to help us make meaning of the present. I think all architects have their own process of filtration that excludes certain memories.

For forty years I have been a desert rat in the American Southwest in Albuquerque, New Mexico. That's the best I can say about myself. I understand my position is a suspicious one, because all around me are living, breathing manifestations of Native American cultures and I really do feel like an interloper. I try my best to understand the place through eyes that aren't inherently connected to it. This approach is evident in one of my first projects, the Fuller House, a true adobe, mud-brick structure, defensive against the low sun angles and westerly dust storms. The pyramidal library evokes the mountains silhouetted on the skyline behind the house.

In Laramie, Wyoming, I won a competition to house an American archive of Western memorabilia on the University of Wyoming campus. It's called the American Heritage Center. I thought of an archival mountain with a village at its foot. The alignment of the archival mountain follows what I call the rendezvous axis. Native Americans had rendezvoused on this site many times; French trappers and American settlers had gathered there as well. So an expression of rendezvous and crossroads aligning with important mountains—Medicine Bow Peak to the west, Pilot's Knob to the east—established the axis of the building. The archival mountain, a black patined copper piece, a mountain alone in a sweeping vista, is framed by distant mountains and the football stadium of the campus. Actually, on another axis, it is seen against the sky. The black patined copper cone evolves, looking almost like an ancient helmet. The interior realm of the stretched cone absorbs the entry area; its center piece is a hearth. Laramie has intense snow and wind, so I imagine this building, with its very controlled apertures in the conical archival mountain, smoking at night, drawing scholars into the archive to gather around the hearth. The concept of architecture as analogous to landscape is something that has interested me for a long time. To demonstrate this, I have skied over the roofs of one of my buildings.

For many people landscape is a collection of views, something to gaze upon. For me, landscape is an artifact of culture. When we first approach a site, I make a collage of photographs, postcards, rocks, animal skeletons—whatever elicits the spirit of the place. The choices I make arise from an attempt to understand that spirit, rooted as it is in both the past and the present. The timeless emanations, the specifics of place, work their way through my process of discovery. Primal shapes, folklore, contemporary technology, cyberspace—they are all included.

The Nelson Fine Arts Center at Arizona State University is a highly processional building. The notion of architecture as an unfolding panorama of episodically linked spaces in great buildings I've visited, and as I've experienced in Jerusalem's Old City, suggests that architecture has so many vantage points. The multiple vantage points in my work are highly critical. It's hard to tell where the front door is; my buildings very often are criticized for that, but I think there's a payoff when you do find it.

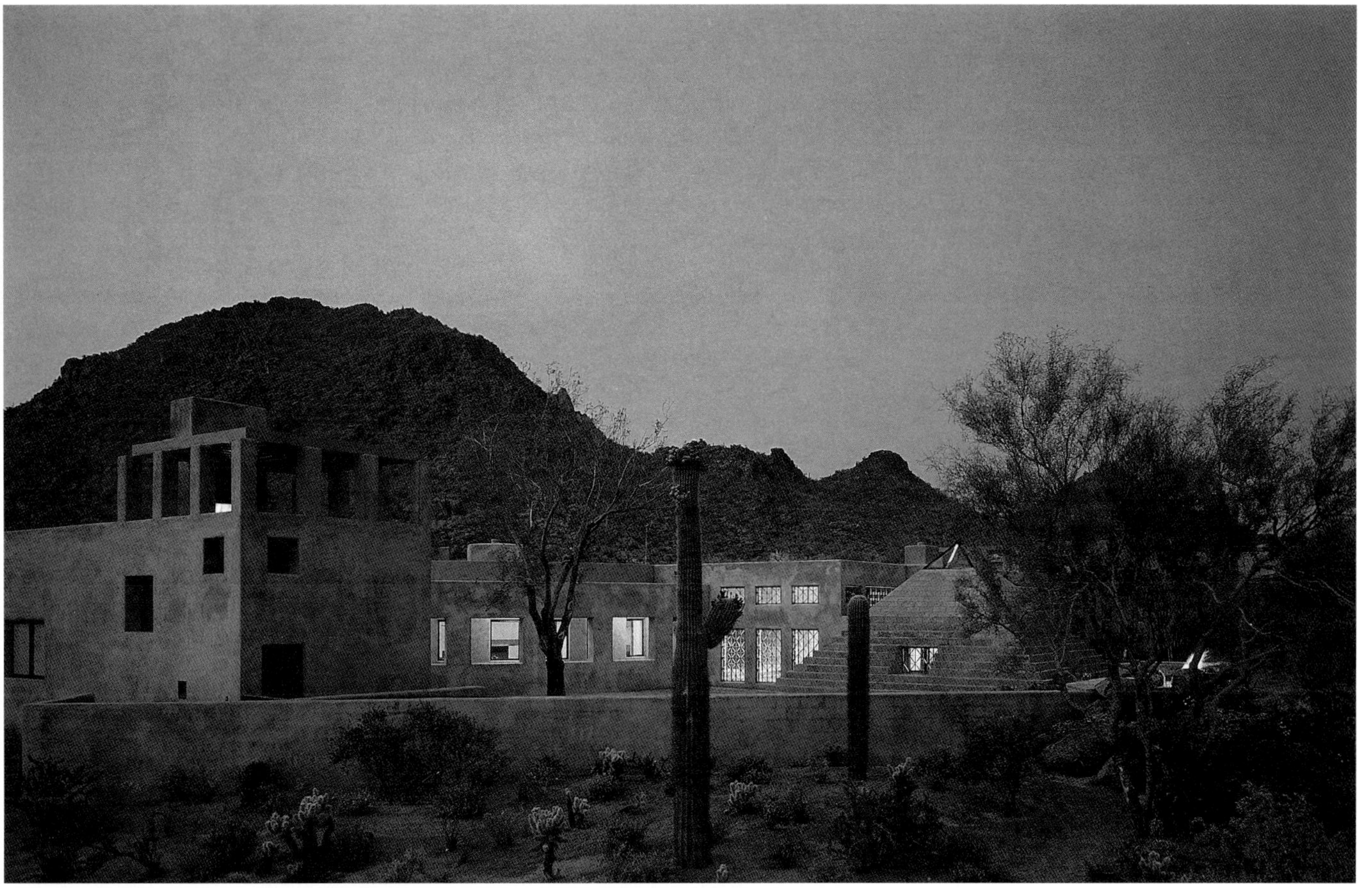

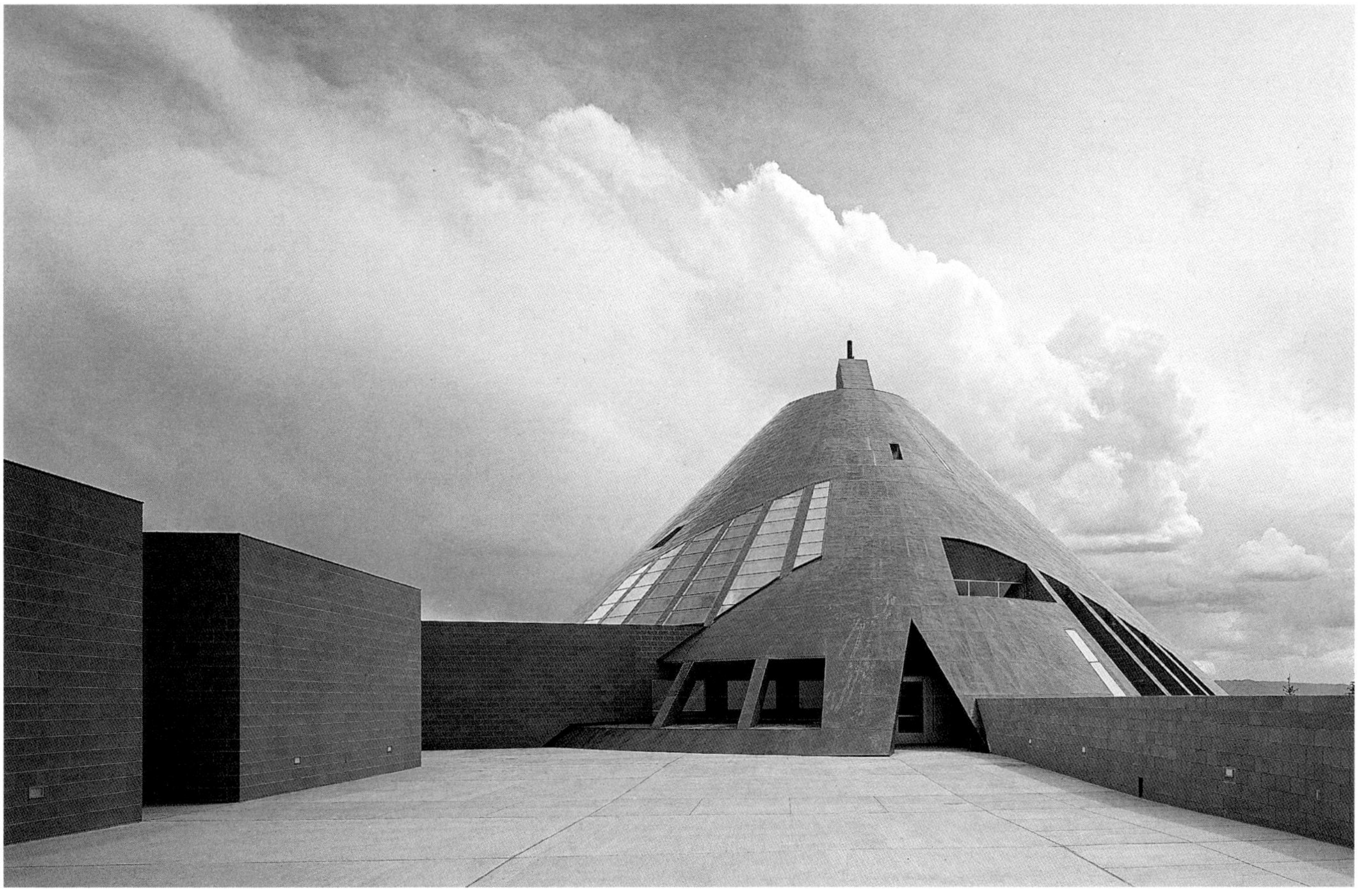

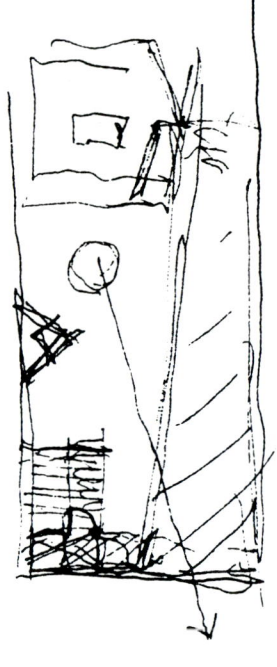

Top
Nelson Fine Arts Center
Arizona State University,
Tempe, Arizona, 1989

Above and right
Venice House
Venice Beach, Los Angeles, California 1991

I did a house in Venice Beach, Los Angeles. The original Los Angeles basin is a great, semi-arid valley with towering mountains five thousand feet above and sparse chaparral landscape. There are native sycamores in the watersheds and riparian plant growth. My proposition was to collapse space and time to encounter the sea from an alleyway on a thirty-by-ninety sort of shotgun site, and to gaze through at the ocean via a diverging perspectival condition that would make the ocean seem closer—perceptually, subliminally—and release the view via a one-ton pivot piece.

I included an armature of concrete as bones along the shore, a great creature. I placed the foreground of polished granite monolith coated with a film of water as a recollection of the bedrock substrate of Los Angeles. The breakwaters are made of this local granite. I thought of the longing for the original place and not the ephemeral Hollywood-invented place. I am getting involved in memory here, but it's not about nostalgia. Nostalgia would be red-tiled roofs with suspect stylistic overtones. I hope this house doesn't have that.

Dallas, Texas, was founded by a developer. We can't even say that there were daring colonists who came through. It was the work of a developer whose predecessors had erased the Native American culture through genocide. There wasn't anything: no Spanish square, no *cardo* or *decumanus* had migrated from Spain to the New World. The site of the house I built in Dallas is great because there's nothing to base anything on, except birds and the land. My clients were intense

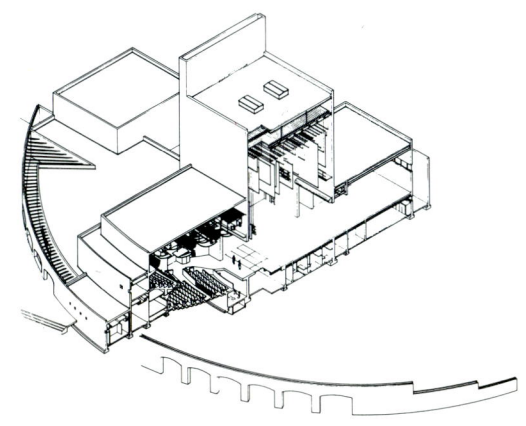

Left
Turtle Creek House
Dallas, Texas, 1993

bird-watchers, so I called the project Theater of the Trees. Theater of the Trees has foreground limestone ledges that allude to the limestone present in the Turtle Creek watershed. The limestone ledges are planted with plants that birds love. When you arrive in your car, the birds greet you. You penetrate through a fissure in the limestone ledges to the realm beyond, the realm of the sky and the birds. The house aspires to the sky. There is a sky ramp, a bridge going nowhere. On the creek watershed side of the house, the sky ramp soars sixty feet into the sky above the watershed, into the trees, toward the levels of the birds' habitat, and there's a thirty-by-thirty-foot-square convex, highly-polished stainless-steel panel. I thought there should be something on the side of the house that created a disquieting relationship between the skin of the house and the space beyond. I thought of fun-house mirrors that make you look fat or skinny. You see a bird approaching the mirror, and the bird suddenly compresses. You see the house being absorbed by itself, devoured by itself. This space of illusion is a kind of Plato's cave, where you are not sure of the reality of the house. I like the idea of the house vacuuming itself in reflection.

We all talk about memory, but you can also just make things up. You can create memories. You can fabricate a site of imagination. There is no obligation to follow the original trail. You can talk about it, but you can also disclaim it, obliterate it, replace it. You can invent memory, you can invent a place in the desert. It is no less improbable than Plato describing Atlantis.

COMMENTARY

Stanford Anderson

Memory in Architecture

John Ruskin perceived architecture as society's primary harbor of memory, more faithful and real than any text. In his *Sixth Lamp of Architecture* he wrote: ". . . for it is in becoming memorial or monumental that a true perfection is attained by civil and domestic buildings." In asserting the memorial role even of domestic building, Ruskin expresses the conservative wish that people maintain their place within a societal hierarchy. Memory, then, can readily serve as a vehicle for maintaining the status quo, for resisting change and criticism. Here, tradition may be opposed to memory. Despite its often conservative usage, "tradition" points forward rather than backward: it allows societal assumptions to be brought to cognizance, criticized, and changed under the imperatives of the present.

Memory and architectural preservation was also the theme of a noted essay of 1903 by the Austrian art historian Alois Riegl titled "The Modern Cult of Monuments." In contrast to Ruskin, Riegl argues that the asserted monument calls for restoration to that original state which makes it, for us, a monument. If for Ruskin architecture seems to speak unproblematically, conveying faithful memories, for Riegl memory and monument are our own constructions, and he was aware of their potential for manipulation and coercion. Most ethnic or national conflicts of our time provide ample evidence of how memory can be used as a vehicle for incitement and control; the repressive regimes of this century have used numerous, oppressive monuments to serve these manipulations. Therefore, the importance of history as a critical means by which to undermine manipulated memories is clear. Conversely, because memory is open to doubt, valid memories, too, are vulnerable to challenge and thus need the support of critical history.

I want to establish a dialogue between social memory, or memory through architecture, and what I would call memory in architecture. Topics concerned with memory through architecture include tradition as opposed to memory; the cult of ruins in the service of memory; memory as the premise for architectural preservation; architecture and memory as coercive forces acting on society; the importance of critical history as a supplement to memory; the intentional monument as a vehicle for unintended subversive commentary; and the status of monument and memory in contemporary society. In this essay, the phrase memory in architecture alludes to "disciplinary memory," which encompasses our relations to earth, sky, fire, and water; the myriad ways we define space and control light; the way we relate materials and structure to systems of order and even to disorder. While all forms of memory may elide, I think there is a history to the distinction of social and disciplinary memory that merits attention. Historically, how has the relation of disciplinary memory to societal memory changed?

In literate or well-established societies, one finds traditional forms of dwelling type and urban fabric that represent the persistence of a particular sociocultural organizational system. In vernacular cultures, tradition (where it still exists) serves to maintain the society's dynamic equilibrium. In this case, social memory and disciplinary memory remain closely associated, so much so that one might speak of "memory without monuments," after Hermann Muthesius, the German architect and historian, or of memory as intrinsic to the act of building.

In the Middle Ages, religious and symbolic references pervaded what I have called social memory. Remembrance within the religion established not only the need, but also the building type, certain key forms, and even the range of options available to the architect. In the eighteenth century, however, with the classical archeological work of architects such as Stuart and Revett, depictions and descriptions attempted to reproduce the visible aspects of the original. Building types such as the classical temple began to be used for domestic purposes, with the effect of gradually draining the original edifice of its "content."

Such attempts to return to origin have largely constituted what has long been regarded as the discipline of architecture, the substance of our disciplinary memory. However, one may argue that these classical archetypes owe their place in our disciplinary memory to something more general than their singular form or specific detail, or the prominence they happen to have held at the time of their making. Architects of all times have worked with such constitutive elements as space, light, and order, a legacy that can be employed imaginatively in the service of society. In modern times this legacy has become increasingly the property of the discipline of architecture, but its continued effectiveness must depend on its ability to awaken responses in all those who experience it. Perhaps such concerns are never wholly absent in any architecture, although in the work of certain architects—Alvar Aalto, Le Corbusier, Louis I. Kahn, Sverre Fehn, Maurice Smith—they have been noticeably and concientiously explored.

Most monuments do indeed fall into oblivion, even vast ones like Grant's Tomb in New York, so we may well be tempted to adopt a dismissive attitude toward commemorative monuments, even though contemporary artists like Krzysztof Wodiczko are able to revitalize the reactionary, received monument of our day by exposing it to a critical light. Moreover, a work like the Vietnam Memorial by Maya Lin reminds us that the monument is not entirely defunct in contemporary society either as an agent of social memory or as a vehicle for architecture.

Societal and architectural memory are no longer as indissolubly connected as they were in previous epochs. Our disciplinary memory has become increasingly autonomous and more inaccessible to society at large. We might say that architecture suffers not only from a certain loss of memory, but also from an inability to transcend the limits of individualism. From this point of view the buildings of Le Corbusier, Aalto, and Kahn are not traditional monuments but explorations of architectural constituents that evoke memory. Conceiving of buildings as a form of aide-mémoire is perhaps the only way for us to write a disciplinary history today as opposed to compiling a mere catalog of monuments. Thus we always need to reconstruct not only the original circumstances of the work but also the principles it embodies in order to construct an internal history of the discipline; we need to cultivate memory in architecture as well as memory through architecture.

Editor's Note
A revised version of this presentation was published as "Memory in Architecture/ Erinnerung in der Architektur," in *Daidalos* 58 (December 1995), pp. 22–37.

COMMENTARY

Kenneth Frampton

The Case for the Tectonic as Commemorative Form

The beginning of modern culture in the Renaissance is associated with the primacy accorded to scenographic representation in the emerging bourgeois world—a mode of representation that introduced ambiguities into Western architecture. Nonetheless, we know that building is as *tectonic* in character as it is *scenographic*. One may argue that building is first and foremost an act of construction rather than a discourse predicated on surface, mass, and plan, to cite the "Three Reminders to Architects" advanced by Le Corbusier in *Towards a New Architecture* of 1923. One may further claim that architecture is as much ontological in character as it is representational, and that built form is a "thing" rather than a "sign," to indulge momentarily in Martin Heidegger's terminology.

I have chosen to concentrate on the theme of the tectonic because I believe that, in view of the present drift toward the commodification of the built environment, it is necessary for architects to reposition themselves. The term *tectonic*, Greek in origin, derives from the word *tekton*, signifying carpenter or builder. This in turn stems from the Sanskrit *taksan*, referring to the craft of carpentry and the use of the axe. It is said that the term acquired a poetic connotation in the sixth century B.C., the time of Sappho, when the *tekton*, the carpenter, became associated with the poet. This etymological evolution would suggest a gradual passage across time from the ontological to the representational.

The term tectonic was first elaborated in a modern sense in Karl Bötticher's *The Tectonic of the Hellenes* of 1852 and in Gottfried Semper's essay "The Four Elements of Architecture," published in the same year. It was further developed in Semper's unfinished study, *Style in the Technical and Tectonic Arts or Practical Aesthetics*, which was finally published in 1868. In another essay, "Four Elements of Architecture," Semper divides the generic building into four components: 1) the podium or earthwork; 2) the framework and roof considered together; 3) the hearth, which is the symbolic, public nexus of the work; and 4) the woven infill framework. He distinguishes between two kinds of wall: the lightweight infill wall (*Die Wand*) and the heavyweight loadbearing wall *(Die Mauer)*. The former appears in the wattle-and-daub construction of the medieval town; the latter in the fortifications and permanent centers of spiritual and secular power— the church, the castle—built in stonework.

Clearly, the term *tectonic* cannot be divorced from the technological means by which to achieve it. Regardless, one may identify three different conditions and/or modes of representation that are evident in built form: 1) the *technological* that arises out of a pragmatic response to a given condition; 2) the *scenographic* that represents abstract mythic or symbolic content as embodied in the surface of a work—the *mask*, as Semper would refer to it; and 3) *the tectonic*, which is capable of synthesizing both the technological and the representational into a single form. If the first of these modes embodies basic construction and the second is a representational skin laid over its surface, then the third is the synthesis of the two, as in the Greek Doric order. As we know, the Doric column was made up out of a series of superimposed stone cylinders held in place by metal spigots. Later it was carved with flutes that render the column as a single shaft while expressing its capacity to carry a static load.

The three conditions identified above relate to Semper's distinction between the symbolic and the technical aspects of construction, a distinction I have attempted to relate to the difference between the representational and ontological aspects of built form. Semper would distinguish further between the tectonics of the tensile frame, in which members are conjoined to encompass a volume, and the stereotomics of a compressive mass, which is constructed through the superimposition of identical units even though it may embody space. One should note that the term *stereotomics* derives from the Greek terms for stone, *stereos*, and cutting, *-tomia*.

Where the implications of the tectonic tend toward the aerial and toward dematerialization, the stereotomic tends toward the earth; where the one presupposes lightness in all its connotations, the other presupposes weight and darkness. Semper's distinction between tectonic and stereotomic recalls arguments recently advanced by Vittorio Gregotti to the effect that marking the ground rather than building the primitive hut is the primordial tectonic act.

> . . . The worst enemy of modern architecture is the idea of space considered solely in terms of its economic and technical exigencies indifferent to the idea of the site. The built environment that surrounds us is, we believe, the physical representation of its history, and the way in which it has accumulated different levels of meaning to form the specific quality of the site, not just for what it appears to be, in perceptual terms, but for what it is in structural terms. . . . The environment is therefore not a system in which to dissolve architecture. On the contrary, it is the most important material from which to develop the project... From this vantage point, new principles and methods can be seen for design. Principles and methods that give precedence to the siting in a specific area. This is an act of knowledge of the context that comes out of its architectural modification. The origin of architecture is not the primitive hut, the cave or the mythical 'Adam's House in Paradise.'
>
> Before transforming a support into a column, roof into a tympanum, before placing stone on stone, man placed a stone on the ground to recognize a site in the midst of an unknown universe, in order to take account of it and modify it. (Address to The Architectural League of New York, October 1982. Published in *Section A*, February/March 1983, p. 8.)

Gregotti explains that architecture's stereotomic aspect is by far the more primordial, not only because it involves the compressive mass of stone but also because it is the essential substance of the earthwork by which the ground is marked. This is not to deny the importance of the spatial construct in architecture but rather to argue that it is inseparable from its foundation in the earth. Situated at the interface between culture and nature, building is as much about the earthwork as about the roofwork. Mario Botta's notion of "building the site," therefore, is of greater critical import than the creation of freestanding objects, for architecture is as much about place-making and the passage of time as it is about the abstractions of space and form. Light, water, wind, and weather: these are the natural agents acting on architecture, causing it to mature over time. To this we may simply add that the ultimate earthworks are, as Adolf Loos put it, the tomb and the monument—the quintessential forms of tectonic commemoration.

Inasmuch as its temporal continuity transcends our individual mortality, building ensures the continuity of the public realm as a civic art form rather than of architecture as a private act. The tectonic is, above all, a poetics of construction. It has nothing to do with immediacy or with the spectacular. Its ultimate value resides in its capacity to withstand the test of time.

COMMENTARY

Joseph Rykwert

History and Memory

The French historian Pierre Nora once remarked that "Memory is life, borne by living societies founded in its name. History, on the other hand, is the reconstruction, always problematic and incomplete, of what is no longer." History, then, is how I reconstruct my past, other people's pasts, the pasts of other nations and cities. It is my reconstruction that puts together and gives meaning to those fragments of the past, whether remote or recent.

Memory, on the other hand, is not something I *do* at all. Memory happens to me; it is involuntary. It is something that I am almost pushed to activate sometimes by external circumstance. Memory is therefore always diacritical and, unlike history (which is always about time), it is always about place, about location. We may recall the two great poets of memory in our time: James Joyce, whose memory was located in Dublin; and Marcel Proust, whose madeleine has almost become a kind of cliché of memory prompts. Though in fact, the source of Proust's paradisical remembrance was not the madeleine itself but rather the experience of standing on the uneven paving stones in the Basilica of St. Mark in Venice. It is the poets and not the historians who provide us with an access to memory and who tell us how memory works.

Architects work in a way analogous to that of historians. Of course, we too hope that we might transcend our day-to-day tasks and be seen as having achieved a poetic result. But this is not something we can strive for consciously; it is something that, if the graces allow it, will eventually happen. It is not for us to make memory places. Instead, our task is to deal with the past through history, because our activity is a conscious activity and can never come directly from those springs of unconsciousness. We can make places that connect us to the past. We can even make places that have historical depth. But we can also make places that obliterate the past and which are deliberately intended to facilitate forgetting.

In general, we must admit that architects have a problem gaining access to the thickness and density of the past, which we always tend to reduce to some kind of textuality. As a result, we seem to live in a time when the place of memory can only be made through defilement and transgression. This all goes back to the 1820s and 1830s, when worry about style, ornament, and the appropriateness of any ornament to the times first began in earnest. The problem of textuality first arose then—we could say after the publication of Victor Hugo's essay "This Will Kill That" (*Ceci tuera cela*), his retroactive prophesy that the book, the printed word, will kill the building. The famous phrase appears in a chapter that Hugo inserted into his best-known novel, *The Hunchback of Notre Dame,* in which he explains that the prevalence of the book, the rise of the text as the most widely-diffused organ of knowledge, will kill what had been the main experience of architecture in the past.

In response to this predicament, a number of architects devised forms whose ornament was based on lettering. Among the first of these was a confidant of Hugo's, Henri Labrouste, whose Bibliotheque de Sainte-Geneviève in Paris, designed in the 1830s, was decorated with seals (like blobs of ink) and panels listing the names of the great authors of history. There are still some blank spaces left around the corner of the building, enabling the director of the library to add names whenever he or she finds this appropriate. Here we have textuality *in se* as the full basis for the ornament. In a sense this is a denial of what had been perhaps the old experience of building as something touchable, as something you can relate to your body. In this respect we may say that Labrouste was the first architect to reduce the essence of a building to a text.

The Vietnam Memorial in Washington, D.C., designed from 1981 to 1982 by a young Chinese architectural student, Maya Lin, consists of a wall conforming to a right angle in plan and treated as art of variable depth cut into the ground. Visitors gain direct access to this cut and its basalt retaining wall via ramped walkways that descend and rise. The entire surface of the polished, black, basalt wall is inscribed with the names of the dead. People come to the wall and leave flowers behind. Sometimes they leave other kinds of mementos—a medal or a flag. However, many visitors were unable to relate to the abstraction of this memorial that consisted of nothing but inscribed names on a wall. This textuality no longer had the power to move them, and their way of relating to it by leaving odd mementos was not adequate to the emotional charge felt during the visit. So they agitated for something else on the site in addition to the wall. This demand was met by providing a figural piece adjacent to but not touching the wall, a sculpture of three soldiers representing the three main ethnic groups in the United States in the 1990s: Asian, Black, and European. As many crowds gather around these figures as visit the original monument itself. If a visitor lost a loved one in the Vietnam war, he or she may want to touch the wall, but at the same time many visitors prefer to see these soldier figures as the ultimate commemorative objects, as something they can relate strongly to—as a sculptural group, in fact, capable of evoking memory.

How do we make places of memory in the high-rise cities of our time? I think this has become increasingly difficult, partly because architecture has been reduced to a surface on which the word is written. Memory places are produced today only at the most extreme moments of emotional tension. Only then does a monument truly become possible, as was the case with the Monument to the Dead of the Concentration Camps, the memorial to the anti-Nazi, anti-Fascist Italian heroes of the resistance during World War II. This monument was erected after the war in the main cemetery in Milan to the designs of Belgioioso, Peresutti, and Rogers (BBPR). Only when an entire people or city is touched by a particularly violent event can a single point be chosen as the focus of our collective memory. Unfortunately, such memory is short-lived, and today this resistance monument is no longer a focus of attention. I am equally sure that the monuments in Washington will not survive the disappearance of the particular moments of tension that produced them. Within this context I would argue that the United States Holocaust Memorial Museum is not a place of memory but a place of history. In this sense, access to memory is always through history, and so it must always be purged by history and thus reconstructed as a historical event. As individuals we make memory places by the touch of the hand, by the recall of a painful or happy experience. But the access to memory in architecture can only be achieved through history.

1992

THE PUBLIC BUILDING: FORM & INFLUENCE

November 8–11
The Jerusalem Theater

Seminar Co-chairmen
Julian Beinart
Arthur Spector

Session Chairs
Elinoar Barzacchi
David Guggenheim
Robert Oxman
David Reznik

Presenters
Henry N. Cobb
Charles Correa
Romaldo Giurgola
Herman Hertzberger
Ram Karmi
Ada Karmi-Melamede
José Rafael Moneo
Richard Rogers
Moshe Safdie

Commentary
Stanford Anderson
Kenneth Frampton
Joseph Rykwert

Editor's Note
Texts on the following pages
are edited excerpts
from full-length
seminar presentations.

Je prends un temps, non comme une chose concertée, mais arrangée, accomodée avec le temps.

INTRODUCTION
Julian Beinart

The Jerusalem Seminar in Architecture series was conceived in 1992 as an international forum for bringing to Jerusalem prominent architects and theorists to examine important topics in architecture and urbanism. The first seminar, *The Public Building: Form and Influence*, coincided with the opening in Jerusalem of the then recently completed Israel Supreme Court building. The focus of the seminar was the contemporary public building, both in terms of how it is shaped in today's public domain and how it in turn affects public experience.

For many, including architects and urbanists, our times are characterized by a decline in the public domain. This, they argue, is to be seen in the weakness of public discourse, in our inability to build beautiful places and safe streets, and in the poverty of meaning with which we endow public buildings and monuments. Yet such a pessimistic reading may fail to see new relationships and opportunities in contemporary society and in its cities and buildings. The conception of what is public and private has never been fixed. In classical Athens at its height, the agora was a public place shaped for the performance of a very specific democracy; over two thousand years later, Rockefeller Center in New York, possibly the best public place designed in our times, was built by one of the world's richest private families. Does it matter today if a private police force protects a citizen, or a highway is sold to a private corporation, or a public square is maintained by its private abutters? Does our understanding of our cities diminish when a law court looks like a commercial building, or an office tower displays classical imagery and monumental proportions? At the seminar, Henry Cobb illustrated these contradictions by showing how the John Hancock Tower in Boston, which he designed, is a major presence in the public domain, yet the use of the building is private and public access to it is quite limited.

Another architect, Herman Hertzberger, expressed deep skepticism about all efforts to delineate a strictly public or private realm. Tested against concepts such as ownership, use control, and meaning, the invited architects and theorists produced complex and nuanced interpretations, in most cases avoiding hard distinctions between public and private. Some presentations included buildings whose form clearly intends to convey the significance of the institutions they house, such as parliaments, law courts, and museums. Other buildings presented, however, included libraries, schools, and train stations, for which their designers claimed less lofty ambitions, but which nevertheless play important roles in a public realm.

The good city was seen as made up of a rich variety of public/private programs, structures, and places, and what matters most is the quality and accessibility of these and how they form an intelligible whole. For Rafael Moneo, the public building, like the city, belongs to everyone, and nothing should constrain access to it. Joseph Rykwert evoked the example of the Cathedral of Florence, where the nave is a public right-of-way, even for donkeys. Charles Correa, in turn, saw a public building as needing to send out an open invitation, not privileging one entrant over another. In his presentation of the Beaubourg museum in Paris, Richard Rogers suggested that the information-loaded facade of this building was designed to attract a large and diverse audience into a public square, and was structured with escalators to continue the public presence up the front of the building. Stanford Anderson cited Adolf Loos's design of a private house in terms of public relations, explaining the impressive simplicity of the building's exteriors as a proper response to the public view.

The ways in which public buildings come about played a secondary role in the discussions. In some cases, architects presented public buildings where both program and design had been subject to extensive public involvement. It was thought that good public participation does not necessarily mean excessive bureaucracy and compromised committee decisions: an architecture of consensus must include the creativity and imagination of the architect. But is this easily achieved? Moshe Safdie spoke of his ambivalence about a public referendum held in Vancouver for his library building, wondering whether the imperatives of democratic politics could be wholly reconciled with the pursuit of the avant-garde.

In our current domain of diversity, contention, and conflict, good public architecture is more likely to be at most a singular attempt to bring together valuable experiences of community. Our society's passion for change, Kenneth Frampton suggested, makes it extremely difficult to build public institutions, and therefore to embody them physically. Yet Frampton saw Romaldo Giurgola set forth four principles for the public building. First, public buildings must stem from the ideas and beliefs of the community, not from individual ideas. Secondly, the building should elucidate this common idea, so that architecture becomes a question of spatial, not stylistic, relationships. The third principle involves the participation of the public in the building, whereby many people join to create multiple experiences. And finally, a public building cannot impose itself where it is not wanted or understood. Public architecture must not be arrogant.

LECTURE
Henry N. Cobb

As I strolled for the first time through the narrow streets of the Old City of Jerusalem and across the stepped platforms of the Temple Mount, a profoundly disturbing aphorism of Franz Kafka came to mind: "The decisive moment in human development is a continuous one. For this reason, those revolutionary movements which declare everything before them to be null and void are in the right, for nothing has happened."

Whether it be true or false—and the evidence of this city oddly supports both judgments—Kafka's aphorism surely explains the self-inflicted amnesia of the modern movement in architecture in which I grew up. This amnesia was legitimized by the entirely defensible claim that a new language of form was required if modern architecture were to make effective use of newly available technical means to achieve newly defined programmatic ends. Because our collective memory now includes modernism and cannot pretend to be innocent of the ideas it postulated, there is in our present engagement with the past an unresolved ambivalence, an uncertainty of intentions, a deep anxiety that decisively separates the postmodern from the premodern. We are today less sure than ever about the answer to one of our oldest questions. This concerns the dynamic interaction—the ongoing dialogue—between memory and invention, between those values associated with understanding or treasuring what is known, and those associated with doubting or probing the unknown.

It should not surprise us that the city—the indispensable theater of our collective memory—now constitutes the principal arena for addressing this question, nor that it is most poignantly brought into focus by the need to accommodate in our cities the proliferation of those institutions that claim to serve the diverse aspirations of our society. In housing these institutions, architecture not only sponsors their existence but represents them in the public realm, decisively shaping their roles as actors on the urban scene. My own preoccupation as an architect has been with exactly this phenomenon: the power of architecture as a representational art—an art of portraiture—portraying the multifarious structure of desired relationships between human beings, their institutions, and the natural world.

The office building, especially the tall office building, has been almost a perpetual presence in my life as an architect. There is no building type that has contributed more to the impoverishment, to the devaluation of the public realm of cities, than the office building. The effort to overcome this condition, to humanize the tall building and give it the demeanor of a good citizen, has preoccupied American architects for more than a century; indeed it preoccupies us still. Ironically, the underlying cause of the problem—the office tower's poverty of program—has actually proved useful in the search for remedies. By its very nature, office space—space that is isotropic, homogeneous, repetitive, and conceptually limitless—constitutes a relatively neutral and quite malleable body that architects have been able to manipulate more or less at will, shaping it into an amazing variety of forms, clothing it in every conceivable stylistic garb, and conjuring up every imaginable architectural metaphor.

"Architecture," as Roland Barthes remarked, "is always dream and function, expression of a Utopia and instrument of a convenience." This is indeed a profound attribute of our art, but its manifestation in office towers is especially vivid owing to the paradoxical situation of tall buildings in the spatial fabric of the city. The tall office building inescapably intrudes as a dominant presence in the public realm, yet it is essentially a very private building, virtually inaccessible to the general public except at street level, and housing no public function that could begin to fulfill the expectations aroused by its assertive bulk and form.

First Interstate Bank Tower (FIBT)
Fountain Place, Dallas, Texas, 1983–1989

Above
Copley Square
Boston, Massachusetts

Above right
John Hancock Tower
Copley Square, Boston, Massachusetts
1967–1976

The act of building is never an isolated event, but always an intervention in the ongoing life of the city, an operation on a living organism that cannot fail to alter its character and its destiny. Viewed in this way, the great challenge and the great opportunity in the design of office towers is to temper their tendency to simply preempt the space of the city by exploiting an opposite potential—that of making *places,* and above all, making *public* places. For if we cannot devise ways to use the enormous economic leverage of tall office buildings—commercial buildings, money-making buildings—to secure and enrich the *public* space of the city, to animate its *public* realm, then we will end up facing a grim future indeed. Commerce Square in Philadelphia, for example, framed by low buildings in a way that admits sunlight and celebrates the pedestrian scale, has added an important new gathering place to the city.

When planning the John Hancock Tower in Boston, I struggled with the relationship between Richardson's Trinity Church and the tower. I reflected on the need to see the tower as a foil to all the characteristics of the church. I wanted the autonomy of the church as a significant object in the round to be preserved. I therefore wanted the tower to be in every way contingent—and to be perceived as contingent—on its relationship to the church. To do that, many oppositions were brought into play: the church is centered, the tower is decentered; the church is highly present, the tower is rendered as close to absent as two million square feet can be; the church is highly volumetric, everything about the tower—its shape, its surface, its detail—is designed to make it read as a plane in space; the church is rough, the tower is smooth; the church is ornamented, the tower is unornamented.

The John Hancock Tower is impoverished in a certain way. It is arguably more a gigantic piece of sculpture than a work of architecture. Indeed, my sculptor friends envied me for having built this building. They thought, "What right does an architect have to make the largest piece of sculpture in North America?!"

In a sense, therefore, as architecture, this building is inadequate, incomplete—and yet, that impoverishment is perhaps what makes it eloquent. If it has a poetry, it is in its self-denial. In that self-denial we may see reflected an unresolved predicament of the society that begat this building.

In a commercial or speculative development, if we want to accomplish either the objective of animating the skyline with a distinctive figure or the goal of animating the fabric of the city with a distinctive space, there is a principle that is crucially important to me: attention to detail. Mies van der Rohe was right when he said, "God is in the details." When we deal with basically minimalist strategies, design strategies in which there are very few moves, each move, and the way it is executed, is critical. The way the building surface is folded to create a particular form; the way the curtain wall is assembled to make that folding possible; the way the water of the water garden is exactly on the same plane as the surface on which you walk, giving the magical feeling, as you move off the street, that you are walking on water—every step is of paramount importance.

Above
United States Courthouse
Boston, Massachusetts,
1991–1998

Above left
Commerce Square
Philadelphia, Pennsylvania,
1984–1987

LECTURE
Charles Correa

Facing page, top
Gandhi Smarak Sangrahalaya
(Gandhi Memorial Museum),
Sabarmati Ashram, Ahmedabad, India,
1958–1963

Facing page, bottom
Bharat Bhavan (art center)
Bhopal, India, 1975–1981

For all of us, Jerusalem is a mythic city, central to human memory. Even the stones, the beautiful stones, are sacred, layered with meaning. When I say sacred, I don't just mean religious, I also mean the primordial, evoking something basic to our nature. This moves me, because in India, too, there is a profound sense of the sacred. Even in a large commercial metropolis like Bombay, every few meters you will suddenly see somebody drawing a little *yantra* (a sacred diagram) under a tree, or performing some *puja* (ritual act). In India, such gestures are part of people's daily lives. They carry memories, and memories of memories, a sort of *invisibilia* present within each person.

We all agreed with Joseph Rykwert when he observed that public art cannot be a private utterance, that architecture must be a shared idea. But it is not just *an* idea, it is *ideas*—and that is the problem. Indian culture is pluralistic; it is highly complex; it has many layers. Thus, the responsibility, the opportunity, for the architect designing a public building is to express this multiplicity of mythic ideas and to clarify them. The consensus we seek will not be achieved automatically; it must be forged. This is the contribution of the architect. Renaissance artists merged two seemingly opposite worlds which seemed on a collision course: the Christian Church and pagan antiquity. In that sense, the magnificent architectural masterpieces of the past are highly polemical. They express very powerfully the central paradigms of each society. Today our buildings are banal; they say nothing. Perhaps this is due to our failing as architects, but it also reflects a modern society that has lost its sense of the sacred, of what awaits expression in the core of its being.

One begins with specific characteristics of culture and then searches for the underlying paradigm. That is what Louis Kahn may have meant when he spoke of Volume Zero. He was looking for the deep structure that engenders the patterns we see.

The sacred buildings of Hinduism are generated by a square diagram called a *vastu-purush-mandala*. The square exists in virtually every culture in the world. I believe it must come from the deep structure of the human brain. We always speak of four primary directions: north, south, east, and west; there is not a single culture that has five directions. It is always four, because that is how we conceptualize space.

In the Hindu *mandala*, the center is always *shuniya* (zero, nothing), but it is also *bindu* (the source of primordial energy). This is a fantastic concept: in the center of everything there exists *nothing* which is *everything*. This is the Hindu perception of the cosmos. I think it describes something that is within each of us, a profound sense of centrality that affects the environment we build.

I would like to mention four projects that treat the issue of public buildings in four different ways. The first one is the Gandhi Smarak Sangrahalaya, a memorial museum to Mahatma Gandhi at the Sabarmati Ashram, where he lived in Ahmedabad. It is very simple: pyramidal tiled roofs grouped around courtyards cover the spaces, some of which are enclosed and some open. It has a meandering character, which critics have perceived as a metaphor for the villages so dear to Gandhi's heart. Of course, I did this intuitively. Like a writer or a musician, when you design, you use reactions and information you don't even know you possess. As Stan Anderson said, architecture might travel, but architects cannot. I imagine it would be very difficult to be in tune with these sensitivities in a new place.

Bharat Bhavan, the art center in Bhopal, is built on a hillside sloping down to the lake in the center of the city. The roof terraces also function as a public garden;

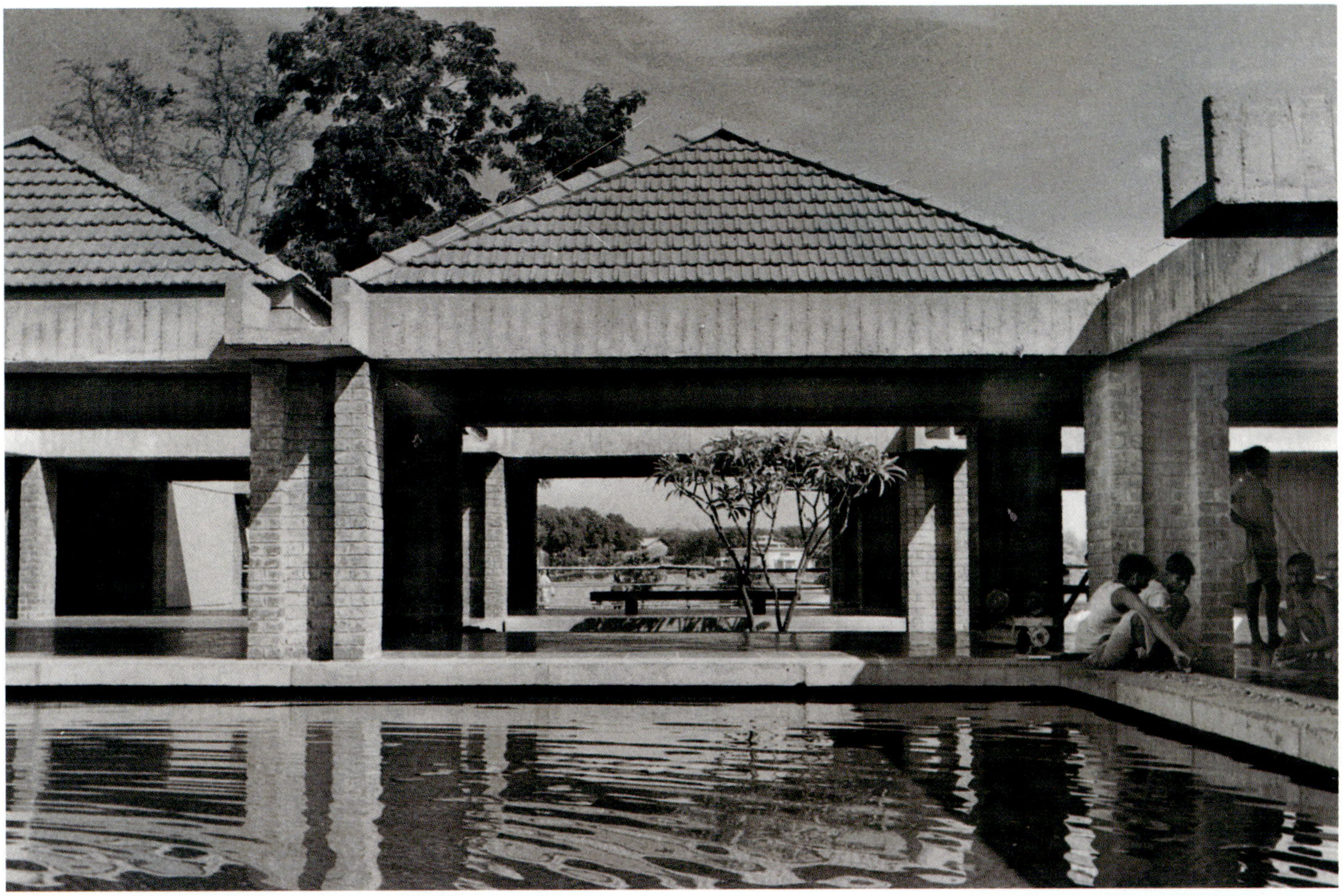

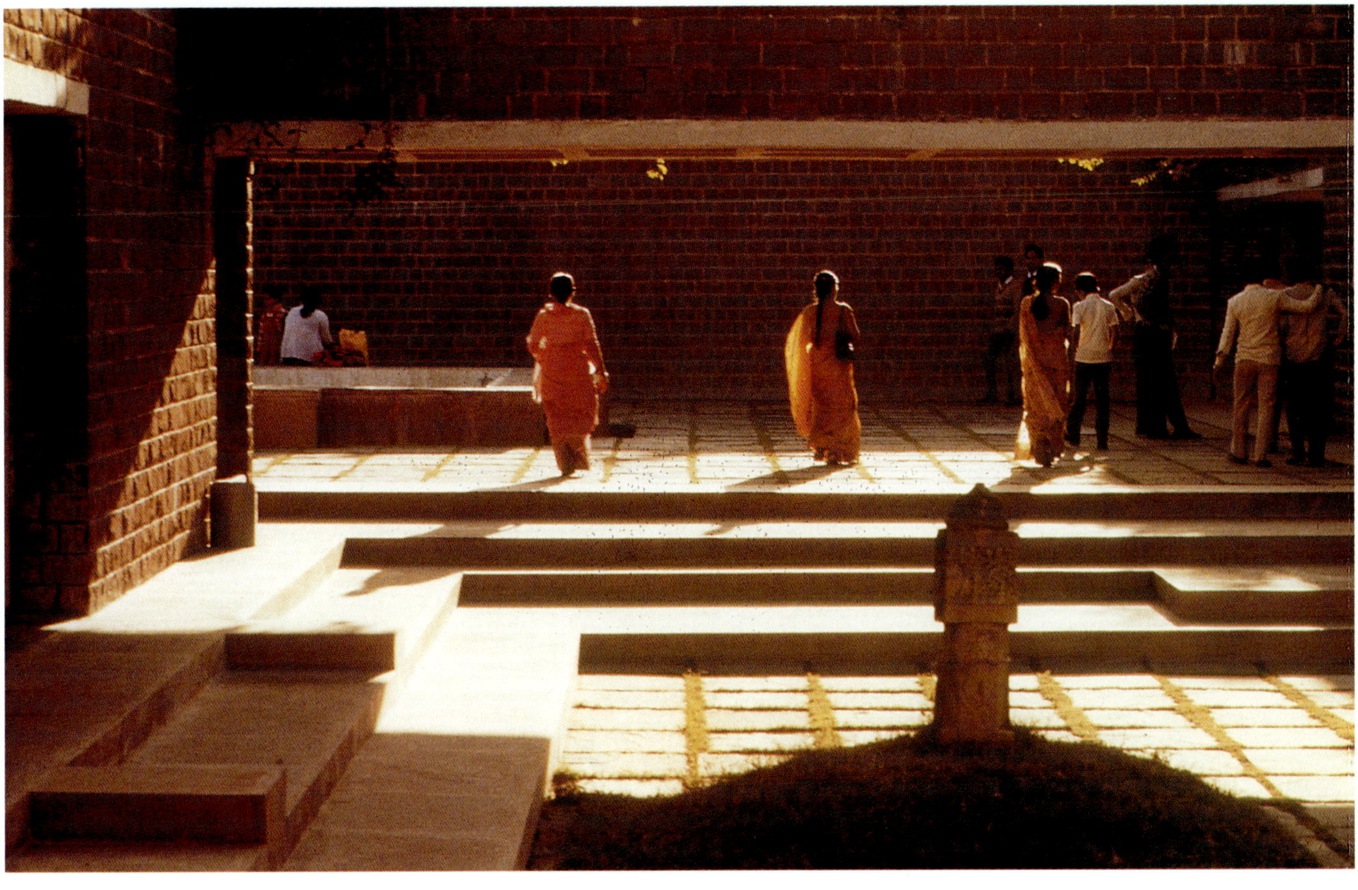

people enter at the top of the site and descend through the complex. This descent does not occur on one continuous slope, but is structured around three courtyards. Off each courtyard one finds various cave-like galleries that house diverse activities, including a museum of tribal art, a contemporary painting museum, a poetry library, and a theater with rehearsal rooms for an in-house repertory company. It is a kind of non-building, with minimal intrusion; only the courtyards are assertively real.

The British Council Library in Delhi is privately owned, but very often a private building can make a public space. The client needed a library, a small auditorium, and some offices. However, we wanted to express something more ambitious: the historic interface between India and England over the last several centuries. Thus, the entire composition is structured around three *axis mundi* that express the mythic imagery of the three principal mind-sets that have prevailed in India: the *bindu* of Hinduism, the Paradise Garden of Islam, and the European Age of Reason. The entrance to this axis is presided over by a Howard Hodgkin mural executed in black stone and white marble, symbolizing the giant shadow of a Banyan tree, as pluralistic and protective as India herself.

The Jawahar Kala Kendra is an arts center named after our first Prime Minister. Like the city of Jaipur itself, it is based on the *Navgraha* (the *mandala* of the Nine Planets). And, like Jaipur, it expresses the mythic imagery of the past through contemporary sensibilities. We took the program and broke it down into nine squares, the nine planets. Each of these squares forms a thirty-meter-square box; its traditional symbols are inlaid in stone, marble, and granite on the outer walls.

In the center is a contemporary version of the traditional *kund* (water tank in front of a temple), which holds no water but serves as an amphitheater. The exterior walls of each planet are finished in red sandstone; the interiors are painted with the mythic images in the auspicious colors of each particular planet.

The building was built by an impecunious state government. Every time we got a little money, we built a planet. At one point, there were four different contractors working simultaneously. This is probably one of the few plans that could lend itself to such a unusual construction program.

The Jawahar Kala Kendra seeks to present architecture as a model of the cosmos. Its form and materials somehow pick up the imagery of the traditional walled cities of Rajasthan. To me, it is also like a big packing case with a sign pointing to the sky, saying, "This side up."

Architecture is not a very pure art, like poetry or music. However, it is the only art whose technology changes every few decades, and thus challenges society to reinvent the expression of its aspirations and mythic values. I think this is the challenge Wright and Sullivan accepted, and in the process they gave American architecture enough energy for an entire century. Had they merely transferred the old images, which would be difficult anyway, the result would have debilitated society. Nations such as India or Israel, where there are so many diverse cultures and different layers of mythic belief, must accept this challenge. I don't think the necessary energy can come from anything less.

British Council
New Delhi, India,
1987–1992,
entrance facade

Jawahar Kala Kendra
(arts complex), Jaipur, India,
1996–1992

LECTURE
Romaldo Giurgola

Tel Aviv City Redevelopment Competition
Jaffa, Israel, 1963

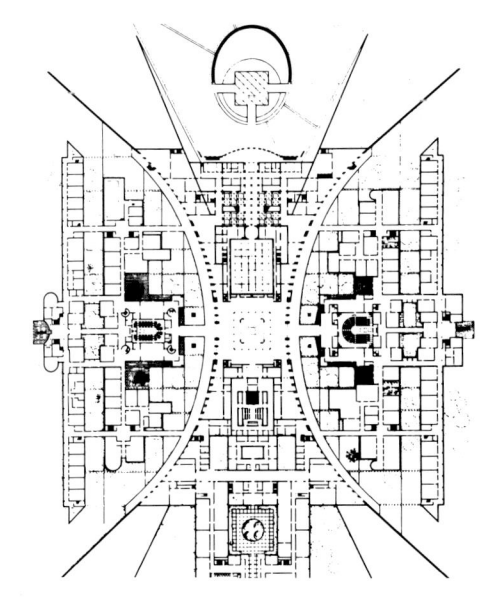

Typical floor plan

Above and facing page
Parliament House
Canberra, Australia, 1979–1988

Public building must be, above all, the embodiment of a shared idea. I mean this in a Socratic sense, where the architect is a midwife of ideas that are not private, self-generated, or discreet, but really belong to everyone. A public building should not confuse the people who use it, but rather elucidate what they are there for. The architecture must reflect what is going on inside the building. Paying taxes is no laughing matter; the design of a municipal tax office should respond to the seriousness of the operation. Architecture should express relationships: a relationship with the order of the land, if it is near nature; a relationship with the order of the city, if it is in an urban environment.

Public architecture has only participants—no mere observers. It is not something that you just pass by in the street. With public architecture, everyone participates, from contributing their tax money to being inside for a meeting, for settling an account, for celebrating, or whatever. Such a high level of participation means that the final form emerges from the confluence of a multitude of experiences, both of those who create the building and of those who use it. The concept of creating is something that should make one quite thoughtful. Everyone involved—from the architect, to the artisan, to the construction worker—should act in a special way when working on a public building.

In 1963 there was a competition for immigrant housing in Jaffa, for higher-density development, and collective or public space. Public building in this area was conceived as a series of alternatives between pedestrian routes and automobile traffic, leading to a little frontage of public buildings and public places of residence. The primary planning principle was to reinforce the linear pedestrian street as a continuous architectural experience, creating a number of urban places along its route. An urban place reveals itself as an alternative to the repetitive fabric of a city, functioning as a reference point that in turn establishes new relationships.

The facade of the San Jose Convention Center is a giant poster, a mosaic designed by Lyn Utzon (the daughter of Jörn Utzon) for the city. It represents an identifiable facade for a significant public building where people come to interact. Structurally, the entire complex is organized along a linear access with activities servicing the major hall of the convention place. The facade-as-art is a means of communicating the shared nature of the building. The universal language of art invites all members of the culture to enter.

In 1991, we finished the St. Thomas Aquinas Parish Church, a little church in Charnwood, near Canberra. The church was done with an extremely small budget of about five hundred thousand dollars. The walls tell the story of what takes place inside: from the baptistery to the altar to the tabernacle. The project incorporates twelve columns representing the twelve tribes of Israel. These define an external gathering space and guide the visitor through the church.

An interior is always a fundamental element in every architectural experience. I don't think of the interior as the partitions producing enclosures inside the building, but rather the enclosures produced by the building itself. An architecture without an enclosure, an interior, is just an object. It remains an object that is not really an architectural experience.

Space is the basic language of the building, not style. Space speaks to people's fundamental urgency. Whether the building is Gothic, Renaissance, or some other style does not have much consequence in comparison to the impact that the space has on the user and on the people who visit it. Jerusalem is the classic example of that. Who cares if something is Byzantine or Roman? The quality of the space is

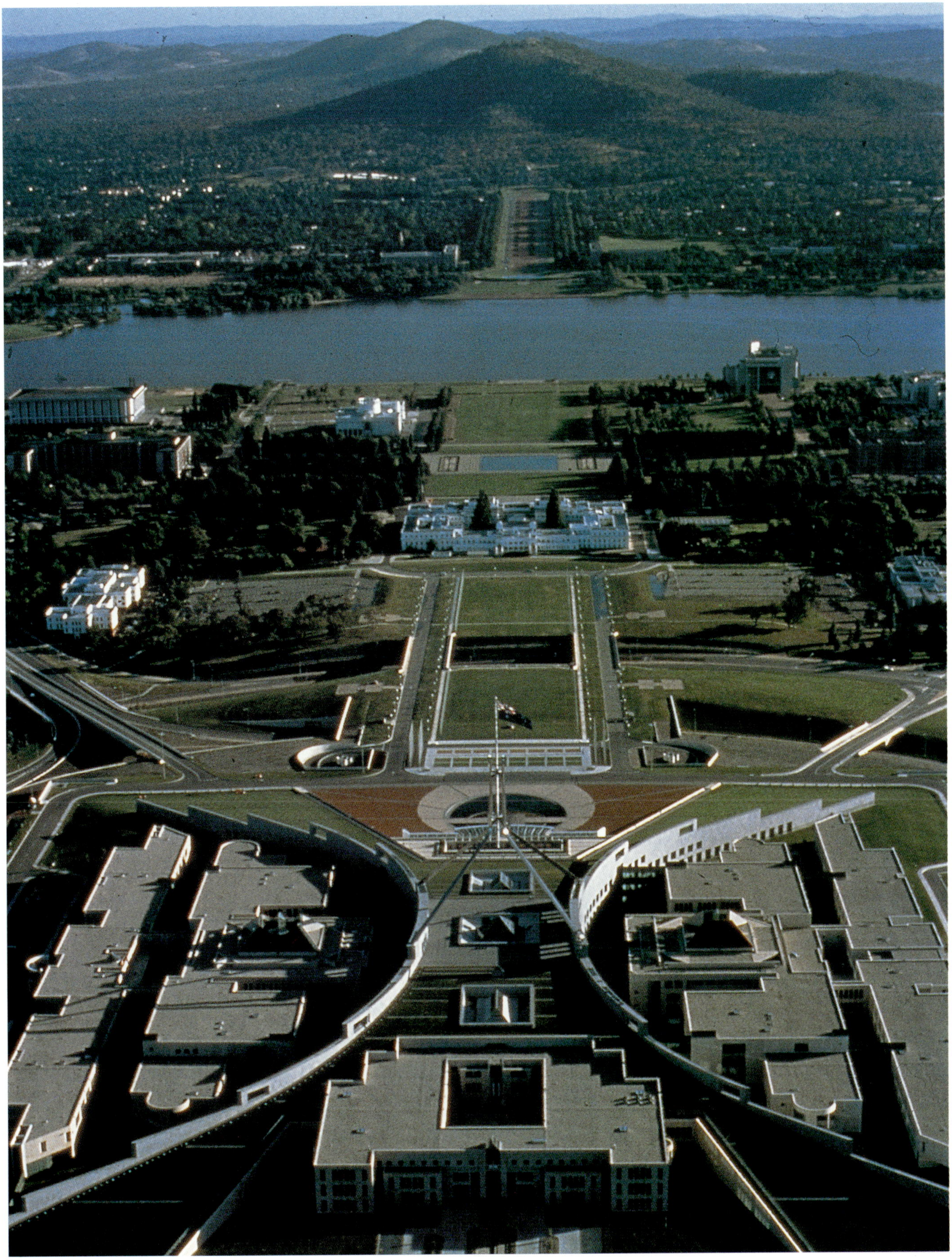

Parliament House
Canberra, Australia, 1979–1988

the enigma of all experience in architecture. Confluence is what makes the space, and that is fundamental in public space and public architecture.

The Parliament House in Canberra was the subject of a competition in 1979. There were more than three hundred entries, and we were fortunate to win the contract. The geometry of the plan of Canberra is unforgettable, and we proposed to extend it. The site is a hill surrounded by two concentric circular roads that make a super roundabout. In Griffin's plan, there is a definite axis that connects the war memorial with a mountain in the background. We were concerned with maintaining both the character of this long axis, which also links the residential part of the city with the more monumental one, and the profile of the existing hill, into which was nested a series of structures.

The Parliament is a building of quite considerable proportions. At times there were ten thousand people working on the project, supervised by an office of one hundred and fifty architects. It was executed with a "fast track" method of construction.

There are no steps for the building entrance. The monumentality was achieved in a different way, by the aura of the material and the sequencing of space. As you march toward the top of the building you have a complete sense of belonging to the rest of the city, seeing all the other areas in front of you.

Parliament House
Canberra, Australia, 1979–1988,
with Australian War Memorial in foreground

This building is almost totally open to the public. The premise of the project was that the building belongs to the public. It was crucial to make that basic idea very clear, although conveying it was difficult. The parliamentarians had always felt that they were the owners of the place. We tried to make them aware that the building belongs to the public and that the members are there as guests for the length of their tenure and nothing more.

The building, a meeting place for the public and the parliamentarians, requires a symmetry with variations according to the needs of both. The parliamentary lobbies of the two chambers are provided with outdoor gardens. This is perhaps the only parliament in the world that has lobbies under the an open sky. The public responds very well to the openness of the building: it receives more than a million visitors a year.

A public building cannot be imposed on a place by an individual; rather, there should be an absence of the arrogance so typical in architecture, and more so because the building belongs to the public. The hubris of being master of the present all the time needs to be defused into a reconciliation with the past (which is never entirely past anyway). The here and now comes very rarely in life, as life itself has a lot of empty space on which the past can make substantial impressions.

LECTURE

Herman Hertzberger

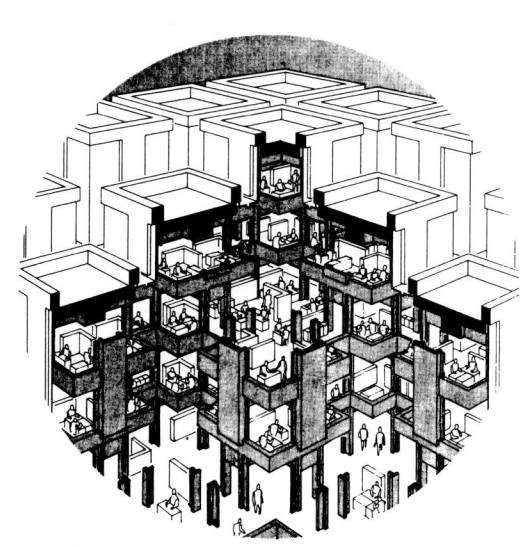

Section perspective

Centraal Beheer Office Building
Apeldoorn, The Netherlands, 1968–1972

Public space is an area that is accessible to everyone at all times, with responsibility for upkeep held collectively. *Private* space is an area whose accessibility and maintenance are controlled by one person or a small group. This dichotomy, private and public, like the opposition between collective and individual, has come to be a cliché, and in fact is as complex and false as the supposed dichotomies general and specific, objective and subjective. Such oppositions are symptoms of the disintegration of primary human relations. I believe there can be no such thing as public and private. As long as we distinguish between them, we will continue to maintain our freestanding buildings like great stones in an alienated terrain. *Public* and *private* must be considered relative terms, delineating a nuanced spectrum of qualities.

The Centraal Beheer building, built in 1968, is composed of sixty-nine towers connected by bridges where people work in groups. The challenge was to take what at that time was a big building for one thousand people, and make it small, dividing it into small pieces. We articulated the function, the work going on in this building, and made building volumes that serve as the envelopes for each work group. Our solution was to design a building with as many entrances as possible from all sides. In hindsight, I suppose I did not want to make a building, I wanted to realize a piece of the fabric of the city. I wanted it to be a city in itself, a settlement.

In designing the Vredenburg Music Center in Utrecht, my objective was to make a concert hall that would be a big shopping center. You should come into the concert hall the same way you would when buying shoes. For me, listening to Beethoven and buying shoes are not similar activities, but I hated the idea of culture as something very high that needs a temple, and buying shoes as something very low requiring a banal structure. The good things in this project are the things that went out of control. For example, some of the benches in the concert hall face the wrong direction. That is because I wanted to create a relationship with the foyers surrounding the hall itself. With the doors open to the foyer, the concert hall becomes part of the foyer. For many people, this seems to be a very comfortable way of sitting. I did not invent this; I perceived it. The non-committal arrangement is something many people love. It expresses an attitude that says, "Maybe I'll leave in a minute," which is quite nice.

The idea behind our competition entry for Mitterand's Bibliothèque de France in Paris was to build a very big glazed hall with just two columns in it. In this hall, all the libraries specified in the program were placed like busses or trucks parked in a garage. We knew beforehand that this program was fake, because it is obvious that in five years the configuration will be obsolete. Growing acquisitions and new trends in information retrieval will require expansion and reorganization. The plan was to arrange all the books in stack sections, each bordering a big public area that is just a continuation of the street. There you would find the information desk, the coffee bar, the catalogues, the meeting areas. You would enter a landscape, stepping up and moving through this space. At the end of your walk you would find a restaurant overlooking the Seine.

With the large, open public space and all the libraries opening onto it, the project had the same organization as an airport. Whenever I enter a library, I feel lost. I see these people who know exactly where they have to go, while I am bewildered. Libraries are always built for the people who already know. I wanted to make a library for people who are just a bit timid like myself, and have to ask the very nice lady for directions. A good airport is clear. Everything is logically organized and clearly marked. You get a boarding card, and if it says you have to be at Gate 8, then you seat yourself at Gate 8. That is the way to organize a library as well.

Top
Centraal Beheer Office Building
Apeldoorn, The Netherlands, 1968–1972

Left and below
Vredenburg Music Center
Utrecht, The Netherlands, 1973–1978

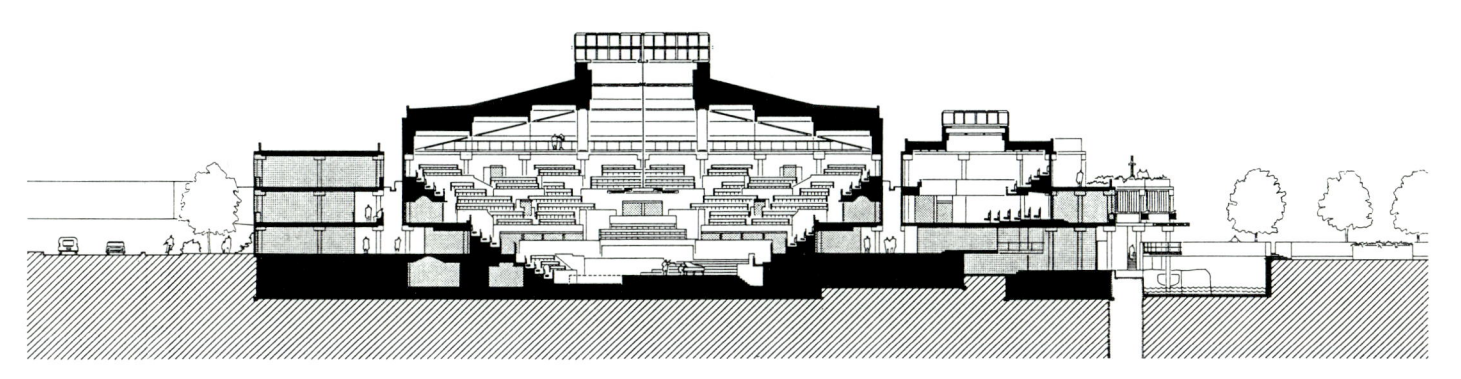

The Ministry of Social Welfare and Employment in the Hague, completed in 1990, was another attempt to make a very big building small by means of articulation. Instead of making one big box, I used recesses to articulate a multiplication of towers, which in themselves are small buildings and together make a small city.

The idea was to repeat these tower units, grouping them around one very big *public* space. It is not public in the sense that it is accessible to the public from outside; but having more than two thousand people working and walking here also qualifies as public. There is a large street on one level, which is the site of circulation, toilets, coffee bars, the library, meeting rooms, and all common facilities. Thus, this is a public space.

I think the inside of a building is more important than the outside. So to me, the amphitheater, with its inside open to the outside, is the ultimate expression of public space. It is the converse of the pyramid. This is my statement about architecture: amphitheaters instead of pyramids. Too many pyramids are built, even if they are not shaped like pyramids. Architecture today is all pyramids and not enough amphitheaters.

You can create cascading waterfalls, plant trees, lay beautiful pavements, create mosaics. You can put all the love, all the care you want into public space, yet you can never make it intimate. What is necessary is to make the private more open and make the public more intimate. It will only become intimate when buildings behave like streets and streets are the buildings, when there is a complete reciprocity of streets and buildings, public and private.

The famous "Threshold" photograph taken by W. Haas illustrates my point. It is of a little child just beyond the protection of the house, in the street, yet aware that

Ministry of Social Welfare and Employment
The Hague, Netherlands, 1979–1990

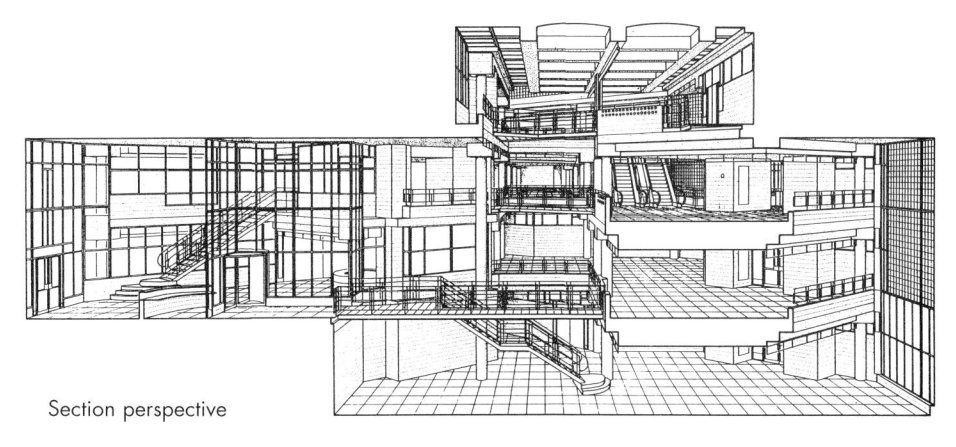

Section perspective

there is protection in the immediate vicinity. Is this a street or is it a house? It is, of course, both street and house, and this is exactly what I am trying to advocate. Architects should provide more in-between zones where private and public overlap. They must soften the strong demarcation between house and street. There must be more areas that are both street and house.

A different facet of my message is represented by the Erechtheion at the Acropolis in Athens: do not look to the female caryatids but rather in between them; be less obsessed by buildings and more by context. Be a little more committed to what is in-between. It is always the official that takes the part of the objects and the unofficial that is the in-between. Architects are too focused on the official and not enough on the unofficial. They are always where the money is, and not where the people are.

LECTURE
Ram Karmi and Ada Karmi-Melamede

Jerusalem is not the result of a sequential or singular design concept. The city was built up around various centers of public activity dating from different historical periods, and it is these nuclei that form its image. The map of the city, like the Supreme Court building, mirrors a distinct hierarchy of those cores implanted in our individual and collective memories. In the harmonious orchestration of these centers, Jerusalem asserts our identity as it narrates our origins and continuity.

With the Supreme Court, we tried to provide a conceptual image of the urban memory and of our deep consciousness of the city in a building whose architecture would reflect the personal map imprinted in each individual. The building was intended to project a feeling of personal possession, just as the city does, and perhaps even of communal possession—in a structure that could suggest cultural orientation and be a source of pride.

The site is at the crossroads where a north–south ridge, connecting the entrance to Jerusalem with the Knesset (Parliament) and The Israel Museum, meets a theoretical east–west axis spanning from the Judean Desert on the east to the Mediterranean on the west. These axes have created an internal urban dimension that divides the complex into four disparate components. The relationship between the private and the public aspects within is one of affinity and confrontation. In the strife between concept and form, the public space creates a balance among the different sections while preserving the identity of each.

Similar to the cardinal axes of roman camps, the *cardo* and the *decumanus* carve out the quarters of the Old City, thus partitioning and delineating them. Each zealously guards its identity, and yet the teeming activity within produces a living connection, a meeting place where differences melt away. The same principle has been applied to the Supreme Court building: the entrance placed at the intersection of the east–west and north–south axes both determines the areas of partition and sets up the interrelations among its parts.

From the outset, we allowed the two axes to divide the courthouse into four sections: the library, the judges' chambers, the courtrooms, and the parking area. Each part, with a "will of its own," vies for attention at the expense of the others. The subdivision into sections was clear, but the large masonry wall, a continuous presence throughout the building, created a new order. As the wall rose, the internal complexity of the building took over, defying its initial simple partition and becoming an experience in itself. With the vertical layering of the building that defined the public, the judges', and the prisoners' levels—each an independent, horizontal plane—the order became even more intricate.

The Supreme Court does not derive its sense from its program. Rather, it is informed by larger themes and higher problems that derive from the nature of the land, the law, and the historical heritage. Law courts have maintained a certain uniformity throughout history, preserving a very narrow borderline between human territory and alienation. Court buildings were traditionally expressed through broad motives such as rotundas, colonnades, and podiums, and were often assembled with a symmetrical order deriving its character from classical models. Such features lend the courts the resonance of timelessness, permanence, and wisdom.

In the Scriptures, justice is figuratively described as a circle: "He leadeth me in the paths [circles] of righteousness" (Psalms 23:3). Curiously, it is also common to find the term justice paired with compassion, no less a value, but often incompatible with its mate. In the Hebrew tradition, justice is an absolute value, to be forever pursued, even if never attained. In contrast, law and truth are described in the Scriptures as a line: "I will apply judgment as a measuring line" (Isaiah 28:17).

National Precinct
Jerusalem, 1992

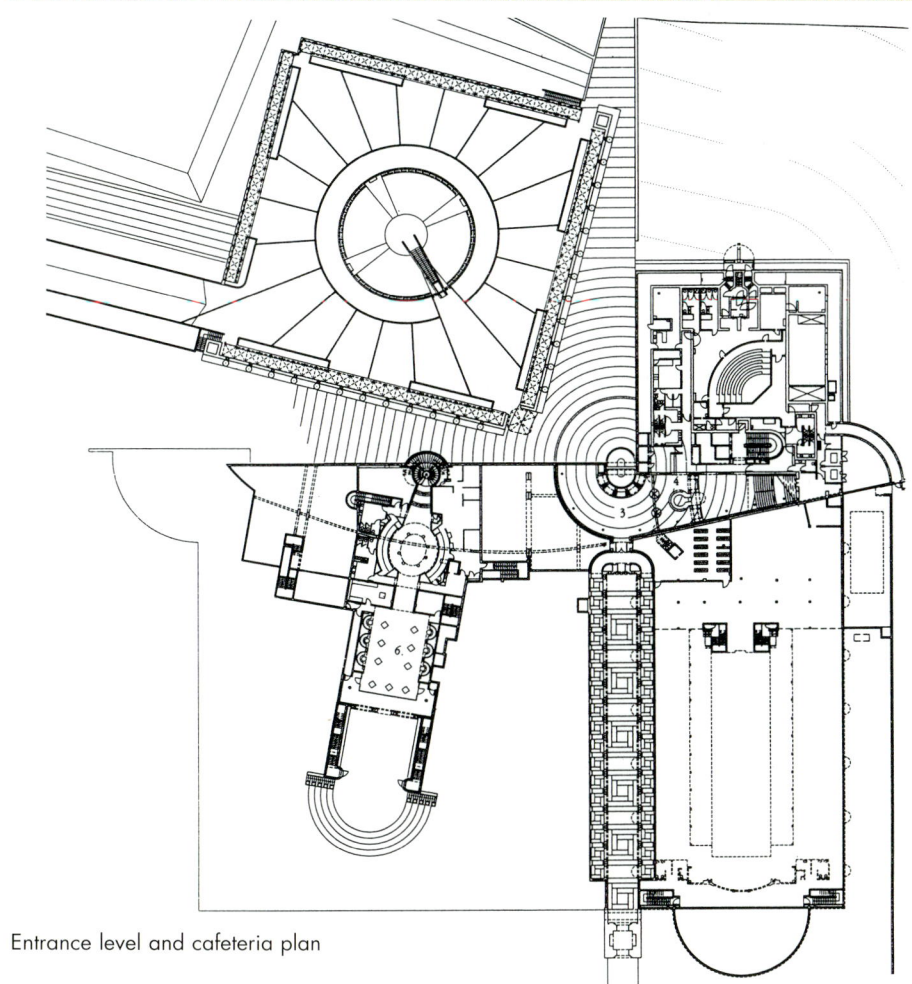

Entrance level and cafeteria plan

Israel Supreme Court
Jerusalem, 1992

Above
View of route to the Knesset
(Parliament), Jerusalem, 1992

Right
Israel Supreme Court
Jerusalem, 1992,
Judges' courtyard (top)
Courtroom Three (bottom)

They are viewed as human concepts, relative values subject to humans' changing perceptions of the world. Truth is deemed relative and law is forever changing. The unresolved conflicts between the relative and the absolute, the line and the circle, the fragment and the object are the conceptual design themes of the building, and we hope to have touched on them in its realization.

The architectural metaphor determines or depends upon a number of "stations" through which the public passes before reaching the courtrooms. The entrance, the large window looking out onto the Nahla'ot neighborhood and Jerusalem, the pyramid, the large hall: the public traverses them as if they composed the main street of a miniature Jerusalem, and in them one encounters the court's various functional parts: the library, the judges' chambers, and the courtrooms. People enter and view these spaces while the court is using them.

The distance between the entrance and the courtrooms, and the changing height along the entire length of the building at the public level, induce reflection. Where do the absolute and the relative begin, and where do they end? How are the eternal, static viewpoints of law and justice presented? Such reflection is part of our attempt to emphasize that the way in which a person makes his way into the building and around it is a combination of linear and circular movements aimed at giving a geometric image to the concept of justice and law as described in our sources.

There are buildings where identification of the edifice's main function is instantaneous upon entry. This is not the case with the public level of the Supreme Court building, inasmuch as it could be the entrance to a bank. The dynamic composition of the space expresses the notion that nothing in the world guarantees that things are organized from the beginning with ironclad logic. Even if there is a certain logic behind them, the essence is always subject to personal interpretation. Emotion, excitement, surprise, and personal association are the mechanisms by which the public experiences and advances through the building.

In the main foyer, the dynamic equilibrium between the stone wall and the opposite row of niches—between a hard, massive material and the seemingly weightless, ascending forms—contributes to the complex composition of the public level. The public moves within a space that provokes a confrontation between the "modern" white components and the "traditional" rough-hewn stone wall, between two sides of our identity as Israelis: the streamlined, the white, the Puritan, the unsentimental as represented by the modern components, and the expanse of the Israeli's great historical experience as called forth by the archaic stone wall.

The light symbolizes the state of pure beginning. White architecture was shadowless architecture, one without memory, without a past, and always new. But in culture there is always a shadow, without which there is no time, no history, no layers. Moreover, there is no unique history. The great contradiction to the claim of perpetual innovation lies in the confrontation of the straight, white wall facing the big, carved stone wall, the backbone of the whole composition, which starts from the entrance and follows the movement of people throughout the building. This stone wall neither reflects light nor radiates the white of eternal youth, but rather "drinks up" the light. The light hovers around the stone wall like a halo, setting it in a ritual context.

LECTURE
José Rafael Moneo

When I received the invitation to participate in this seminar, I thought about what a public building means to me. I realized that, for me, museums, auditoriums, lecture halls, and offices are not exactly what I consider to be public buildings. How, then, do I define the public building? It is quite satisfactory to posit that a public building represents or serves an institution, but I would submit that the public building is something more. The public building is something that belongs to everyone. Who can claim to own a city? The essence of a city is the feeling that it belongs to everyone; no one can assert that this is private property. Something like that happens with what I would call the public building. Such buildings have distinguishing features. Nothing restrains us from entering these buildings. They are not prisons; there are no enclosures. They give voice to a society. Public buildings exceed and overcome their specific purpose as museums, hospitals, or schools. Such institutions *do not* belong to everyone. They always imply restriction, classification, a certain way of saying, "I belong to this group of people and not to that one." Given my criteria, the Logroño City Hall in Rioja, Logroño, and the Atocha Railway Station in Madrid may be considered *public buildings*.

I started work on the Logroño City Hall in 1975, the year of Franco's death. It belongs to a period of transition when we were trying to democratize all of our institutions. Architects were expected to give expression to this new form of democratic life. I was enthusiastic about finding an architectural form that could reflect the novel political possibilities, the innovative ways of seeing life that developed in Spain at the end of the 1970s. I did not want the project to present itself as a symbol of power. I sought a building that could be understood to serve democratic social principles, that was open, accessible, and lacking the rhetoric of a politically inspired building.

The best way I found to do it was to design something that, in the end, becomes the city itself. The building in Logroño strives to inspire a kind of architecture that simultaneously solves both the problem of a building and the problem of the city. The ambition to create an entire piece of the city supersedes the attributes of a simple building.

The building tries to offer the citizens of Logroño an open, clear structure. We worked with a style I will call "collage architecture," assimilated and contained in a rather compact building. We deliberately used architectural elements that stick in people's memories because we wanted the building to be perceived as a public building for everyone—and no one needs to make an effort to see something that strikes out violently at his or her understanding of architecture.

The issue of accessibility was crucial. I wanted a building that did not emphasize the entrance, but that was actually permeable, accessible from multiple points. The building is open to the people and rejects the idea of a building that radiates power. This building attempts to avoid power, or to avoid misrepresentation of power. It creates a structure that embodies and merges with the entire city.

The Atocha Railway Station was opened in the Olympic year of 1992. It belongs to a period characterized by the consolidation of institutions and the establishment of infrastructures. It speaks to Spain's efforts to catch up to Europe and to provide its citizens with new services. A railway station is a functional object, yet it should not be approached as an architectural machine. I like buildings to be in the world of buildings, and here I tried to prevent a mechanistic view from intruding on the city. Instead, this building attempts to revamp a very large section of the city. To this end, the machine-like nature of the building has been blurred, integrated, and merged with the city. The architecture here upgrades the machine aspect of

Above and facing page
City Hall
Logroño, Spain, 1973–1981

Site plan

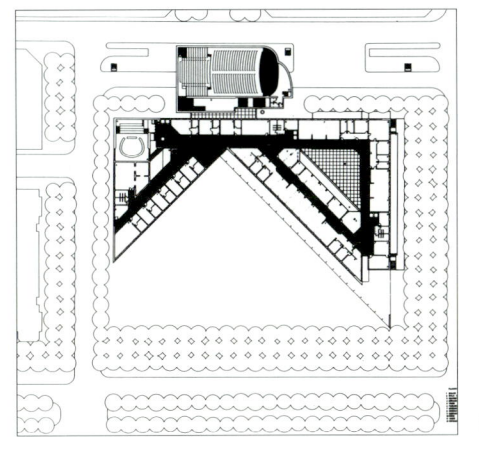

Ground floor plan

the railway station. It continues, yet transforms, the existing context and creates new spaces. Unlike the Logroño City Hall, it works by means of architectural pieces borrowed from the past, which evoke clear associations in our memories.

The Atocha Railway Station overcomes the idea of a *building;* it was designed from the beginning to be a piece of the city, a public space. A building means enclosure, restriction, containment. It seems to me that the space of the late twentieth century speaks much more about intimate places than the contained spaces of the nineteenth century. To understand, to produce public buildings demands a commitment to an appropriate treatment of materials combined with a certain aptitude for design.

The Logroño City Hall and the Atocha Railway Station qualify as public buildings because they aspire to anonymity. I believe the larger the commitment of the public building, the more general its design should be. It must not represent the face of its designer in an obvious way. The designer should take second place, assuming a rather low profile. A public building should allow itself to be clearly perceived, demonstrating an economy of means, soundness of material, and generosity of dimension.

In both projects I was attracted by the idea of dissolving the presence of the building, creating an open plaza reminiscent of many public spaces in Spain. Eventually, the plazas would be surrounded with belts of trees, so the open space would be enclosed. The idea of the large plaza allowed me to address the structure of the city.

In the 1960s, Madrid was spoiled by policies aimed primarily at solving the traffic problem. When a popularly elected administration came into power, the new mayor wanted the railway station to become a gateway from the south of Madrid, where the people with the lowest income live, a population of one and a half million. By enhancing this area, by creating representative buildings, we

Below and facing page
Atocha Railway Station
Madrid, 1984–1992

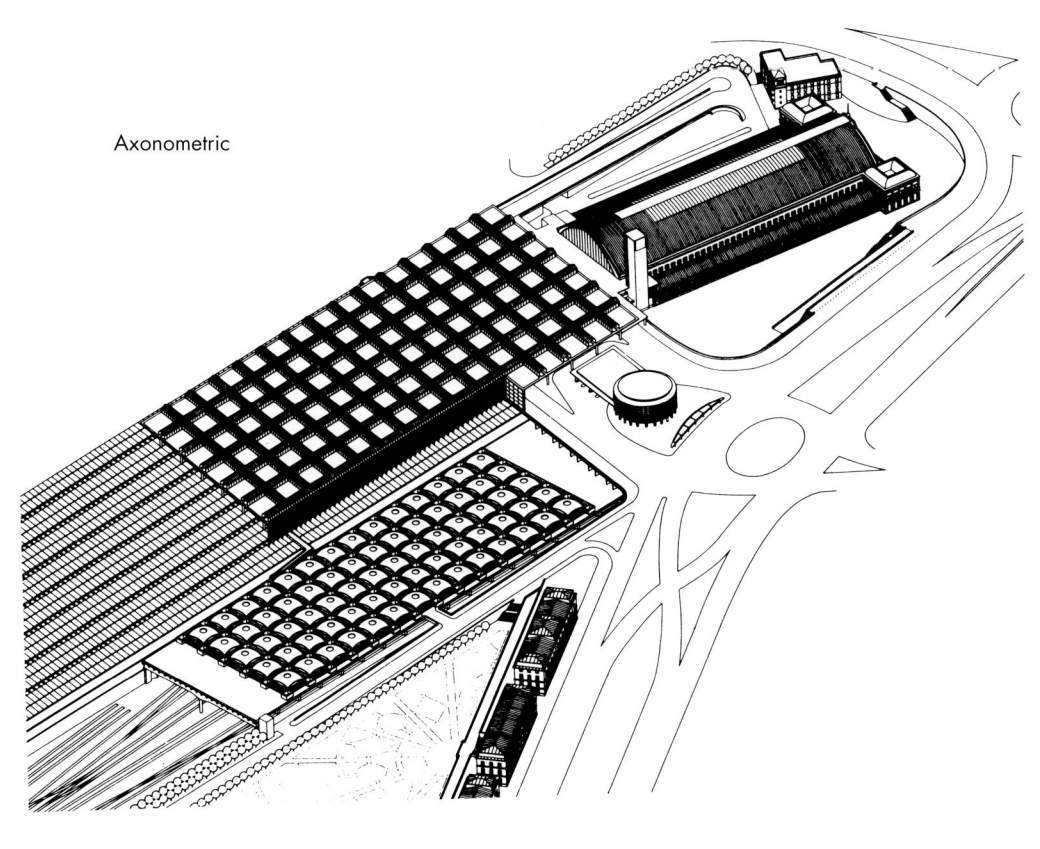

Axonometric

were helping to improve the quality of life for all those in the south of Madrid. So the railway station is something more than a building. It is something that is very much the result of working with different architecture, varying elements, and various pieces, yet having in mind a general strategy for the city.

Democracy implies the ascendancy of individual rights and individual expression. This notion affects every realm of life, including architecture. In recent years, architecture has become so individualistic that it sometimes borders on the idiosyncratic. I do not call for subordination to a set of predetermined criteria and forms. But I do advocate an architecture that possesses a sense of beauty as well as the ability to communicate beyond the narrow purview of a particular moment in time and the individual personality that brought it into being.

LECTURE
Richard Rogers

Facing page
Lloyds of London Building
London, 1978–1986

Cities are the heart of culture. In cities you get the wonderful overlapping of a multitude of activities. Cities are for the meeting of people; that is the single most important purpose cities serve. Nearly every other activity—education, housing, industry—can be dispersed outside the urban area; but you can only meet in great squares with their great explosions of space, in the shade of the market space. There is nothing I enjoy more than sitting in a cafe and watching the people go by. It is a great activity, and an activity that is in danger of extinction, mainly because of private greed. The public zone, the public domain is being steadily eroded. For all the talk about the ease with which we can communicate electronically, it is becoming clearer that now more than ever we still need to communicate face-to-face. In fact, the more we work in an isolated way, the more we need the public domain.

The great cities of the West were designed around expansive, green, wonderful eighteenth- and nineteenth-century parks and grand squares with famous names. These were fantastic public spaces. Today, these wonderful meeting places have become roundabouts, difficult to reach spaces where there is nothing to do but feed the pigeons. There are certainly no nice cafes, no public activities. In the twentieth century, our vast unused spaces have become motorways; the nice little parks or public pedestrian bridges we do have are often unusable. Is this the best we can do with these places? We, at the end of the late twentieth century, with advanced technology and exciting new materials, can certainly do better.

Renzo Piano and I designed the Centre Pompidou as a multipurpose cultural building, a building that houses a wide variety of activities. The aim of the project (from the first sentence we wrote in the report) was a building for all people. It was a building where we wanted to de-mystify "culture" in the sense that we wanted to attract a larger public, not create a place where only a few would go. We talked about it being a cross between a "New York-information-based Times Square" (that was our British image of Times Square in the 1960s, I guess) and an "information-based British Museum." In many ways, the Centre Pompidou reflects the optimism of 1968: it was open-ended, it was a continuation of the public street. We had this idea, this populist vision of breaking the elitism of art. To this end, we created a network of "streets" on the facade of the building which took the visitor from the piazza to the front door of every gallery.

Every day, Lloyds of London becomes a little bit more private, partly due to security. In a way, if the Centre Pompidou is more of a "fun palace," Lloyds is much more of an English club: it is more closed, it is inward looking, they did not really want windows looking outwards. It is a market space, a large market where you buy and sell insurance rather than oranges and lemons. We wanted to create an interesting, layered building that you could not understand at one quick glance, that would unfold as you approached.

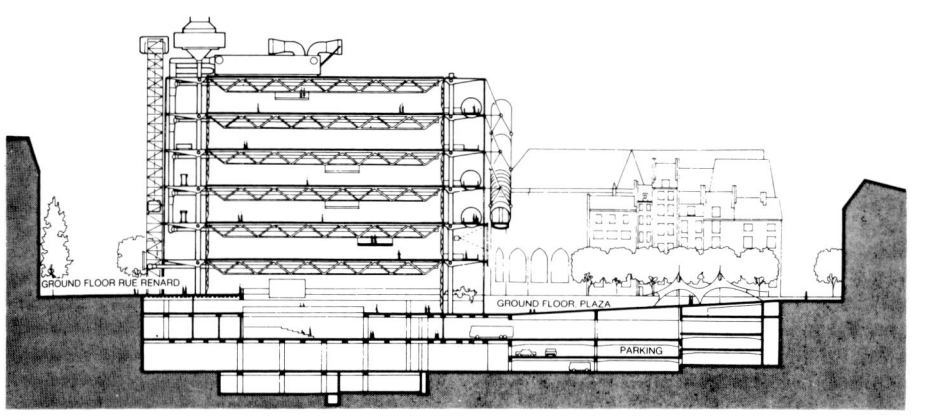

Centre Georges Pompidou
Paris, 1977

Section

Axonometric

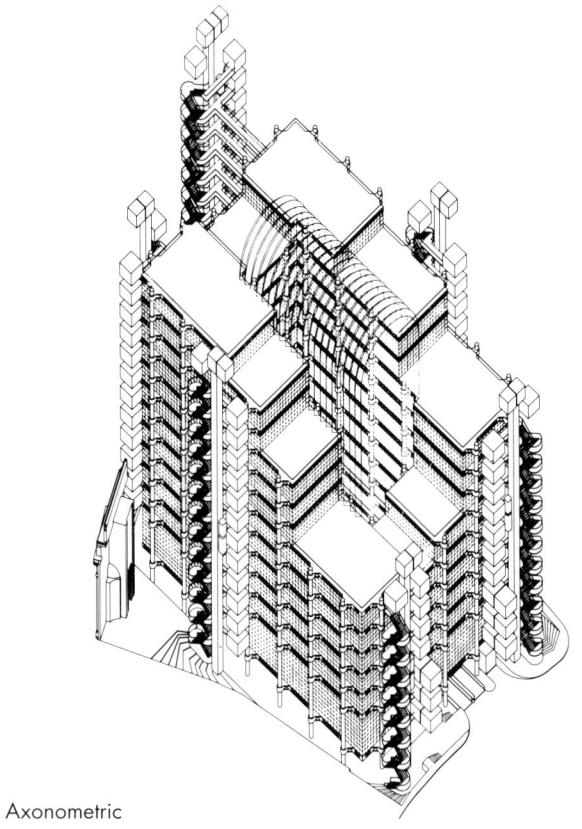

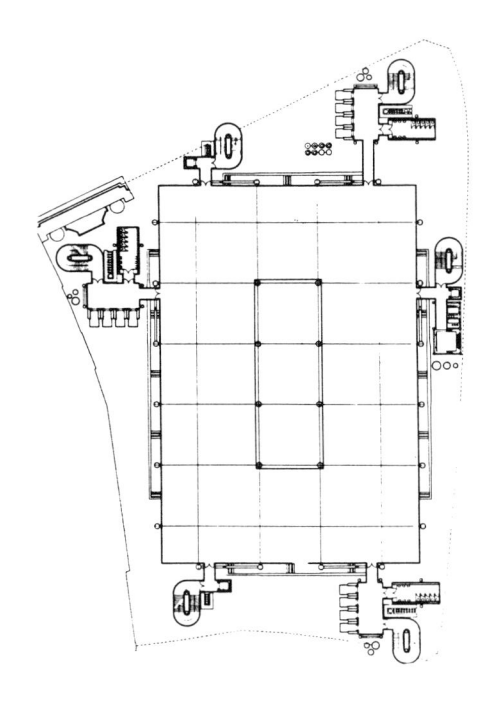

Roof plan

Above and facing page
European Court of Human Rights
Strasbourg, France, 1989–1995

We now tend to construct buildings that are general-purpose buildings, but that is not an excuse for making them boring. It merely means that they have to be easily changeable. Part of our belief as an office, part of our interest, is to create an architecture where pieces of each building can be changed, where the balance can be changed. This represents a big break from classical architecture. Classical architecture emphasized the perfection of a finished building; nothing could be added, nothing could be taken away. At the end of the twentieth century, all dynamic institutions desire to change and grow. So our office is searching for a more flexible form of architecture.

In the Lloyds design, we separated the core from the servant towers. These towers—which have a short life as against the long life of the central part—house electronics, vertical circulation, and lavatories. These elements might have a ten- to fifteen-year lifespan. The objective is to extend the life of the building by making it possible to jettison the servant towers when they become obsolete: you can take them away and the building can still exist in its own right. This, of course, is the functional reasoning. The aesthetic reasoning is to achieve a play of light and shadow between the towers, against what otherwise could be the rather boring, flat facade of a box. We could not put the core in the Centre, because the client wanted an atrium given the way Lloyds works as a market space. So, we created a dialogue between the parts, and between the servant and the master towers.

Approximately thirty years ago, some twenty-five nations signed a declaration of agreement that there would be a High Court for Europe, the European Court. Since construction began in 1994, those twenty-five countries have grown to

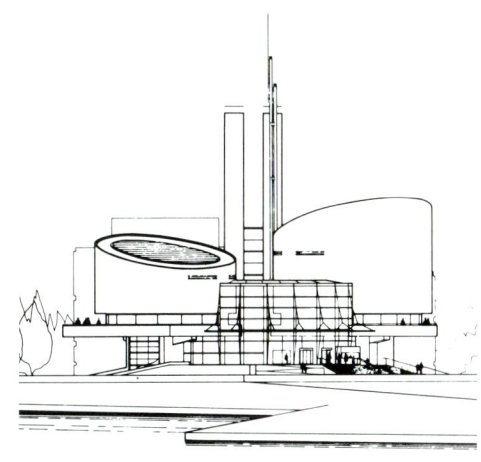

Elevation

forty-something, including many Eastern European countries. Thus, we are actually extending the building as it goes up. The Courts (in reality only two courtrooms), on a fabulous riverine site, is a building that follows the river; it sort of swerves to follow its course. It is a green building. That is, in agreement with the client, it is highly ecological building. We have agreed not to have air-conditioning except in the courtrooms themselves. Ecology dictates the form and the use of the water, and grass is planted all over the site.

I see the future in terms of a highly changeable form of architecture. I think that much of what we are doing now, which is based upon mass and volume, will be the same as Lloyds. The way you have beams and columns, where everything is basically static, will change, and buildings will become more transparent or translucent. Future buildings will respond to nature, they will be seamless; when you use only one part, the electronics systems will allow for that use electronically; the entire building will become environmentally responsive, minimizing the consumption of energy and suiting its uses as closely as possible.

Thus, in the future you will see buildings with highly active facades where, by sending electronic charges through it, you change the density of the glass, automatically allowing more light and more hot or cold air to pass through. In this way, the skin of the building becomes the brains, with the power to make the building. From one moment to the next, this skin can allow the building to become more private or more public. And it will simply hang on a very light structure. So, the future will see buildings become more chameleon-like, and with that, the idea of immutable classical architecture will change.

LECTURE
Moshe Safdie

Below and facing page, top
Yeshivat Porat Yosef
Jerusalem, Israel, 1970–

Facing page, bottom
Hebrew Union College
Jerusalem, Israel, 1976–

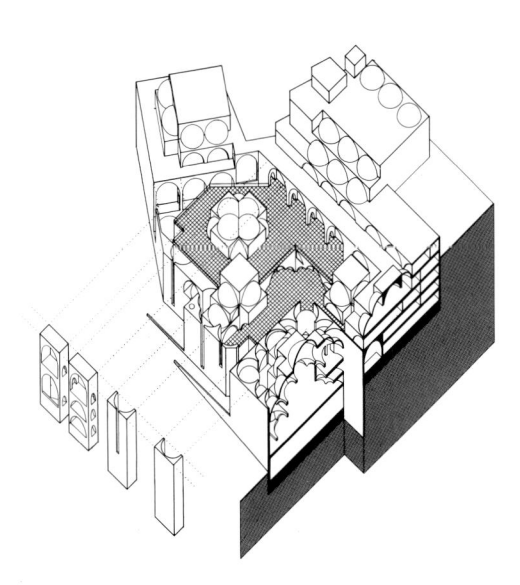

In the nineteenth century, most public buildings were used by relatively few people. They were basically aristocratic places, places for the elite. I think we are moving into an era when public buildings are used by literally everyone. If the black tie was the symbol of a museum or a performing arts building thirty years ago, jeans are no less a symbol today.

This sense of change centers around one key word: access. By access I do not simply mean physical access, but that buildings convey a sense of openness in a more profound way. They invite and draw in the public, rather than intimidate, and they make the public—no matter what their station in life—comfortable.

We must, therefore, reexamine the iconography of public buildings, or at least consider what the appropriate iconography might be and what the nature of its relationship is to the question of power. On the question of monumentality, which we consider synonymous with public buildings, even today we crave a sense of ceremony, but shy away from the statement of power.

Modern pluralistic democracy brings to public buildings the issue of patronage. Who is the client? To paraphrase Louis Sullivan in *Kindergarten Chats*, behind every great building there is a great client. An architect cannot transcend his client, and every client gets the architect that s/he deserves.

For most of us designing public buildings today, the client is not an individual, but rather a committee, often representing a wide cross-section of society. The most extreme case, which I recently experienced, is design by public referendum, a design chosen by public vote—the impact of which is far reaching.

My first experience with the public building was in Jerusalem in the early 1970s. Yeshivat Porat Yosef was an institution to be built in the heart of the Old City, and at that moment, I was concerned with one central theme: the theme of belonging. I felt the issue of belonging was one shared by the public. After all, everything about planning legislation in Jerusalem had to do with the sense of continuity, legislation to build in stone in the traditional way.

I wanted to make a building which felt as if it had always been there, yet was of today. I did not know of a way to achieve this sense of continuity except through the tectonic qualities of the building and through the materials and methods of construction. I continue to be preoccupied with this sense of how a building comes together, how the individual parts are combined to give people the greatest pleasure of an architectural experience. It is this sense of the tectonic that separates the authentic building from the stage set.

The Madaba plan of Jerusalem in Byzantine times embodies much of what is relevant to public buildings today. Not only does it identify the *cardo maximus* as the central street, as a designed public space, but it reveals that all the public buildings, such as the Holy Sepulcher, are plugged into that public domain, creating a hierarchy that gives the city legibility.

The public space itself, the colonnaded *cardo,* is designed with as much will as any individual building. There is a differentiation between the *cardo* and the public buildings that line it, and the general urban fabric of houses and workshops. We see this again in the reconstructed model of ancient Rome, where we have the hierarchy of principal streets and public buildings—the whole being much greater than the parts.

Exploration of the possible dialogue between the past and the present in

267

National Gallery of Canada
Ottawa, Ontario, Canada, 1988

a building continued as we worked on the Hebrew Union College outside the Old City walls. Here I went further in drawing upon some of the archetypes of the city: the courtyard as the major public room, the outdoor room contained by the buildings which accommodate unplanned activity. The juxtaposition of traditional and contemporary construction was emphasized in the building itself. The landscape was integrated with the built environment, and the campus was conceived as a garden, attempting to erase the line between outdoor and indoor. This integration is reflected in the building materials and forms—in the arcades, walls built in stone, prefabricated concrete frames, glass, and aluminum— creating a sense of cold and warm, light and heavy, silver and gold.

In planning The National Gallery of Canada, there was an unstated question: on such a prominent site, how visible should the Gallery be in relationship to the Parliament building? My sense was that the Gallery site had to demonstrate a presence and have a dialogue with the Parliament.

The dialogue between the great hall and the parliamentary library was immediate and conscious. This was an attempt to relate the Gallery to the older building and at the same time contrast the two of them—the transparent juxtaposed with the solid. The public is drawn into the Gallery building. Ascending the colonnade distances the visitor from the city. It is an eight-meter rise along a gentle ramp, creating a sense of possession, of preparation, of transition from the activity of daily urban life to the inner sanctum of the Gallery.

In designing the Vancouver Library, I was preoccupied with a number of questions. One had to do simply with the concept of *library*. What is a library for a large metropolitan city today? It is a place for high-tech storage and exchange of information. But Vancouver needed it to be a significant civic building—a concept that conjured up memories of libraries throughout history.

The design of the Vancouver Library was selected by public referendum. The conditions of the competition required that the three finalists' schemes be exhibited for three weeks, after which the public voted and the results were presented to the city council. Independent of the referendum, a professional architectural jury was convened, without knowing the results of the public ballot, and rendered its own judgment.

Even though we won the competition, I am ambivalent about the concept of a public referendum. My liberal side says we must trust the wisdom of the public. I also realize that in many instances, public intervention has brought major benefit, such as preventing freeways from passing through urban areas, and promoting the heritage movement in the United States. However, design selection by public vote in some ways negates the possibility of the avant-garde. Mahler's Second Symphony was booed on its first performance. Would the Eiffel Tower be selected by referendum? Probably not. The Sydney Opera House? Maybe.

The design of public buildings and their relationship to the city is expressed in the Madaba Plan of Jerusalem—a hierarchical definition of principal streets along which public buildings are located, giving deeper meaning to the civic realm. Their design cannot be considered separately from the public domain that links them.

In Greek and Roman cities, the *cardo maximus* served as the spine of the city. I do not believe that our contemporary city will consist of colonnaded streets. It is clear that the scale and transportation issues of today are new. All the more reason that we must invent an equally compelling concept for an urban public domain of today, a meeting place that connects the parts, a *new cardo* that weaves together public institutions, the building blocks of public life. In this regard, we must be as willful in designing the public place as we are in designing the public buildings that define it.

Vancouver Library Square
Vancouver, British Columbia, Canada, 1995

COMMENTARY
Stanford Anderson
Louis Kahn and
English History

Louis Kahn frequently revealed his concern for institutions. He sought to understand the patterns of human association and their reasons for being. Only then could an architect build properly—whether the great institutions of a society or the more humble institutions of house or street. I propose that Kahn addressed these issues through a reading of English history and law:

> I like English history, I have volumes of it, but I never read anything but the first volume, and even at that, only the first three or four chapters. And of course my only real purpose is to read Volume 0, you see, which has yet not been written. And it's a strange kind of mind that causes one to look for this kind of thing. I would say that such an image suggests the emergence of a mind. Your first feeling is that of beauty. . . . It is the moment, or you might say the aura, of perfect harmony.[1]

Rejecting an idealist position (the beautiful), Kahn attends to what is given (just beauty). Yet Kahn walks a tightrope, seeking "the aura of the perfect harmony." Eighteen months later, Kahn returned to the same theme:

> Then I thought, *What would be a harking back, starting from the beginning?* . . . I'm particularly interested in English history, which fascinates me. Though it's a bloody history, it still has this quality of a search. However, every time I start to read Volume I, I linger in Chapter One, and I re-read it and re-read it and always feel something else in it. Of course my idea is probably to read Volume Zero, . . . just to peer into this terrific thing—man, who has this great capacity for putting things into being that nature cannot put into being.[2]

Kahn's search, his harking back, is the search for a beginning—that which man puts into being and nature cannot. It is the search for the archaic, for the prehistoric, as the number on his impossible book, *Volume Zero*, reveals. The prehistoric is what archaeologists seek in the physical remains of ancient sites. One might imagine an architect with Louis Kahn's turn of mind particularly to be interested in the physical, often architectural, remains of archaic societies. And, of course, Kahn was; he preferred Paestum over the Parthenon.

But why English history? Why should this Jewish architect, who emigrated from Estonia to America as a boy, direct his attention to England? From the second quotation we learn that this reference is more than incidental: He tells us that he is particularly interested in English history because "though it's a bloody history, it still has this quality of a search." The search is now not only Kahn's search for beginnings; he reads English history itself as a search. This must also be a search extended in time and directed forward.

Janus-like, Kahn's search for beginnings is not merely antiquarian nor the identification of sources for imitation, but rather the search for an impulse that may still inform us today. But again, why English history? I suggest two reasons, one quite ordinary and the other more profound. Kahn grew up and worked in a society with English roots. He lived most of his life in Philadelphia and taught most extensively in the eastern United States. His was a society whose English roots were palpable. However, I think Kahn may have had a more profound reason to look to English history: If we look to the European continent, there is written law, Roman laws and Catholic canon law, which are codified and preside over historical change. The English conception of law, however, is a Janus-like construction in which we look back through the succession of events to a time immemorial in order that we may confirm an ancient, unwritten constitution and thus affirm the customs and institutions that also must be adapted as one meets the contingencies of the present and future. The English sense of law, custom, and institution relies on ancient, but constantly renewed, agreement rather than rule—it is the English appeal to the unwritten constitution and to tradition.

Tradition does not exist only in England, however. As J.G.A. Pocock of Johns Hopkins University observed, "Roman law tended to become a tradition in continuous adaptation." Pocock points to a tradition that maintains the authority of the law as *given,* even if newly formulated. Yet there may also come dissatisfaction and the possibility of a fundamentalist revolt, a demand for return to the original sources. Such revolts, at once radical and reactionary, involve the repudiation of tradition. When such questions and revolt arise within a society that possesses a known original form of law or authority, the authority of Janus's backward view may be reaffirmed in ascribing to it a farsightedness and thus a capacity to retrieve and reinstate the fundamentals.

Janus must retreat in time to a moment when custom and tradition are as unsullied as possible. It is this form of learning from beginnings, this imaginative, probing quest that Kahn attempts in reading Volume Zero. How did Kahn invent this notion of Volume Zero? I am told that the six "orders" of the Talmud each begin with page two; that the Talmud contains no page one. Did this absence, suggestive of the absence of the concrete knowledge of ultimate authority, suggest to Kahn a parallel with English history and its unwritten constitution?

Comparing drawings by Kahn with those of other thinkers in architecture clarifies these observations. Viollet-le-Duc, for example, had an immediate purpose different from that of Kahn: He was involved in the restoration of old monuments. He also pursued a different intellectual agenda: the definition of architectural principles as revealed in the original documents in contrast to Kahn's search for the impulse for an imaginative projection. In his drawings of the medieval fortifications at Carcassone, Viollet-le-Duc studied the reality of Volume One to provide the authority for principles he ascribed to that reality. Viollet-le-Duc seeks to know the actual document—Volume One—so thoroughly that it will reveal its principles. As he himself argued, the modern architect should be able to build in his own day as the ancient masters would have done if they were placed in modern circumstances. So every detail of the ancient work may inform Viollet-le-Duc's quest. Kahn, on the other hand, seeks an imaginative projection beyond the detail, beyond the particularity of the ancient monument.

For Kahn, it is institutions that fulfill the Janus role to which I have been referring:

> I know that institutions is not a word to use, but it's an excellent word. It tells you that there is an agreement in back of the making.[3]

Kahn appears as contemporary social critic and traditionalist, as a social inventor and a seeker of beginnings. He sees the institution as the necessary mediating entity of agreement and custom; yet the institution is itself subject to criticism and reformation by the light of its inspiration.

Notes

1. Louis I Kahn, *What Will Be Has Always Been: The Words of Louis I. Kahn,* ed. Richard Saul Wurman (New York: Access Press and Rizzoli International Publications, 1986), p. 151, from a speech by Kahn at Aspen, Colorado, June 19, 1972.

2. Ibid, p. 245, from a speech at Tel Aviv, December 20, 1973.

3. Ibid. p. 156.

Editor's Note:
A revised version of this presentation was published as "Public Institutions: Louis I. Kahn's Reading of Volume Zero," in *Journal of Architectural Education* 49 (September 1995), pp. 10–21.

COMMENTARY

Kenneth Frampton

The Atrium as Surrogate Public Form

I want to broach the theme of the public building through the prototype of the atrium considered as a paradigmatic city-in-miniature. The role of the atrium over the last two hundred years has been to compensate, either consciously or unconsciously, for the gradual erosion of the public realm in the traditional city and even, later, for the disappearance of the traditional city itself. It is significant that Frank Lloyd Wright invariably regarded his public buildings as introspective domains where the representational space and its corresponding public facade were on the interior rather than the exterior. Wright seems to have sensed from the very outset of his career that there was "no more there, there," to coin Gertrude Stein's overfamiliar phrase. He sensed from the beginning that the public realm in the American city was not reliable. This would explain why all of his quasi-public buildings had blank exteriors, from the Larkin Building in Buffalo, New York, of 1904, to the S.C. Johnson Administration Building in Racine, Wisconsin, of 1939; from the Morris Gift Shop in San Francisco, of 1948, to the Guggenheim Museum in New York, of 1959. In each instance, the representative public face of the building was on the interior, as in the traditional mosque.

This phenomenon of progressively internalizing the public realm did not begin with Wright, of course. It first appeared perhaps in the mid-seventeenth century, with Cardinal Richelieu's development of the Palais Royale as a space set apart from the continuous fabric of the city of Paris. The Palais Royale was not just another royal square; it was a microcosmos consisting of a large elongated garden court surrounded on four sides by a continuous open-sided arcade with apartments above. This paradigm was augmented over time by another layer of residential development built during the reign of Louis-Philippe at the end of the eighteenth century, when, as Michel Verne points out, life within the Palais Royale became synonymous with everything one might associate with the French term *commerce*, from trade in luxury goods to prostitution, and from theatrical performances to the organization of political clubs. The Palais Royale was a kind of urban "free port" within which certain license was granted that was not available elsewhere. Hence, it is no accident that Camille Desmoulins would incite a mob to revolution in the garden of the Palais Royale in 1798. The ultimate quintessential glazed gallery or arcade, the so-called Galerie d'Orléans, was built there in 1825 to the designs of Percier and Fontaine.

Over time the Palais Royale became inseparable from the labyrinth of the Parisian arcades extending from it into the interstices of the surrounding urban fabric; the galleries Colbert and Vivienne were typical in this regard. These top-lit *passages*, celebrated by Walter Benjamin in his essay "Paris, Capital of the Nineteenth Century," were superseded after the middle of the nineteenth century by the emergence of the department store, the first of which was the Bon Marché store dating from 1852. Like Wright's Larkin Building, the department store was not only a microcosmos but also a semipublic realm where one went to see and be seen. And, like Charles Garnier's opera house in Paris, it was in fact a surrogate space of public appearance. Other examples of top-lit, ferro-vitreous, surrogate public places dating from the last half of the nineteenth century include, of course, the great railway terminals of the major European capitals, along with mega-gallerias such as Giuseppe Mengoni's Galleria Vittorio Emmanuele in Milan; this last project is inseparable symbolically and politically from the rise of the Italian State.

Once these typological continuities are pointed out, one can easily understand how the atrium came to reassert itself as a type in contemporary practice, even as a way of creating a clearly defined pseudo-public space in what was otherwise a processional urban domain. One thinks not only of Wright's Larkin Building and Raymond Hood's Rockefeller Center in Manhattan (1936) but also of more recent "surrogate" public buildings such as Herman Hertzberger's Centraal

Beheer in Apeldoorn, The Netherlands (1965), or Norman Foster's Willis, Faber, Dunmar Building in Ipswich, England (1975). Both of these were essentially introspective *burolandshaft* office buildings built for insurance companies in the mid-1970s. The link between the internal spaces of Centraal Beheer and the Larkin Building is obvious although the two buildings have quite different plan forms, just as the Foster building and the nineteenth-century department store share spatial and formal correspondences. I have in mind the center void of the "doughnut" plan, with escalators rising inside the void to serve the office floors on all sides. This is a kind of atrium building, and it is clear that a marked sense of commonality is provided by the central volume. Here, this surrogate public space is reinforced by the presence of a restaurant on the roof and a swimming pool on the ground floor, both allocated for use by the employees, as in the Larkin Building. And while the Larkin Building did not provide a swimming pool, it did have a conservatory and restaurant on the roof as well as an organ in the central space.

Other modern atria that come readily to mind are John Portman's Hyatt Regency Hotel at the Atlanta Peachtree Center (1967)—his invention of the "atrium hotel"—or Barton Myers and Jack Diamond's student dormitory block in the form of a top-lit galleria at the University of Alberta (1969). Richard Rogers's Lloyds Building in London (1978–1986) is yet another variation on the same theme, as is Richard Meier's City Hall and Central Library in The Hague, The Netherlands (1986–1995). Here it is clear that the vast atrium of Meier's city hall functions as a totally new space of public appearance within the pre-existing, low-rise brick fabric that until the end of the 1970s made up the basic residential fabric of The Hague. Despite the fact that no one actually lives in the city hall, it is the quintessential "city-in-miniature." It makes up for the fact that the traditional city fabric has been totally disrupted by the rather random superimposition of new office slabs throughout the downtown over approximately the same time. The new atrium of the city hall is able to mediate between the scale of these slabs and the more discreet, tessellated grain of the surrounding city fabric.

COMMENTARY

Joseph Rykwert

The Contemporary Civic
Building and the
Public Work of Art

James Fergusson, a distinguished mid-nineteenth-century historian and architecture theoretician, thought that architecture could be studied as language and that the phonetic aspect of architecture was essentially sculpture and painting. Today we live in a society in which all of this has changed so much that it is difficult to imagine architecture functioning as a frame for art, and vice versa. We also know that whether we are talking about public art or about architecture, the spray-can protester will have his say no matter what happens. I remember that in 1968, a house in Piccadilly, in London, was inscribed by the squatters inside it with the audacious text "We are the writing on your walls." It is worth remembering that whatever we do as architects in our cities of anomie, the spray-can artist will decorate such work with graffiti; with the marks of his possession.

At the same time, the institutions of power in contemporary society have become increasingly invisible. Figures of power today dress just like you and I do, whereas in earlier tribal societies the people holding power at the top of the pyramid were distinguished by their headgear. If you were wearing a crown on your head, or even a top hat, then everybody knew they had to bow down to you. Today, however, we have exchanged the display of hegemony for the reality of it. Personally, I would prefer my dictator to have his chest covered with medals and his epaulets dangling with gold to having him dressed in a suit just like mine, particularly if he had the power to order that I be tortured or shot. If given the choice, I would certainly prefer to know where the power resides. The buildings of the National Security Council in the United States, for instance, one of the seats of real power today, are nothing more prepossessing than ordinary office buildings. There is, of course, nothing much we can do about this condition.

When Napoleon conquered Italy and returned to Paris in victory, he organized a vast triumphal procession in which he displayed the works of art that various Italian states and municipalities had been forced to surrender to him. These works were already commodified by Napoleon's gesture and became, overnight, cultural booty. When the royal art galleries became public property at the beginning of the nineteenth century, such artworks were consecrated and dedicated to the public good. They moved from palaces to museums, which became civic institutions meant to elevate public taste, educate the public, and instill in them a love for the beauty of the past. These collections were housed in monumental buildings which were at the time the greatest structures in the city; in effect, they were the temples of a new cult. Within these public repositories, works of art, torn from their original contexts, were presented partly as commodities and partly as educational objects.

While the museum as an institution still exists today, it is no longer capable of making a decisive physical mark on the city, that is, of establishing its monumental presence. Comparatively speaking, the museum has become a small structure—even such a huge museum as the Metropolitan Museum of Art in New York, which is dwarfed by the skyscrapers around it. High-rise structures that descend abruptly to the ground and have only a simple narrow entrance opening to the street constitute the city today. Such buildings make no connection with the public realm, despite the fact that quasi-public atrium buildings are now being urged on developers by enlightened municipalities. And it is not only the museum that is suppressed in this kind of city: Almost any public institution looks insignificant when compared to the ubiquitous high-rise structure.

How have architects responded to this situation? They have done so in diverse ways ranging from the monumentality of Oscar Niemeyer's Brasilia to Mies van der Rohe's Convention Center in Chicago, which was so neutral in its appearance as to give little indication of its monumental and institutional status. The Federal Plaza law courts complex in New York was selected as a site for a piece of public sculpture by Richard Serra; his infamous *Tilted Arch*, set athwart the central square, challenged the banality of the architecture. However, the violent abstract character of this work was considered offensive. It is interesting to note that Serra defended his work on the grounds of free speech rather than any aesthetic quality. He justified it by saying that the sculpture was site-specific and that removing it would infringe his constitutional rights as an artist. In other words, this sculpture, as an utterance, fell into Fergusson's category of "phonetics"; hence its removal would infringe on the artist's right to speak. That sculpture in fact had to be removed at night in order to avoid protest. Clearly, this is a double issue: the right of the artist to make whatever statement he wants, and the public's right to take offense at what he says.

Other public works by Serra seem to have caused no offense at all, such as the piece commissioned for the Plaza de las Palmeras in Barcelona for the purpose of humanizing an unattractive space situated among a group of rather anonymous buildings. His project consisted of two plastered concrete block walls that curve toward each other but do not meet. The City of Barcelona reinforced this gesture through the paving and through a series of lampposts that echo the curve of the walls. In this instance the work of art was so integrated into the landscape that it virtually disappeared.

Today, when one commissions an artist to do a work for a public space, one cannot say, "I want an image of public virtue," or "I want something that we can all agree on." All one can say is, "I want you to do your thing." If later you decide to remove this thing, then you are infringing on the artist's right to speak. However, what is the artist trying to say? This remains the imponderable question.

It is a sad reflection on our time that there is in fact no contact between the architect and the artist, and that, more generally, there is insufficient contact between the makers shaping the public domain and the general public. The more individualistic the artist, the less enduring his message. If we are to create a new kind of public space, we will have to change our ways very considerably. I think we will have to reflect what we mean exactly by the rights associated with private behavior and by the privileges of the public, because the moment you enter the public realm, you are in a domain in which you cannot simply claim the right to speak. Richard Serra's defense of his *Tilted Arch* seems entirely misconceived to me. Whatever you may think of the work, it is not a private utterance. Every work of civic architecture and art is necessarily a public act. The moment you make your mark in the public realm, you are addressing society as a whole; reciprocally, society demands that you be explicit.

Biographies

Raimund Abraham

Raimund Abraham graduated from the Technical University of Graz, Austria, in 1958 and practiced in Vienna until 1964. During this period he realized a number of private houses in collaboration with Friedrich Gartler-St. Florian. Thereafter he migrated to the United States to join the faculty of architecture at the Rhode Island School of Design in Providence. In 1971 he was appointed to the faculty of the Irwin S. Chanin School of Architecture at The Cooper Union in New York, where he is currently a professor.

After a decade largely devoted to teaching, numerous competitions, and a considerable number of conceptual works, Mr. Abraham returned to practice in 1980, beginning with the conversion of a disused Manhattan law court into Jonas Mekas' Anthology Film Archive. As a participant in the Berlin International Building Exhibition (1980–1981) he went on to realize an apartment building on Friedrichstrasse and, soon after, a large housing quarter in Traviatagasse, Vienna (1987–1991), designed with Carl Pruscha and a number of younger Austrian architects. There followed a mixed-use building in Graz (1990–1993), a bank in Lienz (1993–1996), and his winning design for the new Austrian Cultural Institute in New York (1993), which is pending construction.

Similar to the work of Austrian sculptor Walter Pichler, Mr. Abraham's conceptual work—the hypothetical houses he projected between 1970 and 1984—almost invariably consists of earthworks in one form or another. As such they effect a formal play between the telluric character of the ground and the dematerialized nature of the tectonic structure above it, a dialectic that continues to inform his current realizations.

Stanford Anderson

Stanford Anderson studied architecture in his home state of Minnesota and at the University of California at Berkeley, from which he graduated with a master's degree in 1958. Over the following decade he pursued a course of advanced study in the history of art and architecture in Munich and New York, receiving his Ph.D. from Columbia University in 1968. Professor Anderson has taught continuously at the Massachusetts Institute of Technology since 1963; he served as director of advanced historical and theoretical studies there and is now head of the Department of Architecture.

In addition to his academic pursuits, Professor Anderson has had an extremely varied career as an architect, researcher, and professional consultant, particularly in the field of urban design. He has written extensively and edited two standard texts examining environmental design on a large scale: *Planning for Diversity and Choice: Possible Futures and Relations to the Man-Controlled Environment* (1969) and *On Streets* (1978). The latter book summarized the findings of a research team led by Professor Anderson while he was a fellow of the Institute for Architecture and Urban Studies in New York. Since that time he has carried out a number of related urban studies ranging from a topological reading of the historic core of Savannah, Georgia, to an analysis of the east-west axis in Paris.

In the field of modern architectural history Mr. Anderson is most renowned for his research on the career and work of the German architect Peter Behrens. His most recent historical publication is an annotated translation of Hermann Muthesius's *Style-Architecture and Building Art: Transformation of Architecture in the Nineteenth Century and its Present Condition*. Among his numerous awards are fellowships from the American Association of Learned Societies and the John Simon Guggenheim Foundation.

Dimitris Antonakakis

Dimitris Antonakakis studied at the National Technical University in Athens, where he met his wife and partner, Suzana Kolokytha Antonakakis. The two began to practice upon graduating in 1958, first on their own and after 1965 under the name Atelier 66. The Antonakakises were influenced by Mies van der Rohe via a graduate of the Illinois Institute of Technology, James Speyer, who taught at the university in the 1950s, and by the two main protagonists of the Greek modern movement active during the same period, Dimitri Pikionis and Aris Konstantinidis.

The Antonakakises' earliest houses in Glyfada and Athens were clearly indebted to the work of Konstantinidis, as was the archeological museum they built in Chios in 1965. Their softer, somewhat plastic and labyrinthine work in concrete/concrete block also owed much to Pikionis and is particularly evident in the masterly eighty-story apartment building they inserted into the dense fabric of Benaki Street in Athens in 1972. A considerable number of Atelier 66's projects relate to the Greek tourist industry, including two extended hotel complexes in Hermionis and Lyttos. In addition, they have designed a number of low-rise housing projects and a series of deft insertions into closely knit ancient fabrics, such as a recreation facility for a fortress in Naplion (1969). Over the past twenty years their practice has expanded to include projects for university campuses and various large urban infill schemes.

Dimitri Antonakakis taught at the National Technical University in Athens from 1958 to 1992 and at the Technische University of Delft, The Netherlands, in 1987. Since 1994 he has been a visiting professor at the School of Architecture and Planning at the Massachusetts Institute of Technology. Together with Suzana Antonakakis, he has participated in numerous architecture exhibitions in Greece and at architecture schools in London, Vienna, Zurich, Geneva, and Venice.

Julian Beinart

Julian Beinart is Professor of Architecture at the Massachusetts Institute of Technology, where he teaches the form and design of cities; he also heads Cambridge International Design Associates in Cambridge, Massachusetts. In 1992 and 1994 he was co-chairman of The Jerusalem Seminar in Architecture.

In the 1960s Professor Beinart produced jazz concerts and directed design courses in five African countries as part of a wider study of popular art that was the subject of a BBC film and an exhibition in London. Since 1986 he has designed master plans in Jerusalem for the Israel Museum, the Jerusalem International Convention Center, and the Central Government Precinct with Arthur Spector-Michael Amisar Architects.

Professor Beinart's work is international in scope and includes the St. Petersburg (Russia) Master Plan competition, the Marunouchi downtown study in Tokyo, studies of the long-term effects of hosting the Olympic Games, and projects in southern Africa and the United Arab Emirates. In the United States he has worked on the United States Air Force Memorial in Washington, D.C.; the Dade County (Florida) transportation corridor and the Miami International Airport; the Alliance Airport in Fort Worth, Texas; and a proposed basketball arena in Dallas, Texas.

Professor Beinart has held various academic and research-oriented positions throughout his career. He was a Sir Herbert Baker Rome Scholar; Program Chairman and President of the International Design Conference in Aspen, Colorado; one of the founders of ILAUD (Laboratory for Architecture and Urban Design) in Italy; American editor of *Space and Society/Spazio e Società*, and research director of a Mellon Foundation study of architectural education.

Henry N. Cobb

Henry Cobb graduated from the Harvard University Graduate School of Design in 1949 and thereafter worked in the architecture office of Hugh Stubbins and for the firm of Webb & Knapp, Inc., from 1950 to 1955. He is one of the founding partners of I.M. Pei & Partners, now known as Pei Cobb Freed & Partners. As a design partner Mr. Cobb has been principally responsible for dozens of the firm's projects, including the Royal Bank of Canada Building in Montreal (1962), the John Hancock Tower in Boston (1976), the Portland (Maine) Museum of Art (1983), First Interstate World Center in Los Angeles (1989), and headquarters for the American Association for the Advancement of Science in Washington, D.C. (1996). Among Mr. Cobb's current projects are United States courthouses in Boston and in Hammond, Indiana; the head office of ABN-AMRO Bank in Amsterdam; China Europe International Business School in Shanghai; Tour Hines at La Défense in Paris; and College Conservatory of Music at the University of Cincinnati.

Throughout his career Mr. Cobb has combined professional practice with teaching. He has held the Davenport and Bishop visiting professorships at Yale University and served as Studio Professor and Chairman of the Department of Architecture at Harvard University from 1980 to 1985. Mr. Cobb has been widely honored as an architect and educator. In 1977 he received the Arnold W. Brunner Memorial Prize in Architecture from the American Academy and Institute of Arts and Letters. In 1982 he received the Medal of Honor of the New York Chapter, American Institute of Architects. He has received honorary degrees from Bowdoin College (1985) and the Swiss Federal Institute of Technology (1990). In 1995 he received the Topaz Medallion for Excellence in Architectural Education.

Charles Correa

Born in Hyderabad, India, Charles Correa studied under Buckminster Fuller at the University of Michigan and at the Massachusetts Institute of Technology, where he earned his M.Arch in 1955. He returned to India following his studies in the United States and was a partner in the Bombay firm of G.M. Bhuta and Associates from 1956 to 1958, the year he started his own practice in Bombay. Mr. Correa is a pioneer in the development of low-cost housing for rapidly urbanizing Third World countries. From 1971 to 1974 he was Chief Architect for the planning of New Bombay, an urban center of two million people developed across the harbor from the preexisting city. In 1985, Prime Minister Rajiv Gandhi appointed him Chairman of the National Commission on Urbanization, reporting on urban policies for the Indian government.

Among Mr. Correa's most renowned projects are the Mahatma Gandhi Memorial Museum at the Sabarmati Ashram in Ahmedabad (1963), the Bharat Bhavan Museum in Bhopal (1978), and townships in Karnataka and Maharashtra states. With its sensitive incorporation of low-cost materials and traditional construction techniques, the Mahatma Gandhi museum exemplifies Mr. Correa's approach to building in response to climate and the local culture. His current projects include the U.C. Centre in Mauritius, Cidade de Goa and the Kala Akademi in Goa, the British Council Headquarters in New Delhi, and the Institute of Astrophysics in Poona.

Mr. Correa has taught at several universities in India and abroad and is the author of *The New Landscape*, a monograph devoted to urban issues in the Third World. His honors and awards include the Padma Shri from the President of India (1972) and gold medals from the Royal Institute of British Architects (1984), the Indian Institute of Architects (1987), and the International Union of Architects (1990).

A.J. Diamond

A native of South Africa, A.J. Diamond was educated at the University of Cape Town, Oxford University, and the University of Pennsylvania, from which he graduated in 1962. In 1965, after serving an apprenticeship with Louis I. Kahn, Mr. Diamond moved to Toronto; four years later he founded the partnership of Diamond and Myers, a practice that soon became one of the most distinguished in Canada. In 1975 he established his present practice under the title A.J. Diamond, Donald Schmitt and Company.

Mr. Diamond's work has focused on large-scale planning and infill housing. Among his built works are a dormitory building for the University of Alberta (1975), designed in association with Barton Myers; Toronto Village Terrace Housing (1985); Citadel Theatre, Edmonton (1986); Metro Toronto Central YMCA (1987); Calgary Olympic Arch (1988); Richmond Hill Central Library (1991); and the Jerusalem City Hall (1993). He is currently working on a broadcasting station in Beijing; a winery in Napa Valley, California; a housing project for Beaune, France; and the Visitor and Orientation Centre for the National Capital in Ottawa.

In addition to directing his architectural practice, Mr. Diamond has taught extensively at the University of Toronto, where he founded the M.Arch program, and at numerous other North American institutions, including Harvard University, Princeton University, the University of California at Berkeley, the University of Texas, and the University of Pennsylvania.

The practice has won many awards, including the esteemed Governor General's Award for the years 1985, 1987, 1994, and 1996; and the Toronto Arts Award for Design and Architecture in 1989. In 1994 he was named an Honorary Fellow of the American Institute of Architects, and in 1996 he was appointed an Officer of the Order of Canada.

Balkrishna V. Doshi

Educated at Fergusson College in Poona, India, and the J.J. School of Art in Bombay, Balkrishna Doshi began his career working with Le Corbusier as a senior designer in Paris. He established his own office in Ahmedabad in 1955, and beginning in 1962 he collaborated with Louis I. Kahn on the Indian Institute of Management in Ahmedabad.

Mr. Doshi is a pioneer of higher-quality low-income housing and has built large-scale works throughout the Indian continent. These include the Aranya settlement in Indore and, most recently, the Kharghar development of eighty thousand dwelling units in New Bombay. His most recent works include the Indian Institute of Management in Bangalore (1985), the Sawai Gandharva Smarak Auditorium in Poona (1991), the Bharat Diamond Bourse in Mumbai (1992), and the National Institute of Fashion Technology in New Delhi (1994).

Mr. Doshi founded the School of Architecture and Planning in Ahmedabad in 1962 and served as dean of the school during its first decade. In Ahmedabad he also founded the Centre for Environmental Planning and Technology and the Vastu-Shilpa Foundation for Studies and Research in Environmental Design known as Sangath, which has served as the center of his architectural practice and research for the past twenty years.

Mr. Doshi has taught at several American and European universities; in 1990 he received an honorary doctorate from the University of Pennsylvania. Among Mr. Doshi's numerous honors and awards are the Padma Shree Award from the Government of India (1976), the Great Gold Medal from the Académie d'Architecture in France (1988), and the Aga Khan Award for Architecture (1995).

Kenneth Frampton

After graduating from the Architectural Association in London in 1957 and performing two years of military service, Kenneth Frampton worked in Israel for one year in the offices of Karmi, Melzer, Karmi and Yashar/Eytan. In 1960 he returned to England to join the office of Douglas Stephen and Partners. From 1962 to 1965 he was technical editor for the British magazine *Architectural Design*; thereafter he moved to the United States to become a member of the faculty of architecture at Princeton University.

Since 1972, except for three years at the Royal College of Art in London, Professor Frampton has been a member of the faculty at Columbia University in New York, where he is currently the Ware Professor of Architecture. In addition to his academic work and his role as an architecture critic, Professor Frampton has occasionally worked as an architect, designing a low-rise, high-density housing quarter for Brownsville, New York, in 1972 under the auspices of the Institute for Architecture and Urban Studies (IAUS) in New York.

From 1972 to 1982 he was a co-editor of the IAUS magazine *Oppositions*. In 1980 he published *Modern Architecture: a Critical History*, a synoptic study of the Modern Movement; this was followed by a number of other historical studies, including *Modern Architecture Volumes 1 and 2: 1851–1945* (in collaboration with Yukio Futagawa), and *Modern Architecture and the Critical Present*. In 1983 he formulated his theory of critical regionalism in an essay entitled "Towards a Critical Regionalism" published in the anthology *The Anti-Aesthetic: Essays in Postmodern Culture*. His most recent work is *Studies in Tectonic Culture*, published in 1996 by The MIT Press. Professor Frampton has taught on a visiting basis at a number of universities in Europe and America, including the EPFL in Lausanne and the Berlage Institute in Amsterdam.

James Ingo Freed

A native of Essen, Germany, James Ingo Freed received his architecture degree from the Illinois Institute of Technology in 1953 and worked subsequently in the office of Mies van der Rohe in New York before joining I.M. Pei & Partners in 1956. He became a partner in the firm, now known as Pei Cobb Freed & Partners, in 1980.

Among the well-known works for which Mr. Freed has been responsible are West Loop Plaza in Houston, Texas (1980); 499 Park Avenue, an office tower on the east side of Manhattan (1981); the Jacob K. Javits Convention Center and Plaza in New York (1986); and First Bank Place in Minneapolis, Minnesota (1992). In addition, Mr. Freed played a leading role in the development of Kips Bay Apartments and New York University Towers in New York. In 1993 Mr. Freed realized two key works: the Los Angeles Convention Center expansion and The United States Holocaust Memorial Museum in Washington, D.C., which was widely acclaimed and received numerous awards, including the American Institute of Architects Honor Award in 1994. Mr. Freed's current projects include the Ball State University Alumni Center; the United States Air Force Memorial Museum in Arlington, Virginia; The Israel Museum in Jerusalem; and a United States Courthouse in Omaha, Nebraska.

Throughout his career Mr. Freed has combined his architectural practice with teaching. He was dean of the College of Architecture at the Illinois Institute of Technology from 1975 to 1978, served as the Eero Saarinen Professor of Architectural Design at Yale University, and has been a visiting critic at colleges across the United States. Among Mr. Freed's many awards are the National Endowment for the Arts 1995 National Medal of Arts, the Arnold W. Brunner Memorial Prize in Architecture from the American Academy and Institute of Arts and Letters (1977), and the R.S. Reynolds Memorial Award for Excellence in Architecture (1975).

Romaldo Giurgola

Romaldo Giurgola was born in Rome and obtained a B.Arch from the University of Rome in 1949. He attended Columbia University and received his M.Arch in 1951, then emigrated to the United States in 1954. He is a founding partner of Mitchell/Giurgola Architects, established in Philadelphia in 1958 and in New York in 1966, and of Mitchell/Giurgola & Thorp Architects, based in Australia, where he is Senior Partner. The Australian firm has completed a wide range of projects, including university buildings in Canberra, Adelaide, Sydney, and on the Sunshine Coast in Queensland; as well as a new training complex for the Singapore Armed Forces Military Institute. Mr. Giurgola was principal design architect for Australia's Parliament House in Canberra.

Mr. Giurgola designed many award-winning projects during his years in the United States, including the University of Pennsylvania Parking Garage (1963); the United Fund Headquarters in Philadelphia (1971); the Lang Music Building at Swarthmore College in Swarthmore, Pennsylvania (1973); and the Corporate Headquarters Building for Volvo in Gothenburg, Sweden (1984).

He was a professor at the University of Pennsylvania from 1954 to 1966 and Chairman of the Department of Architecture at Columbia University from 1967 to 1972. He continued at Columbia as Ware Professor of Architecture from 1972 to 1991, and was Thomas Jefferson Professor at the University of Virginia in 1979. Mr. Giurgola was elected to the American Academy and Institute of Arts and Letters in 1977 and to the Accademia Nazionale di San Luca in 1980. From 1978 to 1989 he served as a Trustee of the American Academy in Rome, and in 1989 he received the Order of Australia from the Australian government.

Herman Hertzberger

Educated at the Technical University of Delft, The Netherlands, Herman Hertzberger established his own office upon graduating in 1958 and realized his first project four years later. Over the past thirty years he has been a major influence in Dutch and international architecture. Among his firm's numerous projects are the Students' House in Amsterdam (1966); Centraal Beheer Office Building in Apeldoorn (1972); the Vredenburg Music Center in Utrecht (1978); De Overloop Housing for the Elderly in Almere-Haven (1984); the Polygoon Elementary School in Almere (1992); the Benelux Merkenbureau Offices in The Hague (1993); and the Chase Theater in Breda (1995).

Influenced by the theories of Team 10 and by the Structuralists in the 1960s, Mr. Hertzberger has sought to translate into building his theories on polyvalent form, identity, and structure. He is currently working on several housing projects in The Netherlands and in Cologne, Berlin, and Düren, Germany; urban design/master plans in The Netherlands and in Berlin and Freising, Germany; YKK Dormitory in Kurobe, Japan; the Montessori College Oost in Amsterdam; and the Bijlmer Monument in Amsterdam (with Georges Descombes).

Mr. Hertzberger has had a distinguished career as a teacher and currently holds professorships at the Technical University of Delft and the University of Geneva. He was a visiting professor at the Massachusetts Institute of Technology from 1966 to 1967 and has taught at several other North American universities. From 1959 to 1963 he was an editor of the influential journal *Forum* with Aldo van Eyck, Jacob Bakema, and others. His many honors include the Fritz Schumacher Award (1974), the Richard Neutra Award (1989), the Premio Europa Architettura (1991), the Bond van Nederlandse Arkitekten Award (1991), and the Prix Rhénan for school buildings (1993).

Arata Isozaki

After graduating from the Faculty of Architecture at the University of Tokyo, Arata Isozaki worked with the Kenzo Tange Team in Tokyo from 1954 to 1963, the year he established his own practice. Since that time he has built a large number of widely acclaimed buildings in the United States and Europe as well as in his native Japan. Two of his earliest works, the Oita Prefectural Library (1966) and the Museum of Modern Art in Gunma (1974), received prizes from the Architectural Institute of Japan.

Among Mr. Isozaki's recent buildings in Japan are the Tsukuba Center Building in the new Tsukuba Science City in Ibaraki (1983), the Nagi Museum of Contemporary Art in Okayama (1994), and the Kyoto Concert Hall (1995). His work in the United States includes The Museum of Contemporary Art in Los Angeles (1986) and the Team Disney Building in Orlando, Florida (1990). Isozaki was also the architect for the Sant Jordi Sports Palace, one of the major venues for the Barcelona Olympic Games of 1992, and the Center for Japanese Art and Technology in Krakow, Poland (1993). In addition to architecture, Mr. Isozaki has designed sets for film and stage, numerous art installations and exhibitions, and industrial objects.

Mr. Isozaki has been a visiting professor at Columbia, Yale, and Harvard universities, the University of Hawaii, the University of California at Los Angeles, and at the Rhode Island School of Design. Among the many prizes he has received are the Mainich Art Award, the Chevalier de l'Ordre des Arts et des Lettres; the Asahi Award of *Asahi Shimbun*, the Arnold W. Brunner Memorial Prize of the American Academy and Institute of Arts and Letters, and the Chicago Architecture Award. In 1986 he was awarded the Gold Medal of the Royal Institute of British Architects.

Ram Karmi

Son of the Israeli architect Dov Karmi and brother of Ada Karmi-Melamede, Ram Karmi graduated from the Architectural Association in London in 1956. He was a partner, with his father, in the Tel Aviv firm of Karmi-Melzer-Karmi from 1956 until his father's death in 1962.

Mr. Karmi has built extensively throughout his forty-year career, with works varying from private houses to large housing projects such as Rosmarine Court (1990) and the Gilo housing complexes near Jerusalem (1972, 1993). He has also designed numerous commercial and educational buildings, including the Department of Humanities building at The Hebrew University in Jerusalem (1978), a museum for children of the Holocaust at Kibbutz Lohamei Hagetaot (1993), and the Israel Supreme Court building in Jerusalem (1992).

Among Mr. Karmi's current projects are the master plan for Holyland 2000, a mixed-use complex in Jerusalem (with Arthur Spector-Michael Amisar Architects); Weizman Institute of Science in Rehovot; a cultural center in Mevaseret Zion; and several residential complexes and private houses.

Also known as an architecture critic and educator, Mr. Karmi has taught at The Technion, Israel Institute of Technology in Haifa, since 1964. He has been a visiting lecturer and critic at Columbia University, Princeton University, and the Massachusetts Institute of Technology. From 1975 to 1979 Mr. Karmi served as chief architect of the Israeli Ministry of Housing.

Ada Karmi-Melamede

Ada Karmi-Melamede attended the Architectural Association in London and received her architecture degree from The Technion, Israel Institute of Technology, in Haifa in 1963. Ms. Karmi-Melamede and her brother Ram Karmi grew up with architecture—their father, Dov Karmi, was one of the significant architects of the State of Israel and designed over one hundred buildings. Following their father's death in 1962, Ms. Karmi-Melamede and her brother founded Karmi Associates in Tel Aviv in 1964; however, their winning design for the Supreme Court building in Jerusalem, inaugurated in 1992, was their first joint project.

Ms. Karmi-Melamede has successfully combined careers in both the United States and Israel since the 1970s. In Israel her projects have ranged from the Arel Electronics Industry complex in Yavne (1983), to offices for The Israel Institute for Democracy in Jerusalem (1995), to over ten private houses. Among her U.S. projects are showrooms for textile and furniture manufacturers in Chicago and New York and a Park Avenue apartment renovation in New York (1984). In Israel she is currently working on master plans for The Open University in Ra'ananah and Ben Gurion University in Be'er Sheva, executive offices for the Nilit Factory in Tel Aviv, and Hadassah Residential Complex in Tel Aviv.

Ms. Karmi-Melamede taught at Columbia University from 1969 to 1982 and has served as a visiting professor and lecturer at several other universities in the United States. She received The Sanberg Prize for Research in Art and Architecture in 1985 and several National Endowment for the Arts grants for research projects in Israel and the United States.

Enric Miralles

Following his graduation from the Barcelona School of Architecture and his apprenticeship at the Barcelona firm of Piñon and Viaplana, Enric Miralles opened his own office with Carme Pinós in 1984. Two of his most remarkable works to date were designed during this partnership, although it took a decade for the projects to progress from initial competition entries to completed buildings. These structures are the Morella Boarding School in Castellón, completed in 1994, and the Igualada Cemetery-Park in Barcelona, the first phase of which was completed in 1995. The cemetery, with its inclined prefabricated concrete walls, represents Mr. Miralles's most richly articulated achievement to date, particularly in respect to the relationship between the columbarium that doubles as a retaining wall and the overall topographic form.

The Olympic Archery Range (1992), designed after the dissolution of the partnership with Pinós in 1989, in many ways epitomizes Mr. Miralles's dynamic approach to structure. Herein multiple, folded-concrete plate roofs of varying pitch echo the undulating topographic character of the site. Bounded by hollow brick walls and propped up by steel tubes, this shell-roofed bunker may be seen as reinterpreting the structural rationalism of Eugène Viollet-le-Duc, and in this regard it has much in common with the earlier Catalan tradition of *modernismo*.

While remaining sensitive to the topographic context, Mr. Miralles's later works have tended to stress the expressive capacity of the roof, as in his National Training Center for Rhythmic Gymnastics in Alicante (1989–1994). In addition to his professorship at the School of Architecture in Barcelona and his current directorship of the Master Class at the Städelschule in Frankfurt, Mr. Miralles has held teaching positions on a visiting basis at a number of institutions. He was the Kenzo Tange Visiting Professor of Architecture at Harvard University in 1992–1993 and the Jean Labutut Visiting Professor at Princeton University in 1993–1994.

José Rafael Moneo

José Rafael Moneo graduated in 1961 from the School of Architecture in Madrid, where he studied under the renowned historian Leopoldo Torres Balbás and the architect Francisco Javier Saénz. From 1961 to 1962 Mr. Moneo served an apprenticeship in Denmark with Jørn Utzon, with whom he worked on the Sydney Opera House. Since founding his own practice in Madrid in 1965, Mr. Moneo has realized widely published projects throughout Europe and the United States; among the most important are the Logroño City Hall (1976), the National Museum of Roman Art in Mérida (1986), the Atocha Railway Station in Madrid (1992), the Pilar & Joan Miró Foundation in Palma de Mallorca (1992), and the L'Illa Block in Barcelona (in collaboration with Manuel de Solà-Morales, 1993). Mr. Moneo's current projects include the Barcelona Concert Hall, the Museums of Modern Art and Architecture in Stockholm, Sweden, and the Kursaal Concert Hall and Cultural Center in San Sebastián.

Teaching and criticism have constituted important aspects of Mr. Moneo's professional career. He has been a visiting professor at several universities, including The Cooper Union in New York (1976–1977), the EPFL in Lausanne, and the Architectural Association in London. From 1985 to 1990 he was Chairman of the Architecture Department at the Harvard University Graduate School of Design, where he is now Josep Lluís Sert Professor.

Mr. Moneo's many distinguished honors and awards include the Pritzker Prize for Architecture and the Gold Medal of the International Union of Architects, both awarded in 1996. He received the Gold Medal for Achievement in the Fine Arts from the Spanish Government in 1992; and in 1993 he received the Arnold W. Brunner Memorial Prize from the American Academy and Institute of Arts and Letters and the Schock Prize in Visual Arts from the Schock Foundation and the Royal Academy of Fine Arts in Stockholm.

Glenn Murcutt

After graduating from Sydney Technical College in 1961 and traveling throughout Europe and Scandinavia during the first half of the 1960s, Glenn Murcutt joined the established Sydney firm of Anchor, Mortlock, Murray and Woolley. He started his one-man practice in 1969 and in the following decade also taught architectural design at Sydney University and at the University of New South Wales.

Influenced by the implicit minimalism of Mies van der Rohe and by the folded-metal technology pioneered by Jean Prouvé, Mr. Murcutt's architecture is grounded equally in the climate and the corrugated iron-roofed vernacular of the Australian outback. Mr. Murcutt's later approach has gradually changed from the neo-Miesian style of his early career yet has not lost its essential elegance. It is characterized by corrugated metal roofs of varying profile and rhythmic complexity, beginning with his Marie Short House in Kempsey, New South Wales (1975), and culminating most recently in his Pratt and Simpson Lee houses (1994), which also exemplify his preference for natural ventilating and shading devices. Mr. Murcutt's houses have always been conceived from both an ecological and a cultural standpoint, as is particularly evidenced by his all-timber Marika-Alderton House of 1994, modeled after the aboriginal long house and raised off the ground on short stilts.

With thirty houses designed and built in as many years, Mr. Murcutt has focused professionally on the private freestanding house. When he has ventured beyond this type, as in his Museum and Tourist Centre for South Kempsey (1981–1983), the domestic scale has tended to remain in the overriding format, in this instance, three corrugated-iron vaulted roofs set side by side. Mr. Murcutt has lectured widely throughout the world and has received numerous awards; among these are the Gold Medal of the Royal Australian Institute of Architects (1992), and the Alvar Aalto Medal (1994).

Jean Nouvel

Jean Nouvel graduated from the École des Beaux Arts in Paris in 1972 and thereafter worked in the office of Claude Parent, where he met the influential architect/philosopher Paul Virilio. Parent's radical preoccupation with the oblique in architectural form and Virilio's apocalyptic theories had a lasting effect on Mr. Nouvel's development. He came to prominence as an independent architect in 1987 with the completion of his Institut du Monde Arabe in Paris, a stainless-steel-clad building both inside and out that combined a light scintillating membrane with a feeling for metropolitan density. Selected in an open competition, this work brought Mr. Nouvel international recognition and the coveted Aga Khan Prize, among other awards.

With some two hundred designs to his credit, Mr. Nouvel's most significant works to date have been his major public buildings, notably the Congress Building in Tours (1993) and the Fondation Cartier in Paris (1994). His unrealized Dumont Schauberg office building, designed in 1990 with his associate Emmanuel Cattani, epitomizes the distinct character of his approach: recasting a corporate office building as a lightweight, semi-transparent structure faced with a cantilevered, translucent, hanging sun screen and covered with neon signs. Certain aspects of this proposal reappear in the Fondation Cartier, where a continuous glass "billboard" maintains the frontage of a Hausmannian street. Nouvel displays an equally sensitive response to the agrarian landscape. His Hotel Saint James in Bordeaux-Bouliac (1989), a loose assembly of hotel-sheds covered with steel mesh, flows unassumingly into the landscape of adjacent vineyards and alludes to the traditional tobacco drying sheds of the region.

Mr. Nouvel has received numerous honors and awards, including the Chevalier de l'Ordre des Arts et des Lettres, the Silver Medal from the Académie d'Architecture, the Best French Buildings award, the Chevalier de l'Ordre du Mérite, and the Grand Prix d'Architecture.

Robert Oxman

Robert Oxman is a graduate of Harvard College, the Harvard University Graduate School of Design, and The Technion, Israel Institute of Technology, in Haifa. He is currently dean and professor of architectural and design history and theory at the Faculty of Architecture and Town Planning at The Technion, Israel, where he holds the Gerhard and Gertrude Karplus Chair in Architecture and Urban Design. A widely published author and researcher, he specializes in the history and theory of contemporary architecture and design. In addition to historical and critical writings on the architecture and urbanism of Israel, he is known for his work on the modeling and representation of design thinking.

Among Professor Oxman's recently published works are studies of contemporary Israeli architects, including Moshe Safdie, Ram Karmi, Al Mansfeld, David Reznik, and the landscape architect Shlomo Aronson; and a book on design research in The Netherlands, with a companion volume on design education to be published in 1998. He is currently preparing the book *Design Concepts*, a conceptual history of contemporary architectural thinking, as well as a comprehensive study of Israeli architecture. Professor Oxman is also collaborating on *The History of An Idea*, a volume on the history of the renowned housing and design research institute SAR.

Professor Oxman has held the chairs of Design Methodology and CAAD at the architecture faculty of the Technical University in Eindhoven, The Netherlands, and has been a visiting scholar at various universities throughout the world. In 1997 he was awarded the European Association for Architectural Education prize for original writing on architecture education and an award from the Israel Association of Architects for his contribution to architecture education.

Patricia Patkau

Born in Winnipeg and educated at the University of Manitoba in Canada, Patricia Patkau received a master's degree from Yale University in 1978, the year she and her husband John Patkau established the firm of Patkau Architects in Vancouver, British Columbia. During the past decade, starting with their prize-winning 1986 entry for the Canadian Clay and Glass Gallery in Waterloo, the firm has acquired a reputation for an expressive use of laminated timber construction combined with a particularly sensitive approach to existing topography and to the articulation of the building as an earthwork in relation to its context. This dual principle is dramatically demonstrated in their Seabird Island School in Vancouver, of 1991, where a cradling earthwork is capped by an enormous timber roof that alludes overtly to the houses of the indigenous peoples of the Pacific Northwest. At the same time, the roof's humpbacked profile echoes the silhouette of the nearby mountains.

Similar tectonic principles are evident in the Newton Library, completed in Surrey, British Columbia, in 1992, and in the more complex Strawberry Vale Elementary School in Victoria, British Columbia, of 1995. In these two projects the structure of an inverted pitched roof assumes a more cubistic profile, although in plan the lateral displacement of the space remains relatively organic. In the school, clusters of classrooms are arranged in a stagger formation, almost as a direct consequence of variations in the contours across the site. This tendency to emphasize a split between the aerial, framed character of a timber roof and the telluric monolithic nature of the masonry base culminates in the Barnes House, a private house in Naniamo, British Columbia, completed in 1992.

Renzo Piano

Born into a Genovese building family, Renzo Piano seems to have been predestined to become an architect for whom production would be as important as the spatial conception of the work. Immediately after graduating from the Milan Polytechnic in 1964, Mr. Piano began to design and build a series of small experimental industrial structures in molded stressed-skin plastic (1964–1967) and two housing blocks in the hills outside Genoa in modular prefabricated concrete (1969). During this period he worked briefly with Louis I. Kahn in Philadelphia, and subsequently with the space-frame engineer Z.S. Makowsky in London.

Mr. Piano rose to prominence in 1971, when, in collaboration with Richard and Su Rogers, he won the competition for the Centre Georges Pompidou in Paris (1971), a work that in its time was considered a technological *tour de force*. In many respects it can be said to have realized the neo-Futurist fantasies of Archigram. During his Parisian period, Mr. Piano developed a close friendship with Jean Prouvé, who thereafter exercised a decisive influence on his work.

Returning to Genoa in the late 1970s, he established the Renzo Piano Building Workshop (RPBW), eventually adding branch offices in Paris and Tokyo. Among the approximately one hundred projects that RPBW has designed and realized over the last two decades, certain works are particularly outstanding: the IBM Traveling Pavilion (1984), the IRCAM Center in Paris (1989), the San Nicola Stadium in Bari (1990), Rue de Meaux Housing in Paris (1991), and Kansai International Airport in Osaka (1993).

Mr. Piano collaborated for almost a quarter of a century with the British engineer Peter Rice, and his synthesis of advanced technology with topographic form has effectively put his "high-tech" architecture into a category of its own.

Antoine Predock

Antoine Predock attended Columbia University and established his architectural practice in Albuquerque, New Mexico, in 1967; he currently maintains offices in Albuquerque and in Venice, California. One of his earliest projects—the award-winning La Luz Community in Albuquerque, of 1967—could be seen to embody the forms and concerns that Mr. Predock continues to bring to his work. Sited on a semiarid mesa above the Rio Grande, this adobe-walled complex of townhouses allows views toward the river and the distant mountain landscape and establishes a fundamental connection to earth and sky.

Over the past thirty years Mr. Predock's work has ranged from single-family houses to major academic buildings to master plans for convention facilities and hotels. Between 1987 and 1993 he worked extensively on academic projects, designing buildings for the University of California at its Santa Barbara, Davis, Santa Cruz, and San Diego campuses; as well as works for the universities of New Mexico, Arizona State, Wyoming, and Stanford. He has also designed several cultural institutions in New Mexico, including the Museum of Albuquerque (1979) and the Rio Grande Nature Center (1992). Over the past decade Mr. Predock has been a finalist or winner in fourteen major competitions. He was awarded first place in the competition for the United States Pavilion at the World Expo in Seville, Spain in 1992 (unrealized), and for the Stanford University Center for Integrated Systems Expansion in Palo Alto, California (1993).

Mr. Predock has exhibited his work throughout the world and taught at several universities in the United States. His numerous awards and honors include the Gran Premio Internacional of the Buenos Aires Architectural Biennial in 1989, the Zimmerman Award from the University of New Mexico in 1991, and the Chicago Architecture Award in 1992.

Lord Rogers of Riverside

Lord Rogers attended the Architectural Association in London and the Yale University School of Architecture, where he studied with Norman Foster and was a Fulbright, Edward Stone, and Yale Scholar, receiving his M.Arch in 1962. He first formed the partnership known as Team 4 in 1963 in London with Norman and Wendy Foster and Su Rogers.

In 1970 he formed the partnership of Piano + Rogers Architects and the following year entered the Place Beaubourg competition with Renzo Piano. The partnership won the competition and completed the Centre Georges Pompidou in Paris in 1977. Among the projects executed by the Richard Rogers Partnership are the headquarters of Lloyds in the City of London (1978–1986); Channel 4 Television Headquarters (1990–1994) and the redevelopment of Billingsgate Securities Market (1985–1988), both in London; a laboratory and offices for PA Technology in New Jersey (1982–1985); and the new European Court of Human Rights in Strasbourg, France (1989–1995). The firm's current projects include Terminal 5 at Heathrow Airport and the Daiwa Headquarters in London, and the Seoul Broadcasting Center in Korea.

Lord Rogers has taught at many universities in the United States and abroad, including UCLA, Princeton, Harvard, and Cornell universities, the University of Hong Kong, and Aachen University. He received the Royal Gold Medal for Architecture from the Royal Institute of British Architects in 1985, and the following year became a Chevalier de l'Ordre Nationale de la Legion d'Honneur. In 1991 he was knighted by Queen Elizabeth II and received a life Peerage, becoming Lord Rogers of Riverside, in 1996. Among his awards in the United States is the Arnold W. Brunner Memorial Prize of the American Academy and Institute of Arts and Letters.

Joseph Rykwert

Joseph Rykwert received his architectural education at the Bartlett School and the Architectural Association in London. He earned his doctorate at the Royal College of Art in London in 1970 and currently is Paul Philippe Cret Professor of Architecture at the University of Pennsylvania in Philadelphia.

Professor Rykwert taught at the Royal College of Art before becoming Chairman and Professor of Art at the University of Essex in 1967. In 1979 he was appointed Slade Professor of Fine Arts at Cambridge University, where he was a Reader in Architecture until 1987. He has held visiting professorships and fellowships at numerous European and American universities.

He has received fellowships from the Bollingen Foundation (1966), the National Gallery of Art in Washington, D.C. (1981), the Graham Foundation (1983–1986), and the Getty Center for the History of Art and the Humanities in Santa Monica, California (1990). Other honors include the Chevalier de l'Ordre des Arts et des Lettres (1984), the Alfred Jurzykowski Foundation award (1989), and election to the Accademia di San Luca in Italy. He is an Honorary Doctor of Science at the University of Edinburgh.

Professor Rykwert has written extensively and published twelve books on architecture, including *The Idea of a Town* (1963), *On Adam's House in Paradise* (1972), *The First Moderns* (1980), *The Necessity of Artifice* (1982), and *The Dancing Column: On Order in Architecture* (1996) all of which have been published in several languages.

Moshe Safdie

Born in Haifa, Israel, Mr. Safdie emigrated to Canada in 1955 and received his architecture degree from McGill University in 1961. After working with Van Ginkel and Associates in Montreal and Louis I. Kahn in Philadelphia, he established his architectural practice in Montreal in 1964. He was the architect/planner for the 1967 World Exhibition and designed Habitat '67, the world's first major prefabricated housing project.

Among Mr. Safdie's recently completed projects are the Skirball Cultural Center in Los Angeles (1995); Vancouver Library Square and Ford Center for the Performing Arts in Vancouver (1995); Ottawa City Hall, Ontario (1994); the Harvard Business School's Morgan Hall and Class of 1959 Chapel in Boston, and Rosovsky Hall at Harvard University (1992).

His current projects include the Pantages Place Theater and mixed-use development in Toronto; Exploration Place Science Center and Children's Museum in Wichita, Kansas; the Peabody-Essex Museum in Salem, Massachusetts; a new campus for Hebrew College in Newton, Massachusetts; Mamilla Commercial District in Jerusalem; Ben Gurion 2000 airside terminal in Tel Aviv; and several other projects in Israel.

Mr. Safdie has taught at Yale, McGill, and Ben Gurion universities and directed the Urban Design Program at Harvard University, where he was the Ian Woodner Professor of Architecture and Urban Design from 1978 to 1990. He has published numerous articles and books, including the influential volume *Beyond Habitat* (1970) and *Form and Purpose* (1982). Among Mr. Safdie's numerous awards are the Canadian Lieutenant Governor's Gold Medal (1961), the Order of Canada (1986), Mt. Scopus Award for Humanitarianism (1987), and the Richard J. Neutra Award for Excellence (1993).

Álvaro Siza

A 1955 graduate of the School of Architecture at the University of Porto, Álvaro Siza made his architectural debut in 1963 with a restaurant on the seafront at Leça da Palmeira designed in collaboration with his former teacher Fernando Távora. After realizing a number of private houses and a significant bank building in 1974, Mr. Siza became involved with the so-called Portuguese Spring, designing two well-integrated blocks of workers' housing for areas of Porto. In the early 1980s, he realized two canonical pieces that earned him the European Architecture Award of the EEC from the Mies van der Rohe Foundation—the Avelino Duarte House in Ovar (1984) and the Borges and Irmão Bank in Vila do Conde (1986).

In 1976, Mr. Siza began an extensive low-rise, high-density housing quarter in the town of Évora. This project, together with his reconstruction of the Chiado district in Lisbon (1988–), the Galician Center for Contemporary Art in Santiago de Compostela, Spain (1988–1994), and the new School of Architecture in Porto (1986–1995), are the crowning works in his career to date. Mr. Siza's work often blurs the line between landscape and building. Using the standard concrete block and concrete frame construction of the Mediterranean, he combines in a unique way a series of tropes deriving from Adolf Loos, Alvar Aalto, and the functionalist architecture of the 1920s.

In addition to directing his practice, Mr. Siza teaches at the University of Porto and has been a visiting professor at the École Polytechnique in Lausanne, the University of Pennsylvania, and the Harvard University Graduate School of Design. In 1992 he was recognized as an architect of world stature with the coveted Pritzker Prize for Architecture. He has also received the Gold Medal of the Alvar Aalto Foundation (1988) and the Architecture National Award of the Portuguese Architects Association.

Arthur Spector

After completing his formal architectural education at Rensselaer Polytechnic Institute in Troy, New York, Arthur Spector traveled to Israel as part of a one-year trip abroad. He ultimately decided to remain in Israel, and he established his present partnership, Arthur Spector-Michael Amisar Architects, in 1972 in Jerusalem. Mr. Spector was co-chairman of the Jerusalem Seminar in Architecture in 1992 and 1994 and is currently chairman of the organizing committee.

The Spector-Amisar practice has focused primarily on the planning and execution of public buildings. The firm's work also includes updated master plans for the Israel Museum, the Jerusalem International Convention Center, and the Central Government Precinct, all planned together with Professor Julian Beinart. Recently completed works include the initial stages of the Jerusalem Convention Center (1995), Hemda Science Center in Tel Aviv (1992), a new children's hospital for Hadassah Medical Center (1996), and Bet Gavriel in Tsemach (1992, a collaboration with the office of Ulrik Plesner and Dan Wajnman). Among the firm's current projects is a prototype science-art school to be built throughout Israel, a major addition to the Jerusalem YMCA, a student union for The Hebrew University of Jerusalem, and a library and museum for the Menachem Begin Heritage Foundation in Jerusalem. Spector-Amisar are also the masterplanners and overseeing architects for the Central Government Precinct.

Mr. Spector has taught at the Bezalel Academy in Jerusalem. He was a visiting fellow at the Massachusetts Institute of Technology in 1978 and was a Hallmark Fellow at The International Design Conference in Aspen. The office of Spector-Amisar received the Rechter Prize in Architecture for the Saltiel Community Center in Jerusalem (1987) and for Bet Gavriel (1995).

Kaarin Taipale

Kaarin Taipale studied music at the Sibelius Academy in Helsinki (1964–1967) and graduated as an architect from the ETH in Zurich in 1972. She worked as a practicing architect for almost nine years, first for Wilhelm Fischer, Farner and Grunder in Zurich and then for Kalle Vartola in Helsinki. During the academic year 1981–1982 she earned an advanced architecture degree at Columbia University and thereafter served as an assistant in the office of Robert A.M. Stern in New York.

Ms. Taipale started her own firm in Helsinki in 1985 and practiced architecture until 1988, when she became editor of the leading Finnish magazine *Arkkitehti*. During her tenure at *Arkkitehti*, Ms. Taipale was among the few architecture editors worldwide who continued to assume the responsibility of writing critical editorials in every issue of her publication. In 1993 she relinquished this post to become the Deputy City Architect for Helsinki and subsequently, director of the Helsinki Building Controls Department.

Since leaving *Arkkitehti* she has written occasional criticism for *Uusi Sanoma* newspaper and for the major Finnish daily, *Helsingin Sanomat*. Throughout the 1980s and 1990s, Taipale edited a number of exhibition catalogues, including *Finland Builds 7*, published by the Museum of Finnish Architecture in 1986, and *Stray Paths and Voyages of Discovery*, published by the Finnish Association of Architects in 1992. In 1994 she curated an exhibition in the Jugendsali in Helsinki, "Public Urban Space and Change." Ms. Taipale has lectured extensively throughout Europe, and in 1995 she was voted Woman of the Year in Finland.

Peter Walker

Peter Walker graduated from the Harvard University Graduate School of Design as a landscape architect in 1957 and joined his former teacher Hideo Sasaki to form the practice of Sasaki, Walker & Associates (SWA) in Cambridge, Massachusetts. He promptly established a standing in this field and has worked at a variety of scales for nearly forty years, with commissions ranging from small gardens to the overall design of large university campuses and corporate headquarters.

Mr. Walker first moved to Berkeley, California, in 1975 to establish the West Coast branch of SWA but returned to Harvard to serve as a faculty member in both landscape and urban design. After serving as chairman of the GSD landscape department, Mr. Walker set up his own bicoastal consulting firm in 1983, later joining with his longtime collaborator, William Johnson. In the past four years the two have produced large-scale civic projects and landscape works, including the Harima Science Garden City in Japan with Arata Isozaki, the Euralille Park in France with Rem Koolhaas, Marina Linear Park in downtown San Diego, and the renovation of Exposition Park in Los Angeles with the firm of Zimmer, Gunsel, Frasca.

Throughout his career Mr. Walker has been devoted to the creation of a new and dynamic landscape form—part artwork, part garden, part architectonic structure—and, in some measure, a new kind of regional topography. Perhaps his most successful works to date are his large corporate office parks, where the building is set off by the landscape and vice versa. This strategy is particularly evident in his works for the Upjohn Corporation in Kalamazoo, Michigan (1961), Weyerhaeuser in Tacoma, Washington (1974), and IBM at Solana, near Dallas, Texas (1991).

1996 Moderators

Shlomo Aronson is owner and director of Shlomo Aronson and Associates, a multidisciplinary office of landscape architects and town planners. Mr. Aronson is chairman of the Israel Association of Landscape Architects. Among his numerous prizes, he has received the Rechter Prize for the Suzanne Dellal Center in Tel Aviv and the Sherover Promenade in Jerusalem.

Zvi Efrat is a partner in the firm Efrat-Kowalsky Architects in Tel Aviv and a lecturer at Tel Aviv University, Hebrew University, and Bezalel Academy of Art and Design. In addition, Mr. Efrat is architecture editor of various professional publications and curator of "The Architecture of Statehood: Israel 1948–1967," a retrospective exhibition for the Tel Aviv Museum scheduled for the end of 1998.

Omri Eytan studied at the Rhode Island School of Design in Providence and the Architectural Association in London, graduating in 1980. He worked with the Office of Metropolitan Architecture (OMA) from 1980 to 1981 and has been in private practice since 1984. Mr. Eytan is a tutor and lecturer at the Sadna School, the Bezalel Academy of Art and Design, and Tel Aviv University, and has published numerous critical and theoretical essays.

Pe'era Goldman directs her own architectural practice and teaches at the Bezalel Academy of Art and Design in Jerusalem. A graduate of the Bezalel Academy and of Princeton University, she has taught at the Princeton School of Architecture and at the Harvard University Graduate School of Design, and at the Faculty of Architecture and Planning at The Technion, Israel Institute of Technology, in Haifa, Israel.

Andres Mariasch received his architectural training in Buenos Aires and moved to Israel in 1994. Since then he has worked in the offices of Uri Shetrit, Ram Karmi and Associates, and Kika Braz Architects & City Planners, all in Tel Aviv. Currently he is working in Santiago, Chile.

Arie Rahamimoff is an architect and urbanist who has pioneered many projects in solar energy in Israel. Rahamimoff maintains his own practice in Jerusalem and has taught in Israel, the United States, and Europe. Among his firm's many works are renovations of Sultan's Pool in Jerusalem and the master plan of the Old City of Acre.

Tony Rigg studied at Manchester College of Art & Design and the Polytechnic of North London. After moving to Israel in 1975, Rigg worked for Mandl-Kertesz Architects prior to setting up a private practice in partnership with Ruth Lahav in 1979. Since 1989 they have been directors of the Work Program on Architecture and Energy of the International Union of Architects.

Project Credits

1996

Raimund Abraham / Atelier Raimund Abraham
Transplantation II, project, 1967
House Without Rooms, project, 1974
House for Euclid, project, 1983
Stair Tower, Lanz, Austria, 1985
Times Square Tower, project, 1984
Stair Tower, Graz, Austria, 1990–1993
Austrian Cultural Institute, New York, 1992–

Enric Miralles / Enric Miralles Benedetta Tagliabue
Igualada Cemetery-Park, Barcelona, 1985–1997: with Carme Pinós
Olympic Archery Range, Competition and Training Building, Barcelona, 1989–1992: with Carme Pinós
Unazuki Meditation Pavilion, Unazuki, Japan, 1991–1993
Copenhagen Auditorium, Copenhagen, Denmark, 1993
National Training Center for Rhythmic Gymnastics, Alicante, Spain, 1989–1993: with Carme Pinós

Glenn Murcutt / Glenn Murcutt & Associates
Magney Country House, Moruya, New South Wales, Australia, 1982–1984
Simpson-Lee House, Mount Wilson, New South Wales, Australia, 1989–1994
Marie Short House, Kempsey, New South Wales, Australia, 1974–1975 and 1980 (extension)
Visitors' Information Center and Park Headquarters, Kakadu National Park, Australia, 1992–1994: with Troppo Architects (Darwin, Australia)
Marika-Alderton House, Yirrkala Community, Eastern Arnhem Land, Australia, 1991–1994

Jean Nouvel
Institut du Monde Arabe, Paris, 1981–1987: with Gilbert Lezenes, Piere Soria, Architecture Studio
Fondation Cartier, Paris, 1991–1994: with Emmanuel Cattani & Associés
Lyon Opera House, Lyon, France, 1986–1993: with E. Blamont (competition and design development) and Emmanuel Cattani & Associés (construction)

Patricia Patkau / Patkau Architects
Seabird Island School, Agassiz, British Columbia, Canada, 1988–1991
Canadian Clay and Glass Gallery, Waterloo, Ontario, Canada, 1988–1992: with Mark Musselman McIntyre Combe, Inc.
Barnes House, Nanaimo, British Columbia, Canada, 1991–1993
Strawberry Vale Elementary School, Victoria, British Columbia, Canada, 1992–1995

Renzo Piano / Renzo Piano Building Workshop
Renzo Piano Building Workshop, Genoa, Italy, 1989–1991
The Menil Collection Museum, Houston, Texas, 1982–1986
Rue de Meaux Housing, Paris, 1987–1991

San Nicola Football Stadium, Bari, Italy, 1987–1990
Kansai International Airport, Osaka, Japan, 1990–1994
Jean Marie Tjibaou Cultural Center, Nouméa, New Caledonia, 1993–
Padre Pio Pilgrimage Church, Foggia, Italy, 1995–

Álvaro Siza
Housing in Évora, Portugal, 1976–
House in The Hague, The Netherlands, 1984–1988
Chiado District Restoration, Lisbon, Portugal, 1988–
Galician Center for Contemporary Art, Santiago de Compostela, Spain, 1988–1994
Aveiro University Library, Aveiro, Portugal, 1988–1994
School of Architecture, Porto, Portugal, 1986–1995

Peter Walker / Peter Walker William Johnson and Partners
Upjohn Corporation World Headquarters, Kalamazoo, Michigan, 1957–1961: Sasaki, Walker Associates (landscape architect); Skidmore, Owings & Merrill (architect)
Weyerhaeuser Corporate Headquarters, Tacoma, Washington, 1974: Peter Walker, Sasaki, Walker & Associates (landscape architect); Skidmore, Owings & Merrill (architect)
Burnett Park, Forth Worth, Texas, 1983: Peter Walker (The SWA Group)
Plaza Tower, Costa Mesa, California, 1991: Peter Walker and Partners (landscape architect); Cesar Pelli and Associates, CRS Sirine, Inc. (architects)
Marina Linear Park, San Diego, California, 1988–present: The Office of Peter Walker Martha Schwartz (landscape architect); Austin Design Group (urban design)
Center for Advanced Science and Technology (CAST), Harima Science Garden City, Hyogo Prefecture, Japan, 1993: Peter Walker William Johnson and Partners (landscape architect); Arata Isozaki and Associates (architect)
IBM Japan Makuhari Building, Makuhari, Chiba Prefecture, Japan, 1991: Peter Walker and Partners (landscape architect); Taniguchi and Associates, Nihon Sekkei, Inc. (architects)
Grand Axe Competition Entry, La Défense, Paris, 1991: Peter Walker and Partners
IBM Solana, Westlake Southlake, Dallas, Texas, 1985–1991: Peter Walker and Partners (prior to 1990, The Office of Peter Walker Martha Schwartz)

1994

Dimitris Antonakakis / Atelier 66
Lyttos Hotel, Anissaras, Crete, 1977
School of Humanities, University of Crete, Akrotiri, Crete, 1981
Technical University of Crete, Akrotiri, Crete, 1982

A. J. Diamond / A. J. Diamond, Donald Schmitt & Co.
York University Student Centre, Toronto, Ontario, Canada, 1987
Jerusalem City Hall, Israel, 1993

Balkrishna V. Doshi
Sangath (Vastu-Shilpa Foundation), Ahmedabad, India, 1979–1981
Vidyadhar Nagar, Jaipur, India, 1984–1986
Indian Institute of Management, Bangalore, India, 1977–1985
National Institute of Fashion Technology, New Delhi, India, 1988–1994
Bahrat Diamond Bourse, Mumbai, India, 1992–1998
Hussain-Doshi Gufa, Ahmedabad, India, 1992–1994

James Ingo Freed / Pei Cobb Freed & Partners
Los Angeles Convention Center Expansion, Los Angeles, California, 1986–1993
United States Holocaust Memorial Museum, Washington, D.C., 1986–1993

Arata Isozaki / Arata Isozaki & Associates
Tateyama Museum of Toyama, Toyama, Japan, 1989–1991: with So Architects Associates
Team Disney Building, Orlando, Florida, 1987–1990: with Hunton Brady Pryor Maso Architects, P.A.
Tsukuba Center Building, Tsukuba Science City, Ibaragi, Japan, 1979–1983
Art Tower Mito, Ibaragi, Japan, 1986–1990: with Seiichi Mikami & Associates
The Museum of Contemporary Art, Los Angeles, California, 1981–1986: with Gruen Associates

Antoine Predock
Fuller House, Scottsdale, Arizona, 1987
American Heritage Center and Art Museum, University of Wyoming, Laramie, Wyoming, 1993
Venice House, Venice Beach, Los Angeles, California, 1991: Antoine Predock
Nelson Fine Arts Center, Arizona State University, Tempe, Arizona, 1989
Turtle Creek House, Dallas, Texas, 1993

1992

Henry N. Cobb / Pei Cobb Freed & Partners
First Interstate Bank Tower (FIBT), Dallas, Texas 1983–1989
John Hancock Tower, Boston, Massachusetts, 1967–1976: (I. M. Pei & Partners)
Commerce Square, Philadelphia, Pennsylvania, 1984–1987
United States Courthouse, Boston, Massachusetts, 1991–1998

Charles Correa
Gandhi Smarak Sangrahalaya, Sabarmati Ashram, India, 1958–1963
Bharat Bhavan, Bhopal, India, 1975–1981

British Council, New Delhi, India, 1987–1992
Jawahar Kala Kendra, Jaipur, India, 1996–1992

Romaldo Giurgola / Mitchell/Giurgola & Thorp Architects
Tel Aviv City Redevelopment Competition, Israel, 1963: (Mitchell/Giurgola Architects, Philadelphia)
Parliament House, Canberra, Australia, 1979–1988

Herman Hertzberger / Architectuurstudio Herman Hertzberger
Centraal Beheer Office Building, Apeldoorn, The Netherlands, 1968–1972
Vredenburg Music Center, Utrecht, The Netherlands, 1973–1978
Ministry of Social Welfare and Employment, The Hague, The Netherlands, 1979–1990

Ram Karmi and Ada Karmi-Melamede / Karmi Associates
National Precinct, Jerusalem, Israel, 1992
Israel Supreme Court, Jerusalem, Israel, 1992

José Rafael Moneo
City Hall, Logroño, Spain, 1973–1981
Atocha Railway Station, Madrid, 1984–1992

Richard Rogers / Richard Rogers Partnership
Centre Georges Pompidou, Paris, 1977: (Piano + Rogers Architects)
Lloyds of London Building, London, 1978–1986
European Court of Human Rights, Strasbourg, France, 1989–1995: with Atelier Claude Bucher

Moshe Safdie
Yeshivat Porat Yosef, Israel, 1970–1983
Hebrew Union College, Jerusalem, Israel, 1976–1984
National Gallery of Canada, Ottawa, Canada, 1988
Vancouver Library Square, Vancouver, British Columbia, Canada, 1995

Illustration Credits

Numbers refer to page numbers. Photographs and illustrations not credited below are courtesy of the architects and critics.

1996 Presenters

Raimund Abraham
© Debbie Cooper: 276 (top)
© Tugmann Photo: 27

Enric Miralles
© Debbie Cooper: 279 (top)
© Duccio Malagamba: 40 (bottom)
© Domi Mora: 44–45
© Hisao Suzuki: 37
© Giovanni Zanzi: 40 (top)

Glenn Murcutt
© Debbie Cooper: 281 (bottom)
© John Gollings: 64–65

Jean Nouvel
© Debbie Cooper: 282 (top)
© Georges Fessy: 77, 79
© Philippe Ruault: 84–85 (photos), 88, 89, 92
© Von Schaewen: 80, 81, 87 (photos)

Patricia Patkau
© Debbie Cooper: 282 (bottom)
© James Dow: 96–111

Renzo Piano
© Richard Bryant: 120
© Michel Denance: 122, 123 (left), 125 (top)
© Fregoso & Basalto: 119
© Stefano Goldberg: 283 (top)
© Alastair Hunter: 121
© Shunji Ishida: 123 (right)
© Yutaka Kinumaki: 125 (bottom)
© Publifoto: 133
© Skyfront: 126–27
© William Vassal: 130–31

Álvaro Siza
© Luís Ferreira Alves: 149
© Roberto Collovà: 139, 148
© Debbie Cooper: 284 (bottom)
© José M. Rodrigues: 145

Peter Walker
© Gerry Campbell: 159–161, 163 (top)
© Jim Hedrich: 169 (bottom)
Courtesy Maguire Partners: 171, 174
© Oliver's Photography: 169 (top)
© Pamela Parker: 163 (bottom), 167 (top), 172 (bottom)
© David Walker: 164–165, 172 (top), 173
© Eiji Yonekura: 167 (bottom)

1994 Presenters

Dimitris Antonakakis
© D. Georgantopoulou: 207

A.J. Diamond
© Steven Evans: 209–211
© Debbie Cooper: 278 (top)

Balkrishna V. Doshi
© Yatin Pandya: 213, 214 (top), 278 (middle)
© John Panikar: 214 (bottom)

James Ingo Freed
© Debbie Cooper: 279 (top)
© Alan Gilbert: 217 (top)
© Jeff Goldberg/ESTO: 216
© Timothy Hursley: 217 (bottom), 219

Arata Isozaki
© Mitsumasa Fujitsuka: 221 (top)
© Yasuhiro Ishimoto: 222 (bottom), 223 (left)
© Tomio Ohashi: 222 (top)
© Eiichiro Sakata: 280 (top)

Antoine Predock
© Timothy Hursley: 225–227
© Robert Reck: 283 (middle)

1992 Presenters

Henry N. Cobb
© Nathan Benn: 277 (middle)
© Gorchev & Gorchev: 240 (left)
© Nathaniel Lieberman: 241 (left)
© Norman McGrath: 239 (top)
© Richard Payne: 239 (bottom)
© Steve Rosenthal: 240 (right)
© Eric Schiller: 241 (right)

Charles Correa
© Pranlal Patel: 243 (top)
© Ram Rehman: 244, 245 (bottom)
© Mahendra Sinh: 245 (middle)

Romaldo Giurgola
Courtesy Australian Information Service, Department of Foreign Affairs and Trade: 247
© John Gollings: 248, 279 (middle)
© Alison Taylor: 249

Herman Hertzberger
© Arnold Meine Jansen: 252–53
© Chanine Odes: 279 (bottom)

Ram Karmi and Ada Karmi-Melamede
© Albatross: 255 (photo)
© Richard Bryant/Archaid: 256
© Debbie Cooper: 280 (middle and bottom)

José Rafael Moneo
© D. Biaggi: 259 (top)
© Lindman: 258, 259 (bottom)
© Duccio Malagamba: 261 (left)
© Francisco Otañón: 281 (middle)

Richard Rogers
© Richard Bryant: 263 (left)
© Janet Gill: 263 (right)
© Katsuhisa Kida: 264
© Sekiya Masaaki: 283 (bottom)
© Morley von Sternberg: 265

Moshe Safdie
© Timothy Hursley: 268 (bottom), 269
© Malak Photographs, Ltd.: 268 (top)
© Michal Ronnen Safdie: 267 (top), 284 (midddle)

Critics/Essayists

Stanford Anderson
© Debbie Cooper: 276 (middle)
Villa Comunale dell'Olmo, Como, Italy: 182
Reprinted from *Der Architekt Adolf Loos* (Vienna: A. Schroll, 1964): 183, 185 (lower photo), 188
Reprinted from *Grossherzog Ernst Ludwig und die Darmstädter Künstler-Kolonie* (Darmstadt: A. Koch, 1901): 184 (top)
AEG-Arhive, Frankfurt: 184 (bottom)
Reprinted from *Adolf Loos: Leben und Werk* (Salzburg: Residenz, 1982): 185 (top), 186
Reprinted from *Architettura*, May 1965, p. 62: 187

Julian Beinart
© Debbie Cooper: 277 (top)

Kenneth Frampton
© Dorothy Alexander: 278 (bottom)

Robert Oxman
© Debbie Cooper: 282 (middle)

Joseph Rykwert
© Debbie Cooper: 284 (top)

Arthur Spector
© Debbie Cooper: 285 (top)

Kaarin Taipale
© Debbie Cooper: 285 (middle)